# FROM AXIS VICTORIES VICTORIES TO THE TURN OF THE TIDE

# FROM AXIS VICTORIES TO THE TURN OF THE TIDE

## WORLD WAR II, 1939–1943

Alan Levine

Potomac Books
Washington, D.C.

**Library of Congress Cataloging-in-Publication Data**
Levine, Alan J.
  From Axis victories to the turn of the tide : World War II, 1939–1943 / Alan Levine. — First Edition.
      p. cm.
  Includes bibliographical references and index.
  ISBN 978-1-59797-711-1 (hardcover) — ISBN 978-1-59797-795-1 (electronic)
  1. World War, 1939–1945—Campaigns.  I. Title.

  D743.L49 2012
  940.54′1—dc23

                                          2012012053

Printed in the United States of America on acid-free paper that meets the American National Standards Institute Z39-48 Standard.

Potomac Books
22841 Quicksilver Drive
Dulles, Virginia 20166

First Edition

10 9 8 7 6 5 4 3 2 1

# Contents

# 1

# The Catastrophe

On May 20, 1940, the German Army reached the English Channel. Fighting in France went on for another month, but the success of the campaign that had begun ten days earlier was assured. The Dutch had already surrendered, and the northern wing of the remaining Allied armies—the entire Belgian Army, the British Expeditionary Force (BEF), and the strongest element of the French Army—had been cut off. Although the forces in the northern pocket were not all as hopelessly trapped as it seemed, the defeat in the north left the French so weak that they had no prospect of holding out against the Germans when the latter turned south. Victory in the western campaign, achieved within the first ten days, had completed the Nazis' domination of Europe west of the Soviet frontier.

Adolf Hitler had risen from the gutters of Vienna to master an empire greater than that of Napoleon Bonaparte. Many feared that eventually, perhaps even soon, the Nazis would conquer the rest of the world.

In only seven years, Hitler and the Nazis had established a totalitarian regime with wide popular support, restored prosperity to Germany, thrown off the limitations imposed by the peace settlement after World War I, rearmed, broken down the alliances the French had constructed after World War I, absorbed Austria and the Czech lands, and established German domination over eastern and central Europe—all without firing a shot. Then, in less than a year of war, the Nazis had more than reversed the outcome of World War I. They had accomplished it all despite Germany's near helplessness in 1933 and the warnings that the world read in Hitler's own writings in *Mein Kampf* and in those of the eloquent ex-Nazi Hermann

1

Rauschning. Again and again, Hitler had taken his enemies by surprise. Among the Germans and others, even those who had little use for Nazism, Hitler had established a reputation as a virtual magician.

Hitler's personal ideology—the product of what historian Stanley Payne described as a "rather powerful but delusory mind"—which became the official doctrine of the Nazi Party, determined the aims and even the strategy of the war. The ideological quirks of Hitler and the Nazis would be more important in determining the nature and outcome of World War II than is generally recognized even today. (For that matter, the delusions of their enemies—whether they concerned Joseph Stalin's ideas about Hitler or those of Western liberals and leftists who saw the Spanish Civil War as Armageddon or who imagined that Stalin would be a reliable ally—were of no small impact either.) Hitler was driven to move fast, partly by his fears that America would intervene and that he would die at an early age, and that no successor could "save" Germany.

For Hitler, and for most Nazi leaders, his hatred of the Jews, his convictions about the racial inferiority of the Slavs, and his aims of eastern conquest and colonization were all tied together. The Nazis held that the superior Aryan race, of which the Germanic peoples were the purest representatives, had created what was most valuable in human culture and was menaced by inferiors and the satanic Jewish "counter-race." The Aryans, and especially the German speakers, were too few in numbers and too confined in space. Germany occupied too small and exposed a territory, facing threats from the west by the French, who would always be hostile to Germany, and from the east by the more numerous Slavs, who might close the German lead in technology. (The Nazis, though, believed that some of the Western and South Slavs were of German origin and should be "re-Germanized.") Germany needed more space (lebensraum), which must be found in the east. The Nazis' race doctrine was further tied to their anti-communism. They maintained that Soviet communism was the product of an uprising by the inferior Slav majority under Jewish leadership against the old Russian ruling class, which had itself been of Germanic origin and had created the Russian state, providing the organization and leadership that had shaped the inferior mass of Slavs into a formidable opponent. Although the Nazis felt that the Soviet regime was the most extreme and horrible form of Jewish rule, they saw it as only a limited threat because the Jews, fundamentally inferior and capable only of destruction, could not effectively replace the older rulers. By destroying the latter the communist rulers actually had eliminated the only real obstacle to German expansion eastward, which would be the starting point for its world empire.

Thus Hitler, at least until the crisis on the eastern front in late 1941, did not take Soviet power seriously. This had the seemingly paradoxical result that while Hitler's primary aim was conquest in the east, Germany's main opponent was in the west. As historian Eberhard Jäckel observed,

> When Hitler reflected on how this war [against the USSR] was to be won, his thoughts were from the beginning not really directed toward the actual opponent, for the Soviet Union was supposed to collapse swiftly under a German attack. Rather, his thoughts were directed toward establishing a diplomatic constellation, in which Germany could not be prevented by other powers from achieving success. In Hitler's eyes, their intervention was the real problem.

Even non-Nazis regarded the French Army, rather than the Soviets, as the most formidable army in Europe. Professional pride and their respect for the French Army led non-Nazi German generals to the same conclusion.

Apart from the point that the Western powers should be subjugated eventually, the Nazis saw a clash with them as inevitable because France, at least, would oppose Germany's eastern expansion or would strike while Germany was tied down in the east. Although Hitler may have hoped, perhaps as late as 1937, to split Britain from France, he always assumed that it would be necessary to fight France simply to gain freedom of action in the east. Hitler's supposition that the Western powers were the more formidable opponents had an important corollary: if they were defeated easily, the Nazis would have nothing much to worry about when facing the Red Army. Both his readiness to take on the Soviet Union in 1941 and his failure to prepare adequately for that war were thus embedded in Hitler's long-standing assumptions. So was his desire to dispose of the racial enemy as well as Germany's internal weaknesses. It was no accident that on the day Germany invaded Poland—September 1, 1939—Hitler initiated the "euthanasia" program for destroying mentally ill (non-Nazis) and handicapped people in Germany. Shortly afterward, he began annihilating the Polish upper and middle classes. Both efforts, incidentally, served as pilot projects for eradicating the European Jews and the even bigger slaughters envisioned for the Slavs.

Hitler was undoubtedly delusional. Despite the repulsive nature of his character and ideas, however, he was highly intelligent and almost inordinately imaginative. He was remarkably persuasive in dealing with individuals and had a dreadfully accurate insight into the darker side of human nature. He was an important source of strength for the Nazi regime. He was not without military ability, at least when he was able to attack. Yet once Germany was on the defensive, the results were worse. He played an important part in promoting the growth of airpower and armored forces. His ideas about strategy played a major role in the early German victories, although his rigidities later aided Allied advances.[1]

## The Prewar Advances

The initial aims of the Nazi program—"revising" the peace settlement, rearming, and acquiring some of the German-speaking areas outside the current German frontiers—received overwhelming support from non-Nazis in Germany, and many outside Germany also accepted them. The bitter criticism of the Versailles settlement that had become popular in the 1920s and the dogma of "self-determination" seemed to leave little ground for opposition, while the more threatening parts of the Nazi program were brushed away.

The Western democracies were dominated by a mood for which the term "appeasement" is inadequate. War weariness, compounded with the fear that another war would resemble World War I, created wishful thinking that if people in democracies were scared out of their wits, this state would preserve peace. The dogma of the virtues of "self-determination" and the identification of this fetish with democracy had the paradoxical effect of sanctifying totalitarian expansion in central Europe. Regret and guilt over the Versailles settlement were common, as were antimilitarism and pacifism. Most Socialists opposed a draft and military expenditures until the war began in 1939 or even later. Communist parties in the West unsteadily supported defense between 1935 and 1939, or as long as it suited Stalin's maneuvers, which aimed at an arrangement with Germany. Although generally not inclined to make excuses for the Axis powers, as was all too common on the prewar Right, the democratic Left effectively opposed any serious attempt to cope with the fascist threat.

Those not inclined to ideological thinking of one sort or another were conscious of American isolationism. The British had never liked France's alliances with countries east of Germany, which, they feared, would draw Britain into conflicts in which it had no stake. (Czechoslovakia's abandonment at Munich was implicit in British policy long before 1938.) They also knew that the British Empire was dangerously stretched, facing threats not only from Germany and Italy but also from Japan and less immediately the Union of Soviet Socialist Republics (USSR). Nor did the empire contribute much to its own defense. Indeed, what were then bluntly called the White Dominions—which included Canada, Australia, New Zealand, and South Africa—did little to help. They spent little on defense and were, except for New Zealand, more ardent supporters of appeasement than was the British government.

Indeed, the tendency in favor of self-delusion and collapse in the face of Nazi aggression was so great in the 1930s that it almost seems surprising that this thinking was ever reversed. The Western democracies attempted to find or placate available allies to bear some, or all, of the burden of opposing Nazi Germany. Keeping or regaining Benito Mussolini's Italy as an ally was the pet idea of the political Right, while Soviet help was the favored idea of the Left and of the otherwise realistic Winston Churchill and a few appeasers, like British home secretary Samuel Hoare. Since neither of these ideas had any basis in Italian or Soviet policy, the democratic countries were on their own.[2]

Step by step, Hitler broke the limitations of the 1919 peace settlement. More or less neutralizing Poland, at first the country most ready to take action against him, he cleverly justified open rearmament in 1935 and the reoccupation of the Rhineland in 1936 as reactions to such feeble efforts as the French had made to counter German power—increasing the length of military service in the first case and establishing a weak alliance with the Soviets in the latter. Reoccupying the Rhineland was a decisive watershed. The Belgians reacted by withdrawing from their alliance with France and proclaiming their neutrality, unhinging the defensive front in the west and leaving the Germans strong enough to discourage any French action to support their eastern allies. Various other distractions aided Hitler: the Italian conquest of Ethiopia, the Spanish Civil War, and the Japanese invasion of China. Much attention also focused on the Germans' relations with Italy and Japan, although Hitler concentrated on breaking down the opposing alliance system rather than forming a counter system of his own. The Western powers' incoherent combination of appeasement and empty gestures of sympathy for the Ethiopians merely smoothed the way for Mussolini's basic inclination to join the Germans.

Despite the trend in the Nazis' favor, Hitler reluctantly concluded by late 1937 that Britain could not be split from France. In November of that year, he decided that while Britain and France would let him gain Austria and Czechoslovakia without a major war, they would not allow further

German expansion eastward. Therefore, he deemed that the Western powers had to be conquered before launching the major drive against the Soviet Union, which was to occur no later than 1943–1945. Because of that stance, he let slip the opportunity of forging an early alliance with Japan, whose leaders, until 1940, were unwilling to sign one aimed at the Western powers as well.

Over the next year and a half, Hitler acquired Austria without war and gained control of Czechoslovakia, although not quite in the way he expected. He had wanted an isolated war against the Czechs, taking their country in one bite. International developments forced him to take Czechoslovakia in two bites, without "trying out" the Wehrmacht.

The second stage of this process, bringing about Slovakia's secession and occupying the Czech lands, however, was such an outrage and a spectacular violation of his most recent pledges that it destroyed appeasement. British policy drastically changed; however, Hitler failed to appreciate it. The Western powers now guaranteed Poland, Romania, Greece, and Turkey against attack, incidentally increasing Stalin's bargaining power.

Hitler wrongly supposed that he could force Poland into satellite status. To isolate the Poles and the Western powers, and to discourage the latter from helping Poland, he gave Stalin what the latter had long sought, a pact dividing Eastern Europe with the USSR. But the Western powers did not yield. When Germany invaded Poland, it found itself at war with the West as well. Hitler was not a little dismayed. He had not wanted all-out war with the West—at least not yet.[3]

## Preparations for War

Nazi preparations for war had been erratic, especially of its economic base. Rearmament had started slowly, although the Nazis had intensified its effort by the late 1930s, reaching an extraordinary 23 percent of Germany's gross national product (GNP) in 1939. Contrary to a later myth, it was geared to an eventual long war, although not one as early as 1939, and not to a series of short blitzkrieg campaigns. The rearmament effort was not, however, always intelligently directed. Hitler was ignorant of economics, while Hermann Göring, his nominal deputy and theoretical director of the economy, did not know much about his job and was too lazy to learn. The military buildup, until 1942, was hampered by poor coordination, quarrels between agencies and Nazi Party factions, and excessive military intervention in the production end of weapons procurement. The latter continued even after Dr. Fritz Todt, the able Nazi construction boss, and his successor,

Albert Speer, began rationalizing the economy in 1941–1942. There were always too many types of equipment in production and too many projects in development. Even though the economy was fully mobilized and civilian consumption was cut after war began, poor management resulted in enormous waste and a less than expected output of weapons. Todt and Speer did not increase the overall war effort, but they made it more efficient.

During the 1930s, the Nazis had launched several critical programs to make Germany independent of its normal sources of some items that would be inaccessible in a long war. They built huge industrial complexes to make synthetic oil, rubber, fibers, and nitrogen. They carefully dispersed critical weapons industries, moving some to central Germany, farther from western air bases. The aircraft industry was especially well protected, with new production sites located outside cities and well spaced in strongly constructed buildings and with most processes duplicated. But other preparations, notably stockpiling raw materials, were erratic. Germany's railroads, for example, were not in good shape at the start of the war.[4]

## The German Armed Forces

The armed forces had not prepared consistently or always intelligently for war. The German Army had maintained its reputation as the world's best army, with an unmatched expertise at the level of tactics and operations, a supremely able staff, and outstanding cooperation of arms: infantry, artillery, and now airpower and tanks. Hitler had promoted the development of panzer and airborne forces and airpower. The German armored forces were superior to their enemies in tactics, organization, and training. Although they lacked heavy tanks or armored personnel carriers and their tanks had inferior guns and armor to at least the better types of French tanks, German tanks were faster, more mobile, and equipped with better radio and optical equipment than were the Allies' tanks. However, panzer and fully motorized infantry divisions formed only a fraction of an army largely supported by horse-drawn vehicles. Maintaining and supplying new equipment were such strains that the number of trucks in the non-motorized units had to be reduced soon after the war began. The army had skimped on artillery development, and in 1939 its ammunition reserves were low. Nor did it have enough signals units. Its trucks were not suited to bad roads, and even its horse-drawn vehicles proved too heavy for Russian and eastern European roads. Field Marshal Gerd von Rundstedt later remarked that it had been fortunate that the Polish campaign had been fought in dry weather.

Some of the army's weaknesses were long-standing and infected the other services. The German Army had downgraded intelligence and logistics. Although well informed about Germany's neighbors on the European mainland, it knew less about the British and was remarkably ignorant about the Soviet Union. A basic problem was that intelligence was often regarded as a minor factor in planning operations, and supply issues were often scanted. German supply problems in previous wars had usually been relatively simple, for Germany usually had fought its immediate neighbors and had an excellent railroad network. Thus, the Germans did not consider supply until after deciding on their war plan.

Perhaps closely related to this issue was the army's actual weakness in the field of higher strategy. The Prussian/German General Staff was oriented toward planning and winning campaigns and not plotting the grand strategy of entire wars—far less so than were the British, Americans, or Soviets. In the war against Napoleon, Prussia had been only one partner in the victorious coalition, fighting on one front, and had not supplied the larger strategy of the war. In the wars of unification, under the guidance of the civilian Otto von Bismarck, Prussia had fought on one front. In World War I, the disastrous and perverse strategy of the Schlieffen Plan brought Britain into the war, put Germany on the wrong side of world opinion when the Central Powers had a good claim to be the injured party, and failed to defeat France. The General Staff then wasted a year dithering before attacking Verdun in 1916 and then sanctioned unrestricted submarine warfare in 1917, bringing the United States into the war. Finally, it had muffed Germany's last chance to win in 1918. As a bitter internal critic, Gen. Moritz von Faber du Faur remarked in the 1950s that the General Staff had produced "good technicians, capable of turning out one plan of campaign after another, and then letting fate run its course." The planners banked on quick victories, without pondering their larger impact or what would happen if a campaign failed. Hitler, however inadequate his own war direction, operated in a strategic vacuum. The result was that his army won many battles and whole campaigns, sometimes against extraordinary odds, but lost wars.

Moreover, the factor of corruption—moral and intellectual—in the history of the General Staff cannot be ignored. Reaching its peak under the elder Gen. Helmuth von Moltke, it had deteriorated into a much narrower institution, with its members often quite ignorant outside their own professional interests. By the time of the First World War, some officers were surprised to learn that German was spoken at all in Austria-Hungary, Germany's main ally (and the center of German culture up to the late nineteenth century), while others assumed that all inhabitants of the multinational empire were Germans. In the 1930s, the German officer corps agreed with many of the Nazis' initial aims. The professional soldiers did not like Hitler or the Nazis (although there were exceptions), and Hitler detested them as part of the "upper ten thousand" of pre-Nazi society, but they were slow to resist him. Later, Hitler tamed or bribed many generals with money or estates, while firing or easing out the more obstreperous figures. Thus an innovative institution that German liberals founded to fight the tyranny of Napoleon ended as the servant of a tyranny a thousand times worse. It entered World War II without an overall strategic plan for victory.[5]

The Luftwaffe, or German Air Force, in 1939 was not merely one of the strongest but one of the most advanced air forces in the world. It had well-trained pilots, an excellent, if short-ranged, single-engine fighter in the Messerschmitt (Me) 109, and effective medium bombers and dive-bombers. Unlike most air forces, it had at least attempted to acquire a long-range escort fighter, although the Me 110 ultimately proved unsatisfactory. It was, compared to its rivals, well prepared with navigational aids and electronic guidance systems for bombing. More than any other air force, it was mobile and well suited to move to forward bases, backed by a large air transport force and a strong complement of effective antiaircraft guns. It also had an efficient air-sea rescue service. Most important to Germany's early victories, it had perfected support for army operations. Only later would its limitations and mistakes become clear.

However, the Luftwaffe was not intended to be solely, or perhaps even primarily, a "tactical" air force. Its development into what Field Marshal Wolfram von Richthofen later bitterly described as the "Army's whore" was unwanted by its founders, who had been strongly interested in strategic bombing. The ultimate neglect of acquiring four-engine heavy bombers stemmed partly from the pressure of more immediate needs and from basic limitations of German industry accentuated by mistaken technical decisions. Early designs for heavy bombers were abandoned for lack of suitable engines, one effect of the Versailles Treaty's military limitations. Moreover, these limitations of Germany's aircraft industry and fuel supply would have prevented developing a large fleet of heavy bombers comparable with those of the Royal Air Force (RAF) and U.S. Army Air Force (USAAF) during World War II. Nevertheless, a modest force of heavy bombers could have been built and would have been a major asset for the Germans in the Battles of Britain and the Atlantic.

The fumbling technical direction of the Luftwaffe's later development aborted this possibility. Göring, the nominal head of the air force, was a technical ignoramus, although his laziness left considerable scope to its real founders—Gen. Walter Wever, who was extremely capable, and State Secretary for Air Erhard Milch. But after Wever's death in 1936, the Luftwaffe never enjoyed a competent chief of staff again. Ernst Udet, the head of technical development, was unsuited to direct the poorly organized department. Udet and others promoted dive-bombing, insisting that not only small, single-engine planes such as the Junkers 87 Stuka but also much heavier aircraft be capable of steep dive-bomb runs. That requirement greatly delayed the development of the Luftwaffe's best bomber, the Junkers 88 medium bomber, and reduced its performance. (In actual operations it rarely dived at a steep angle.) The mania for dive-bombing was absurdly imposed even on the four-engine bomber design, the Heinkel 177, requiring adherence to the plane's original design, which yoked two engines in a single nacelle to drive one propeller. Originally chosen to reduce drag in normal flight, the configuration proved unworkable, but the dive-bomber obsession prevented changing over to an arrangement of four separate engines.

In general, the Luftwaffe's later designs, which should have provided the second wave of planes for World War II, proved unsuccessful. The Messerschmitt 209 and 210, Heinkel 177, Heinkel 129, and others all proved failures. Only the Focke-Wulf 190 was an exception. The course of the war also exposed less obvious weaknesses in Germany's initial equipment. Good as the Messerschmitt 109 was, it may have been inferior to its rival design, the Heinkel 112, and the Nazis (possibly because of prejudice against Ernst Heinkel, wrongly believed to be politically unreliable or of Jewish descent) did not procure the follow-on design, the Heinkel 100, although it showed better performance and safety than the Me 109 did. Procuring the Stuka may have been a mistake in the long run. While the specialized dive-bomber was highly effective in the early campaigns of the war, a more versatile fighter-bomber might have been a better choice. The Luftwaffe did not have enough fighters. Its reliance on the Me 110 as a long-range escort proved mistaken, while drop tanks to extend the range of the Me 109 were not developed until too late. The Luftwaffe's production program proved inadequate.

The director of air intelligence, Josef Schmid, was a drunkard with little knowledge of foreign matters. Intelligence about the French and the other air forces of Germany's immediate neighbors was adequate, but the Luftwaffe neglected, then fumbled, collecting intelligence about Britain and the RAF. It neglected radar development and ground control. Further, Göring not so much neglected as actually opposed cooperation with the navy. When the war began, the Luftwaffe suffered an acute shortage of bombs and was not even well fixed for fuel.[6]

The navy was even more erratically directed than the air force was. It suffered, perhaps inevitably, from a low priority. Adm. Erich Raeder, its conservative and unimaginative head, was the wrong man in a preposterous position. An even bigger liar in his memoir and in his postwar testimony than most outright Nazis, he was a "battleship admiral" heading a navy almost without battleships. Although U-boats had proven its most effective weapon in World War I, the dominant element in the navy tended to believe, as did the British, that convoys and sonar had largely nullified the effectiveness of the submarine. Raeder also showed little interest in airpower. He concentrated instead on building a huge force of modern surface ships. The "Z Plan" for war against Britain and ultimately the United States envisaged a force of big-gun ships, and the navy scheduled construction of only two small aircraft carriers, with two more anticipated by the plan's completion in 1948. This fleet was not balanced, even by the standards of the 1930s or even compared to the British Royal Navy, which was itself too dominated by the big-gun school. Nor did Raeder prepare effectively for the war that actually broke out, well before the Z Plan was anywhere near complete. Although German surface ships were well designed and formidable opponents for their generally much older British counterparts, the German Navy simply did not have enough of them. Even had the Z Plan been realized, it would not have secured success against the Anglo-American carrier force.

Apart from the Germans' underestimation of the submarine, Raeder tried to force large, clumsy U-boats heavily armed with deck guns on the submarine service. Its head, Adm. Karl Dönitz, successfully fought Raeder, emphasizing a more versatile craft, although the standard Type VII Atlantic U-boat he favored proved too small.[7]

## Allied Weakness

While the political and psychological weaknesses that had helped bring about the war faded quickly, Britain was in fact not a colossus straddling the world (as widely imagined) but a medium-size industrial power with serious economic problems and a strategically overstretched set of colonies. India, Burma, and Ceylon were well on their way to independence, while the few colonies that were economic assets to Britain—Malaya, Singapore, and British Borneo—were the most exposed to attack. India and the White Dominions would be a real help but only after lengthy mobilization. Important British industries, notably shipbuilding, had already decayed seriously. Many shipyards had closed, while those remaining had obsolete equipment. Britain's light engineering and machine tool industries were relatively weak, while its aircraft industry was less advanced than those of the other major powers, probably owing to the backwardness of British civil aviation.

The Royal Navy was one of the world's three biggest fleets, but it had fallen behind technically. Many ships were old and worn. Although the Royal Navy had pioneered the development of the aircraft carrier, the big-gun element dominated it more than in the U.S. or Japanese navies. Its air arm was in poor shape. Its few carriers were mostly old and had small plane capacities, accentuated by practices that made less use of space aboard the carriers than did the Americans and Japanese. The Fleet Air Arm's planes were obsolescent at best. Its only advantage—but a big one—was that its airmen were well trained and efficient. The Royal Navy was not well prepared for antisubmarine warfare. Overconfident about the effectiveness of sonar (asdic), it assumed that escort ships could be built quickly if necessary. It could not count on much help from the RAF's small and poorly equipped Coastal Command.

The Royal Air Force, until late in the 1930s, focused on strategic bombing rather than on maritime cooperation, tactical support for the army, or even air defense. Late in the 1930s, however, it built an excellent air defense system, including a fine force of up-to-date fighters, but in other ways the RAF was still not well prepared for war. The attention given strategic bombing did not produce an effective bomber force. Bomber Command was composed of medium and light bombers, mostly of poor design, with not particularly well-trained crews. They could not bomb accurately even in daylight and would prove practically helpless when the RAF switched to night bombing shortly after the war began. British bombs were small and weak. The RAF had not even tried to develop a long-range escort fighter, believing it impossible to do so and that its bombers could fight their way to their targets without one.

If the RAF and Royal Navy had themselves fallen behind, then the British Army had been the stepchild of rearmament. The British government had been reluctant until late in the 1930s to contemplate mounting another British Expeditionary Force. The army was short of new equipment, especially effective antitank and antiaircraft guns. Except for some heavily armored "I" tanks, its tanks were unsatisfactory. Most were weakly armored and early in the war carried only machine guns. Emphasizing mobility, the British had not paid enough attention to the ability of their tanks to fight other tanks. Worse, if possible, the standard "cruiser" tanks were unreliable, often breaking down. Heavy losses in France delayed improving British tank design, which caught up with the Germans' designs only near the end of the war. The British armored force was split between the old Royal Tank Corps and a few reluctantly mechanized cavalry units that only slowly adjusted to the change from horses to armored vehicles. Meanwhile, "all-tank" fanatics who eschewed cooperation further hampered the units' development. Although fully motorized, unlike most German divisions, ordinary British infantry divisions had less firepower in automatic weapons, mortars, and artillery than their German counterparts had. Last, the British officer corps was not as professional as was its German counterpart.[8]

## The Early Victories

Although not nearly as well prepared for war as generally imagined, the Germans' strength was overwhelming in relation to that of the Poles; and given the passivity of the Western powers, this force was sufficient. The Germans were free to concentrate the Luftwaffe and their mechanized forces in the east and risk leaving their Western front weakly defended, so much so that had the French struck quickly they might have reached the Rhine in 1939. The Polish forces were so poorly equipped, having only a few obsolete planes and tanks, that they were easily beaten despite heroic resistance. Airpower and armor secured an inevitable German victory.[9]

The Germans' next victory was the conquest of Denmark and Norway. Seizing Denmark was easy. The conquest of Norway was a stunning blow that toppled the government of Prime Minister Neville Chamberlain in Britain, which led to Churchill's becoming prime minister. The British retreat was a humiliating defeat for the Royal Navy and a spectacular manifestation of Nazi power.

Yet, as with other German victories early in the war, the conquest was a bit less impressive than it seemed and succeeded by a narrower margin than was supposed. The Germans depended on surprise, on quickly gaining air superiority, and on the extreme weakness of the Norwegian forces, which were small, not alert, and used obsolete equipment. The Norwegians had no modern fighters or bombers, tanks, submachine guns, or even grenades.

The Germans achieved surprise despite that a move against Norway had been long anticipated. On April 8, the British began mining the Leads, the inshore route sheltered by islands off the Norwegian coast, that ships used to carry iron ore from northern Sweden to Germany. The Allies expected that the Germans might react by landing in Norway, and the British had embarked troops aboard some warships to counter this maneuver. The Admiralty (except for Vice Adm. Max Horton, the head of the submarine service) misread the movements of the German fleet as portending not an invasion of Norway but a breakout by a surface raiding force into the Atlantic. The British troops went ashore, and the Home Fleet moved to counter an Atlantic sortie. Although evidence quickly piled up that an invasion was under way, the Admiralty was slow to react. The four infantry battalions available, if rushed to Stavanger and Bergen, might have retaken those ports from the Germans. The German forces got through the danger zone, and seized most of the Norwegian ports, including Oslo, and vital airfields. British bombers could only reach a few Norwegian targets without fighter escort. Only in the north at Narvik, far from German air bases, was the British navy able to react quickly and effectively, demolishing the German naval force there, which included nearly half of the German destroyers. The Allies tried to retake Trondheim in central Norway, but their decision making remained sluggish. The weak, poorly equipped forces landed at two small ports flanking Trondheim but were soon forced to evacuate. While the Luftwaffe was not that effective at this point of attacking ships (they had no torpedo bombers or heavy bombs available), the British had little air cover and weak antiaircraft armament. The Allies eventually retook Narvik but only after the front had collapsed in France and right before they had to evacuate Norway entirely.

Norway, however, did not prove a particularly rewarding conquest for the Nazis. To gain it, most of their surface fleet was sunk or so heavily damaged as to be out of action for months. Victory in France made securing access to Swedish iron ore less important and gave the U-boats far more useful bases than those in Norway. Last, to hold Norway against Allied invasion proved costly and involved pinning down hundreds of thousands of men and coastal defenses for the rest of the war.[10]

## Western Europe

The greatest German triumph, which decisively shaped the rest of the war, was the conquest of Western Europe. Although accomplished by a narrower margin than ordinarily assumed, it was achieved with an ease that surprised the Germans themselves and helped produce a disastrous overconfidence.

The traditional narrative holds that the Nazis must have won through overwhelming strength or, alternatively, because of some inner social rottenness endemic to France. More recently, it has become fashionable to regard the German victory almost as a fluke.[11] But the Germans' victories over their immediate neighbors were no more accidents than their later failures against more distant enemies.

Hitler had wished to strike in the West soon after the Polish campaign, despite the extreme reluctance of his generals and a dissatisfactory plan of campaign, involving a wide sweep to outflank the French Maginot Line through the Netherlands and Belgium. Few expected complete victory as this move would run headlong into the Allies' main point of strength. At most, a partial victory might be achieved, inflicting serious losses on the French and British and providing bases in the Low Countries for the air and sea war against Britain. But most felt it was unlikely to knock France out of the war. And despite Hitler, many German generals still respected the French Army. The effectiveness of the Luftwaffe and panzer forces in Poland pleased the generals, but most thought that the lessons of Poland were of limited applicability against the better-equipped western European armies.

The Allies, for their part, never envisaged anything other than a long war in which a major land offensive should be launched in the west only after blockade and other measures—possibly including land action in Scandinavia and the Balkans—seriously weakened Germany. If the Germans launched an offensive in the west, they thought, it would be exactly the sort of attack the Germans planned in 1939.

Fortunately for Hitler, bad weather enforced delay after delay in the offensive, and during late 1939 and early 1940, German strength increased faster than that of the Allies did. By the spring of 1940, Germany was far better equipped than it had been in 1939. The Germans were also forced to change their strategy. The original plan had fallen into Allied hands in early 1940; moreover, Hitler and others had long had misgivings about it. As early as October 1939 Hitler had suggested shifting the main point of attack well to the south. He may only have sought a softer spot to strike. But thinking independently on similar lines, Gen. (later Field Marshal) Erich von Manstein, the ablest soldier in the German Army and the chief of staff of Gerd von Rundstedt's Army Group A, developed a subtle, full-blown plan of campaign.

Field Marshal Fedor von Bock's Army Group B in the north, originally slated to be the main force, would strike into the Low Countries with just enough strength to appear to be the main attack. The Allies would move north to meet it. Meanwhile, Army Group A, with most of the panzer divisions, would strike in the Ardennes, a forested and rugged area much farther south, where the Allies would not expect an assault. Traversing the Ardennes as quickly as possible, the panzer forces would cross the Meuse River, principally around Sedan; sweep west far behind the Allied forces moving into Belgium and the Netherlands; and cut off the whole Allied northern wing. German intelligence at this point, and through the French campaign, was excellent. Reading some Allied ciphers, they were well informed of Allied dispositions, which played right into their hands.

The Allied command system was muddled and illogical. The French dispersed authority among three widely separated headquarters with poor communications. Bad communications would be a common feature of the campaign, slowing the already sluggish reactions of the Allied generals and worsening relations between the Allies. The French commanders were all elderly men who were slow to adapt to new or rapidly changing situations, even compared to the senior German generals like Rundstedt. The French commander, Maurice Gamelin, was on bad terms with his chief subordinate, Gen. Alphonse Georges, and the division of authority between them was unclear.

Expecting an assault on the Low Countries, much as the Germans had originally planned, the Allies argued about how far to go to meet it. Gamelin insisted on advancing as far as possible and deployed much of his mobile reserve on the far left to push to Breda in the Netherlands. That arrangement made some, like Georges, uneasy, and the overcommitment of forces behind the Maginot Line, which the Germans never considered attacking, left the Allies without a strategic reserve. Only weak forces held the Meuse, while the French and Belgians dismissed the Ardennes as unsuitable for deploying large forces. Each assumed that that the other's covering forces would take care of the area. The Dutch and Belgians refused to concert planning with the British and French, although the Belgians at least covertly exchanged full information with France. The French, however, ignored warnings from Swiss intelligence that the Germans were shifting the main point of their attack farther south.

Contrary to popular opinion after the war, the Germans had no quantitative advantage in May 1940 over the Allies except in the air. Some 141 German divisions faced about 144 Allied divisions (counting the Dutch and

Belgians), mustering 2,445 German versus 3,383 Allied tanks. (Some have given even higher estimates for the Allies' strength.) The Germans, however, had immense qualitative advantages. The Dutch and Belgians were not well armed; their air forces were small and almost entirely obsolete. Army Group B stood an excellent chance of smashing them before the Allies could come to their aid. The French and the BEF were far better equipped; still, the Germans had a considerable advantage. At almost every level, their tactics, training, discipline, command, and communications were better than those of the Allies, as was much of their equipment. One exception was the tanks. In important respects, most French tanks were superior to their German counterparts and featured heavier armor and guns, especially the Somua and "B" tanks. As their Allied counterparts found later in the war when fighting the Panther and Tiger tanks, the Germans could stop the B tanks only by blowing off their tracks or hitting the small, vulnerable points presented by the radiators in their sides. However, few French tanks had radios, and those available were poor. Even the big tanks had one-man turrets, with the same man serving as commander and gunner. German tanks were thus better controlled. Overall, the Germans felt French tank units used poor tactics, reacted slowly, and were poorly trained. Much of the French armor was dispersed in direct support of infantry units. Only a portion was concentrated in newly formed mechanized and armored divisions, whereas the Germans had concentrated all their tanks in such divisions. The sole British armored division had not yet arrived. The French and British, unlike the Germans, had few antitank or antiaircraft guns and antitank mines.

In the air, the balance of numbers is not quite clear, since the effective strength of the French Air Force remains uncertain. It appears that some 2,589 German aircraft were operational against only 1,413 Allied planes. The poorly led French Air Force was caught while transitioning to new aircraft and was short of pilots, but the French command, expecting a long struggle, may have held back a considerable part of its strength. Qualitatively, the French Air Force was inferior, with too many types of planes. All French fighters were inferior to the Me 109, and only the latest, the Dewoitine D520, and the American-built Curtiss Hawk 75 were at all competitive. French warning and ground control systems were inadequate; moreover, their bombers and their fighter tactics were mostly obsolete. The French and British still flew tight three-plane "vics," or *V*-shape formations, while the Luftwaffe used the far superior four-plane "finger-four" formation. An improvement over the French fighters, the British Hurricane—the newer

Spitfire was held back in Britain—was still inferior to the Me 109. The British bombers based in France were all obsolete planes with very small bomb loads. Further, unlike their German counterparts, Allied airmen were not trained or equipped to support ground forces.

## The Attack

On May 10, the Germans struck. With three panzer divisions and all available airborne forces, Army Group B's attack appeared to the Allies to be the German's main effort. It was strong enough to force the Dutch into surrender within five days.

As the Allied forces of Army Group 1 and the BEF surged forward in the west, Army Group A pushed through the Ardennes. The Allies neither sent Allied aircraft to attack the traffic jams there nor paid attention to air reconnaissance that showed bridging moving forward in that area. (The Allies, further west, were impeded by huge traffic jams of their own, as millions of Belgians and Dutch refugees, and later the French, flooded south.) The French did not recognize the main attack over the Meuse until it was too late. The Germans fell on the French Ninth Army and its neighbors—comprising the weakest and worst divisions in the whole French Army—which had only some light tanks and a few antitank guns.

Nevertheless, the Germans found crossing the Meuse on May 13–14 difficult. Their success stemmed from the Luftwaffe's overwhelming, concentrated effort. Very heavy Stuka attacks knocked out French artillery and communications and neutralized, although they did not destroy, the pillboxes defending the south bank. Only now did the Allies act, after the Germans had strong concentrations of antiaircraft guns around the bridges thrown over the Meuse. The British and French suffered enormous losses from German fighters and flak, trying to knock out the bridges at low level. The British planes carried only 250-pound bombs, unlikely to do serious damage even if they hit. Meanwhile, the Germans expanded the bridgeheads.

Gen. Friedrich von Mellenthin later wrote, "Even after our initial breakthrough at Sedan, the French would still have had a fighting chance if their High Command had not lost its head and had refrained from counterattacks until all available armor had been assembled for a decisive blow." Instead, the Germans defeated their belatedly arriving armored divisions, scattered and disorganized in the process of moving to the front, piecemeal and drove them west toward the sea.

Now, the only question was whether the Allied forces in the north, or some of them, could escape. A successful breakout to the south might have been possible as late as May 21 had the French command acted swiftly. The prime minister had replaced the hapless Gamelin on May 19 with another elderly general, Maxime Weygand. He may have been professionally more competent, but his belated appointment and the time needed to return from his previous command in Syria further postponed and modified the plans Gamelin had sluggishly made for a major attack. By then, Weygand's plans were hopelessly outdated and unrealistic. He counted on Belgian and British movements that were now impossible, to release eight divisions that could not have moved in the time available, and on French forces that no longer existed. The commander of Army Group 1, Gen. Gaston Billotte, had been mortally injured on May 21 but was not officially replaced until May 25, the day the counteroffensive was to take place. Lord Gort, the BEF commander, confirmed his suspicion that he would have to evacuate his troops by sea.[12]

Since no successful stand could be made in France once the forces in the north were gone, the British government faced a critical decision. It was now a governing coalition led by Winston Churchill. Brilliant, energetic, erratic, and eloquent, he was the exact opposite of his predecessor, Neville Chamberlain, and ideally suited to rally the British people and inject new energy into the war effort.

# 2

## The British Carry On

*Dunkirk through the Battle of Britain*

As the Germans swept far behind the Allied northern armies, Lord Gort, commanding the British Expeditionary Force, had become worried, far more so than his superiors in London were. He knew that the Belgians on his left and the French armies on his right were in bad shape. By May 19, 1940, Gort saw that there was a serious chance that he would have to fall back northwest to the Channel coast and evacuate by sea. Many in London still expected a counteroffensive to cut off the German advance or thought that, if anything, the BEF would retreat southwest over the Somme. After meeting Gen. Gaston Billotte that day, Gort lost any faith in launching a counteroffensive, and the Germans soon ended the latter illusion.

Gort's warnings led London to start planning an evacuation. Gort himself prepared a final defensive line along the Aa Canal south of the port of Dunkirk and formed provisional units from rear area troops to man it. Elements of the BEF that were not absolutely needed—bluntly called "useless mouths"—began leaving for England.

The British had already begun removing ships and boats of all sorts from Dutch and Belgian ports. They demolished the ports and oil stocks there, to the extent possible, and later extended these efforts to harbors in northern France. Although not originally part of the preparations to save the BEF, these actions proved important to the operation. The most important prizes secured during the evacuation were fifty 200-ton Dutch *schuyts* (shallow-draft motor coasters).

On May 20, Lord Ironside, the chief of the Imperial General Staff, met Billotte. Shaken by the state of the French Army, Ironside saw that Gort's assessment was right. The French and British agreed to contribute two divisions each to a counterattack in the Arras sector to brake the German advance. (This move was not the major counteroffensive that was supposed to cut off the whole German thrust toward the Channel; its exact shape had not yet been determined.) Although the Germans reached the Channel that day, Weygand imagined for several more days that only "light enemy units," not the main weight of the German Army, were in the rear of Army Group 1.

The Allied counterattack of May 21 dribbled down, with only two British tank battalions and two infantry battalions accompanied by some small detachments of the French Third Mechanized Cavalry Division executing it. But the attack, hitting Erwin Rommel's Seventh Panzer Division, caused serious damage out of proportion to the losses inflicted. The Germans found that their standard antitank guns could not stop British I tanks, some of which had two-pounder guns that could trade fire with the German tanks. Only 88mm flak guns could destroy them. The Germans became more cautious. The panzer group commander Col. Gen. Ewald von Kleist cancelled plans to send panzer divisions straight to Boulogne, Calais, and Dunkirk and ordered the Tenth Panzer Division, slated for Dunkirk, into reserve for a time. Nevertheless, on May 22, the Germans swung north and northwest deep into the rear of Army Group 1, nearing Boulogne and Calais and cutting the BEF's supply line. The following day the BEF went on half rations and retreated from Arras. Gort now warned that he definitely would have to evacuate his troops. Strong British forces entered Boulogne and Calais to slow the German movements.[1]

But the German pressure abruptly lessened. Army Group A's commander, Gen. Gerd von Rundstedt, had issued a halt order, and the group largely held on the Aa Canal line as the panzer units stopped. (Bock's Army Group B continued to attack from the east.) Rundstedt and his chief of staff Georg Sodenstern still feared an Allied counteroffensive to pinch off Army Group A. Col. Gen. Günther von Kluge, whose Fourth Army controlled the panzer groups, was also uneasy. Kleist's group reported half of its tanks were out of action, although most would be repaired in a few days, and wanted a rest. Rundstedt thus halted the panzer groups, but the II and VII Infantry Corps continued advancing. The attack on Boulogne and Calais went ahead.

On May 23 Göring suggested to Hitler that destroying the forces around Dunkirk could be left to "his" Luftwaffe. Some Luftwaffe commanders, notably Gen. Albert Kesselring and Gen. Wolfram von Richthofen, on hearing of Göring's boast, warned that the Luftwaffe alone could not stop a seaborne evacuation, but it is not clear whether Hitler knew of their views. A factor in many Germans' thinking during this period, often ignored, is that they seem to have greatly underestimated the number of French and British forces in the northern pocket at only 100,000 men, or a quarter of the real total.

Gen. Franz Halder, the army chief of staff, and most of Rundstedt's subordinate commanders regarded the halt as unnecessary. Along with Bock, they saw no threat of a counteroffensive. Halder intervened to end the halt and to shift the Fourth Army from Army Group A to Bock's command. On May 24, however, while visiting Rundstedt's headquarters, Hitler vetoed the change and sustained Rundstedt on the halt order.

Why he did so was later viewed as highly controversial. After the war, when the decision to stop was universally seen as a mistake, Rundstedt and his later chief of staff and biographer Günther Blumentritt, seconded by some other generals, ignored or deliberately obscured Rundstedt's responsibility for the original decision to halt and put all the blame for the (second) halt order on Hitler. Many argued that Hitler had stopped the advance to let the BEF escape, in the belief that if he did so, the British would be readier to make peace. As Albert Speer remarked, however, anyone who thought that Hitler wanted to let the British escape "didn't understand the Fuehrer very well."

The evidence sustains Hans-Adolf Jacobsen's conclusion that the generals' claims about the halt order were a "postwar fantasy." Hitler wanted the BEF destroyed, not evacuated, as his Directive 13 stated, and the Luftwaffe and the German Navy's motor torpedo boats, the only naval units available, tried to stop the evacuation. The halt order had other, circumstantial explanations. Hitler's own contemporary explanation for sustaining the halt order was his evident belief—possibly prompted by Gen. Wilhelm Keitel, head of the nominally interservice Oberkommando der Wehrmacht (OKW)—that the wet Flanders terrain was unsuitable for tanks. (In fact, in May 1940, it was quite dry.) Hitler himself had served in Flanders in World War I and, with vivid memories of the Flanders mud, readily accepted the idea. He, Rundstedt, and Kluge were anxious to conserve tank strength for the coming showdown with the remaining French armies after the northern Allied pocket was wiped out and the Germans turned south. Hitler also believed Göring's promise that the Luftwaffe would do the job in the north.

The issue, however, did not seem as crucial at the time as it did later. Halder grumbled at the halt order and Hitler's refusal to allow the transfer of Fourth Army to Bock, but he was not terribly concerned, remarking in his diary entry of May 25 that "the battle will be won, this way or that." On May 30, he blamed the halt, and the bad weather that grounded the Luftwaffe, for "countless thousands of the enemy . . . getting away to England right under our noses." Still he and other Germans, as previously noted, underestimated the numbers involved. Indeed, some did not seem to think that a large-scale evacuation by sea was even possible, a view that even Adm. François Darlan, the head of the French Navy, shared.

Halder was also right about the failure to shift the Fourth Army to Army Group B, which was, in part, responsible for the poor coordination of later German attacks on the perimeter around Dunkirk. On top of the Germans' caution on May 22, the halt order gave the Allies an important respite. Had the Germans continued, they would have inflicted far greater losses on the British but would not necessarily have destroyed the BEF. The British, in that case, would have started withdrawing at least a day earlier and based their evacuation on Ostend rather than Dunkirk. Ostend was a longer trip by sea and farther from British air bases, but the British still could have gotten their men out.[2]

Dunkirk, in fact, was not entirely desirable as an evacuation point. Although the third biggest port in France, it had serious limitations—a narrow harbor entrance and a strong tidal current—and was vulnerable to bombing. In fact, the harbor proper was unusable by the time the main evacuation started. Northeast of Dunkirk, however, are sixteen miles of accessible beaches, and the surrounding canals, rivers, and flooded areas obstructed the Germans' advance.

On May 25, Gort—this time without consulting his government or the French—shifted his Fifth and Fiftieth Infantry Divisions, which were slated for the counteroffensive Weygand was still planning, from the south to his northern flank to plug a dangerous gap between the BEF and the Belgians, who warned that they were near collapse. Following a previous withdrawal without notice in the Arras sector, Gort's actions further poisoned relations with the French High Command that were already difficult due to bad communications. Weygand and some other French leaders began making the British, and/or the Belgians, the scapegoats for their inevitable defeat.

The Germans had made little progress over the previous two days, taking only Boulogne, which the British Navy had managed to evacuate. On May 26, Hitler lifted the halt order, although the Germans did not get major attacks under way for another sixteen hours. The Germans did take Calais.

The British, in the hope of winning valuable time, had sacrificed a first-class force (part of their First Armored Division) to hold the place. That decision was probably a mistake, but the stand at Calais tied up the Tenth Panzer Division and a considerable air effort.

## The Dunkirk Evacuation

On May 26, the British began an all-out evacuation. By now, the perimeter around Dunkirk had hardened. The French III Corps under General Benoît-Léon de Fornel de la Laurencie, for whom the British, in spite of growing inter-Allied recriminations, had the highest praise, took an important role in Dunkirk's defense. But the situation was clearly desperate. The British expected that, at best, they could get out no more than 45,000 men over two days, and they foresaw taking out only their own men. They could not save any equipment. Peculiarly, Weygand failed to tell Gen. Georges Blanchard, now commanding Army Group 1, of the evacuation. Nor did Weygand authorize French forces to take part in it for another two days. Meanwhile, Adm. Jean-Marie Abrial, commanding the French naval forces in the north, envisaged holding a permanent bridgehead and not totally withdrawing under fierce air attack.

The Royal Air Force, now flying from Britain, sent in fighters and even bombers (some obsolete) to cover the evacuation. Both the Allied air forces and the Luftwaffe were stretched, operating at extreme range from their bases, and tired after two weeks of continuous fighting. Fortunately for the Allies, the weather often interfered with German air operations, while calm seas favored the evacuation. On May 27, the British threw in Spitfires, the first time the British fighter saw serious combat. The German pilots were perturbed by a fighter as fast as the Me 109 and more maneuverable. Luftwaffe attacks, however, had made Dunkirk harbor unusable. To pick up the men, the British shifted to using the long "East Mole"—an artificial barrier that protected the harbor and had never been intended to berth ships—as an embarkation point and focused on getting men off the beaches. They also began calling up private craft to help, resulting in the famous fleet of "little ships" that braved the Channel.

The perimeter was now under heavy pressure, mitigated by the fact that nearly half the French First Army, still holding out in a pocket around Lille, pinned down German forces for four more days. On the night of May 27–28, however, the Allies suffered two heavy blows. First, the Belgians surrendered. King Leopold, the effective Belgian commander in chief, with far more power than the usual constitutional monarch, had warned that

Belgian resistance would soon end, but he did not consult with the Allies before taking the final step. The Belgian forces were backed against the sea, and the next German attack would smash into an area jammed with civilians. The British learned of the Belgian surrender only belatedly, owing to a communications failure. Only a desperate effort by British armored cars and engineers and French mechanized cavalry plugged the twenty-mile gap opened in the Allied line, long enough for substantial forces to come up.

Leopold's behavior in the hours before the surrender was often exaggerated. His actions, along with his unpleasant character, his unfriendly demeanor toward the Allies throughout, and his later conduct under the German occupation, made him, and even the Belgians in general (who had fought hard), scapegoats for the Allied defeat. A second blow to the Allies was self-inflicted. A badly written order led the British Second Antiaircraft Brigade to destroy all its heavy antiaircraft guns, leaving only some 40mm Bofors guns to oppose the Luftwaffe.

Fortunately, the German air effort, while strong, was unimaginative. The Luftwaffe failed to concentrate on ships or the approach to the East Mole, from which a majority of the men embarked. Instead, it wasted many bombs on the already ruined town and the beaches, hitting the latter with high-explosive bombs, even though fragmentation bombs would have been far deadlier against troops.

The British were able to continue the evacuation much longer than originally expected. On May 28, with air fighting more intense, they began sending over several squadrons at a time but at the cost of leaving longer intervals between patrols over the beachhead. The Dutch schuyts, manned by the Royal Navy, arrived with badly needed food, water, and ammunition and helped bring men off the beaches. By this time, the Germans had pushed so far into terrain unsuited for tanks that they began to withdraw them.

On May 30, after unpleasant incidents with the French, Churchill insisted that thereafter French and British troops must be saved in equal numbers. The next day, the sea got rougher, making it harder for ships to berth at the East Mole or to approach the beaches. But the mass of small craft ferried men from shore to the bigger ships. This work, in fact, was their main contribution to the evacuation, as destroyers and transports took most of the men. The Allies improvised jetties by driving trucks into the surf. That day, the French surrendered at Lille.

On June 1, air attacks became so fierce that embarkation was limited to the nights. The BEF's evacuation was completed, but the evacuation of

French troops continued through the night of June 3–4, when further rescues became utterly impossible. Some 30,000–40,000 French were left behind. (The exact number is uncertain since the Germans may have conflated those captured at Dunkirk with those taken prisoner at Lille.)

Overall, the operation had been far more successful than the British had expected. They had transported 198,224 British (not counting the earlier removal of the "useless mouths") and 141,445 Allied soldiers. The cost, however, had been great. The British had lost 226 of their own vessels and seventeen Allied craft. Most of these were relatively small civilian craft, but six valuable British destroyers and three French destroyers were sunk, along with eight British transports and smaller warships. No less than nineteen other British destroyers and nine transports had been damaged badly enough to be put out of action, when destroyers in particular were desperately needed in the Battle of the Atlantic and to counter a possible invasion of Britain. The Luftwaffe seems to have suffered heavily in the air fighting, although this information is less certain. In all fighting in the west during the evacuation, the RAF apparently destroyed 240 German planes and lost 177 of its own and eighty valuable fighter pilots.

The BEF had lost practically all of its equipment except small arms. Replacing it was difficult, and the need to continue producing even obsolete equipment, especially tanks and antitank guns, meant British weapons in those categories remained inadequate. The men, however, had been saved, without whom the British war effort on land would have been permanently lamed.

Dunkirk often was viewed later as a miracle of salvation. It is, however, most unlikely that the Germans could ever have destroyed the BEF completely. The Allied force in the northern pocket was too large and had too many alternative routes of escape, although the Germans could certainly have trapped a large part of the BEF if not for their errors. And while the evacuation was extremely important, it was not decisive in ensuring that Britain would continue the war against Germany.[3] That question had already been decided, when it seemed doubtful that many men would get out of Dunkirk.

### The British Carry On

Even as the Germans reached the Channel, the British came to grips with the possibility that French resistance might collapse and laid plans accordingly. Although they were not sure that early and total defeat was certain until June, and even then hoped that the French would continue fighting from North Africa, they soon recognized that they would face a German-controlled Europe alone. Churchill, in a message to President Franklin D. Roosevelt (FDR) on May 15, envisaged fighting the war on this basis.

So did the British military. On May 16, Air Chief Marshal Hugh Dowding, the head of Fighter Command, sent a letter to the undersecretary of state at the Air Ministry. Stressing the need to keep sufficient fighter strength in Britain, Dowding remarked, "I presume that there is no one who will deny that England should fight on, even though the remainder of the Continent of Europe is dominated by the Germans."

On May 19, the chiefs of staff began work on a paper blandly titled (for security reasons) "British Strategy in a Certain Eventuality." Submitted on May 27, it assumed French defeat. The study also assumed that merely a small part of the BEF could be saved, that Italy would join Germany in the war, that France would not only be occupied but that its territories in North Africa would be "accessible to the enemy," and that Spain, Portugal, and the Balkan countries, except for Turkey, would be under German domination. It assumed that the Mediterranean would be lost. But despite these worst-case scenarios, the authors believed that with American help Britain could survive and even win. They hoped to defeat Germany by blockade and air attack, causing the German economy to crumble. The Germans were thought to be short of food, oil, and some other vital materials. Attacks on their economy, plus widespread revolt in the occupied countries, would cause a collapse. The British were overconfident in the ability of bombing to hurt German oil production and transportation, which they correctly saw as vital spots in the German war effort. In the long run, they were right, but in 1940–1941 they did not have the planes, the bombs, or the ability to find such targets accurately. Thus the British, even while pondering the chance that their situation would be even worse than it proved to be, were confident in their ability to hold out against attack and overconfident in their ability to hurt Germany.

During 1941, it became apparent, if only because of leaks through Vichy French territory and the Soviet Union, that the blockade was less effective than expected and that the bombing effort thus far was a failure. To be sure, in 1940 many British may already have believed they needed America's entry to the war to ensure victory. On May 22, 1940, in response to urgent appeals from the British and French, Roosevelt took the daring step of reclassifying much of the ridiculously small U.S. Army's reserve stockpile of World War I weapons and ammunition as surplus and rushed it to Britain. On June 6, a considerable number of obsolete but working aircraft followed. Complicating Anglo-American relations, however, were Joseph

Kennedy, the American ambassador in London and an extreme isolationist who could not be relied on to convey his government's views to the British, or vice versa, accurately, and William Bullitt, the ambassador to France and a staunch anti-Nazi who was prone to pass on erroneous French opinions and uncritically swallow French complaints.

While they were reluctant to stipulate that American entry would be required for victory, a fair amount of evidence shows that in 1940 many British leaders, including Churchill, believed that the United States would enter the war. Further, they thought it would do so much sooner than it in fact did—if not once Britain came under serious air attack, at least once President Roosevelt was reelected that fall.

By contrast, the British did not rely on Soviet help. Although they tried to persuade the Soviet government to a policy that was at least not actively hostile, they did not expect or depend on success in this endeavor. Nor did they think much of the Soviets' military capability if the Soviet Union entered the war, willingly or unwillingly. At most, the likelihood that the Nazis and Soviets must fall out, eventually, was a comforting thought.[4]

## Whether to "Make Peace"

Churchill wrote in his war memoirs, in 1949, that "future generations may deem it noteworthy that the supreme question of whether we should fight on alone never found a place upon the War Cabinet agenda." It was, he insisted, "taken for granted." Many years later, when the British cabinet papers from this era were made available, clearly this assertion was true only in a highly technical sense. Making peace was not on the agenda, but it was discussed. Indeed, this disclosure, which seemed to contradict sharply what had become a strong British patriotic tradition, caused an aftershock in which some leaped to the conclusion that, as Professor David Reynolds put it, "contrary to patriotic mythology, it was not inevitable that Britain fought on in the summer of 1940." Others, more extreme, have at least implied that continuing the war was a near matter and a highly personal accomplishment of Churchill's and even that "making peace" would have been the rational thing to do. Not a few commentators, such as the famous military historian B. H. Liddell Hart, suggested that fighting on was an expression of British bulldog stupidity and irrationality that "just happened" to work out well. In the 1990s, a school of thought surfaced suggesting that Britain *should* have made peace.

But the debate in the War Cabinet was really a minor affair. On May 26, when it still seemed that few men would get out of Dunkirk, the War

Cabinet examined the prospect if the French left the war. Foreign Secretary Lord Halifax brought up an offer by the Italian ambassador to arrange an armistice and raised the possibility of considering German proposals, "provided our liberty and independence were assured." Churchill admitted that he would be glad to get out of the present situation on such terms, even at the cost of giving up some territory, apparently meaning Malta, Gibraltar, and the African colonies Britain had taken from Germany in World War I. But he simply did not believe in the prospects of such a deal. Some of the subsequent discussion was not recorded at all, but Halifax suggested that Hitler might not insist on "outrageous terms." Churchill, however, insisted that the Germans would not offer decent terms and that the British could still resist. Chamberlain agreed and backed Churchill throughout the discussion. (Chamberlain and Halifax, who had been the chief alternative candidate to succeed him, were still much more popular in the Conservative Party than Churchill was.) The formal submission of the simultaneously pessimistic and optimistic "British Strategy in a Certain Eventuality" almost certainly reinforced the tough line taken among the political leaders.

The following day, Churchill strenuously opposed any approach to Italy. He argued for fighting on. To accept German domination of Europe meant reducing Britain to satellite status. Halifax maintained that he merely agreed with what Churchill had said the day before and was prepared to discuss terms if the British retained what was essential. He admitted that "the issue was probably academic, since we were unlikely to receive any offer which would not come up against the fundamental conditions which were essential to us." Churchill grumbled about discussing an issue that was "quite unreal and which is most unlikely to arise." If Hitler was ready to make peace on the basis of restoring Germany's colonies and limiting himself to the overlordship of Central Europe, that was one thing. But it is quite unlikely that he would make such an offer. The minimum terms Halifax and Churchill envisioned were evidently a complete German evacuation of western Europe. Halifax was apparently angry at Churchill and perhaps considered resigning, something Churchill wished to avoid.

On May 28, when the situation at Dunkirk was still desperate, Churchill flatly opposed giving in to French desires to use Italian dictator Mussolini as an intermediary. When Halifax took the opposite position, Churchill warned that once the British got to a conference table, any terms Hitler offered would touch British independence and integrity, and the resolution to oppose such terms would be lost. Both the War Cabinet and the full cabinet strongly supported Churchill. That ended the matter. Halifax seems to have been almost alone, at least at the top of the government, in his views. Only a minority in Parliament and the country—possibly larger than people later cared to recall, but still a small minority—favored giving up on the war. The importance of this debate has been wildly exaggerated, revolving, as it did, around a possibility even Halifax admitted was highly improbable. Churchill's later desire to keep it secret was probably because he wished to refrain from publicizing anything that could hurt British morale, even in 1949; to preserve Halifax's reputation (he was a successful and well-liked ambassador in Washington); and to avoid embarrassing the Conservative Party.

The possibility of Hitler offering acceptable terms was not improbable; it simply did not exist. While he did wish to make peace of a sort, temporarily, with Britain, even his minimum terms would not have coincided with Halifax's. He would undoubtedly have insisted on continuing to occupy the Low Countries and part of France. He already envisaged annexing the Netherlands, Belgium, and the Lille and Burgundy areas of France, as well as Alsace-Lorraine. A permanent peace settlement of the sort Churchill's later critics envisaged was even more out of the question, as Hitler expected to focus on the British once he defeated the Soviets.

Churchill was wise to insist on a course that would ensure that Hitler did not get another opportunity to tackle his enemies one at a time and at the moments he considered most convenient. As the German official historians have argued, "The importance of Britain's determination to continue the war can hardly be overestimated. . . . Britain's refusal during these months to accept German domination of Europe was an important, if not the most important, factor in determining the ultimate fate of the aggressors." It was Britain's fighting on that led, fairly directly, to America's entry into the war and, though it did not cause the attack on the Soviet Union, limited the resources the Germans could commit to the Eastern campaign. Without these conditions, the Soviets might have been defeated.

But a peace agreement, even a temporary one, was not a real possibility. In his memoir, Field Marshal Manstein argued that Churchill should have sought an arrangement with Germany in order to profit from the Nazi-Soviet war when the inevitable clash between the totalitarian powers came. Even Manstein, however, conceded that it was doubtful if Hitler, "already drunk with a belief in his own infallibility, would have been ready to accept a peace based on reason and justice" and that, given his previous actions, no one could have trusted him anyway.[5]

However, while any British attempt to come to terms with Hitler would have been extremely dangerous, as Churchill recognized, it is not quite certain that the results would have been inevitably fatal, as is often assumed. In the wildly unlikely event that Hitler, in the interest of an interim arrangement, curbed himself sufficiently to offer reasonable terms or a British government, headed by Halifax or someone similar, agreed to terms that had previously been deemed unacceptable (e.g., German control of the Low Countries), the results would probably have resembled the attempt to come to terms with Napoleon in 1802. Any arrangement would have been no more than an armed truce, and the British, at least half of whom would have bitterly opposed it from the start, would have seen it that way. Even Halifax would have been on his guard, and it is most unlikely that, as Churchill suggested, Britain would have somehow become a satellite state of Nazi Germany. The most likely result would have been that the Nazis would have defeated the Soviet Union, although only after a lengthy campaign, during which it would have been hard for them to prepare properly for a struggle with the British. If war with Britain did not resume even before the Soviets were defeated, as might well have happened, the issue would have been fought out between an alert Britain, almost certainly backed by the United States, and a Germany perhaps still not well prepared for an air-sea war against the Western powers.

## The Mediterranean and Middle East

An important accompaniment to Britain's resolve to fight was its decision to hold on to the Mediterranean and the Middle East, despite the grave dangers to Britain itself and its Atlantic supply line. This course was not chosen all at once, but evolved gradually from late May to early August. In late May, with the prospect of the Italians' intervention and French defeat, the British had reinforced their Mediterranean Fleet based in Alexandria. In June, the British chiefs of staff considered withdrawing it entirely, but Churchill strongly opposed this option. They decided to wait until the status of the French fleet was clarified. The fleet remained. At the end of June, the British formed a new Force H at Gibraltar to replace the French fleet, which the Allies had previously depended on to control the western Mediterranean. It later fell to Force H to deal with the French fleet at Oran.

The Mediterranean Fleet was further reinforced instead of being withdrawn. Although Britain itself faced invasion, the government made the truly daring decision, on August 10, to send important ground and air reinforcements to the Middle East Command immediately. Leaving only 250 in Britain, 102 cruiser and infantry tanks were sent along with 52 light tanks and an assortment of artillery, antitank and antiaircraft guns, and modern aircraft. Later, while the Battle of Britain still raged, the British undertook a joint expedition with the Free French against the Vichy-held port of Dakar in West Africa in an attempt to roll up the French West African colonies. This operation ended less happily.

The commitment to the Mediterranean–Middle East, on top of the closure of the Mediterranean to ordinary traffic as Italy entered the war, was expensive, not only in terms of sea, air, and ground forces, but also in shipping. The long route around Africa increased the requirement for ocean escorts against German surface raiders and depended on scarce fast liners and cargo ships to get troops and supplies to their destination in a reasonable time. This effort tied up 150 of Britain's best ships.[6]

## The French Armistice

Surprisingly, the British reinforced the small British forces already in France that had not been swept up in the Dunkirk pocket. When the Germans struck south, most of the Fifty-first Division was lost. In a new series of evacuations, running down the French coast all the way to the Spanish border, 191,000 British and Allied troops were brought out. A horrendous disaster occurred on June 17 when an air attack sank the liner *Lancastria*, and 5,000 people lost their lives.

Although the French fought with more skill in June than they had previously exhibited in the north, and harder than the Germans expected, they were hopelessly outnumbered. It was apparent even to the biggest optimists that they could not resist much longer in France itself. The French now had to decide whether to fight on from overseas, with a government in exile. The British and Americans tried to discourage France from seeking an armistice or at least insure that the Axis would not seize the French fleet. But Roosevelt had no answer for French prime minister Paul Reynaud's pleas that the United States enter the war, while Britain's dramatic offer of a "Declaration of Union" with France, fusing Britain and France into one superstate, inspired little French enthusiasm. Reynaud was under intense pressure to seek an armistice.

In sharp contrast to the situation in Britain, French military leaders opposed fighting on. They wanted the earliest possible armistice to save French lives. Weygand and Marshal Philippe Pétain, the greatest French hero of World War I, bitterly opposed a purely military surrender in France and continuing the fight overseas. Weygand even argued that this option was dishonorable although the Poles, the Norwegians, the Dutch, and the Belgians had not thought so. He dismissed a war effort based on the French Empire with the contemptuous comment, "The Empire is just a pack of blacks over whom you'll have no control from the moment you're beaten." This observation seems more far-sighted in the twenty-first century than it was in 1940, as the empire remained mostly quiescent under both Vichy and Free French rule during World War II. Weygand and most French leaders believed that the British would soon be beaten, too, if they were "foolish" enough to carry on the fight.

Gen. Charles Noguès, the governor of Morocco and commander in chief in North Africa, however, opposed an armistice. He was so confident about his ability to hold his domain, that the "softs" later deposed him from the North African command when they gained power.

Despite the views of most of the French military, it seems that France may have been much closer to continuing to fight overseas than the British ever were to giving up. It appears that Reynaud resigned, on June 16, under the mistaken impression that most of his cabinet wanted an armistice, but in fact that was not the case. The move might not have been fatal, had he not made the additional error of recommending Pétain as his successor. He believed that Pétain, whatever his other limitations (he was a semi-senile royalist and hostile to the republic), would at least resist the more extreme German demands, something Reynaud did not trust the weak democratic alternative of Camille Chautemps to do. Reynaud may have calculated that the Germans would demand the outright surrender of the French fleet, that Pétain would refuse, that the armistice talks would break down, and that Pétain would then resign. Afterward, Reynaud and the "hards" would return to power and carry on the war from North Africa. This gamble proved a miscalculation.

On June 17, Pétain asked for terms. As a result, French resistance began to collapse, while Hitler proved cleverer than Reynaud had anticipated. Hitler did not expect to obtain the French fleet and was satisfied with neutralizing it. Indeed, he would not have greatly minded the French scuttling their fleet. He offered an armistice on terms that seemed, by his usual standards, moderate and left much of France "unoccupied" and under control of a government situated at Vichy in the south. There, prompted by Pétain and the authoritarian right, the French Republic committed suicide. That left only a weak movement overseas, led by Gen. Charles de Gaulle, to fight the war at the side of the British. "Unoccupied France," with only a tiny so-called Armistice Army, was indefensible. The remnants of French independence soon became a sour joke, as the Vichy regime sank more deeply into ethical slime than most of Germany's outright allies did.

Defenders of the armistice, and some German critics of Hitler's decision to grant it, later argued that it ultimately proved fortunate for the Allies because it neutralized northwest Africa until the Allied invasion of November 1942. Had the French fought from North Africa in 1940, they argued, the Germans would have pursued them, encouraging or forcing Spain to enter the war, which would have led to a complete German victory in the Mediterranean and Middle East. Germany, however, could not have waged such a campaign while it fought the Battle of Britain. Further, it is most doubtful that even if they had concentrated on attacking North Africa, they could have defeated the Allies there, as the French officer André Truchet showed after the war. Had the maximum forces possible been evacuated to North Africa, the French there would have been strong, possessing more modern fighters than the RAF had. Indeed, German historians have suggested that the likeliest consequence of France's fighting on would have been the early elimination of the Axis foothold in Africa in Libya.[7] It is conceivable, however, that a French decision to continue the war might have worked against the Allies for another, rarely mentioned reason: had the French pushed on, even Hitler might have found it hard to gather the nerve to attack the Soviet Union in 1941.

The British did not receive timely notice of the armistice terms and felt the French had disregarded their minimal interests; notably, the latter failed to honor a promise to hand 400 captured German airmen over to the British before an armistice. Now Britain faced, or thought it did, a difficult problem—namely, the French fleet. On June 22, they refused French warships then in British-controlled ports permission to leave.

The armistice provided for French ships to be demobilized in their home ports, at least implying that the fleet's main units then in North African bases would return to France. There, the British feared, the Axis might seize them, even against French resistance; and the leaders in London did not trust their French counterparts any longer. On June 27, they took what Churchill considered the "most unnatural and hateful" decision of his career: to use force, if necessary, to eliminate the French fleet as a threat. On July 3, in a series of operations, French ships in British harbors were seized, while Force H delivered an ultimatum to the principal French naval force at Oran in French Algeria. The British insisted that it either join the British or carry out one of several courses of action that would eliminate it as a factor in the war. The French refused. In a full-scale battle, several French ships were sunk or wrecked, and 1,300 French sailors were killed. The British naval commanders suspected the attack was a mistake, probably rightly. The Germans did not think that an attempt to seize the French fleet would work, while the Vichy government was unlikely to throw away one of the few cards it held by letting it happen.

French commanders had been ordered, in no uncertain terms, to take no chances and not let their ships fall into Axis or British hands. That Vichy would go wholly over to the Axis was unlikely, and even the most extreme collaborationists must have wondered whether orders to turn French ships over to the Axis or to fight alongside the Axis would be obeyed. Although probably an error, the British action was an understandable mistake under the circumstances. It did prove the British determination to fight on at any cost. But it had a high price in French lives, in alienating French opinion, and in greatly harming de Gaulle's Free French movement.[8]

### The German Dilemma

Had the British leaders, in May–June 1940, been able to see into German councils they would have been vastly encouraged. The Germans lacked almost any appreciation of the true strategic and political situation and were almost completely unprepared to finish off Britain. They were sure that the British would come to terms. Churchill's stirring speeches of June 4 and June 18, vowing to carry on the struggle to the end, and the British reaction to them went unnoticed or were written off as the ravings of a doomed, drunken politician. Even after it was apparent that Britain would not succumb, American intervention remained below the Nazis' mental horizon for some months. As late as October 15, Hitler remarked that the war was won, and ending it was only a question of time.[9]

Hitler instead focused on another problem, the next war against the Soviets; and when the Germans faced the fact that Britain would fight, they discovered that they had neither appropriate plans nor the forces to deal with the recalcitrant island. Mesmerized by their triumph—faster and cheaper than expected—over the French Army, the Germans supposed that neither the British nor the Soviets would be hard to defeat.

Some Germans indulged in grotesque dreams of acquiring at least chunks of the western European empires. Hitler was mainly interested in bases on the Atlantic, presumably to deal with Britain and the United States. For him, regaining Germany's old colonies was primarily a matter of prestige. The navy and other elements closer in mentality to the more extreme German expansionists of World War I than to the orthodox Nazis, however, dreamed of a vast central African empire. The navy even wished to add not only Madagascar but also the Dutch East Indies (Indonesia) and British Borneo, oblivious to the point that these goals cut right across the aims of Germany's most powerful prospective ally, Japan.

In theory, three possible ways to defeat Britain seemed to exist after the fall of France: an outright invasion, an air-sea blockade of the ocean supply routes (i.e., success in what became known as the Battle of the Atlantic), and an indirect approach, involving the conquest of the Mediterranean–Middle East. Only a successful invasion could defeat Britain quickly. Although Hitler in 1939 had believed that Britain would be defeated by blockade, in 1940 he lacked the means to accomplish this goal quickly if at all. Germany's surface fleet, already small, had been largely crippled in Norway, while the U-boat fleet was only about a fifth the size its commander believed was necessary for victory. The Germans had only a few planes—converted airliners—with enough range to attack ships far out at sea. A Mediterranean approach, if effective at all, would also consume a great deal of time.

The German armed forces had made only sketchy preliminary studies of how to invade Britain, during which, typically, the navy and the Luftwaffe fell out over the plans. The complications of an amphibious operation and the need for landing craft and other specialized equipment were barely acknowledged.

On May 21, Hitler and Adm. Erich Raeder did discuss the problem of dealing with Britain. Hitler indicated that he agreed with Raeder and preferred a blockade to an invasion if the British continued to fight. On June 2, he told some generals that if Britain made peace, as he expected, he would be free to turn against the Soviets. On June 13, in a rare interview with an American reporter, he indicated his desire to make peace with Britain; the only condition he referred to was the return of Germany's colonies.

Hitler remained confident that the British would come to terms, but he began pondering the need to bring some pressure—perhaps by bringing in Spain, capturing Gibraltar, and seizing bases in Morocco, which he also wanted for more long-range purposes against the United States. On June 23, he again mentioned attacking the Soviet Union, this time even if Britain remained at war with Germany. On June 30, Col. Gen. Alfred Jodl, the brains in OKW, produced a memorandum reviewing the strategic problem, "Continuation of the War Against England." Jodl concluded that a blockade was not promising. An attack on the "periphery"—which is how the Germans tended to refer to the British position in the Mediterranean and Middle East—aimed at capturing Gibraltar and Suez with Spanish and Italian help might be useful, but it did not promise to be decisive. Jodl may have regarded this option as a course to be pursued parallel with an invasion or blockade strategy, perhaps even in the case of a successful invasion of Britain to shut out potential rivals. (Hitler found troubling that other powers stood to gain more from partitioning the British Empire than Germany did if he smashed Britain.) Jodl regarded invading England as a difficult operation to be launched only after air attack and blockade had seriously weakened it.

In late June, Erhard Milch had suggested an early invasion of England with an airborne landing in Kent to seize an "airhead," followed by a seaborne attack. General Kesselring seconded this idea, as did Gen. Kurt Student, the commander of the airborne forces. Others saw that Milch's proposal did not account for the Luftwaffe's need to rest and recuperate after the French campaign, and many thought it simply unworkable. Hitler appears to have known about Milch's idea but dismissed it.

Despite his earlier coolness to invasion, on July 2 Hitler accepted Jodl's suggestions and ordered planning to go ahead, indicating that a landing might be made as a last resort if complete air supremacy were attained. The chief of the General Staff, if not enthusiastic, did not find the idea all that daunting. Raeder continued to urge a blockade rather than invasion. Hitler made a major peace appeal on July 19 but expected it would fail. The British staunchly refused this approach. The British Broadcasting Corporation (BBC) "unofficially" jeered at it the same day. Halifax officially and vehemently rejected it personally on July 22.[10]

On July 16, meanwhile, Hitler had issued a detailed directive for the invasion code-named Operation Sea Lion. It envisaged crossing the Straits of Dover and the upper part of the English Channel, as far south as the Isle of Wight, with protection on either flank by elaborate mine barriers and support from long-range guns and the Luftwaffe, which had to secure complete control of the air. Hitler was not enthusiastic, for he recognized that an invasion would be risky and expensive. Unlike army planners, he realized that the action would not be just an unusually big river crossing but a major naval operation involving unique problems.

Hitler was convinced that Britain fought on in the hope of receiving Soviet support. That notion became an additional justification (although certainly not the main one) for his decision, which he officially made only on July 31 but had probably already settled on, to attack the Soviet Union even if Britain was still at war with Germany. This decision to strike the Soviets was not an indication that he cared less about beating Britain or that Sea Lion was simply a bluff. Indeed, the invasion preparations were costly and disruptive to the German economy. If anything, Hitler wanted to conclude the war in the west as soon as possible, precisely to avoid interfering with the attack in the east, and he was willing to incur serious costs and risks to do so. He was, in fact, most reluctant to abandon Sea Lion as the year went on.[11]

In a series of interservice conferences and meetings with Hitler on July 30 and 31, invasion plans were thrashed out further. On the first day, the navy was so obviously unhappy that the army leaders agreed among themselves that an invasion was not feasible. As a substitute they pondered efforts on the periphery aimed at Gibraltar and the Suez and possibly encouraging the Soviets to advance on the Persian Gulf oil fields. Although he favored postponing an invasion of Britain until 1941, Raeder conceded to Hitler the second day that it was possible but not before September 15. Hitler—not wildly enthusiastic but not particularly pessimistic either—set the invasion for that date, provided that the Luftwaffe could secure air superiority. He showed little interest in taking Gibraltar or proposals to send two panzer divisions to Libya, although planning for these actions went forward. That same day, he set the invasion of the Soviet Union for May 1941 but repeatedly affirmed that Sea Lion had overriding priority.

The Luftwaffe was not particularly thrilled about an invasion of Britain. Gen. Otto von Waldau, the chief of staff for operations, doubted its ability even to cover an invasion fleet, while Göring and others seem to have believed that they could beat Britain by air attacks alone. The army became the chief advocate for the invasion. It gradually accepted the navy's severe limitations on what could be done, discarding its original picture of the invasion as a huge river crossing on a broad front. Under navy pressure, it narrowed the attack by Rundstedt's Army Group A to a sixty-mile front across the Straits of Dover. A first wave of six divisions, with altered organization and special equipment, would land on two short stretches of coast in Kent and Sussex, supported by airborne landings at Brighton and on high ground north of Dover. The Germans would secure a fifteen-mile-deep beachhead for a buildup and then attack north toward the Thames, eventually cutting off London from the south and west.

Rundstedt had no faith in the invasion plan but gave his able subordinates, who were more optimistic, a free hand to do what they could. The Germans made remarkable if belated progress in working out the problems of amphibious operations and developing some equipment such as amphibious tanks and Siebel ferries, air propeller–driven, shallow-draft craft. But while gathering an enormous number of barges, tugs, coasters, and fishing craft—enough transports to seriously disrupt Germany's economy—they still lacked proper landing craft and the kind of naval gunfire support Allied landings later took for granted. The principal substitutes for landing craft were hastily modified and clumsy *prahms* (barges) designed for inland waterways. Most had to be towed. They were unsuited to work at sea, terribly vulnerable to bad weather, and very slow. The inadequacy of the prahms alone rendered the invasion's success doubtful, even with air superiority.

Preparations for the subsequent occupation of Britain also proceeded. Contrary to the supposition that Hitler and the Nazis were soft on the British, their proposed policies were considerably harsher than those instituted on the western European mainland. These tactics included deporting all able-bodied men ages seventeen to forty-five to the mainland and confiscating property. The British would also come under the tender care of Dr. Franz Six and several Schutzstaffel (SS) Einsatzgruppen (special action groups).[12] However, it was never likely that Six would get to work on the British. He and his men exercised their peculiar talents in Russia, where he was in charge of the element of Einsatzgruppe B slated to deal with Moscow. But he never reached Moscow, either.

## Dealing with the Invasion Threat

It is still widely, although not universally, supposed that in 1940 Germany came close to invading and defeating Britain and that a terribly outnumbered Royal Air Force barely stopped the Luftwaffe from gaining air superiority over England, which would have made an invasion possible. Given the impotence of surface warships in the face of air superiority and the weakness of the British Army, nothing could have stopped the Germans from crossing the Channel had the RAF lost. And it won by an extremely narrow margin. As we shall see, these accepted beliefs are far from the truth.

At the time, most British leaders were not all that worried about a German invasion. Churchill himself wrote, "Few British and very few foreigners understood the peculiar technical advantages of our insular position, nor was it generally known how, even in the irresolute years before the war, the essentials of sea and latterly air defence had been maintained." He was sure that the RAF could defeat the Luftwaffe and realized that the Germans had no proper landing craft. Retrospectively, he deemed the German invasion plan a "bleak proposition," but he was skeptical of the invasion threat even at the time. As he wrote, "Those who knew the most were the least scared." He did not fear an early invasion; rather that Germany, with its superior resources, would slowly grind the British down and especially threaten its overseas traffic. It was the U-boats, not the Luftwaffe, that worried him. During the worst phase of the Battle of Britain, on August 29, the British chiefs of staff assured the Americans that an invasion was unlikely to succeed and spoke with some confidence of eliminating Italy and exploiting Germany's weakness in oil.[13] To be sure, the British military took the danger seriously. After Dunkirk, British land forces were weak. After suffering enormous losses in France, they had few heavy weapons and were especially short of artillery pieces, antitank guns, and tanks. In fact, most of the available tanks were light. The military launched a frantic effort to rearm and rebuild the British forces, which were supplemented by the newly raised Home Guard.

The War Office and Churchill initially took the view that the main danger of invasion was on the east coast, while Lord Ironside, correctly, held that the main threat was to the south. Like Field Marshal Rommel, defending against an Allied attack four years later, Ironside believed that given the state of his forces, his only chance was to halt a landing on the beaches. He emphasized keeping the maximum force well forward, depending on static defenses. His critics favored a more conventional defense, with a thin delaying crust on the beaches and strong reserves for counterattacks. When Lt. Gen. Alan Brooke replaced Ironside he came to realize that he had been right, at least about the likeliest site for a landing. Brooke soon had more to work with, and to carry out a more orthodox defense, than Ironside had had.[14] Whether an invasion would be attempted depended on the outcome of the air battle.

## Prelude to the Battle of Britain

The most critical decision in the Battle of Britain may have been made weeks before it began, during the battle for France. As early as May 13, Air Marshals Cyril Newell and Archibald Sinclair had warned against sending more fighter units to France, lest Britain be left undefended. Dowding, of Fighter Command, agreed. He needed a minimum of fifty-two fighter squadrons but had the equivalent of thirty-six. "I believe that if an adequate fighter force is kept in the country, if the fleet remains in being, and if Home Forces are suitably organized to resist invasion, we should be able to carry on the war single-handed for some time, if not indefinitely. But, if the Home Defence Force is drained away in desperate attempts to remedy the situation in France, defeat in France will involve the final, complete, and irremediable defeat of this country." Churchill, however, seems to have supposed that the minimum required for an ultimate defense of Britain was only twenty-five squadrons. It was a dangerous misunderstanding, for he was under heavy pressure from Gort and Reynaud to commit more fighters to France.

On May 16, Newell and Churchill agreed to send a maximum of eight half squadrons to France. But after meeting Reynaud on May 16, Churchill—who was always emotionally pro-French—asked the War Cabinet to release six more squadrons for service in France. Many have maintained that such a move would have lost the Battle of Britain in advance. Newell strongly opposed it as too dangerous. In any case, he agreed with Arthur Barratt, the RAF commander in France, that the British bases there could hardly handle more than an additional three squadrons anyhow. He reluctantly let six Britain-based squadrons—three in the morning and three in the afternoon—stage through French bases and fly over France. They began operating this way on May 17.

But on May 21, the German advance forced the RAF to start pulling out of its French bases, and Churchill agreed that no more fighters should go to France. To some extent, the issue had to be readdressed in early June, as the French begged for help against the final German offensive. By then, three fighter squadrons assigned to Barratt had returned to bases in France. The War Cabinet reluctantly agreed to base two more squadrons there and allowed four more to operate from British bases. By then even Churchill suspected that the French were taking advantage of him and that they were not using their own planes. The commitment to France remained strictly limited.[15]

### THE BALANCE OF FORCES
British losses over France and the Low Countries had been high, even higher than they would be in the Battle of Britain: at least 931 aircraft (possibly as many as 959), including 386 vital Hurricane fighters and 67 Spitfires, and 1,526 RAF killed, badly wounded, captured, or missing. German losses also had been considerable, with estimates ranging from 1,300 to 1,428 planes. Even the lower figure was 30 percent of the Germans' strength at the start of the campaign. At least 355 were fighters. (Tank losses, incidentally, numbering 753, had also been considerable.) Heavy losses and the general exhaustion of the Luftwaffe were factors in how sluggish the preparations to attack Britain were.

Both sides had an interval in which to rebuild their strength. By the start of the Battle of Britain, usually dated as July 10, 1940, the RAF had 754 single-seat fighters (Hurricanes and Spitfires); 149 two-seat fighters of little value (Defiants and Blenheims); 560 bombers assigned to Bomber Command, and 500 bombers and patrol planes in Coastal Command, versus the Germans' 1,107 single-seat fighters (all Me 109s); 357 twin-seat, twin-engine fighters (Me 110s); 1,380 level bombers; and 428 dive-bombers. Less than 75 percent of each side's planes were operational. A variant set of figures for the Luftwaffe estimates that by July 20 the air fleets operating against Britain had 809 Me 109s, 246 Me 110s, 1,260 bombers, and 316 dive-bombers, with again about three-quarters of these being serviceable.

The British built up their forces faster. By August 10, the opening of the main, critical phase of the battle, the Luftwaffe deployed 3,358 aircraft. Of the 2,550 operational planes, there were 805 Me 109s, 224 Me 110s, 998 level bombers, 261 dive-bombers, and 31 ground-attack planes, along with 151 reconnaissance and 80 coastal reconnaissance aircraft. (These figures do not include night-fighters and transports.) The British, as of August 3, had 708 operational fighters and 1,434 pilots ready to go. The Germans had 1,126 Me 109 pilots alone, but only 869 were classed as "operational." The meaning of these figures is another problem. The British fighters—and overwhelmingly the Hurricanes and Spitfires—would largely fight the battle against German fighters and bombers of all types. The British bombers, generally inferior to their German counterparts, had largely been converted to night bombing (which they could not usually do accurately) and would largely be confined to attacking the invasion force assembling against Britain. The most crucial balance of all would be that between the fighters and especially the single-seat, single-engine fighters of each side. The Me 110 proved of relatively little value; likewise, the British twin-seat fighters were practically worthless. In the effective balance of fighter strength, the Luftwaffe outnumbered the RAF about 4 to 3.[16] Although the Luftwaffe outnumbered the RAF about 2 to 1, the Luftwaffe's low ratio of fighters to bombers restricted the full use of its considerable bomber strength by day.

Both air forces had limitations, but those of the Luftwaffe proved more serious in the Battle of Britain. Its flexibility, excellence at supporting ground forces, mobility, and ability to operate in bad weather and at night were not factors, for the coming battle would be fought from static bases for daylight air supremacy. Meanwhile, the RAF's faults—its lack of a real strategic bomber force, in spite of its considerable investment in one, and its belated development of maritime cooperation—did not have an immediate impact. Since 1936, the Luftwaffe had not been particularly well led; its organization was chaotic; its intelligence, beyond Germany's immediate neighbors, was poor; its production program was inadequate; and although it had the world's most advanced electronic navigation and bombing systems, it made little use of radar. Its equipment, although in many ways ideal for supporting the campaign in France, was less suited for the struggle against Britain. It lacked enough fighters and had no real long-range escort fighter. (No other air force except the Japanese naval air arm had considered such a plane a practical possibility.) The Me 109s were too few and their range too short. The Luftwaffe had overemphasized the specialized dive-bomber, but even the original Stuka, while effective and accurate, was vulnerable and required heavy fighter escort if encountering any serious opposition in the air. Even French fighters had massacred Stukas when they caught the latter away from fighter protection. Its medium bombers, although as good as those of any other air force, were not armed well enough. Last, it did not have any four-engine heavy bombers. Although this factor alone was not decisive in the Battle of Britain, most German survivors of the battle thought it a significant weakness. While the Germans could have neither built nor provided fuel for a strategic bomber force comparable to those that the British and Americans built later, they could have created a modest force of heavy bombers large enough to have given invaluable support to the German Navy in the Battle of the Atlantic. In the Battle of Britain, their heavier bomb load, greater range, and ability to attack from higher altitudes would have made the RAF's task far more difficult.[17]

## THE FIGHTERS

As noted earlier, the crucial aircraft for both sides were the single-seat, single-engine fighters: the British Hurricanes and Spitfires and the German Messerschmitt 109s. Although the Spitfire is better known, most British fighters were Hurricanes. The most maneuverable of the three fighters, it was definitely inferior to the others, but not by a great margin. A good pilot in a Hurricane stood a reasonable chance against an Me 109. The Hurricane was rugged, reliable, easy to repair when damaged, and easy to fly.

The Spitfire used the same engine but in a far more innovative airframe, with distinctive elliptical wings. It was a brilliant piece of engineering although not easy to mass-produce. The basic Spitfire design was better than that of the Me 109, as it had more "stretch." Both went through many models, and some versions of the Me 109 temporarily overtook contemporary models of the Spitfire, but the last models of the Spitfire considerably outperformed the later Me 109s. The Spitfire was much easier to fly and far safer. It had wider landing gear than that of the Me 109, which was always prone to take-off and landing accidents, and the placement of the Spitfire's fuel tanks was much safer for its pilots either in air combat or crashes. Last, it had far better cockpit visibility, with an advanced semi-bubble canopy.

The Spitfire I, the model most used in the Battle of Britain, was close in performance to its counterpart, the Me 109E. The German fighter was generally considered to perform better at the highest altitudes and the Spitfire at low altitudes, but at the medium heights, where most fighting over Britain took place, both were evenly matched. The Spitfire II, which arrived in small numbers late in the battle, was definitely better than the Me 109E. While Spitfires were more maneuverable than the Me 109, the latter was far better in a dive than the British fighters were. The Spitfire did not accelerate much in a dive in any case, but the carburetors in the British planes cut out briefly when they nosed over, unlike the fuel-injectors used in the Me 109. This characteristic alone caused the great German ace Werner Mölders, who test-flew captured Spitfires and Hurricanes and admitted they were simpler to fly compared to German planes, to reject them as "miserable" fighters. While British pilots generally depended on a tight turn to get out of difficulties, the dive, or half-roll and dive, was the favorite move for German pilots to escape from an unfavorable situation until 1943. Later in the war, however, diving away, which became a seemingly ineradicable habit, proved fatal against other Allied fighters.

The Me 109E was also better armed than the Spitfire, with a mixture of well-placed cannon and rifle-caliber machine guns. The British fighters depended on eight light machine guns delivering less weight of fire. The British did introduce 20mm cannon during the battle, but they were so prone to jam that they were not an improvement until later.

All three fighters, by later standards, were short ranged. The Hurricane had a longer endurance than the others did, but a limited range would be far more important for the Germans. Incredibly, the Germans had not fitted the Me 109 to use drop-tanks, although earlier German fighters had carried them in Spain. Only near the end of the Battle of Britain did the Me 109E4 model, capable of carrying a belly tank, reach German fighter units. As a result, their ability to escort bombers over England was limited to the southeastern part of the country. London was about the limit of the Me 109s' effective radius; they could not stay and fight there for more than twenty minutes. Many German fighters would run out of fuel on the way home and end up in the Channel.

Not all German fighters had such short ranges, but unfortunately for the Luftwaffe, the Me 110, which constituted a substantial fraction of German fighter strength and attracted the elite pilots, proved ineffective as a long-range escort. As with most twin-engine fighters during World War II, it was no match for single-engine interceptors. Although well armed and safer and easier to fly than the Me 109, it was slow and unmaneuverable. With an escort, it proved an adequate fighter-bomber but was only used on a small scale by a special and effective unit, Erprobungsgruppe (Test Group) 210. The Me 110, however, performed far better than did the Defiants and Blenheims, which were a small fraction of Fighter Command's strength.

The Defiant was an odd design, an attempt to revive the two-seat fighter that had had some success in World War I. A single-engine plane with the same power plant as the Hurricane and Spitfire, it was slightly bigger, but instead of forward firing gun, it only had a powered gun turret mounted behind the pilot. It had some success over Dunkirk when Germans mistook it for a conventional single seater, but it proved virtually useless after the Germans discovered its abilities. The two squadrons equipped with the Defiant were withdrawn from day combat in July and turned into night fighters. Fighter Command had a few squadrons of Blenheim light bombers fitted with belly packs of machine guns in an attempt to turn them into fighters. They were not normally used by day in the Battle of Britain.

Immediately before the battle, the British introduced 100-octane gasoline; the Luftwaffe never got beyond 97-octane fuel. The British fighters went through many modifications during the battle. Engineers made small alterations to their engines, and they received three-blade, constant-speed propellers; rear-view mirrors; self-sealing fuel tanks; armor plate; and bulletproof windscreens. Meanwhile, German bombers were given additional armor and up-gunned.[18]

## TACTICS AND FORMATIONS

While the Germans enjoyed no great superiority in the quality or number of their fighters, they did have better tactics. The Germans had perfected a modern fighter formation with two pairs flown in "finger four" formation during the Spanish Civil War, and were prepared for fighter versus fighter combat. The RAF, in France, had flown the tight, three-plane vic and later modified it to provide "weavers" flying behind to give somewhat more warning of any attack from the rear. RAF pilots were trained in complicated formal attacks designed to down unescorted bombers. Tactical training during the Battle of Britain tended to disappear, although the RAF adopted the pair, flown in line astern, as its basic formation. The Germans contemptuously referred to it as the "idiot's row." The last man in the line astern, as with the weavers, was prone to be shot down. Later in the battle, some RAF squadrons copied the Luftwaffe formation.

From the RAF, the two-plane element and four-plane flight gradually spread to other Allied air forces. The U.S. Navy hit on the two-plane element, or "section," as it called it, independently in 1939 but was slow to adopt it until mid-1941. It then flew pairs in relatively clumsy six-plane flights ("divisions") shortly before converting to four-plane divisions. The U.S. Army Air Force switched from three-plane Vs to pairs flown in six-plane flights shortly before the attack on Pearl Harbor, and switched to four-plane flights in 1942. (The American Volunteer Group in China, the "Flying Tigers," used pairs and four-plane flights from its inception.)[19]

## RAF CONTROL

The British defense had a great advantage, an excellent system of radar detection and fighter direction. The system depended on twenty-one "Chain Home" and thirty "Chain Home Low" radar stations covering the approaches to Britain, with the latter, as their name indicated, picking up planes flying at low level. The radar stations and visual observers reported to Fighter Command headquarters, where enemy attacks were plotted. From there, data was passed to the four groups that actually directed tactical operations. The most important was 11 Group, defending southeast England, and the next most important, 12 Group, covered the Midlands region and, at least in some cases, could intervene in the 11 Group area. The group headquarters decided which squadrons intercepted which attacks. Below them, sector stations, the lowest level of control, directed the fighters once they were airborne.

The well-designed system had much redundancy and repair capability but also had limitations and vulnerabilities. Radar warning over Kent was only about twenty minutes, for example, and it took four minutes for radar data to reach the plotting board at headquarters. Spitfires took thirteen minutes to reach 20,000 feet, a typical height for an enemy approach; Hurricanes took three minutes longer. Moreover, the radar of 1940 was not good at estimating heights. During much of the Battle of Britain, fighter units thought the plotters tended to underestimate the enemy's altitude.

Also, the number of squadrons that groups and sector stations could handle was limited. Finally, the small sector stations did not make good targets for deliberate attacks, and the Germans did not understand the British control system well enough to seek them out. Thus, the radar stations were not particularly vulnerable. Intense attacks, however, could put them out of action for a time, and the lower levels of tactical direction were exposed. While Fighter Command and 11 Group headquarters were located safely underground, the critical sector station operation rooms and radio stations—with the exception of a concrete bunker at Tangmere—were aboveground in relatively flimsy buildings on forward airfields; so attacks on Fighter Command bases housing sector stations could put the local control system temporarily out of action. The danger was unnecessary. Sector stations and vital communications easily were relocated away from the airfields as the battle progressed.[20]

One weakness in the British defense was their lack of antiaircraft guns. In contrast to the outstanding German flak force, Britain was short of antiaircraft weapons of all sorts, especially the light guns needed to defend airfields against low-level or dive-bomber attacks. It so bad that the British salvaged machine guns from downed Stukas to beef up their defenses. British planes on the ground, however, were dispersed in well-built revetments. Only about thirty fighters were lost on the ground in the whole battle.

Another extraordinary British weakness was that the RAF had no air-sea rescue service. Coordination with other services was inadequate, so many RAF downed pilots were lost at sea. Only late in 1940 did the British copy the German air-sea rescue service.[21]

## INTELLIGENCE

The British enjoyed better intelligence than their enemies gathered, although they gained little from decrypting high-grade German ciphers during the Battle of Britain. While they had steadily read the Luftwaffe's ciphers from May 22, most important signals went along landlines. Intercepts did warn of preparations for the attack on Britain, enabling the British to scale down their exaggerated earlier estimate of German numbers, although they still overestimated the Luftwaffe's strength. They occasionally got advance notice of individual attacks but not necessarily in time to be of use. Low-level intercepts, however, alerted them that German planes were about to take off. At least they understood the Luftwaffe's basic structure, strength, and weaknesses; it was more than the Germans knew about the RAF.

The Luftwaffe's estimate of the RAF, submitted on July 16, offered little guidance to planners. It correctly estimated Fighter Command's current strength but underestimated British plane production. It overstated the Me 109's superiority over British fighters and overrated the Me 110, claiming that it was better than the Hurricane and conceding only that it was inferior to "skillfully flown" Spitfires. Worse, the Germans did not understand the importance of radar or how the British control system worked. In addition, while they identified British aircraft factories, the Germans do not seem to have correctly gauged the relative importance of particular plants. They did not exploit the fact that the Merlin engines for British fighters were only produced in two plants and that Spitfires were built in only two localities. With one as yet in full-scale operation, most Spitfires were still built at Southampton on the south coast. The Germans appear to have confused these plants with one building bombers.[22]

## PRODUCTION AND PILOTS

While German aircraft production stagnated, the British leaped ahead of schedule. Already in May, they had given all-out priority to building fighters. The production feat was often credited to the energy of Lord Beaverbrook, whom Churchill had made head of a new Ministry of Aircraft Production, taking the job away from the older Air Ministry. It appears, however, that the spurt was mainly owing to the pay-off of earlier developments—previously, Spitfire production, especially, had been unduly delayed—and the frantic efforts of workers who knew what was at stake. Some maintain that Beaverbrook's bullying may have actually hurt production efforts.[23]

The British thus had plenty of planes. They could have put a hundred to two hundred more fighters in the air had they had the men to fly them. Although losses over western Europe had been more than replaced, Fighter Command remained below "establishment" strength in pilots. Once heavy fighting began, it would be hard put to replace losses. Training times were cut to the bone. The British frantically ransacked other services for pilots. In June, fifty-eight navy pilots were transferred to Fighter Command, and in August, fifty-three volunteers from light bomber units went into fighter training.

Not all pilots were from the British Empire. A sizable number of Poles and Czechs and smaller numbers of Belgians, French, and Americans served in the Battle of Britain. Eventually five Polish squadrons and one Czech squadron were formed; the top-scoring RAF ace was a Czech, Sgt. Josef

František, serving in a Polish squadron. In September, the RAF began forming the first American Eagle Squadron.[24]

The Germans, by contrast, made little use of their allies. For reasons of prestige, Mussolini sent an Italian force of light bombers and fighters, but the latter were obsolete. (Half were biplanes.) The Italians arrived only after the Battle of Britain had been decided and the invasion was postponed indefinitely. Although Italian planes and tactics were poor, the pilots were reasonably good. While the Germans had no Me 109s to spare, they might have rearmed the Italians with French fighters.

## GERMAN PLANS

The initial fighting in the Battle of Britain—the Germans usually list its start as July 3 and the British as July 10—actually preceded the Luftwaffe's development of plans to fight it. The belated German planning went forward in an atmosphere of general overconfidence. To win, they had to smash the RAF while retaining enough strength to cover the invasion fleet. By contrast, the RAF needed only to avoid too heavy losses and stay basically intact, so it could oppose an invasion. And it had the advantage of fighting over its homeland—RAF pilots who were shot down but survived could fight again, while Germans downed over England became prisoners.

Alone, sufficiently prolonged bad weather—common over northern Europe even in summer—could prevent the Germans from achieving air superiority and make crossing the Channel impossible. Col. Theodor Osterkamp, the commander of the Jagdgeschwader (Fighter Wing) 51 (until Göring fired him, perhaps because of his annoying realism), calculated that the Germans could not afford any net decrease in their fighter strength if they were to cover the invasion. Osterkamp correctly maintained that the Germans underestimated the strength of Fighter Command and the quality of the Spitfire.

Several factors delayed the opening of the battle. Apart from the Luftwaffe's recuperation from the French campaign and its concentration on bases in northwest France and the Low Countries, there did not seem to be a rush. The invasion was many weeks away. Further, Göring calculated that he needed only a month to defeat the RAF. He, and some others, hoped that its collapse might cause the British to give up without a landing or only a token one. Last were the incoherence of the Luftwaffe's planning, Göring's own laziness, and the Luftwaffe's poor intelligence. Hitler did not intervene far down in the planning process. He limited himself to issuing a few broad directives that were actually more sensible, as far as they went, than the ideas generated farther down the chain of command. The Luftwaffe's ideas largely originated at the level of the air fleets, Kesselring's Luftflotte 2 and Gen. Hugo Sperrle's Luftflotte 3, which were seriously at odds about what to do.

Göring and others at first favored attacking London. They thought this tactic would force British fighters to enter into a fighter versus fighter battle that the Germans would win. Göring dropped the idea, but it would be revived later. Others suggested attacking British aircraft plants but soon realized that most of the targets involved were beyond the range of German fighter escorts. Sperrle favored attacking shipping and ports, while Kesselring tried to cut down the number of targets to an essential minimum. Göring had not completed planning when Hitler, on July 30, ordered that he should be ready to launch the crucial offensive on twelve hours' notice; the next day Sea Lion was set for September 15. On August 1, Hitler and the OKW issued directives for the offensive. The OKW stipulated that gaining air superiority ought to take eight to fourteen days after a start expected around August 5. Hitler stressed concentrating attacks on the RAF, its ground installations, and the aircraft industry. He reserved a decision to make "terror attacks in reprisal" for himself. He also discouraged attacks on civilian targets, above all London, for another month despite considerable pressure from below. At this time, he placed a greater emphasis than many of his military advisers did on concentrating on military objectives. As historian Gerhard Weinberg has suggested, Hitler's deferring on bombing London was not influenced by any tenderness for the British; rather, he believed a "Rotterdam"-type of attack on London should come immediately before a landing, causing people to flee the city, jam the roads of southern England, and assist the invasion.

Hitler's decrees forced Göring to finally settle on a plan, which took almost another week. The resulting scheme, Adler (Eagle), was supposed to start August 10. It was muddled, had far too many targets and no proper priorities, and omitted some important targets. Göring envisaged attacks in three series of three to five days each. They were to start at the coast; progress inland, primarily against RAF bases; and conclude with attacks on bases around London. A preliminary series of low-level and dive-bombing attacks on the radar stations, aimed at knocking them all out between Portland and the Thames, would precede the main effort.[25]

## THE CHANNEL BATTLE
Fighting, sometimes fierce, had occurred over the English Channel and the Straits of Dover from July 10 to August 11. The Luftwaffe had probed

Britain's defenses and hoped to weaken it economically by attacking ports, other coastal targets, and shipping. The Germans mainly struck at coastal convoys, which were important to the British economy. Some convoys suffered serious losses, and covering them proved costly for the RAF in terms of sorties flown but not in losses of pilots and planes. The Luftwaffe also showed the vulnerability of the Defiants, wiping out most of a squadron on July 19; the RAF withdrew them from day fighting. The Germans, however, did not note that the Channel fighting also showed the inadequacy of the Me 110 and the Stuka. Their attacks were effective enough to stop the convoys for a time, on July 25, but they were resumed on August 5.

During the Channel battle, the RAF lost 162 planes and the Germans 301 from all causes. The RAF's pilot strength, however, had continued to increase. The Luftwaffe, meanwhile, had wasted a whole month.[26]

### The Battle of Britain: The Main Fighting Begins

Göring finally set Operation Adler for August 13. On August 12, the Germans launched the preliminary attack on coastal fighter fields and radar stations. The latter were hit by severe attacks, especially by the fighter-bomber unit Erprobungsgruppe 210, which proved effective. The radar towers proved less vulnerable than either side expected. Only one of the six stations attacked, at Ventnor, was knocked out. It was only out for three days after suffering damage to its power supply rather than its antennas or electronic gear. The British masked the gap in the radar chain by sending out signals on the radar wavelength even though no equipment picked up the reflections. (Later, mobile stations promptly filled such holes.)

The main offensive on August 13 largely misfired because of bad weather. The Germans mainly attacked bases that Fighter Command did not use. Not one attack on a Fighter Command field succeeded. The Germans did bomb Southampton, but they aimed at and hit the dock area, rather than the Spitfire plants. The RAF inflicted heavy losses, downing forty-two German planes for thirteen British losses. The weather also prevented important attacks on the following day.

On August 15, the Germans made the greatest effort of the whole battle. The Scandinavian-based Luftflotte 5 intervened for the first and last time, launching a diversionary attack on northern England. A small force of Me 110s, weighed down by auxiliary tanks, and a few fighter versions of the Junkers 88 bomber escorted the bombers. The Germans had supposed that practically all British fighters had been sent south, but Dowding carefully kept the north covered, using the area to rest squadrons from the main theater in the south. Although the Germans hit a Bomber Command base hard, they suffered disastrous losses in the northern attack. Gruppe 210's fighter-bombers scored heavily in two attacks on southern airfields. Its second attack of the day mistakenly hit London's Croydon Airport and neighboring factories, which suffered heavy losses. Me 110 and Stuka damages were especially bad, with the Luftwaffe losing seventy-five planes—its worst loss of the whole battle—to the British thirty-four. Göring now concluded that attacking radar stations was probably not worthwhile.

On August 16, variable weather hampered German operations. They nevertheless destroyed an unusual number of British planes on the ground, but of the eight bases they hit, only three belonged to Bomber Wing. Despite good weather, the Germans stayed home on August 17. The next day, they concentrated on two targets: the important bases at Kenley and Biggin Hill. They planned to launch a carefully coordinated, mixed attack on Kenley. First, Junkers 88s would dive-bomb the base. A conventional high-level attack would follow and provide a diversion for the squadron of Dornier bombers from Kampfgeschwader (KG [Fighting Squadron]) 76, which was the only specially trained low-level unit apart from Gruppe 210, to conduct a low-level strike. The timing got mixed up, and the Junkers hit the wrong airfield. While the low-level strike arrived first by mistake, causing considerable damage, the Germans' losses were so horrendous that the unit was rarely employed again. Despite Göring's opinion, the Stukas struck a radar station as well as an airfield but incurred terrible losses. One group was practically wiped out, and sixty-nine German planes had been destroyed for thirty-four British.[27]

Weather then interrupted operations for several days. On August 19 Göring made several major changes in policy, some sound, some not. While shaken by the heavy losses, he was still basically overconfident, supposing that the Germans had inflicted heavier losses on British fighters and installations than they had. The Germans now estimated Fighter Command's strength at just half the real figure. They withdrew the Stukas from the battle, reducing effective German bomber strength by a nearly a third, and directed that Me 110s would be used only with Me 109 support or to take bombers to targets beyond the Me 109s' range. They discontinued further low-level attacks, except by Gruppe 210, and attacks on radar stations. The Me 110s of Luftflotte 5 went south to join the main battle. More important, most Me 109 units were transferred from Sperrle's command to Kesselring's Luftflotte 2 and based as close to England as possible. The Luftwaffe would concentrate on fewer targets and on Fighter Command proper. But it would reduce daylight bomber operations, which were regarded mainly as a means to force RAF fighters to fight. The Germans would send bombers in smaller forces with closer escort. At night, bombers would strike RAF installations, aircraft plants, and oil refineries and storage facilities at Thameshaven east of London. Small forces of bombers might also attack aircraft plants by day but only in bad weather.

Göring's orders were usually interpreted as insisting on tightly shackling the fighters to the bombers so closely as to deprive the fighter pilots of the initiative. (This interpretation of his orders may have been overly narrow, but he failed to correct the misconception.) The insistence on closer escort resulted from the earlier heavy losses that the bombers had suffered; they also caused Göring to rule that only one officer would ride in any bomber. Göring also replaced the commanders of many fighter units with younger men. Except for his decision to end attacks on radar stations and insistence on tying the fighters close to the bombers, these changes considerably increased the pressure on the British. The more numerous tightly escorted bomber formations snarled radar plotting and fighter direction and tended to nullify the British policy of concentrating on attacking bombers and avoiding, when possible, German fighters. The British now had to resort to more complicated tactics. Spitfires would try to deal with the escort while Hurricanes tackled the bombers.[28]

A long spell of bad weather prevented major operations until August 24. Then the hardest part of the Battle of Britain for the RAF began, with continuous attacks on its most important bases and tougher air fighting. The addition of Me 109s to Kesselring's force enabled him to add high cover above the close escort. The British fighters found it harder to pursue the German bombers, although they still did so, especially on August 26. Despite the German fighter pilots' dislike of the closer escort, the ratio of German to British losses narrowed. Indeed, on one or two occasions the RAF would lose more planes, although not pilots, than the Luftwaffe would.

There was grumbling at the situation in Fighter Command. Air Vice Marshal Keith Park, commanding 11 Group, was angry that he did not get more support from Trafford Leigh-Mallory's 12 Group, which he had called on to cover some of his airfields, but, it seemed to him, was doing other things. 12 Group had its own ideas. The well-respected squadron leader, Douglas Bader, backed by Leigh-Mallory, favored using "big wings," assembling three or more squadrons in the air under one commander, to intercept the Germans. Bader, who already led the unofficially constituted "Duxford wing," and Leigh-Mallory argued that it was necessary to meet the Germans with as many concentrated fighters as possible. Hopefully, they would hit after 11 Group had disrupted a German attack, but the implication was that it did not matter much if German bombers struck once as long as the British shot so many down that they could not return.

Bader thought 11 Group should also employ big wings. Park and Dowding disagreed. They thought a big wing took too long to assemble and was too hard to control in the air. Furthermore, they believed it was essential to hit the Germans before they drop their bombs and prevent as much destruction and disruption as possible. Bader's and Leigh-Mallory's critics suspected that the Duxford wing exaggerated its results. They were correct, although it was not Bader's fault; he was honest and an extremely capable leader despite the errors of the big wing idea. The claims simply resulted from the normal effect that the more fighters engaged in a single battle, the more success they tended to claim. Park thought that two squadrons at most could be assembled in time over Britain and perhaps even properly controlled in the air at all; however, even that did not seem to have particularly good results when tried. Concentrating the fighters was, of course, desirable, but should be orchestrated by ground controllers, not one pilot on the spot tediously assembling and leading big formations in the air. Later experience showed consistently that Park and Dowding's views were correct for air defense—even under offensive conditions two squadrons were the most even the best leaders could handle in the air. Other, later critics thought that instead of keeping many units in reserve in the north, Dowding should have packed a far larger number of squadrons with all available Spitfires into 11 Group for a decisive showdown there. But, apart from other considerations, that was probably beyond the capabilities of the existing control system.

As it was, that control system was frayed. August 30 and 31 were particularly bad days. The important base and sector station of Biggin Hill was especially hard hit. Effective low-level attacks by Gruppe 210 on August 30 and the special low-level squadron of KG 76 the next day damaged Biggin Hill so badly that two of its three squadrons had to move to other bases. On August 31, the RAF lost 39 planes, the worst single day's loss of the battle, to 41 German aircraft destroyed. On September 1, German losses in the air were actually less than the RAF's—14 to 15, respectively— but the British continued to fly a high level of sorties while the German effort had begun to fall off sharply. The constant pounding was still worrying. Five forward airfields and six of seven sector stations had sustained considerable damage, although the control system at individual stations was only briefly out of action. Over the next week, the Germans lost 189 planes to 161 British. Dowding and Park were concerned. Although individual airfields and sector stations might only be knocked out for a few hours at a time, the system as a whole seemed degraded, and Fighter Command seemed, albeit slowly, to be wasting away. From August 24 to September 6, 295 fighters had been destroyed and 171 damaged; meanwhile, only 269 new or fully repaired planes had arrived, although many were still in reserve. The British believed that 103 pilots had been killed or were missing and 128 wounded, while only 260 new pilots, not fully trained by earlier standards, had arrived. The older pilots were tired. Even time off and a rotation to the north did not seem to rest them enough. "Fresh" squadrons full of replacements suffered heavy losses, stemming at least partly from the RAF's continuing to teach obsolete tactics, to the extent tactics were taught at all. Even Dowding and Park, however, were not as pessimistic as was later widely claimed by those who thought that the British were now losing the battle—only to be saved by German blunders often blamed, as usual, on Hitler.[29]

Things were not as bad as they looked. Although the Germans still both overestimated the damage their bombing caused and the number of RAF planes they shot down and underestimated the RAF's ability to replace its losses, the Luftwaffe's men were at least as tired as those of the RAF, as British interrogators of prisoners noted. They were actually worse off for replacement aircraft, and the number of planes that the Luftwaffe sent actually fell. Despite their early optimism and miscalculation of RAF losses, the Germans were not all that confident. They feared that the RAF might pull back from bases south of London and fly from fields to the north, beyond the Me 109s' range. That move would nullify the Luftwaffe's hopes to draw the RAF into an all-out air battle and destroy it and would still allow the RAF to contest the air in the event of an invasion. In fact, some German leaders were surprised that the British had not relocated its planes already.

The Germans cast about for a new strategy to try. One idea was to attack British aircraft plants within fighter escort range. Göring, with the Luftwaffe staff's prompting, had finally approved the plan on September 2. But this program competed with another, worse idea that had lurked for weeks but Hitler had ruled out—an early attack on London.

Several developments led Hitler to change his mind. On August 25 German night bombers aiming at oil storage tanks at Thameshaven inadvertently hit the heart of London. The British responded by bombing Berlin over several nights. (Previously, Bomber Command had been bombing, or trying to bomb, industrial targets in western Germany.) On August 30

Hitler lifted the ban on attacking London. Contrary to common opinion, he may not have acted purely out of political or emotional reasons but because he also was anxious over the continued RAF resistance. The invasion date was near. He was well aware of the military arguments for striking London. He left the final decision on when to hit London to the air force, but Göring was not inclined to cross Hitler's wishes, which many in the Luftwaffe agreed with.

On August 31 preliminary plans for a day attack on London were prepared. At a meeting on September 3, Kesselring revived the old argument, which he had favored from the first, that bombing London would force a big air battle that the Germans would win. He felt that British resistance was weakening. Much damage had already been done to the bases south of London and any more might lead the British to retreat to the north. Sperrle, less confident about the damage done to the RAF, favored continuing attacks on Fighter Command bases. Göring predictably sided with Kesselring. Hitler, surprisingly, was still a voice of reason, vetoing deliberate attacks on civilians and favoring attacks on military objectives in the capital for the time being. Attacks to cause mass panic should come later. In fact, given the inaccuracy of bombing at the time, and the mingling of military objectives—that is, port facilities and industry—with residential areas, especially in London's East End, this directive was not much of a distinction.[30]

The German High Command had ordered shipping to the Channel ports. On September 3 the earliest date for launching the invasion was fixed for September 20; the landing would take place the next day, on September 21. A final go-ahead, however, had to be given ten days in advance, or on September 10 or 11. It is often said that Hitler was not determined to launch an invasion, but the preponderance of evidence shows that despite well-founded anxieties, he was ready to go ahead. After the British bombed Berlin, he gave a particularly violent speech to an audience of hysterical nurses and social workers and joked that the English were asking, "Why doesn't he come?" He answered, "Be calm. He's coming!" He promised terrific reprisals for the attacks on Berlin, remarking, "England will collapse, one way or another." This speech clearly indicates that he expected early victory either by invasion or, a possibility he privately referred to several times over the next few days, by Britain's collapse precipitated by bombing. On September 6, Admiral Raeder, although expressing a brief and unusual flicker of optimism about the invasion, perceived that Hitler expected such a collapse.

On September 10, without enough progress in the air and the navy reporting delays in assembling the invasion fleet owing to the weather and RAF bombing, Hitler postponed the go-ahead signal for the invasion until September 14. On September 12, he seemed to have cold feet. The next day he told Field Marshal Walther von Brauchitsch that he hoped for victory through bombing, and others believed he seemed to be thinking about abandoning the invasion. On September 14 he seemed much more determined. Although Raeder warned that the air situation was not yet suitable and Hitler agreed that the prerequisites for the invasion had not yet been fulfilled, he did not cancel it. He remarked, as Halder recorded, that a successful invasion would end the war. He postponed a final decision until September 17, which allowed an invasion on September 27. Given the tides and phases of the moon, it was the last possible date before October 8 if fall weather left it possible at all.

British attacks, however, seriously interfered with the Germans' invasion preparations. One factor in postponing it from the original target of September 15 was a successful attack on the Dortmund-Ems Canal on August 12. While six bombers made diversionary runs from a high altitude, five others went in low. Two were lost, but the canal, a main route for barge movements, was out of action for ten days. Coastal Command harassed dockyards, shipping, airfields, and oil storage targets. Further action against the invasion fleet awaited the movement of barges to the invasion ports in early September. The main strength of both Coastal and Bomber Commands was turned loose against those ports. The readily visible break between land and water made them a target that could be bombed with reasonable accuracy at night even in 1940, and the Royal Navy shelled them from the sea. The attacks caused the Germans considerable trouble, putting 21 of 168 transports and 214 of 1,697 barges out of action by the time the invasion was cancelled. That factor alone was not enough, however, to have prevented an invasion.[31]

## The British Victory

Hitler's erratic moods owed something to the equally erratic results of German air operations. The decision to hit London was finally implemented on September 7, much to the relief of Dowding and Park, as it took the pressure off Fighter Command's ground installations. But it marked the beginning of a terrible experience for Londoners and especially for the people of London's East End. Many cities would be more heavily bombed later in the war, but none suffered such continuous attack as London experienced over the next few months.

The September 7 attack was a maximum effort for the Germans, in relation to their now-reduced capabilities. Three hundred bombers set out, escorted by 600 Me 109s and Me 110s, with a much higher proportion of fighter escorts to bombers incidentally than American attacks later enjoyed over Germany. The German bombers and fighters flew higher than they had before, with improved escort tactics. The switch to London, however welcome to the British commanders, still took them by surprise, and the RAF was somewhat out of position. The plotting of the attack was confused and it was mistaken for yet another strike against Fighter Command bases and Thameshaven. The Germans reached their targets without much interference. The belated RAF interception did not go well, although it downed 37 Luftwaffe planes for 23 British fighters lost.

Although aimed at industrial targets, such as the Woolwich Arsenal and shipyards, and the docks, the bombing caused terrific destruction in the adjoining slums. The following night's attack by Sperrle's air fleet was even more indiscriminate and, given the weakness of the night defenses, could hardly be disrupted at all.

On September 8, there was no major daytime attack. The Germans returned to London on September 9 but with a force smaller by a third than that used on September 7. Effective interception disrupted the bombing and inflicted heavy losses on the bombers, with 28 German planes going down for 19 RAF. The results were another factor leading to Hitler's postponing the invasion decision.

Weather prevented a major effort on September 10, but on September 11 the Germans returned to London. They also began jamming British radars, although this effort ultimately had little effect. The German escorts were unusually effective, and Fighter Command lost more planes than the Luftwaffe. Bad weather then prevented much activity until September 14. The RAF again came off badly, each side losing 14 planes.

On September 15, the weather improved. The Germans made a maximum effort but had exhausted their bag of tricks. The nearest British radars watched as the Luftwaffe took an unusually long time to assemble over the Calais region. With plenty of warning, the RAF mounted an exceptionally effective interception. Every squadron in 11 Group came up, followed by Bader's Duxford wing, which performed better than usual. The result was the big fighter battle the Germans had sought but a big British victory. It was marred by overclaiming, precisely because of the huge scale of the fighting; the British claim of destroying 185 German planes led to this date becoming "Battle of Britain Day." Actually, they had shot down 56 and lost 28 planes. The RAF had in fact destroyed more German planes on other days. But this day was decisive. The German High Command had to recognize that it had failed; its long-sought all-out battle had misfired. In the lower ranks, the visible failure, on top of weeks of heavy losses and repeated assurances that the next attack would encounter the "last 50 Spitfires," was a serious blow to morale.

With air superiority not in sight, Hitler postponed the invasion indefinitely on September 17, although he let preparations continue. On September 19, the Germans stopped assembling the invasion fleet and began dispersing ships and barges already in the invasion ports to avoid further damage. Sea Lion was now a bluff that the Germans maintained for its psychological effect on the British and, increasingly, as a disguise for the attack on the Soviet Union. On October 12, it was formally postponed until May 1941.[32]

The air battle over Britain did not end suddenly; even the daylight struggle simply petered out. (British historians usually date the end of the Battle of Britain, rather arbitrarily, at the end of October 1940, while the Germans hold that it lasted until May 1941, encompassing the night bombing campaign the British called the Blitz.) Göring would not admit defeat and insisted on continuing daylight attacks, of reduced size, even after Sea Lion was dead. In the fewer intervals of good weather, the Luftwaffe mounted smaller day attacks on London. The last, on September 28 and 30, consisted of only 30 Junkers 88s protected by 200–300 fighters. Afterward, medium bombers did not go to London during the day at all. Reinforced by Gruppe 210, Sperrle's air fleet had some belated successes attacking British aircraft plants in carefully planned operations assisted by diversions. On September 26, after several misfires, a mixed force including Gruppe 210 finally hit the Spitfire plants at Southampton, a target the Germans should have struck at least two, if not three, months earlier. A serious blow to Spitfire production, it came much too late. By this time, the long-delayed Spitfire plant at Castle Bromwich, far to the north, was in full production. After October 7, medium bombers made no serious day attacks at all, instead flying almost entirely at night. The Germans pointlessly tried to exert some pressure by day by sending over fighter-bombers, occasionally including a Junkers 88 in the attacking formations. They did not operate as Gruppe 210 and fighter-bombers usually did—that is, by dive-bombing or attacking at low-level—but dropped their bombs while flying straight and level at high altitudes, hardly aiming at anything in particular. Dealing with them was difficult, as they flew above the best altitude for the Spitfire. The British pilots found them very tiring, but they were simply nuisances. By giving the British the opportunity to shoot down these German pilots, Göring's misuse of his fighter force worked in favor of the British and the Soviets.[33]

The night attacks of the Blitz (September 1940–May 1941) were a real ordeal for the British. Their ability to defend against night attacks was slight, but they had early developed extremely effective techniques to jam the most accurate electronic guidance systems the Germans had for directing night bombing. Lesser guidance systems; the short distances to British targets, most of which were on or near the sea; and the especially exposed position of London, close to German bases and on a bending river right above a wide estuary that made it easy to find, made the Luftwaffe's attack on Britain more effective than the Allied bombing of Germany would be until 1943. Nevertheless, the Germans could not usually effectively single out a particular factory for attack. Their inaccurate bombing and poor target selection—they only occasionally struck cities such as Coventry and Birmingham that contained the industries most critical to the British war effort—and the British people's endurance and determination prevented the night bombing of Britain from doing decisive harm, although it did more damage to British war production than is generally realized.[34] But the Blitz, on top of the Battle of Britain, was costly for the Luftwaffe. The heavy losses of the summer of 1940 permanently damaged it, costing experienced airmen who were never fully replaced. The Luftwaffe was never as strong as it had been in July 1940.[35]

## Analysis

The Germans were never close to winning the Battle of Britain. Many, including the official British historians writing in the 1950s, later maintained that the British had been close to disaster from August 24 to September 6 and were saved at the last minute by the blunder, often wrongly ascribed to Hitler alone, of shifting the attack to London. But this assertion was not true. As Telford Taylor summed up the situation, Fighter Command was "badly strained, but still basically intact." The research of historian Roger Parkinson and others showed a more optimistic picture than earlier accounts allowed. Comparing Fighter Command's own returns with the Air Ministry's figures, he showed that the latter apparently exaggerated its losses of RAF pilots. No airfields or sector stations were out of action for more than a few hours, even after the worst attacks. German airmen were at least as tired as the RAF's pilots; their morale sagged as much or probably more. British replacement pilots, while not well trained, were not as badly trained as sometimes claimed and kept pace with losses. Writer Stephen Bungay concluded that had the Germans continued bombing airfields, and British losses mounted at the worst rates inflicted in late August and early September, the RAF would still have had 725 Spitfires and Hurricanes ready to fly in the third week of September 1940.[36] While the number of operational RAF fighters hardly dropped at all during the battle, the number of German operational aircraft, both fighters and bombers, diminished fairly steadily throughout the campaign, and the number of Luftwaffe sorties fell steeply during the first few days of September, before the Germans focused on London.[37] Parkinson concluded that the battle "never came near to being lost by Fighter Command; the postwar belief that the 'few,' battling for Britain's very survival came within days of defeat, is totally false." He also contended that no switch in tactics would have changed things for the Germans.[38]

Some authors, notably Air Marshal J. E. Johnson and Bungay, have contested the latter point, arguing that the Luftwaffe had the equipment to win but did not use it properly. By concentrating from the first on radar stations and Fighter Command bases and especially by using the low-level tactics demonstrated by Gruppe 210, the Germans could have won air superiority over southern England. Bungay has argued that the entire Me 110 force should have been retrained for work as low-level fighter-bombers. With cross-Channel commando raids, they could have knocked out the radar stations, at least temporarily, leaving Fighter Command vulnerable to attacks on its airfields and control system by further Me 110 attacks, orthodox high-level attacks by medium bombers, and strafing fighters. He also pointed out that the Luftwaffe should have attacked the aircraft plants, especially the Spitfire plants at Southampton, much earlier. Johnson suggested that Stukas could have struck the radar stations nearest the European mainland; Me 110s and Junkers 88s could have hit the farther sites and, together with strafing fighters, struck airfields; and night bombers could have hit sector stations and aircraft plants. The British early warning and control systems could not have been destroyed once and for all, but repeatedly knocking them out for a few hours at a time would have been enough. Johnson thought that such a course, resolutely followed, would have given the Luftwaffe air superiority over southeastern England in two weeks.[39] But such actions do not appear to have occurred to anyone on the German side.

The Germans made so many mistakes, some quite grotesque, that it is hard to say what would have happened had they done things differently.

Poor intelligence, erratic target selection, the failure to concentrate attacks on British radar stations and aircraft plants (especially Spitfire plants) at an early date, and the failure to relocate all Luftwaffe fighters on bases as close as possible to Britain—all were notable flaws. Undoubtedly, however, low-level attacks would have been extremely costly. Gruppe 210 and the special squadron of KG 76 suffered heavy losses on the occasions when they tried them, and the British would have massed machine guns around their bases once a shift to low-level attacks became clear. The British could also have abandoned the most exposed bases while still continuing to contest the air over southern England.

The Luftwaffe's chief problems—its general orientation toward ground support, its lack of a heavy bomber or well-armed medium bombers and a true escort fighter, the vulnerability of the Stuka, the insufficient number of Me 109s, and above all, the short range of the Me 109 and the failure to develop drop-tanks for it—were built in long before the battle began. The Me 109's range was so short that even with the tactics suggested by Johnson and Bungay, the Germans could never have won complete domination of the air over southern England. Even had far greater losses been inflicted on Fighter Command and its bases in the south had become untenable, the British fighters could have flown from bases outside the range of the German fighter escort that were immune to serious bombing. From such bases, the RAF could still have operated over the south and the Channel.[40]

Even if by some fluke the Luftwaffe had won undisputed control of the air over the Channel and the projected beachhead, an invasion of England would still have been impossible. It is usually assumed that had the Luftwaffe gained air superiority, it could have stopped the Royal Navy from interfering with the invasion fleet.[41] Experience during World War II seemed to show that surface warships without fighter cover were helpless against planes. That was true, however, only against properly equipped attacking aircraft. Destroying heavy warships, especially, was a specialized task requiring heavy armor-piercing bombs or torpedoes. The Luftwaffe had only a few clumsy floatplane torpedo bombers in 1940. Gen. Dietrich Pelz, the Luftwaffe's dive-bombing specialist, later declared that even in the best conditions, with the weapons then available, the Luftwaffe could not have stopped the British fleet from annihilating an invasion force.[42]

Given these facts, it is almost a waste of time to discuss the German invasion plan, but it should be noted that by September 1940 the British Army was not the almost unarmed mob that had returned from Dunkirk.

It had a force of 800 tanks and might well have pushed the Germans, who planned to invade with only 310 tanks, into the sea.

Some observers have argued that the Germans' whole approach to the invasion problem was simply belated or misdirected. They should have struck right after Dunkirk, when the RAF was weak and no serious defense on land could have been mounted. Moreover, it is argued generally by the same critics that it was a mistake to embark on a long, drawn-out campaign for air supremacy. Instead, the Luftwaffe should have aimed to cover the invasion force and win an air battle during the Channel crossing.[43] However, neither an early assault nor all-out concentration on "one single battle" would have defeated the Royal Navy. An invasion in June or July was never possible, aside from the point that such a move would have had to have been planned months in advance and only sketchy preliminary studies of the invasion problem had been made.

The German historian Cajus Bekker (Hans Dieter Berenbrok) also pointed out that the Germans found virtually no seaworthy craft in the Channel ports; this detail alone shows they could not have launched an early pursuit of the British across the Channel. Barges and other craft had to be tediously brought from Germany to the invasion ports, which British demolition parties had heavily damaged. In any case, the Luftwaffe too, had suffered heavily in the French campaign, its exhaustion and losses being partly responsible for the BEF's escape from Dunkirk. Many bomber units had less than half their nominal strength of planes operational.[44] In short, there was no lost opportunity for an early or for any German conquest at all in 1940.

# 3

# The Battle of the Atlantic I

## *1939–1941*

The fight to defend the Allies' lifeline in the Atlantic, mainly against German U-boats, lasted throughout the war and ultimately spilled over into the Indian Ocean and the Pacific. It dragged on until the last U-boats surrendered to the Allies or were seized by the Japanese at Jakarta in May 1945. It was the longest campaign of the war, one on which the success of all other western Allied endeavors turned. As Churchill wrote, "The only thing that ever really frightened me during the war was the U-boat peril." He elaborated, "The U-boat attack was our worst peril. It would have been wise for the Germans to stake all upon it." Many historians who never thought that the threat of an invasion of Britain in 1940 was serious later maintained that the Western powers came close to disaster in the Battle of the Atlantic. The oft-quoted view of Stephen W. Roskill, the official British historian of the war at sea, was that Britain narrowly escaped defeat by the U-boats in the spring of 1943. Of the British naval leaders, Roskill wrote, "They must have felt, though none admitted it, that defeat stared them in the face."[1]

An island unable to feed itself, Britain depended on the sea for imports to survive, for transporting British forces and supplies to overseas theaters, and for Allied support while Britain served as the vital base for operations against the European mainland. The U-boats caused enormous damage and tied up huge resources in defensive efforts. It has been estimated that the Allies had to put three times the resources into antisubmarine warfare as the Germans put into the U-boat campaign.[2] The Germans were in a race not only against antisubmarine measures but also against a vast shipbuilding effort. It is doubtful that they came close to breaking the transatlantic supply line.

The issue of whether they were ever close to success is a complex one, for the Germans might well have built up the U-boat force faster or employed it more effectively. Several times in late 1941 and 1942, Hitler diverted many U-boats to the Mediterranean and the Arctic. There they caused major losses but sank fewer ships than they would have in the more crucial Atlantic. And part of the effectiveness of the Allies' antisubmarine effort, in the last half of 1941 and after December 1942, depended on a delicate foundation—that is, reading German naval ciphers. Had German signals specialists been less arrogantly confident of the security of their ciphers, the Allies would have lost a major source of intelligence. Yet during the most intense fighting in the Battle of the Atlantic, the Germans also read important British ciphers. The cryptographic efforts of the two sides may have neutralized each other.[3]

## Prewar Preparations

Neither side prepared well for the Battle of the Atlantic. Many senior German and British naval officers believed that the submarine was a weapon of limited effectiveness to which the main countermeasures—convoys and escort ships carrying sonar, which the British developers called asdic—were already known. The German Navy and especially Raeder were obsessed with big gun surface ships and discounted U-boats and aircraft. Hitler gave Raeder a largely free hand, but Raeder's defective planning, Göring's hostility to the navy, and the latter's low priority left Germany in 1939 with a small fleet of high-quality surface ships, soon put out of action in the Norwegian campaign, as well as an inadequate force of only fifty-seven U-boats, many small and short ranged. Only in July 1940 did U-boat construction get top priority. Adm. Karl Dönitz, the head of the submarine service (and Raeder's replacement in 1943), calculated that he needed three hundred U-boats (only a third would be in action at any one time) to force Britain to its knees.

Dönitz's confidence in his force was based partly on his belief that British antisubmarine measures would be far less effective than others thought and on high expectations for his own system of tactics and strategy rather than radical new technology. Torpedoes remained temperamental, and to be sure of getting a hit, a submarine normally had to penetrate the escort screen of a convoy. German submarines, until late in World War II, were not radically different from those of World War I and lacked the electronic gear that greatly helped American submarines in the Pacific. With better power plants, welded construction, better steels, and improved radios, World War II U-boats were faster and could dive faster and deeper, but they remained submersibles rather than true submarines. Their effectiveness, in fact, depended on their ability to operate on the ocean's surface. A submerged submarine, operating on battery power, was slow and moved slower than a convoy of merchant ships. It rarely got more than one shot at a convoy before it passed out of range and was vulnerable to sonar detection. (Later, U-boats running at shallow depth on diesels, using the snorkel breathing tube, were even slower than fully submerged submarines using batteries.) But a surfaced U-boat, running on diesels, was faster than the great majority of merchant ships and even some escorts. A surfaced U-boat was almost invisible to sonar, hard to detect on early radar, and extremely difficult to see at night. It could travel 320–370 nautical miles a day—the average convoy, only 240—so it could keep up with a convoy, and even get ahead of it. Quick transit to and from operational areas also depended on staying on the surface most of the time.

Dönitz counted on this capability. His favored tactic was the night attack on the surface. When possible, whole groups of U-boats, or wolf packs, spread out in patrol lines, with the U-boats sailing eight to fifteen miles apart to find convoys. Allied convoys could often slip through U-boat patrol lines unseen. U-boats normally did not communicate directly with each other. Instead, the first U-boat to sight a convoy reported its position to U-boat command onshore, then trailed it, while the U-boat command directed other boats to converge on it. Therefore, Dönitz's system of operations depended on the ability of U-boats to stay and attack on the surface, where they were vulnerable to improved radar and aircraft, and on an extremely centralized system of communication, highly vulnerable to direction-finding. U-boat contact reports were so stylized that even when the ciphers involved could not be read, the British could determine that one of their convoys had been spotted.[4]

Dönitz's overall "integral tonnage" strategy was also questionable. It was based on the idea that the Germans must sink as many ships as possible to cut the whole Allied shipping pool below the level at which Britain could be supplied. He not only overestimated the losses the Germans could inflict, but he erroneously assumed that sinking ships in westbound Atlantic convoys and losses in areas far from Britain (e.g., the Indian Ocean) hurt Allied supply as much as sinking ships eastbound across the Atlantic. This strategy also left the Germans little recourse once the Allied shipbuilding effort shot past the point at which the Germans could hope to reduce the Allied shipping pool to a fatal level.[5]

In terms of real damage to the Allies, losses inflicted on the transatlantic convoys that ran east from North America to ports in Britain were far more important than ships sunk elsewhere. The only traffic at all comparable in importance was that of the oil tankers running from the Gulf of Mexico, the Caribbean, and the East Coast of the United States to Britain. The Germans would attack these convoys, with considerable effect, only in 1942, after the United States entered the war.

Dönitz had been bitterly at odds with Raeder not only about the priority the U-boats and how many to build but also about what types were needed. Dönitz preferred what became the standard Type VII submarine of about 750 tons displacement, for he believed it was most suitable for North Atlantic operations. Raeder had wanted much larger, more heavily armed, and longer-range craft that could reach distant waters. He forced Dönitz to accept the construction of a few large Type X minelayers and Type XIs with overgrown deck gun armament of little use in actual warfare. Much of the U-boat fleet consisted of the more useful Type IXs, which were less clumsy than the Type Xs and XIs, but were still suited for long-range operations. Although requiring more construction time compared to the Type VIIs, the Type IXs proved of some value later, and Raeder may have been right to force them on Dönitz. They enabled the Germans to carry on the war against Allied shipping, to some extent, even after the fight in the North Atlantic was lost.

Dönitz's own judgment in pushing the Type VII was open to question. Early Type VIIs had serious design flaws. The improved Type VIIC, by far the most common German U-boat (661 were built), although strong and reliable, lacked sufficient range even for North Atlantic operations and carried only eleven torpedoes. U-boats never acquired effective air search radar and only belatedly received radar search receivers to warn that Allied radar was scanning them. They also lacked air-conditioning, which reliable electronic gear probably required in those days, and even by the standards of other submarines, they were cramped and uncomfortable. Clay Blair, an American submariner who served in World War II, commented that the Type VIIC was "overtouted" and that the Germans should have built a slightly larger submarine with three instead of two diesel engines.

Apart from questions of priority and what to build, it is doubtful that the Germans could have built a three-hundred-boat U-boat fleet in time to affect the outcome of the war and without evoking a British reaction. Even after open rearmament began, the German Navy wasted six months in securing contracts for U-boat construction. Historian Jürgen Rohwer, however, has calculated that even using its shipyards and resources to the maximum extent, only seventy-two U-boats could have been ready by September 1939. A three-hundred-boat fleet could not have been ready before 1942, and there might not have been enough diesel fuel for it.[6] The lack of air support also seriously hampered the U-boat campaign. Between Raeder's indifference and Göring's hostility, the elements of the Luftwaffe assigned to reinforce the navy and especially the U-boats were poorly equipped and supported.[7]

For their part, the British also made many mistakes. They gravely underestimated both the need for shipping and the U-boats' effectiveness. Indeed they were more worried about the relatively few German surface raiders. Although U-boats had made some night surface attacks late in World War I and British submarines had practiced such attacks in prewar exercises, the Royal Navy was oriented toward countering the inherently limited, submerged day attack. Strapped for money, it was acutely aware that German surface ships were up-to-date and better than their British counterparts and emphasized replacing aging large ships, which took a long time to build. The navy assumed that antisubmarine escorts could be built quickly in converted civilian yards. Besides overestimating the efficacy of sonar, it also failed to train enough sonar operators. (The U.S. Navy did an even worse job.) In addition, the Royal Navy underestimated the effectiveness of air escort of convoys, although they were of great service in World War I. And Coastal Command, the RAF's maritime arm, was poorly equipped with obsolete planes. Although radar sets were installed in the planes in 1940, they were inefficient. Moreover, the planes had no effective antisubmarine weapons until August of that year.

The Royal Navy was short of escorts. What it had in 1940 was of mixed worth. It had procured the excellent Black Swan sloops (forty-two were built), but they were too complex to be mass-produced. To have enough escorts, the British resorted to using the small Hunt class destroyer and the corvette, a modified whaler that ordinary shipyards could mass-produce. The Hunt class destroyers were a failure—top heavy, dangerously unstable, with too little fuel, carrying too few depth charges. The early Flower class corvettes (214 were built), while reasonably safe and stable, were almost unendurable in bad weather. Later, the British built larger and improved Castle-class corvettes and bigger frigates; however, the corvettes remained rather slow. Until 1943, Flower class corvettes, sloops, and a mass of generally inadequate destroyers largely waged the Atlantic battle. Apart from the Hunts, the British depended largely on old V and W class destroyers.

Even after extensive modifications, they were poor escorts, as were the fifty World War I–era American Town class destroyers that the British received in 1940. About the same age as the *V* and *W* class destroyers, they were, if anything, even worse. In 1941, the Americans transferred ten Coast Guard cutters to the British; like the sloops, they were excellent ships.[8]

## Early Wartime Operations

The Battle of the Atlantic started slowly. Apart from the small size of the U-boat force, Hitler, apparently hoping that restraint might make an early peace with Britain possible, did not immediately allow unrestricted submarine warfare. By November 1939, it was well under way. The Germans also had the new magnetic mine, which seemed a more formidable weapon than the U-boat torpedo and at first could not be swept. U-boats, surface ships, and planes laid the new mines around the British Isles, and for several months they were extremely dangerous.

U-boats, despite their small numbers, achieved two spectacular successes in 1939. The British foolishly used some of their few aircraft carriers in ineffective submarine-hunting groups. One encountered the sub *U-29*, which sank the carrier HMS *Courageous* that September. In a carefully prepared special operation, *U-47* slipped into the Home Fleet anchorage at Scapa Flow and sank the battleship HMS *Royal Oak* in October. But an early experiment with wolf pack tactics misfired. U-boats in this period usually made submerged day attacks.

The British quickly started a convoy system, although it was rudimentary and of short range by later standards. At first, they had only about sixty escort ships, forty Sunderland flying boats, and some short-ranged, land-based planes to guard convoys.

Fast transatlantic convoys (HX) for Britain formed at Halifax, Nova Scotia. Starting in August 1940, the far more vulnerable, dangerous, slow convoys (SC)—nominally 7.5–8.0 knots in speed but usually even slower—formed at Sydney on Cape Breton, Nova Scotia. Later, in August 1942, all Atlantic convoys were shifted to New York, but it became so jammed that in the spring of 1943 SC convoys were transferred to Halifax. Westbound fast and slow convoys, initially designated OA and OB, assembled at Liverpool or, sometimes, out in the North Channel; later these were redesignated ON and ONS. Convoys from Gibraltar to Britain were HG; outbound to Gibraltar, OG. Ships coming from further south joined SL convoys at Freetown, Sierra Leone. Ordinary outbound convoys in the reverse direction were OS, while troop and major supply convoys from Britain to the Middle

East were WS, or "Winston's Specials." The latter required especially heavy escort, as did the PQ and QP convoys to and from North Russia after Germany attacked the Soviets.

Managing the convoy system was a complex job. By 1942, in the most important part of the system, normally four HX and two SC convoys, averaging fifty ships each, headed for Britain at any one time, and as many ON and ONS convoys were en route to North America. Later, in 1942–1943, after the United States entered the war, convoys were extended along the coasts of the Americas and later through the southern oceans. Important additions to the convoy system were CU and UC tanker convoys running from the Caribbean to Britain and back. After the North African invasion in November 1942, OT and TO tanker convoys shuttled between the Caribbean and North Africa to support the military campaign there, while UGS-GUS convoys ran between the United States and North Africa. On average, a ship in convoy could make just six round trips a year between the United States and Britain and four between the Caribbean and Britain. The only thing more wasteful of shipping than sailing in convoy was *not* sailing in convoy. Only a very fast ship had a fair chance of getting through U-boat waters without an escort.

Until July 1940 convoys leaving Britain received antisubmarine escort only as far as 15 degrees west, or about three hundred miles west of Ireland; in that month, the escort was extended to 17 degrees west. Then the antisubmarine escort broke off to meet an incoming convoy. Ocean escort consisted of an auxiliary armed merchant cruiser, a fast merchant ship outfitted with guns, or sometimes, when German surface raiders were feared, cruisers or even battleships. The small Royal Canadian Navy escorted convoys about four hundred miles out of Halifax. Convoys received air cover only when close to Britain.

The results of the U-boat campaign were not great, however, before it was broken off so submarines could support the Norwegian invasion. In that campaign, five U-boats were lost for little gain. The Germans did learn that their torpedoes didn't function properly; they ran too deep and their magnetic exploders did not work. Later American submarines would encounter similar defects in the Pacific.[9]

## Wolf Packs

The conquest of Norway and western Europe completely changed the situation in the Atlantic, although the U-boat force comprised only fifty-one boats in June 1940. The Germans quickly put Norwegian and French bases into operation. The latter extended the operational area far to the west, increasing the effective strength of the U-boat fleet by up to 40 percent. The British had lost the help of the French fleet, while the Germans now had Italy, with its seemingly formidable (if only in numbers) submarine force, as an active ally. The British had lost many destroyers, especially at Dunkirk, and for months many of the rest were pinned down to counter the invasion threat. Coastal Command, too, concentrated mostly on anti-invasion tasks. The closing of the Mediterranean further stretched shipping and the Royal Navy, forcing ships headed to the Indian Ocean and farther east to undertake longer voyages. Around Britain itself, all shipping had to pass through the northern approaches and use western ports to unload. Extending escorts farther west meant little, for most convoys from July to October had only one escort.

The U-boats now switched to night surface attacks and, in September 1940, to wolf packs. At night with their decks barely above water, they were safe from sonar and barely visible. They could slip through a thin escort screen to strike repeatedly, diving only to escape counterattacks. They could follow convoys for days and take advantage of other U-boat attacks that drew escorts from one side of a convoy and exposed the other side to attack. Switching Atlantic convoys to the North Channel to avoid German air attacks made them easier to find. Sailing from Norway, even the small Type II boats could reach that area. It was an easy voyage for Type VIIs from the new French bases, and the toll rapidly mounted. Beginning in early September, an attack on convoy SC 2 was a massacre. Late in September, HX 72 lost twelve of forty-one ships. SC 7 lost twenty of thirty-four ships, the worst single loss to a convoy in the whole Atlantic struggle; and HX 79 lost a dozen ships. In one month, the Germans sank as many ships as they had in the previous four months.

The British responded by forming permanent escort groups of radar-equipped ships that trained and worked together and began improving air cover. The early metric wavelength radars were not effective, however; the British had mounted their antennas too low and they were useless in heavy seas. The British also extended the escorts to 19 degrees west. Sunderland flying boats, the only long-range planes then available, made the North Channel area untenable for the U-boats in October and the convoys harder to find. Although few in number and hard to maintain, the Sunderlands impressed the Germans. Near Britain, they were supported first by the short-ranged Ansons and then Lockheed Hudsons.

In November 1940, as air cover pushed the U-boats farther out, beyond 15 degrees west, Royal Navy destroyers were released from anti-invasion work. As the wave of U-boats sent out in September and October returned to base, the effort fell off, and greater difficulty in finding convoys, increased air cover, and bad weather then reduced U-boat sinkings. Only four to six boats were usually at sea at any one time. Although a nightmare for convoys and escorts, especially the corvettes, bad weather hampered U-boats even more, making it hard to sight ships or to aim, and could throw torpedoes off course. After sinking sixty-three ships of 352,000 tons in October, in November they sank only thirty-two ships of 147,000 tons. The force grew to seventy-three boats, but only twenty-seven as yet were operating out of French bases in December. The British knew, however, that this drop in activity was only temporary. Churchill wrote to Roosevelt on December 8 of the "mortal danger" of shipping losses.[10]

Fortunately for the Allies, the twenty-seven Italian submarines sent to operate from Bordeaux proved of limited value. Italian submarines accomplished little even in the Mediterranean and were totally unsuited to the Atlantic. Noisy, clumsy, and unmaneuverable, they were slow on the surface, slow at diving, and had large silhouettes that made them easy to see. (Later, the conning towers were cut down.) Their periscopes were too short. They had no external air intakes for their diesels, so they had to run with a hatch open on the surface. In rough seas, water poured inside. Their poorly trained crews were totally unready for night or surface attacks and showed little inclination to learn. They could not provide the Germans accurate or even intelligible reports. Later on, though, the Italians achieved successes against ships sailing independently in the central Atlantic and in distant areas such as the Caribbean and South Atlantic.[11]

The U-boats received more support from other German forces. Raeder sent his large warships out on lengthy raids, which enjoyed considerable success in late 1940 and early 1941. The battle cruisers *Scharnhorst* and *Gneisenau* sank twenty-two ships on a cruise in early 1941. In home waters, the British suffered considerable losses to German motor torpedo boats. Diesel powered, with better hull forms, they were more formidable than their British counterparts. Bombers also sank many ships along the British east coast; coastal convoys did not get adequate air cover until April 1941.

The Luftwaffe did have a plane that could range far into the Atlantic, the Focke-Wulf 200 Kondor. Its only four-engine bomber was a rather fragile converted airliner that could only carry a relatively light bomb load. Few were available, and the rate at which they could be kept operational was low. They seemed to offer an otherwise unavailable source of recon-naissance for the U-boats. Göring typically fought cooperation with the navy, so Hitler intervened and put the only Kondor unit under the navy's control. The Kondors, flying out of Bordeaux (and later shuttled between Bordeaux and Norway, flying around Ireland), proved to be disappointing scouts for the U-boats. Their navigation was poor; U-boats usually steered Kondors to targets rather than the other way around. Kondors, however, were surprisingly effective as attack aircraft. In October 1940, one Kon-dor crippled the huge, converted liner RMS *Empress of Britain* (the biggest troopship sunk in the war) so that a U-boat could destroy it. The Kondors' biggest success was sinking seven ships out of convoy OB 290 on Febru-ary 26, 1941. They became such a menace that the British, lacking enough aircraft carriers, developed the catapult aircraft merchantman (CAM) ship. From a catapult installed on the ship's bow, the CAM ship could launch a Hurricane fighter for one flight to counter an air attack. Afterward, the pilot flew to a land base, if one was in range, or ditched in the sea.[12]

Already, in late 1940, the British had begun evasive routing of convoys and of all ships sailing independently farther north to keep them out of Kondor range and to make them harder for U-boats to find. Later they spread convoy movements over a wider sea area. This was an additional factor in the relative lull in losses during the winter, but by February the Germans found the new route. British losses, which were only twenty-one ships of 122,000 tons in January, shot up to thirty-nine ships of 197,000 tons in February. That month, the U-boats also began operating in distant areas, sending Type IX boats against shipping in the South Atlantic, where de-fenses were weak and targets easy. By March 1941 the U-boat force grew to ninety-nine boats.

The British had made a serious blunder in December that helped the Germans: they reduced the speed limit for ships sailing independently from 15 to 13 knots. This change resulted in heavy losses, for even when wolf packs were most successful against convoys, they scored dispropor-tionately higher against ships traveling independently or straggling behind convoys.

The British were losing ships at twice the rate they were being re-placed. They desperately tried to strengthen their defenses. RAF Coastal Command was put under the navy's operational control. Six new Hudson squadrons were formed, units were transferred from Bomber Command to Coastal Command, and new airfields were built. Coastal Command began to receive American-built PBY Catalina flying boats, which had almost as much range as Sunderlands but were far easier to maintain. The remarkable expansion of the Canadian navy began to pay off as well. Escort ships obtained very high frequency (VHF) voice radio for better communication, more radars, and bigger depth charges.

On March 6, with more than three million tons of shipping gone in the last eight months, Churchill issued an overall directive on the Battle of the Atlantic that allotted still more resources to antisubmarine efforts. Bomber Command shifted almost its entire effort to maritime targets, especially the German heavy ships now at French bases, while more squadrons (ultimately seventeen) moved to Coastal Command. Churchill arranged for better methods to using the available shipping, handling their cargoes, and repairing the huge backlog of damaged ships.

A certain check on the Germans' success became evident even in March. The Germans inflicted heavy losses on OB 293 and HX 112, but five U-boats and their three best captains were lost. The Germans temporarily abandoned the northwestern area. Working farther south, they soon sank ten of SC 26's twenty-two ships. In April, the British finally made effective use of Iceland as a base, first for surface escorts, enabling convoy escort to 35 degrees west, and then for planes. The U-boats moved out of range of Iceland-based planes but improved their methods. On May 8, instead of maintaining nearly stationary patrol lines, they took up wider search patterns, moving both east and as far west as the Grand Banks off Newfoundland. That led to the discovery of HX 126 and the sinking of nine ships. Moving west, however, the U-boats entered the Americans' patrol area, which was advancing east. It extended from 60 degrees west to 30 degrees west on April 18 as the Americans occupied Greenland. As early as April 10, the destroyer USS *Niblack* (on a reconnaissance mission to Iceland outside the patrol area) dropped a depth charge aimed at a U-boat.[13]

### Surface Raiding

During the spring of 1941 the struggle against the German surface raiders reached a climax. The British were desperate to keep *Scharnhorst* and *Gneisenau*, now at Brest, from striking again. They were prime targets for air attack. On April 6, 1941, a Beaufort torpedo bomber seriously damaged *Gneisenau* when the ship briefly left the protection of torpedo nets. The Beaufort was shot down; its crewmen had understood that they had practically no chance of survival. Their sacrifice may have prevented a major disaster. From then on, the battle cruisers, although usually in dry dock and immune to sinking, were kept almost continuously out of action by periodic bomb hits. In February 1942, they finally escaped to Germany through the English Channel. Mines damaged both in the process. Shortly afterward, *Gneisenau* was damaged beyond repair by RAF bombs.

In late May 1941, the new battleship *Bismarck* went out on a raid. On May 24 *Bismarck*, breaking out into the Atlantic between Iceland and Greenland, sank the British battle cruiser HMS *Hood* and damaged the new battleship HMS *Prince of Wales*. In a dramatic chase, torpedo bombers from the carrier HMS *Ark Royal* damaged *Bismarck* enough so the Home Fleet could catch and sink the battleship. It was a narrow victory for the British; if not for a lucky hit that jammed its rudder, *Bismarck* almost certainly would have reached France. On June 13, a Beaufort seriously damaged the pocket battleship *Lützow* off the coast of Norway before the ship reached the Atlantic.

That ended serious raids by major warships in the main theater, although they sometimes seriously threatened the North Russia run. Earlier losses, a shortage of fuel oil, the enforced escape of the battle cruisers, and Hitler's fears of an invasion of Norway—all discouraged later German attempts to break out into the Atlantic. The *Bismarck*'s sister ship, the *Tirpitz*, and the rest of the German surface fleet represented primarily a local threat to the Russian convoy and a "fleet-in-being" that pinned down a large part of the Royal Navy that otherwise would have been released to fight in the Mediterranean and against the Japanese. It was to free ships of the Home Fleet rather than eliminate a major threat, that the British from 1942 to 1944 devoted considerable effort by heavy bombers, Chariot manned torpedoes, midget submarines, and carrier air strikes to crippling or destroying the *Tirpitz*.

After the spring of 1941, the Germans' big warships were no longer a serious asset in the Battle of the Atlantic. For the rest of 1941, however, the U-boats received distant support from disguised merchant raiders or auxiliary cruisers, big and fast freighters with armament comparable to that of a light cruiser but hidden so that they could sneak up on independently sailing ships. Nine were sent out, with six operating at the peak of activity in the spring of 1941. Although having no direct impact on the crucial battle in the North Atlantic, they caused considerable losses in distant areas and captured a whole Norwegian whaling fleet in the Antarctic. The most successful auxiliary cruiser, the *Atlantis*, sank twenty-two ships. More such ships would have been a better investment than recklessly sending out the big ships, but they too were a wasting asset. With the extension of Allied air patrols and the convoy system, they became less viable and were vulnerable to the British breaking of German ciphers. The British never read the raiders' ciphers, but attempts to concert raider operations with other forces, such as the U-boats, whose ciphers were read, sometimes led to their destruction. After 1941 the remaining raiders were not successful.[14]

## Enigma and Ultra

The destruction of some surface raiders was a modest side effect of a more significant development. The Germans used various models of the Enigma electromechanical cipher machine to protect their communications. Portable and battery powered, it resembled a typewriter with a screen mounted above it. When an Enigma operator pressed a key, a current went through a set of several different movable rotors, and a letter on the screen, the enciphered version of the letter being typed, lit up. A second man wrote down the illuminated letters for transmission. The rotors used and the order in which they were placed varied. Early in the war, the operators inserted three of five different rotors at any one time; eventually the German Navy used five of seven types of rotor. The way the rotors were set up was the critical element, or the "key," to the system. Batches of keys were issued in advance for a whole month, but operators used each key for only twenty-four hours and changed them each midnight. So, to some extent, Allied cryptographers had to start fresh each day.

Because of the complexity of the rotors themselves, their arrangement, and the short life of the keys, the Germans were sure that their ciphers were unbreakable. They believed that if the Allies captured an Enigma machine or even a complete key for a certain period, it would do them little good. And owing to their success at breaking Allied ciphers early in the war, they were confident that they would quickly find out if the Allies did read their messages.

Learning to read the ciphers was a daunting task. As the British mathematician Gordon Welchman, one of the critical figures in breaking the Enigma ciphers, commented, it "would have been impregnable if it had been used properly," and "enforcement of a few minor security measures could have defeated us completely." He thought the Allies "were lucky." Fortunately, Welchman observed, German procedures always proved defective in some way, or the operators made mistakes that gave the Allies vital clues. Welchman thought some simple changes to the Enigma device would have foiled the Allies' code-breaking effort even had the Germans never corrected their procedural errors.

The struggle to defeat the Enigma, in use since the 1920s, long predated the war. Polish mathematicians Marian Rejewski, Jerzy Rozycki, and Henryk Zygalski, aided by documents that French military intelligence had obtained, first broke the Enigma ciphers in 1932. The Poles were able to read German messages until 1938, when the Germans introduced improvements in the Enigma machine and procedures. The Poles shared their work with the British in July 1939 shortly before Poland was overrun.

The Western powers found that the Luftwaffe's signals service was the most careless of the German forces and, in May 1940, began reading its general-purpose cipher, which the British called Red, which disclosed much information on army operations. The British read this cipher almost every day, with little delay, for the rest of the war. (The qualification "with little delay" is important, because even when some other ciphers were broken, reading them often took so much time that that by the time a message was understood it was of little value.) Breaking Red came too late to help France, but from then on Enigma traffic was a major source of information. The British centered cryptographic work at the Government Code and Cypher School at Bletchley Park. They expanded the first break to read other ciphers and built electromechanical "bombes" based on earlier Polish designs and greatly improved by Alan Turing and Welchman. These devices duplicated the Enigma's scrambling units and enabled apparent "cribs," or clues, to be tested quickly, which the Germans had not expected. This line of endeavor led to a major technological breakthrough. Deciphering became more difficult in early 1943, as the Germans made alterations to the Enigma device and to their methods. To speed the work and handle the more elaborate Siemens Geheimschreiber (secret writer) already used for some high-level messages, which, the Allies feared, would replace the Enigma, the British built the first electronic digital computer, Colossus.

To distribute communications intelligence—code-named Ultra—and to ensure its secrecy, the British developed a system of carefully camouflaged Special Liaison Units attached to field headquarters throughout the world. They passed on messages deciphered at Bletchley Park and enforced rules designed to protect the Ultra secret.

Nevertheless, Ultra remained a fragile achievement. Aside from the points noted by Gordon Welchman, some of the French and Poles who had worked on the Enigma problem earlier remained in France. The Gestapo captured five of the Poles. Had any revealed their work, even the complacent Germans could not have failed to react decisively.

Reading naval Enigma ciphers remained particularly difficult and required special efforts and some luck. Some commando raids on occupied Europe, notably that on the Lofoten Islands off Norway in February 1941, were aimed partly at seizing cipher materials. In the Lofotens, the British captured some Enigma rotors and documents that allowed some limited reading of the German "Home Waters" cipher (which the British called Hydro) in March 1941, although it did not prove of much help. Suspecting that weather-reporting ships received cipher materials in advance to cover a considerable time, the British decided to try and capture some. They took valuable materials aboard the weather ship *München* on May 7. The following day, an unplanned seizure proved even more helpful. The British forced *U-110* to the surface and captured it. Although it sank under tow, a boarding party had retrieved its cipher books and an Enigma machine. The British seized another weather ship the *Lauenberg* on June 28 and retrieved more important Enigma documents. Afterward, the British did not undertake further operations of this sort lest the Germans get suspicious. Thanks to the captures, the British read the Home Waters cipher, which the U-boats used until late 1941, with a delay of only three to seven days in May. In June and July, code breakers read the cipher currently, although the Germans introduced a more complex system of coding positions at sea, causing some trouble. From August 1941, the cipher was read on all but two days of the war, although there were delays of up to thirty-six hours in December 1941.

The success at deciphering naval Enigma enormously aided evasive routing, letting the British slip convoys past U-boat patrol lines. It also enabled the British to destroy eight supply ships that had gone out to support the *Bismarck*, preventing them from supplying U-boats.[15]

### The First Defeat of the U-boats

Shipping losses fell from more than 300,000 tons a month in May and June 1941 to less than 100,000 tons a month later that year, which was still a serious loss but far less than before. More effective evasive routing was only one factor in an abrupt turn against the U-boats. In May, the British reversed the erroneous decision to lower the speed limit for independently sailing ships. They returned to a limit of 15 knots, greatly reducing the number of sitting ducks for the U-boats. Protests also stopped Spain from letting German ships in the Canary Islands supply U-boats. The greater antisubmarine efforts also had effect. The British and Allied escort force had grown to 250 destroyers, 150 corvettes and sloops, and 300 smaller craft, while Coastal Command now had 582 planes (although not all of them were on antisubmarine missions). Canadian forces had expanded so that beginning with HX 129 in June 1941, convoys were escorted all the way across the Atlantic. During the summer, Canadian-manned Catalinas and Digbys (obsolete American B-18 bombers) began flying four hundred miles out from Newfoundland.

The Germans also had to operate more cautiously in the western part of the Atlantic in a futile effort to avoid incidents with the Americans. The evidence suggests that reducing independent sailings was much more important than the contributions of Ultra, though estimates indicate that the latter saved 300 ships of 1.5 million tons. After losing 61 ships of 310,000 tons in June to a U-boat fleet of 138 boats, the British lost only 22 of 94,000 tons in July and 23 of 80,000 tons in August.[16] The Germans failed to respond to the Allied intelligence breakthrough, although they suspected something was wrong. They realized that the Allies knew details of their operations but attributed this development to other causes than to the reading of their messages. For a time, they suspected improved direction finding from shore bases but eventually dropped this idea. (They never realized the effectiveness of Allied shipborne direction finders.)[17]

The British, meanwhile, began to heed scientists' advice. Coastal Command, in the spring of 1941, brought in operational researchers under the leadership of the great physicist P. M. S. Blackett. Operational research was not directed toward devising new weapons but the less glamorous and often more effective task of using available equipment better. Blackett was especially adept at learning how to use aircraft more effectively. He discovered how bad Coastal Command's navigation and use of radar were. (The main contribution of airborne radar, in fact, had been to help British planes find not enemy submarines but the convoys they were to escort.) He found the radar operators poorly trained, improperly positioned within the planes, and overworked; later an additional operator was added to each aircrew. Blackett also determined that the planes patrolled at altitudes that were too high and that their depth charges were set to go off too deep to catch diving U-boats and should have been spaced more widely. His work quickly paid off. New, shallow-set depth charges destroyed U-452 on August 25. He also suggested improved paint schemes to make planes less visible to U-boat lookouts. Later, Blackett shifted to working for the Admiralty, producing more effective search and depth-charge patterns for surface escorts.[18]

Although the Germans had several times as many U-boats as they had six months earlier and the force continued to grow, their sinkings of Allied ships fell. Dönitz countered "end to end" escorts by shifting U-boats back toward the British Isles. This move proved unsuccessful during July and August and simply brought the U-boats up against British-based air patrols. In August, he even resorted to the desperate expedient of giving attacks on escorts higher priority than attacks on merchant ships. This also proved ineffective. Even when the U-boats found the convoys, attacks on the latter were not particularly effective.

Dönitz concentrated some effort farther south against the Gibraltar convoys, and this endeavor was somewhat more successful. Found with the help of the Luftwaffe's more effective tracking, OG 69 lost seven ships west of Ireland. With the U-boats focus around the British Isles on the whole deemed a failure, Dönitz moved them out into the Atlantic and spread them over wider sea areas, as far as Newfoundland, and with smaller, looser patrol lines. They found a weak spot southwest of Greenland, where a wide gap still had no air cover and the Canadian-based surface escort was weak, inexperienced, and not well equipped, reflecting the price of the Canadians' remarkable naval expansion. Even where Newfoundland-based air cover was available, it was hampered by extremely poor visibility and headwinds when flying eastward. In early September the Germans sank sixteen ships out of convoy SC 42 and lost *U-501*. U-boats from this patrol line that still had torpedoes left also attacked SC 44 and sank four freighters and a corvette. But even this success seems to have been uncharacteristic.

Moreover, the danger and reality of clashes with the Americans grew. Beginning with HX 150, they were escorting convoys as far as Iceland. On September 11, Roosevelt issued the "shoot on sight order": "From now on, if German and Italian vessels of war enter the waters the protection of which is necessary for American defense, they do so at their own risk."[19]

Whether the Battle of the Atlantic was at a stalemate is not quite certain, for the situation changed once again. In September, Dönitz came under severe pressure to divert U-boats from the Atlantic to help the hard-pressed Axis forces in the Mediterranean. Hitler himself intervened for the first time in the Atlantic battle to overrule Dönitz and ordered a massive shift of effort to the south. Sixteen U-boats went to the Mediterranean. This move not only represented a serious diversion of effort from the main theater in the North Atlantic but also meant that the U-boats sent would probably never return to the ocean. British forces at Gibraltar made it hazardous even to enter the area, and the adverse current sweeping into the Mediterranean made it extremely dangerous to try to get out again. The British spotted the Germans' move and strengthened their forces at

Gibraltar. U-boats still in the Atlantic concentrated on convoys to and from Gibraltar. Although U-boats in this area enjoyed the support of Kondors, they also faced constant British patrols, while Gibraltar convoys consisted of mostly small freighters and were not profitable targets either in terms of Dönitz's integral tonnage strategy or for supporting the Axis forces in the Mediterranean. During November, practically the whole U-boat effort was diverted to the Gibraltar route and the Mediterranean.

After some disappointing weeks, U-boats operating on the Gibraltar route finally found what appeared to be a profitable target, namely, convoy HG 76 bound for Britain. The British, well aware of the U-boat concentration building on HG 76's route, delayed sailing until an unusually heavy escort could be provided. It left Gibraltar on December 14 with thirty-two cargo ships and an escort of nine corvettes, five sloops, three destroyers, and the escort aircraft carrier HMS *Audacity*. The latter was the first, although not good, example of a new class of small carriers converted from merchant ship hulls and designed to protect convoys. The *Audacity*, particularly small, lacked a hangar deck and carried only six Martlet fighters (the British designation for the U.S. Navy's Grumman F4F Wildcat), which posed no direct threat to U-boats. They could spot surfaced U-boats but did not carry bombs or depth charges, although the U-boats did not know that and promptly submerged on sighting them. The *Audacity* had previously helped save the otherwise weakly protected OG 74 from heavy losses.

HG 76 led to a terrific running battle between the *Audacity*'s planes, the surface escort, and the U-boats. The convoy lost two merchant ships—a destroyer and the *Audacity*. Dönitz, who was following the action, made the carrier a prime target, although its sinking by *U-751* may have come because it was accidentally lit up by a British Snowflake illuminating rocket. Toward the end of its run, the convoy came under the protection of the newly arrived, long-range Liberator bombers of Coastal Command's 120 Squadron. Despite the loss of *Audacity*, the battle was a notable reverse for the Germans, who lost five of the nine U-boats that reached the convoy and four Kondors. The experience with HG 76 made clear that a counter to the U-boat—escort groups of ships that had trained and worked together and combined with air support—already existed, and when Allied resources were brought to bear, they would win.

Dönitz's staff now doubted that the U-boats could foil the convoy system. But he disagreed, blaming the defeat on the unusual strength of the escort, which he maintained was possible only over a relatively short route and on weather unfavorable to the U-boats. He believed his still-growing fleet could sink Allied ships at the rate of 700,000 tons a month and would bring about the Allies' collapse. In fact, the U-boats had sunk only thirty-two ships of 157,000 tons in October and thirteen ships of 62,000 tons in November, although overall Allied shipping losses still exceeded replacements. Dönitz had convinced himself, but as former Royal Navy escort commander Donald Macintyre pointed out, the Germans' successes in 1942–1943 were achieved only because of the Allies' inability to profit by the example of HG 76.[20]

The lessons of HG 76 coincided with other dramatic events, some favorable to the Germans. Nevertheless, on top of the declining effectiveness of the U-boats in the Atlantic even before their diversions to the Mediterranean and the Gibraltar route, the HG 76 battle points to the conclusion that the U-boat war was already lost, even if the Germans enjoyed local or temporary successes thereafter. Many experts later concluded that the U-boats' only chance of success was in the first two years of the war or, even, up to the spring of 1941. As historian Marc Milner put it, the period from the spring of 1940 to the spring of 1941 was the only time the U-boats could have achieved decisive strategic results, and the Americans' intervention then made their task hopeless. Cajus Bekker also concluded that the German Navy's prospect of victory existed only in the first two years of the war.

But that chance was probably nonexistent, for, as noted earlier, the Germans could have built up their seagoing forces only marginally faster than they did. Further, Britain's survival was likely not dependent on the admittedly fragile achievement of reading the Germans' ciphers. The evasive routing that the intelligence made possible saved many ships, but perhaps it was less important than reversing Britain's self-inflicted mistake of letting many ships sail independently and their throwing more resources into the Atlantic struggle. Indeed, they could have put additional resources into the Atlantic. Had the British faced the imminent breaking of their transatlantic lifeline, they would probably have reduced their commitments in the Mediterranean and Middle East, which were extremely costly in terms of shipping. They did not wish to do so and were glad to avoid that, but they would have done it had the only alternative been famine and the loss of the war.[21] It is also likely that had the British been harder pressed, the Americans would have intervened in the Atlantic struggle sooner.

Meanwhile, the Germans enjoyed some good fortune at the end of 1941. The U-boat fleet was still growing, rising to 236 boats, with 86 operational by December. Although the full-blown entry of the United States into the war was disastrous, in any long view, it ended the need for restraint in dealing with the U.S. Navy and opened the whole Western Hemisphere to U-boat assault, while the Japanese would divert American resources. Moreover, the intelligence struggle turned in their favor. The Germans began reading the British Naval Cypher No. 3, which revealed convoy movements, and took new measures to protect their own messages. Periodically, they had suspected that the British knew at least some of their moves as soon as they were broadcast to the U-boats and were particularly perturbed by the loss of *Bismarck*'s supply ships. Although the "experts" reassured him that the ciphers could not have been more than temporarily compromised even by capturing Enigma machines, Dönitz decided on September 28 to take further steps to protect the ciphers, if only against leaks or traitors. In addition to tighter security procedures, a new model of the Enigma would be introduced, using four rotors instead of three and with other improvements. U-boats operating in the Atlantic from France would also use a new, separate cipher called Triton (which the British called Shark), while U-boats based in Norway, along with other forces, continued to use the Home Waters cipher.

The four-rotor Enigma machine and Triton went into operation on February 1, 1942.[22] The Allies could no longer read the U-boat messages in the critical Atlantic theater. That loss of intelligence, the growth of the U-boat fleet, the vulnerability of the Americas, and the Allies' mistakes would lead to horrendous shipping losses and delay the victory in the Atlantic that had already been visible with the battle of convoy HG 76.

# 4

---

# The Russian Campaign I

*To Moscow*

With the invasion of the Soviet Union, the Germans initiated a struggle that they could not finish. It ended with the catastrophic reversal of the Nazi dream, with the Red Army in command of half of Germany and Europe. Not surprisingly, it is widely but wrongly believed that Hitler's invasion of Russia was the fatal mistake of his career, the one that forfeited the Axis powers' victory in the whole war.

Alternatively, common wisdom holds that had the Russian campaign resulted in a Nazi victory, Germany would have won World War II, but that assertion is equally dubious.[1] Some German and other authorities who think Germany had no real chance of defeating the Western powers do regard a complete German defeat of the Soviet Union as within the realm of possibility. After the war, many, or most, German generals were happy to heap all the blame for the Russian campaign, and its failure, on Hitler.

## The Decision to Wage War

An examination of Hitler's decision to attack the Soviet Union suggests that it was not the result of some specific contingency, narrow tactical solution, or an avoidable mistake. Rather, it flowed quite directly from Hitler's worldview and ideas he shared with most Nazi leaders. The need for lebensraum in the east, the supposed ease of acquiring it, and the desire to destroy Bolshevism, which the Nazis saw as the prime expression of the Jewish world conspiracy, reflected Hitler's most deeply held beliefs. In his mind, the notion of "Jewish Bolshevism" tied the Russian campaign to the destruction of the Jews, whom he hated more than anyone else. Planning the "Final Solution" was closely correlated with the development of Germany's attack on the Soviet Union, and it is no accident that the outright destruction of the European Jews began on occupied Soviet territory (although the Nazis had already started starving the Polish Jews to death). It would have been hard indeed for Hitler to forgo an attack on the Soviets once he felt free to initiate it.

This does not necessarily explain the immediate decision to attack Russia in 1940 and involve Hitler in the two-front war that he and all other Germans rightly feared. In 1939 he had restrained his hatred of the Soviets long enough to sign a nonaggression pact with them. Moreover, Göring, Raeder, and a fair number of generals were unenthusiastic about the decision to invade the Soviet Union. Although they did not as strongly oppose attacking the Soviets as they later pretended, it is probable that had either Göring or the professional military made the decision, the invasion of the USSR would not have taken place, at least not in 1941.

Hitler's statements in June and July 1940 suggest that after the fall of France he considered destroying the Soviet Union his next logical move whether Britain made peace, was conquered, or fought on. When Britain chose not to capitulate, Hitler continued to push toward war with the Soviet Union.

Paradoxical as it may seem, Hitler's decision to attack the Soviet Union may have preceded his decision to prepare an invasion of Britain, and the initial steps in planning the eastern campaign ran roughly parallel with that of Operation Sea Lion. Indeed, the two offensives were intertwined and were not simply alternatives or contradictory, as is often supposed. Nor was Sea Lion a bluff, as has sometimes been suggested. Hitler's reluctance to cancel Sea Lion—which he had originally hoped to avoid and which he rightly regarded as difficult, costly, and risky—seems to have been due to his desire to end the war with the British before he attacked the Soviets. That goal was desirable although not absolutely vital.

As early as June 2, 1940—right after Dunkirk—Hitler told Field Marshal Gerd von Rundstedt and others that if Britain made peace, his hands would be free for the destruction of Bolshevism. On June 23, he indicated to Field Marshal Walther von Brauchitsch, the army's commander in chief, that if Britain remained at war with Germany, the British would be fighting on in the hope of gaining Soviet support. Gen. Franz Halder learned of Hitler's inclination to attack the Soviet Union at the end of June. Halder considered the plan for such a campaign over the next three weeks. On July 29 he commissioned Gen. Erich Marcks, the chief of staff of the Eighteenth

Army, to make a serious study of the problem. Marcks had already outlined a plan for defense against a Soviet attack.

At this point, Halder and Brauchitsch (the chief of staff was the stronger character) did not seem to have been unduly worried about war with the Soviets. The tone of Halder's diary suggests that he regarded the invasion of Britain as the more immediate and the more difficult problem. Indeed, for a time, Brauchitsch even contemplated attacking the Soviets in the fall of 1940, a possibility Hitler had mentioned on June 21; but even Hitler was more prudent than that and came down in favor of striking in 1941. On July 29, Col. Gen. Alfred Jodl indicated to members of the Oberkommando der Wehrmacht (OKW) staff that Hitler had already decided on war. On July 31, Hitler made clear to the OKW and the Army General Staff that he intended to launch a properly prepared attack on the Soviets in 1941. The "psychohistorian" Robert Waite has suggested that Hitler had privately made the final decision on seeing *Die Götterdämmerung* at Bayreuth on July 23.

The spring of 1941 was the earliest period in which the Germans could concentrate enough forces and count on a full campaigning season and the last time they could hope to attack the Soviets without the Americans intervening. Any invasion of Britain, the Germans thought, would surely be finished by then. By late July, it was certain that Britain would not make peace any time soon and doubtful that it could be invaded or quickly starved into surrender. Moreover, the grave danger was that a prolonged war in the west would invite economic blackmail by Stalin, for Germany depended on the Soviets for oil and other important materials. Should Germany suffer serious defeat in the west, Stalin might attack. Moreover, maintaining the strong ground forces needed to defend against such a move would hinder the war effort against the British and Americans. If Germany destroyed the Soviets, however, it would have the materials it needed and be free to develop the air and naval strength necessary to win the war in the west. Further, by demonstrating German power and increasing Japan's strength in the Far East, defeating the Soviets might deter the United States from entering the war. (Destroying the Soviets thus converged with the drive for a full-scale alliance with Japan that had culminated in the Tripartite Pact of September 1940.) Even if the Americans entered the war, the European Axis powers and Japan, controlling a vast Eurasian bloc, could face this prospect with confidence—as indeed they could have if the Western powers had not acquired nuclear weapons first.

While some of Hitler's arguments, especially that the Soviets were a threat, smack of rationalization or insincerity, he seems consistently to have assumed that conquering the Soviet Union was the solution to his problems. Lebensraum was both a broad goal of Hitler's policy and a panacea in grand strategy, even a requirement. He told Jodl on December 17, 1940, that Germany must solve all continental problems in 1941, for from 1942 on the United States would be in a position to intervene. He apparently reasoned also that although Britain was still fighting, he would not really be engaging in the dreaded two-front war, because Britain could not open a serious land front against Germany in Europe. The considerable forces he left in Western Europe and the Balkans in 1941, however, suggest that he was not really secure about this conclusion.

Most other German leaders had no basic problem with this prospect, even if they were less enthusiastic about attacking the Soviet Union than Hitler was. Only Admiral Raeder flatly opposed war with the Soviets. Although Göring and Foreign Minister Joachim von Ribbentrop disliked the idea—the former preferred a Mediterranean campaign against the British, and the latter disliked the implicit repudiation of "his" (really Stalin's) diplomatic masterpiece, the Nazi-Soviet Nonaggression Pact—neither man had the stomach to stand up to Hitler. Among his generals, only Rundstedt's chief of staff, Sodenstern, was genuinely upset by the idea, although Rundstedt himself seems to have been lukewarm if not hostile.

But even those who disliked the proposal did so because they thought it a strategic mistake, but not a fatal one, to tackle the Soviets before finishing the war with Britain. At worst, it was rushing off in the wrong direction. No one seems to have visualized the war ending with the Red Army in Berlin. None seem to have disagreed with the disastrous idea that the Soviets could be smashed in one short campaign in 1941, nor considered what would happen should that fail to occur.

Halder, overcoming his initial willingness, decided that a Soviet war would not help defeat Britain and would harm Germany's economy, while Rundstedt and some others may have suspected that a Russian campaign would not be as easy as most supposed. But practically all leaders, including Raeder, thought that Germany would win such a war, even if it went against conventional wisdom to initiate the battle while still fighting Britain. If Germany had been able to defeat the French Army and the British Expeditionary Force more easily than anyone expected, there seemed no particular reason to fear the Red Army. Even those generals who were not hard-core Nazis were strongly anticommunist, tended to regard Slavs in general and Russians in particular as culturally inferior to Germans, and seem to have assumed that some sort of showdown with the Soviets was only to be expected. A war against the Soviets was more "natural" than one against Western opponents whom they tacitly accepted as civilized. Like many western Europeans and Americans, Germans thought of the USSR as a backward, undeveloped country not all that different from imperial Russia, which they had beaten handily. If this war proved dangerous, it would be so only if Germany were tied down elsewhere. Few, if any, realized that they would be fighting an advanced industrial country as powerful or more powerful than Germany, run by a regime that was rather more rational but as ruthless and as determined to prevail as Hitler was, and no more likely to be easily toppled than the Nazis. There was some similarity to American and British tendencies to underestimate Japan before Pearl Harbor, although the Germans' racial attitudes toward the Slavs were far more extreme.

Occasionally some have argued that Hitler's decision of July 31 was not final or absolute, that he at least was willing to consider drawing the Soviets as allies into a variation of the continental bloc against Britain, and that he only finally decided on war in late 1940 after unsatisfactory negotiations with the Soviets in November. The indications are that he did not regard such an arrangement as anything other than an outside, unwanted possibility—one that might be forced on him in certain circumstances (perhaps if the United States entered the war at an early date) but one that he neither wanted nor expected. Indeed, in the 1940 negotiations, Hitler likely hoped to trick the Soviets into waging war on Britain and invading the Middle East, putting off Soviet suspicions (had he *not* tried to win the Soviets as an ally against his current active enemy, Stalin would have wondered why) and simplifying Germany's task in conquering the USSR in 1941. Had he succeeded, it might even have led to a Soviet defeat. Such a hope may also help to explain his relative disinterest in a Mediterranean campaign. Why use German forces to destroy the British position there when Stalin might be maneuvered into doing it for him? Hitler was not always optimistic about succeeding in this endeavor, however, telling Mussolini in October that he doubted he could divert the Soviets to the south. Ironically, some evidence indicates that the Soviets were actually preparing to invade Iran in 1941, partly for their own reasons and partly to appease the Germans, although they hoped to avoid outright war with Britain.[2]

## Military Geography of the Campaign

The geography of the western part of the Soviet Empire strongly shaped German plans. It was apparent from the start that a long advance would be required even to reach what the Germans deemed the Soviets' vital centers. They had to take an area the size of France simply to approach Moscow, Leningrad (St. Petersburg), or the Donetz Basin. And the attack would cover a wide front: the western Soviet frontier, aside from Finland, covered some 1,300 miles from the Baltic to the Black Seas, and the main front, between the Baltic and the Carpathians, alone stretched 700 miles. The distances would continue to grow as the Germans advanced eastward from the relatively narrow "throat" between the Baltic and the Black Sea. The width of the front, to be sure, at least initially favored the attacker, but as the Germans spread out, they would grow more vulnerable to Soviet counteroffensives.

The western part of the Russian theater was split in two by the Pripet Marshes, a huge swampland 150 miles wide and 300 miles long, in which offensive operations would be difficult. The main route to the Moscow region, which contained not only the capital but much of Soviet industry and the main railroad center west of the Urals, ran through Belorussia (Belarus) and western Russia and north of the Pripet Marshes. The Minsk–Moscow highway was practically the only modern all-weather road in the country. Most, although not all German planners—Hitler himself was a notable exception—considered Moscow the logical prime objective and were apt to see its capture as the blow likely to topple the Soviet government. However, Belarus and western Russia were not particularly promising terrain, with much forest and swampland.

To the south, between the marshes and the Carpathians, the narrow corridor of Galicia gave access to Ukraine, whose rich agricultural lands and industrial Donetz Basin the Germans regarded as the main economic prize in the east. Ukraine was also the path to the oil resources of the Caucasus. Hitler attached particular importance to Ukraine. A few German planners favored making the main attack there, although even Hitler did not go that far. While not as well served by roads and railroads as Belarus and western Russia, the terrain of Ukraine was relatively more suited to armored warfare. Farther south, Romania offered another avenue of access to Ukraine, but for supply reasons this route had to remain secondary to a drive through Galicia. In the north, the Baltic region led to Leningrad, the second city of the Soviet Union and a major industrial center. An attack through the Baltic states enjoyed some advantages—proximity to Germany, relatively good roads, and the possibility of supply by sea—but as the Germans drove north and east they would run into more and more swampy areas and dense forests.

Some Germans, notably Rundstedt, nevertheless favored making Leningrad, rather than Moscow, the primary objective. Capturing Leningrad would offer an early linkup with the Finns, eliminate the Soviet Baltic Fleet, and offer the advantage of supply by sea. Once Leningrad was theirs, they could use it to supply an advance on Moscow from the northwest as well as the west. One disadvantage, however, was that the terrain between Leningrad and Moscow was filled with even more forbidding forest and swamp than elsewhere. Although Hitler was fascinated by capturing Leningrad, the original "cradle of Bolshevism," he nevertheless rejected this idea.

German planners in general overestimated the economic importance of the Baltic countries to the Soviets, just as they did, with more reason, that of Ukraine. They believed that both were so significant that the Soviets would hold on to them at virtually any cost, exposing them to flanking thrusts from the center of the front. Why German planners made this assumption about the Baltic states is not entirely clear, since the Soviets had struggled along without controlling Lithuania, Latvia, or Estonia up to 1940. The planners' beliefs may have reflected the influence of relations with the Baltic German minority and misleading memories of imperial Russia. Then, Riga had been an important center of heavy industry, but it had decayed since. Hitler was to take this premise about the Baltic states further and, perhaps being more imaginative than the army planners, would extrapolate from it a radically different concept of how the campaign should go. Possibly, he hoped to repeat the success of May 1940 when the Germans sliced off the Allied northern wing with a drive to the sea.

Inside the Soviet frontier, the German routes of advance would have to cross two obstacles—the Western Dvina and Dnieper Rivers, flowing into the Baltic and Black Seas, respectively. It was important to quickly reach the watershed between them—the fifty-mile gap variously known as the Orsha land bridge or the Vitebsk or Smolensk gate through which the main road to Moscow passed—before the Soviets retreated through it or set up a strong defense. And it became more and more clear that it was vital to defeat the main Soviet forces west of the Dvina and Dnieper. Once east of those rivers, the Germans' capacity to supply their forces would sharply decline.

## Planning the Attack

The Germans were hampered by poor intelligence that reinforced their assumptions about the ease of defeating the Soviets. They had no agents beyond the 1939 Soviet frontier. Their sole sources of information were air reconnaissance and poorly equipped radio intercept stations that did not pick up anything beyond the Baltic states and the area west of the Dnieper. They even lacked good maps and, despite considerable air reconnaissance, learned little about the Soviet forces in the western Soviet Union. The Germans grossly underestimated, both quantitatively and qualitatively, Soviet military strength while overestimating the proportion of it that was vulnerable to early destruction. For example, the strength of the Red Army was underestimated by about a third, while the portion of it in the Soviets' western military districts was overestimated by 30 to 50 percent. The Luftwaffe underestimated the Soviet Air Force at a bit more than half its real strength.

The Germans were overimpressed by the Soviets' poor performance in the invasion of eastern Poland and Finland in 1939. They seem to have ignored the earlier Soviet victory, under the future marshal Georgi Zhukov, over the Japanese at Khalkin Ghol in August 1939. The Germans, and others, did not realize that the Finnish experience was misleading; the Soviets had started the Finnish war at the wrong time, with poor planning, and unprepared units against an opponent that, in the peculiar Finnish terrain, was superior to both the Soviets and the Germans. The Germans, and the rest of the world, ignored the well-prepared offensive with which the Soviets ended that war. Although the German Army's handbook on the Red Army warned that it would fight more determination in defense than it had against the Finns, the Germans did not seem to take this caution seriously.

The Germans also discounted the Soviets' ability to retreat into the interior and bring reinforcements from the Far East. They underestimated Soviet industrial resources and the extent to which industry had been developed east of its traditional centers, in the Urals and Asia, and did not consider the possibility that the Soviets might evacuate much industry eastward. Above all, the Germans overwhelmingly assumed that the Soviet Union was a "rotten structure" that would collapse under attack. The Nazis, and many others, miscalculated the extent to which people would obey or even support "their" government, however bad (even though the Nazi Party had profited from it in Germany). Many people, especially in the newly Sovietized regions—not only non-Russians and even many Jews—were so embittered that they initially welcomed the Nazis as liberators. But even Stalin's monstrous tyranny had not killed Russian patriotism or even loyalty to the Soviet government, and the horrors of Nazi rule soon became obvious. The Nazis did not consider that their own plans for the occupied Soviet Union virtually guaranteed that the Russians, if not all Soviet subjects, would fight on, even if Stalin was overthrown or the Soviet regime toppled. If anything, a military regime with popular support would have been even less likely to surrender or make a deal with the Nazis than Stalin was, assuming Hitler himself was willing to make one. Stalin's generals, at least, had never regarded Hitler as a reliable ally.

Even those Germans who did not expect an earlier victory tended to think that resistance would collapse and the regime would fall once Moscow was taken. Some did question this assumption. The General Staff's Military Geography Branch, as early as August 1940, drew attention to the industrial development of Soviet Asia and warned that the Soviets could fight on even if they lost Leningrad, Moscow, Ukraine, and the Caucasus. German diplomats in Moscow warned against anticipating an early Soviet defeat, while the army's quartermaster general, Eduard Wagner, privately doubted that the army was logistically capable of taking Leningrad, Moscow, or the Donetz Basin without some sort of Russian collapse, which he still seems to have expected. The head of the OKW's War Economy Branch, Gen. Georg Thomas, at least initially doubted that Germany could successfully exploit a conquered Ukraine. The diplomats who warned against expecting Soviet failure and some civilian officials in Germany shared Thomas's view. It also became clear at an early date that an attempt to appropriate Ukraine's resources would spell mass starvation for its people.

In the spring of 1941, Thomas's office studied the problem of exporting Caucasian oil and determined that only 100,000 tons of oil a month could be brought overland to Germany, even if the oil fields were taken intact. The river tankers on the Danube were already fully employed hauling Romanian oil, so further oil shipments from the Caucasus by water would require using a sea route through the Black Sea and Turkish Straits to Mediterranean ports. To secure that route, however, the Germans would have had to eliminate British air and sea power from the Mediterranean. The requirements for using Soviet oil—complete military successes, some improbable, and the use of scarce means of transport in two different and competitive military theaters—were thus enormous.

The German planning process focused initially on the offhand work of Marcks, the chief of staff of a single army. The army group commanders who had played an important part in planning the western campaign did not have such a role in the Russian campaign and were consulted only at a late stage. Nor did Gen. Erich von Manstein, although the author of victory in France in 1940 would have been worth hearing. As German historians have commented, Marcks's scheme, submitted on August 5 after only a week's work, the starting point for the operation's planners, replaced a necessary sober assessment of the situation with "a string of speculative assumptions"—notably that losing the western border areas would result in a collapse of the Soviet war economy and that this threat would force the Soviets to fight a decisive battle there to halt the Germans on a line south from Riga and along the Dnieper, which would suit the Germans. Marcks assumed that Moscow was the ultimate objective; if it fell the USSR would collapse. Thus, the Germans would deploy two army groups, concentrating their strength in the center and north of the Pripet Marshes. A subsidiary drive would split off from the central advance to reach Leningrad, while a secondary, independent drive went through Galicia to Kiev. From there it would push on to Kharkov. A "final" line would be attained from the Northern Dvina (running into the White Sea) to the middle Volga (Gorki [Nizhni Novgorod]) and to Rostov on the lower Don. They expected to reach this line in about eleven weeks, including a three-week pause to rest, refit, and straighten out the supply lines, but thought the campaign might take as little as nine or as many as seventeen weeks. Marcks conceded that a subsequent "pursuit" to the Urals might be necessary. He even noted later that the Soviets might fight on and the United States might join in, but he did not address this possibility.

Halder altered Marcks's scheme. He made the subsidiary drive on Leningrad separate from the first carried out by another army group. He also reduced the reserves that Marcks envisaged; instead, he would commit a much larger force from the start.

As a check to the Oberkommando des Heeres (OKH) study, OKW initiated its own plan. Lt. Col. Bernhard von Lossberg, who probably saw Marcks's plan before submitting his report to OKW on September 15, used the same basic materials. This study was broadly similar to Marcks's ideas and anticipated some of Halder's modifications. But while envisioning a concentration in the center, it attached less importance to Moscow, suggesting that progress beyond the Orsha-Smolensk area ought to depend on the situation on the flanks. It introduced the possibility of having forces from the central army group turn north to cut off the Soviet forces in the Baltic region and emphasized the desirability of capturing the Baltic coast to enable seaborne supply. These ideas considerably influenced Hitler.

A war game was conducted between November 29 and December 3, based on the modified Marcks scheme. The results impressed the participants with the need to destroy the Red Army west of the Dvina and Dnieper Rivers, the need for a major pause, and the difficulty of supplying forces east of the rivers.

Hitler now intervened in the planning, introducing ideas apparently derived from Lossberg's study. Downplaying the importance of Moscow, he emphasized taking the Baltic area for the sake of seaborne supply, by turning forces from the center to the north, and occupying Leningrad before driving on Moscow. He also placed greater emphasis on the advance in Ukraine and a drive southeast to the Black Sea. Halder, the General Staff, and most others did not like these ideas, wishing to keep the emphasis on Moscow and the overwhelming concentration in the center. They did not contest Hitler's ideas, however, and the directive for the Russian campaign, codenamed Operation Barbarossa, issued on December 18, 1940, naturally registered the dictator's views. But the planning was left vague. When and how the Germans would turn north to the Baltic was unclear. The field commanders strongly disliked this idea, but Halder kept them quiet. He and the others hoped to get their way later, avoiding the turn north and aiming at Moscow. In any case, the generals involved do not seem to have regarded the problem as a critical one. All expected to defeat the Soviets west of the Dvina and Dnieper Rivers. Where the German forces went afterward did not seem to be all that vital.

Yet, in early 1941, a growing unease surfaced about the supply problems in Russia, and some tended to revise upward the estimates of enemy strength. Field Marshal Fedor von Bock, who would command the central army group, and others feared that the Soviets might escape total defeat in the western area and fight on after Leningrad or Moscow, and the resources of the southern USSR would be lost. Any idea of postponing an invasion of Russia, however, receded. Hitler was sure that America would be in the war by 1942.[3]

## Logistical Preparations

The Germans' ignorance of the Soviet Union and its armed forces largely stemmed from the difficulty of finding out what was going on there but also from the tendency of the German Army to downgrade the intelligence and supply functions. The army considered both elements as serving operational planning instead of being integrated with the latter. The German supply system was "small and primitive," as historian Barry Leach put it.[4]

That was partly the result of the desire to keep its combat units as strong as possible and its "tail" as small as possible, but fundamentally the German Army was suited only to wage war over relatively limited distances in nearby countries. In spite of Hitler's long-standing obsession with conquest in the east, the army had not been designed with the special problems of a war with the Soviet Union in mind.

The German leaders did understand, in a general way, that conditions in Russia would be different from and worse than those they had encountered in the west. Hitler had not been pleased by the supply system's performance even in France. It undertook special preparations for the Russian campaign, but they proved grossly inadequate. Indeed, there was no attempt to ascertain the special supply requirements of the expected operation and to ensure they would be filled; rather, the army assumed that fuel and ammunition expenditures would be similar to those in the western campaign and merely hoped that whatever measures it took would be enough.

The main problems were that the few major roads in the Soviet Union were bad, and over long distances the Germans depended on railroads for supply. Because of the difference between the wider gauge of the Soviet railroads and the standard European gauge, there would be a gap before captured rail lines could be converted and brought into service. Even then, the less dense Soviet network would provide only one railroad line for each of the three German army groups instead of the usual German standard of one per army. As an interim measure, the Germans built 170 small, gasoline-powered locomotives of Soviet gauge to get some use out of the Soviet tracks before they were converted. The Germans increased signal and railroad troops, but the latter were never allotted the fuel, motor vehicles, and communications gear they needed. Before the invasion, they were used to improve railroads in Poland at the expense of preparing for tasks beyond the Soviet frontier.

The Germans knew their motor transport would be strained to supply the advance before the railroads were brought into operation. They had already concentrated it to support the "fast forces," or the panzer and motorized infantry divisions in the Panzer Groups. To keep the Panzer Groups going, some supply vehicles—fully loaded with fuel, rations, and ammunition—were incorporated into the advancing panzer units themselves. This applied to a technique developed by Col. Kurt Zeitzler (who was later promoted to general and chief of the General Staff) for Panzer Group Kleist in the 1940 campaign, which had made the great advance to the English Channel possible. This "suitcase" of supplies would support the initial advance. The trucks would dump the remaining supplies at supply points and then race back to their original base to reload, while the rest of the heavy motor transport units created dumps 100 kilometers inside the Soviet frontier and went back to reload. A second set of dumps, 200 kilometers in, would be up set upon the fifth day of the campaign. Eventually, though, the relay system would be stretched to the breaking point, well before the railroads were ready.

The Germans tried to strengthen the supply of the ordinary infantry divisions and issued two hundred Polish *panje* wagons (one-horse carts) each to seventy-five divisions. These small carts proved more rugged than the standard German horse wagons, which, like German trucks, tended to come apart on the poor Russian roads. As they marched into the USSR, the Germans seized many more panje carts.

They bolstered truck transportation by buying more trucks in Switzerland and formed three new heavy transport regiments by drafting heavy tractor-trailers and other long-haul civilian vehicles and their drivers into the army. They replaced German-built civilian vehicles at home with confiscated French vehicles, but because German truck production was inadequate, captured French and Czech vehicles had to be used in Russia too, complicating the supply of spare parts. Most heavy German trucks, lacking all-wheel drive, proved inadequate on the bad roads in the east. Civilian and French vehicles proved even worse.

The Germans were short of fuel, tires, and spring steel for their vehicles. They had only enough to support a brief campaign. They did not anticipate the problem of driving in the muddy seasons of late fall and spring, much less the intervening winter, when even tracked vehicles found it hard to keep going. The already strained German motor vehicle industry could not have built enough fully tracked supply carriers for the job, even had the need for them been realized.

Ammunition and fuel consumption and truck losses all proved far higher than expected, and the rate of conversion of the railroads far slower. Because of oversights by the General Staff, not Hitler, the German Army was not prepared for a winter campaign with the necessary clothing and equipment, which were not ordered until much too late. Moreover, German locomotives proved unsuited for extreme cold. They were not properly insulated, and their main water pipes ran outside their boilers rather than through them, causing them to burst when the water inside froze. During the severe winter of 1941–1942, 70–80 percent of German locomotives in the east were put out of action.

The Germans made relatively small improvements in their combat forces for the Russian campaign. The army doubled the number of panzer divisions in 1940–1941, but it did so by splitting existing divisions and halving their tank strength. In effect, it reduced the tank strength of the panzer force in ratio to that of its infantry and artillery components. Most German generals thought this reorganization was an improvement. German tank production remained so low that it could barely replace losses, much less increase overall armored strength. Hitler was justifiably enraged when the Army Ordnance Office sabotaged one of the few real improvements he had ordered—upgunning the obsolescent Panzer III medium tank with the L60 high-velocity 50mm cannon—and substituted the less effective L42 gun instead, apparently assuming the better weapon unnecessary. Some divisions still had obsolete Czech tanks. The army did get more half-tracks and some 250 of the new assault guns. (Not in the British or American army's arsenal, the assault gun was essentially a turretless tank, carrying a high-velocity tank-type gun mounted in the front of its hull. Often carrying a bigger gun than tanks of comparable size did, it could be even more dangerous and harder to see.) Moreover, the Waffen (Armed) SS was tripled in strength, although it was still small compared to the regular army. In all, in 1941 the Germans' effective strength was little more than it was in May 1940.[5]

The Germans had allies, but they did not add much strength. The Germans themselves only respected the few but proven Finnish fighters, who were eager to retake the territory they had lost to the Soviets in 1940. Hitler expected them to be a big help in taking Leningrad, but the Finnish leader Marshal Carl Mannerheim had no desire to take part in such an operation. Germany's other European allies were not especially promising. Mussolini sent a corps to Russia for prestige purposes, but the Germans were well aware of the Italian Army's weaknesses. Nor were most Italians eager to take on another enemy. Only a little more willing to fight than the Italians were, the Hungarians and Romanians hated and feared the Soviets, but they hated each other more. The Germans would have to take special precautions to keep Hungarian and Romanian units apart lest they fight each other rather than the Red Army. Hitler disliked and distrusted the Hungarians, so he did not bring them into the campaign until it was under way. He found the Romanians more trustworthy and cooperative, but like the Hungarians, they did not have a well-equipped modern army. Apart from their equipment deficiencies, which the Germans were in no position to supply from their own production, the Romanians in particular had a poor officer and noncommissioned officer corps and bad relations between officers and their men. As Manstein sniffed in his memoirs, "Such outmoded practices as flogging [abolished in the Prussian Army in 1807] were unlikely to improve the quality of the rank and file." In March 1941, Brauchitsch bluntly warned the German Army group commanders that the Romanian Army would be useless, but it proved an exaggeration.

Most important, the Germans did not try to coordinate plans with a far more powerful potential ally. Hitler's policy in 1941 was to encourage the Japanese to attack Britain's position in Southeast Asia rather than attack the Soviet Union. Until much too late, the German leaders supposed that Japanese help would not be needed against the Soviets. They did not even alert the Japanese to their intentions. Although they offered some broad hints to Foreign Minister Yosuke Matsuoka in April 1941 and to Ambassador Hiroshi Oshima later, these remarks seemed to have passed unnoticed. The Japanese instead secured an agreement with the Soviets in April 1941 to insure themselves a free hand against the western democracies. Their attention was focused on Southeast Asia when the Nazis attacked the Soviet Union. The Nazis' deviousness in concealing their plans to attack the Soviets, as they had also hidden their moves toward the Nazi-Soviet pact in 1939, embarrassed those Japanese leaders who were pro-German or favored attacking the USSR. Only in July did Ribbentrop urge Japan to attack the Soviets as well as the British.[6]

Without the Japanese the Germans nevertheless amassed a considerable force—about 75 percent of the German Army's combat strength and 65 percent of the Luftwaffe—against the Soviets. They had allotted 145 to 149 divisions (not all had reached the theater when war began), including 19 panzer and 15 motorized infantry divisions, with 3,050,000 men, 625,000 horses, 600,000 motor vehicles, 3,350 tanks, 250 assault guns, 7,184 artillery pieces, and 2,770 planes. The Luftwaffe force in the east, however, was definitely weaker than it had been in the French campaign, and the air arm was probably actually weaker overall. The Romanians contributed 150,000 men in 14 divisions and three brigades, all understrength. Eight more German divisions, along with 500,000 Finns in 14 divisions, were allotted to the separate Finnish front. The Germans nevertheless left strong forces elsewhere; 38 divisions in France and the Low Countries, 8 in Scandinavia, 7 in the Balkans, and 2 in North Africa. The small force in Libya represented a sizable fraction of Germany's armored strength, but the units deployed elsewhere were often second rate. Nevertheless, the German forces in the west were much more than what was needed to hold western Europe, which the British were in no position to attack, and also unnecessarily strong in the Balkans, which at that point the Germans could safely have left to Italy and Bulgaria to control.[7]

The forces on the main front in the east formed three army groups. Field Marshal Wilhem von Leeb's Army Group North, the smallest, comprised the Sixteenth and Eighteenth Armies and Gen. Erich Hoepner's Fourth Panzer Group. (Panzer groups were often referred to after the names of their commanders. During the campaign, they were renamed panzer armies.) Army Group North had three panzer and three motorized divisions of 26 overall. Bock's Army Group Center, the largest, contained 50 divisions—9 of them panzer and 6 motorized in two groups, the Third Panzer Group under Gen. Hermann Hoth and the Second Panzer Group under Heinz Guderian—along with the Fourth and Ninth Armies. Later in the campaign the Second Army also joined Bock's command.

Rundstedt's Army Group South—the second strongest with 41 divisions, 5 of them panzer and 3 motorized—was deployed in two separate groupings. The main force, on the left in Polish Galicia, comprised Col. Gen. Elwald von Kleist's First Panzer Group and the Second, Sixth, and Seventeenth Armies. The weak German Eleventh Army was with the Romanian forces well to the south and lacked tanks. At one point, planners thought to provide the Romania-based force with an armored component, but this idea was dropped, perhaps mistakenly, at a late stage of planning. Rundstedt had almost all the non-German forces participating in the campaign under his command. Some 28 divisions, including 2 panzer and 2 motorized divisions, were in the Army High Command's reserve.

A final but by no means minor preparation was the establishment of four SS Einsatzgruppen—one allotted to each of the North and Center Army Groups and two to Army Group South's sector—for exterminating Jews, Communists, and Asian prisoners of war. From Hitler's point of view, their job would perhaps be as important as the military task in the east. In addition, the Germans expected early famines to destroy much of the Slav population. Planning to feed the Wehrmacht in the east from local sources and to extract food for use elsewhere, they expected to seal off cities and starve the entire urban population of the conquered Soviet Union to death in short order.

## The Balkan Factor

The Germans had originally hoped to attack the Soviets on May 15. Several factors delayed it until June 22. The need to overrun Yugoslavia and Greece forced a five-week postponement, but bad weather—a late thaw and the flooding of eastern Polish and Russian rivers—would have slowed the Germans' advance until at least the first weeks in June in any case. Thus the Balkan invasion in itself probably cost the Germans no more than two or three weeks' campaigning time in the east.

Although the Germans experienced few losses in the Balkan campaign, it caused appreciable wear and tear on tanks and other vehicles and delayed the return of two panzer divisions and an SS motorized infantry division to Army Group South, costing it one-third of its tank strength in the first stages of the invasion of Russia. The Luftwaffe suffered heavy losses of airborne troops and transport planes at Crete, rendering airborne forces unusable in Russia. The long-run effects of the Balkan campaign were perhaps more serious, pinning down substantial German forces later in the war, but they were already at least a serious nuisance in 1941.[8]

## Soviet Preparations

The actual and potential strength of the Soviet Union should have made a German victory impossible. Instead, Soviet blundering, for which Stalin was largely responsible, played into Hitler's hands and made the Russian campaign a more equal struggle than it should have been. Had the Soviets been alert, taken reasonable precautions, and adopted a rational strategy, the Nazi invasion would have misfired immediately. Stalin's failures cost the Soviets enormous losses and may have jeopardized the survival of his regime.

Stalin ignored many warnings, almost to the last minute. He had the benefit both of the extremely effective Soviet intelligence system and warnings from many governments, even some (such as Vichy) that were not at all friendly to the Soviet Union but nevertheless wanted the Red Army to have the best chance to take Germany down a peg. Stalin had a touching faith in Hitler and discounted all forecasts of attack as "disinformation." He thought the warnings were either British and American subterfuge designed to embroil him in a war with Germany or possibly "provocations" from reactionary elements of the German military, which he suspected wanted war with the Soviets.

The Americans were the first to secure good information on the Nazis' intentions. It came from a well-placed friendly German, Erwin Respondek,

and Undersecretary of State Sumner Welles passed it on to the Soviet ambassador on March 1, 1941. Churchill also had concluded that a German-
Soviet war was near, but until early June, even in the American and British
governments, many could not believe that the Nazis would attack the
Soviets. If anything, the possibility seemed too good to be true, although
such thoughts were tempered by the belief that the Soviets would be easily
beaten and the Nazis would gain enormous resources. The Allies still
feared a German invasion of Britain, and even if it was not an immediate
danger, in the spring of 1941 it seemed likelier that the Germans would
follow up their victories in the Balkans and North Africa by invading the
Middle East rather than take on a whole new enemy. Many in the British
Foreign Office and military intelligence also thought an early conquest of
the USSR unnecessary even from a Nazi point of view, because they believed Stalin would cave in to almost any German demand. As intelligence
agents tracked the movement of German air and ground units, however,
virtually everyone in the British government became convinced Germany
was about to attack.

Stalin, meanwhile, gripped by wishful thinking, ignored reports from
his own sources of German and Romanian preparations for the attack. In
the hope of avoiding war, he practically groveled to the Nazis while neglecting to take precautions lest they seem provocative. Only at a late stage
did he reluctantly allow some elementary actions. The Soviets believed that
before an invasion, a final German deployment would be readily detected
and an invasion would probably be preceded by an ultimatum or negotiations.[9]

The German attack caught the Soviets at an awkward moment, with
poor plans and preparations. This would have been astonishing even a few
years earlier. The Soviet armed forces had been not only the numerically
strongest in the world but also one of the most advanced, being preemi-
nent in the development of tank and airborne forces. Stalin's hostility to the
professional military and new and unorthodox ideas, and his purge of the
armed forces had wreaked havoc. The purges of 1937–1938 had eliminated
at least 30,000 of the 75,000–80,000 men in the officer corps, including three
of the five Soviet marshals; all commanders of military districts, the commanders and chiefs of staff of the navy and air force, and all admirals; 14
of 16 army commanders; 60 of 67 corps commanders; and 136 of 199 divisional commanders. The purges were by no means over when the war began. Ivan Proskurov, the far-sighted and able head of military intelligence,
was fired in 1940 for failing to report what Stalin wished to hear and then

killed as a scapegoat. The purges resulted in low morale, a crippling shortage of trained commanders and staff officers, and an actual regression in
military doctrine and organization.

The Soviets concentrated, as they always had, on preparing an offensive war. Poorly trained, they lacked defensive weapons such as mines.
The mechanized corps were dismantled, and no large armored formations
existed for a time. Only in July 1940 were mechanized corps belatedly reorganized; many were still forming when the Nazis struck. The Soviets
were also badly off for equipment, even though they had more tanks and
as many planes as the rest of the world combined. In the mid-1930s, their
tanks, planes, and other equipment had been up-to-date, but now they were
obsolete. While the mass of older tanks was not necessarily inferior to the
Germans', many were in poor repair. New equipment had been delayed.
Still, some 1,861 new KV-1 and T-34 tanks—the best in the world, being
heavily armed and armored with broad tracks that gave them superior
mobility in mud and snow—had been delivered by June 22, 1941. Most,
however, were mistakenly scattered among older tanks in the mechanized
corps of the forward military districts, and the mechanized corps themselves were dispersed. Their supply arrangements were poor, and individual tank crews were inadequately trained.

The ordinary Soviet infantry (rifle) divisions, as with other elements
of the Soviet forces in the midst of reorganization, slowly received new
small arms, but most lacked their complement of tanks, vehicles, artillery
ammunition, and repair facilities. They had few and mostly light antiaircraft weapons. Artillery units often lacked tractors and supply vehicles.
The Soviets vastly overemphasized horse cavalry, which, in the peculiar
conditions of the eastern front were not entirely useless, but the thirteen
divisions they had were hardly needed.

The Soviet Air Force was procuring a substantial number of new
planes, including bombers and ground attack aircraft, notably the famous
Il-2 Sturmovik; but even its latest fighters—the Yak-1, LaGG-3, and MiG-3—
were not as good as the Luftwaffe's planes. The new aircraft were only a
fraction of the force. Moreover, tactics were rigid and poor. Soviet fighters
flew rigid, tight three-plane formations. Bombers flew too high to bomb
accurately and too low for reasonable protection against German flak. In the
border military districts, Soviet planes were jammed on crowded forward
airfields, and orders to camouflage them came too late to be implemented.

Instead of holding his main forces well back and using the newly annexed areas as a buffer, Stalin scattered the Red Army along the new fron-

tiers. He believed that this arrangement would deter the "provocations" that the German generals supposedly planned. The old frontier defenses were stripped to build up defensive positions on the new border, but the latter were still incomplete. He was sure that any German attack would be concentrated in the south (an idea his military advisers had originally shared but came to doubt), so the strongest Soviet forces were massed under Col. Gen. Mikhail Kirponos's Southwest Front in Ukraine.

Only in April 1941 did Stalin reluctantly allow some precautions to be taken against attack. He declared a limited "special threatening military period" but began only the first stage of a precautionary mobilization and not the full-blown preparation that the military had advised. Nearly 800,000 reservists were called up, an intake of new recruits was conducted, and some purged officers were rehabilitated. The deployment along the frontiers, however, negated the effect of these actions, and until the last minute he allowed nothing more, fearing a high state of readiness would provoke war. Although the Soviets had treated the people of the newly annexed areas with the utmost brutality, he ignored warnings that the Baltic armies, which had been incorporated bodily in the Red Army with just a slight change in uniforms, would turn against the occupiers and he did not remove them to the interior.

Stalin rejected Marshal Zhukov's suggestion on May 15 for a preemptive attack on the Germans before the latter could strike. He still hoped to avoid war or at least delay it until 1942. Kirponos and the commanders of the Soviet Baltic and Black Sea Fleets managed to get around Stalin's inertia to some extent and brought their forces to a higher state of alert than the rest, but the results of this effort were limited. It was not until June 21, when German preparations were obvious, that Stalin agreed to Zhukov's arguments for a full alert. The weak Soviet communications system ensured that the alarm did not reach many units before the Germans attacked. Still, the Soviets were a formidable foe, numbering more than five million men in 303 divisions—198 rifle, 31 motorized rifle, 61 tank, and 13 cavalry—and 16 airborne brigades.[10]

## The First German Victories

With Stalin's help, the Nazis took the Soviets by surprise. The Luftwaffe, in particular, secured air superiority with ease. It caught the Soviet Air Force on the ground, on its jammed forward bases, and destroyed an enormous number of planes—twelve hundred on the first day alone—and suffered few losses. It only became clear later that the Soviets had lost mostly obsolete equipment and few trained airmen, but Luftwaffe commanders were already perturbed by the discovery that the Soviet Air Force was far bigger than they had expected. And the Luftwaffe had not knocked out it entirely. Soon Soviet planes frequently, albeit ineffectively, harassed the Germans. They were lucky that Soviet bombing was inaccurate.

The forces of the Soviet West Front were jammed into the Bialystok salient. A military formation, a Soviet front was the equivalent of a Western army group. Soviet forces were usually grouped in from five to nine fronts in 1941 and 1942; occasionally, in brief periods in 1941, several fronts were combined into "directions," or theaters. Soviet armies were usually the equivalent of Western corps.

The German forces plunged deep into Soviet territory, their superior command and tactics leading to victory after victory even when obsolescent German tanks encountered Soviet armored units equipped with T-34 or KV tanks. The Fourth Panzer Group alone advanced more than 200 miles in five days. Army Group Center quickly bit off the Bialystok salient, drove 250 miles, and closed a huge encirclement at Minsk on June 28. It then destroyed Gen. Dmitri Pavlov's West Front, taking 290,000 prisoners, 2,500 tanks, and 1,800 guns when the pocket was cleared on July 3. Hitler and Halder, in early July, both remarked that the war in the east was already won.

The Minsk success, however, had already seen considerable friction between Hitler and Field Marshal Bock. The latter had wished to drive far deeper and close the first pocket round Smolensk. Hitler, more cautious, had ruled in favor of a shallower envelopment that he thought could be more securely closed. In this case, events vindicated Hitler, as they were to do several more times during the 1941 campaign. The deeper envelopment that Bock envisaged at most would have added two more Soviet armies—the Nineteenth and Twentieth—to those snared with West Front, if the larger encirclement could have been closed at all. The German infantry, even in the Minsk operation, had found it hard to catch up with the advancing armor and close the pocket, despite exhausting marches of twenty-five miles a day in hot weather. Moreover, during the Minsk encirclement, many Soviet soldiers slipped out at night through the forests. The Germans found that encircled Soviet forces did not give up as quickly as forces usually had in the west; instead, they fought on for a considerable time. The lesson became apparent that at least under Russian conditions, it was possible to envelop too much at a time.

Hitler's caution let the Soviets commit five new armies to the Vitebsk–Mogilev line, where they were trapped in Army Group Center's second great encirclement battle around Smolensk that was completed on August 5. The Germans took 300,000 more prisoners and the Orsha land bridge. They were two-thirds of the way to Moscow, although the Soviets continued to launch powerful counterattacks in the Smolensk area. To many observers in the rest of the world and to most German generals, the way seemed open to Moscow. The next advance should take the Soviet capital.

But the other German Army Groups had been less successful. After its remarkable initial advance, Army Group North became more hampered by forest and swamp. Its operations had not been well planned after the first moves, and the two corps of the Fourth Panzer Group were dangerously separated. Although the Baltic troops had defected to the Germans, by mid-July the Soviet armies facing Army Group North had escaped encirclement and formed a relatively stable front. On July 26, Manstein, whose LVI Panzer Corps had been chiefly responsible for the first dash to and across the Dvina, advised Halder to remove the armored elements from Army Group North. Such an assessment, from Germany's ablest soldier, was evidence that the situation in the north was not promising. But Army Group North had been too weak. As historian Albert Seaton pointed out, even had Fourth Panzer Group reached Leningrad, it would not have had the infantry to clear such a great city or hold it once it had been taken.

The Panzer Group stayed in Army Group North and received reinforcements, but the advance there was slow, with the Germans severing Leningrad's land connection with the rest of the USSR only in mid-September. That began the great siege (1941–1944), in which a million people in that city died. Lake Ladoga was Leningrad's only precarious lifeline. Supplies coming across it were interrupted when it froze on November 11, resuming only when a road was laid across the ice late in November.

Army Group South had had even greater difficulty, falling behind schedule from the start. Facing the strongest, most alert Soviet forces, it met tough resistance and was hit by a serious counteroffensive. It had broken through only belatedly, accomplishing a major encirclement at Uman on August 5. The Germans in general suffered heavy losses of men and trucks. The combat losses of tanks were no worse than expected, but their wear and tear was extreme. Supply difficulties were apparent by late July. Gasoline consumption was twice as high as expected and railroad conversion slower. The Germans had captured less food and transportation equipment than they had counted on, and only fortunate seizures of fuel and railroad rolling stock at Baranovichi and Minsk had enabled them to keep going as fast as they had. Army Group North was the best off of the army groups for supplies, owing to its relatively short supply line and the better transportation system of the Baltic region. It was also more successful at capturing Soviet supplies and transportation facilities, but even it was strained.

Halder, by early August, was showing some unease about the Soviets' effectiveness. On August 11, he confided to his diary that the Germans had underestimated them; the Germans had reckoned on meeting 200 Soviet divisions but had now identified 360. Bock, on August 12, wrote in his diary, "If the Russians don't soon collapse somewhere, the objective of defeating them so badly that they are eliminated will be difficult to achieve before winter."[11]

## What to Do Next: Hitler's Decision

The Germans had never entirely settled what to do after the initial operations. Hitler's directive for the invasion envisaged taking Leningrad before Moscow and assumed that forces from Army Group Center would move toward the north to envelop the Soviet forces in the Baltic region and help Army Group North. But when and where that turn would take place had never been decided, and the army had never loved the idea. It never made detailed plans for such a move, hoping either that quick victories elsewhere would avert the need for it or that Hitler would forget about it. Actually, the idea may not have been a bad one, but the time for it was already passing. General Hoth, commander of the Third Panzer Group, wrote after the war that it could only have been successful if it had been ordered between July 1 and July 10. After that, the battle was too far east, and the terrain did not favor it.

Hitler had also considered taking Ukraine and the Donetz Basin before Moscow. On July 4, he reaffirmed the idea of pausing in the center and talked of diverting the Third Panzer Group to assist Army Group North and the Second Panzer Group to the south to help take Ukraine. But he wavered. On July 8 he spoke to Halder and Brauchitsch of diverting the Second Panzer Group south once it was across the Dnieper, but he did not order it. He also indicated that he would probably have to order the Third Panzer Group north but that he preferred to avoid doing so. Generals Halder, Brauchitsch, and Bock made it clear that they disliked these ideas, although on July 12 in the privacy of his diary, Halder contemplated both movements. Halder soon resumed his stance as the fiercest opponent of anything but an all-out concentration in Army Group Center on Moscow. Clearly the question was crucial and concerned more than how to direct a "pursuit" after the Red Army had been broken.

Hitler on July 17 again raised the idea of diverting the Third and Second Panzer Groups north and south, respectively. Directive 33, issued on July 19, specified using the Second Panzer Group and "strong infantry forces" from Army Group Center to drive southeast and cut off the Soviets in Ukraine. It did not clearly indicate how to use Third Panzer Group but ordered it to turn north, cut communications between Moscow and Leningrad, and protect Army Group North's right flank. Army Groups South and Center would also cooperate to destroy the Soviet Fifth Army, which was holding out in the Pripet Marshes and threatened their flanks. This directive suggests that Hitler was becoming uneasy.

Conferring with Field Marshal Leeb on July 21, Hitler discussed using the Third Panzer Group to ensure that Leningrad would be isolated. (On July 8 he had ruled that the city was not to be captured but sealed off and destroyed and its people exterminated. He later issued a similar order about Moscow.) On July 23 the supplement to Directive 33 reaffirmed the diversion of the Second Panzer Group and much of the Third Panzer Group, which would assist Army Group North and attack the Leningrad area.

Halder fought this directive tooth and nail with support not only from Brauchitsch and Bock but also Jodl and the OKW, normally toadies of Hitler's. Halder now pointed out that the terrain the Third Panzer Group would have to cross, first to reach the Leningrad area and then to drive southeast toward Moscow, was unsuitable for tanks. He urged at least limiting the Third Panzer Group to cutting the Moscow–Leningrad railroad. As an alternative, he presented a plan for Army Group Center to assault Moscow without diversions. The normally compliant Jodl's backing for Halder's views may have made Hitler uneasy. He carefully considered what to do. His next directive, number 34, on July 30, spoke of deferring the distant objectives he had set earlier; instead, Army Group Center would go on the defensive to release its Panzer Groups for rehabilitation. He did not specify where they would go thereafter. In early August, he visited the headquarters of Army Groups Center and South and decided that he had been right in the first place. The supplement to Directive 34, issued on August 12, made Moscow the next objective, to be captured before winter but only after Army Group South took Ukraine and the menacing enemy concentrations on both flanks of Army Group Center were eliminated. It seemed to omit the idea of putting the Third Panzer Group under Army Group North. On August 15, Hitler made clear that only XXXIX Panzer Corps and the supporting VIII Air Corps of the Third Panzer Group would move from Army Group Center to Army Group North. The army still opposed sending the Second Panzer Group (withdrawn from the front on August 8) into Ukraine, arguing that a Moscow offensive could start by the beginning of September. On August 26, however, Hitler flatly insisted on sending the Second Panzer Group south. Afterward, Halder talked the group's commander, the tank pioneer Guderian, into seeing Hitler personally to persuade the führer to change his mind. Hitler convinced Guderian instead.

With the Second Army's support, the Second Panzer Group turned south against the Soviet Central Front on August 25 and took the Soviets, who had expected an attack toward Moscow, by surprise. The First Panzer Group struck north from a bridgehead over the Dnieper at Kremenchug to meet Guderian's drive. Now Stalin again played into Hitler's hands. Rejecting Zhukov's advice to abandon Kiev, he insisted that the Southwest Front hold the Ukrainian capital. He replaced Zhukov for his unwelcome suggestion and refused to listen when his old crony Semyon Budyonny, the theater commander, and the latter's political commissar, Nikita Khrushchev, urged a retreat. On September 16, the Germans trapped four Soviet armies with 665,000 men around Kiev. The pocket took ten days to clear. The Germans soon overran eastern Ukraine.

In terms of prisoners, Kiev was the biggest German victory of the whole war, yet many critics insisted later that Germany lost the war by diverting forces that could have taken Moscow. This assertion is highly doubtful. Despite Halder's optimism about an early attack on Moscow, it seems that the army could not have launched one before late September or early October. The true cost of the Kiev operation was to postpone a renewed offensive in the center by at most one or two weeks. By contrast, in supply terms, the Second Panzer Group was well placed to move south. As Barry Leach commented, "In view of the logistical situation, the envelopment of Kiev was probably the only major operation feasible in the late summer of 1941." A direct advance on Moscow, without the diversion to Ukraine, would have had substantial Soviet forces on its flanks, and "the envelopment of the enemy between Viasma and Briansk with two Panzer Groups would probably not have achieved a greater success than that conducted by three Panzer Groups in October. [By then, the Fourth Panzer Group was available from Army Group North.] Thus, even if the Germans had reached Moscow they could hardly have inflicted losses upon the enemy as great as those that resulted from the battle of Kiev and the operations that followed it." The German forces would have been extended in a great salient and in a poor position to deal with threats to their flanks. Nor would taking Moscow alone have been decisive. The Kiev victory and the resulting capture of the Donetz Basin seem to have been the maximum damage the Germans could have inflicted on the Soviets; and although Hitler's reasons may not have been entirely rational, the results justified them. This staggering victory appears to have convinced many generals, even anti-Nazis, that Hitler was indeed a genius.[12]

## Soviet Recovery

In spite of their early defeats, the Soviets had launched measures that ensured the recovery of their forces and of war production. Despite the confusion and chaos of the early days of the war, they created a sound higher apparatus for its direction and inaugurated another reorganization of the Red Army. Disbanding the corps level of organization, the Red Army reorganized into smaller field armies comprising stripped-down divisions, which gave up specialized units such as antitank and antiaircraft battalions to centralized army control. It disbanded the clumsy mechanized corps, made the leaner tank divisions the largest armored organizations, and while existing tank divisions were preserved, smaller tank brigades were the only new armored units formed. Vast new rifle armies, tank and infantry brigades, and horse cavalry divisions were created. No fewer than thirteen new armies were formed in July, fourteen in August, one in September, four in October, and eight in November–December. By December 1, the Soviets had created 199 new divisions. In October, contrary to German expectations, the Soviets had also begun transferring well-trained units from the Soviet Far East to the European front, including eight to ten rifle divisions, with a thousand tanks and as many planes. By the end of 1941, the Soviets had fielded 688 divisions and the equivalent of 133 more in brigades, or more than four times what the Germans had expected to see, even if many had been destroyed.

After the first days of the war, the Germans captured little equipment or installations of much use, because in yet another measure the Germans had not bargained for, the Soviets conducted a massive evacuation of industries from threatened areas in the Urals to Siberia. Their success was even more remarkable because the Soviets had not prepared this operation before the war and it was not properly planned until August. The Soviets moved 1,523 plants, with 1,360 classed as "heavy," along with massive amounts of railroad equipment. The factories were back in operation so amazingly fast that the production of weapons and ammunition—much of it new equipment, including T-34 and KV tanks, the Katyusha mass-fire rocket launcher, and the Il-2 Sturmovik—actually rose by the first three months of 1942. The Soviets concentrated on producing a few types of tanks (two major ones) and five main types of planes with limited modifications. While they could not entirely focus on the best equipment, they strove to make the most effective ordnance. They made T-60 light tank and its improved version, the T-70, although not particularly useful, simply because they could be readily built in car and truck plants that were not convertible to making heavier armored vehicles. The promise and then the arrival of American trucks through the president's Lend-Lease program allowed the Soviets to reduce their own truck production in favor of making combat vehicles. Soviet production of planes and tanks, in 1942, would exceed that of the Germans. Moreover, the Soviets expertly demolished locomotives that could not be moved eastward, as well as locomotive repair shops and electric power stations. By early November, the Germans calculated that they had taken only 500 Soviet locomotives and 21,000 railroad cars, or only a tenth of what they had expected to get.[13]

## The German Fall Offensive

Even as Army Group South followed up the victory in Ukraine, the Germans regrouped quickly in the center. Fewer than half their tanks and a bit more than three-fourths of their trucks were in working order. The Second Panzer Group's equipment, after long marches back and forth, had been particularly hard hit. For the offensive on Moscow, the Germans not only returned the Second Panzer Group to Army Group Center but also transferred the Fourth Panzer Group, although not all of its corps, from Army Group North as well. Finally, the Germans had barely stocked enough supplies.

The Second Panzer Group initiated the offensive on September 30; the main attack, farther north, followed on October 2. The usual breakthrough and encirclement resulted. On October 7, the pincers snapped shut around Vyazma, trapping most of Lt. Gen. Ivan Konev's West Front, with six armies, while a smaller pocket was formed around Bryansk and almost all of Ivan Yeremenko's Bryansk Front. The Vyazma pocket took almost a week to clear and produced almost as many prisoners (663,000) as the Kiev victory. The Germans reported the capture of 1,242 tanks and more than 5,000 guns. The Bryansk pocket's forested areas took until October 25 to clear, and while many Soviet soldiers escaped, the Germans took 100,000 prisoners. As the extent of the defeat became clear, panic gripped Moscow. In mid-October, for a brief moment, the Soviet government may have trembled on the brink of disintegration. Had the Nazis had reasonable war aims and a suitable line of propaganda, they might have exploited the situation (but then, they would not have been Nazis). But they could not exploit their victories militarily. Apart from the time taken to clear the pockets, the weather had broken. Even as the Vyazma encirclement was closing, rains and even the first snow had fallen and ushered in the *rasputitsa* (mud season). It was not cold but mud that stranded the German forces and prevented a further major advance. The German commanders, who had looked forward to a spectacular Soviet collapse, thereafter became more pessimistic.[14]

## The Battle for Moscow

The Germans had a strong argument for halting for the winter. Even after the ground was dry, there would be only a short period in which mobile operations would be possible before winter fully set in (normally mid-December in the Moscow region.) The Germans' combat efficiency was poor, their men were tired, and divisions one-third to half strength. Their supply situation was bad and not likely to improve. Army Group Center's southeast flank was already exposed.

Of all the senior officers, Rundstedt alone favored shutting down operations for the winter then and there, although Bock thought that he lacked the requisite forces and adequate supplies to support the force. Rundstedt felt the army could at most make minor gains and only if the weather was favorable. Others wanted to exploit the short interval of reasonable weather while the Soviets were still weakened. They thought they could at least take Moscow, about forty miles from the nearest German positions, and maybe precipitate a collapse of resistance; however, by this time even Hitler conceded that the war would go on into 1942. The field commanders apparently thought that despite Hitler's order that Moscow should not be occupied but sealed off and destroyed, they would wind up occupying the city, which would shelter at least some German troops and installations. Halder was even more enthusiastic. He envisaged reaching a line far east of Moscow, or about 160 miles beyond it as a minimum. The army group commanders, their staffs, and even the OKW, not to mention those lower down the chain of command, were far less confident. As Colonel von Liebenstein, the chief of staff of Guderian's Panzer Group, tartly complained, they were not fighting in France, and this was not the month of May. The more realistic elements finally persuaded Halder to rein in his objectives and aim at a line immediately east of the Soviet capital. Bock, however, may have not expected even to reach that goal and simply seize Moscow itself.

They had received reports that well-trained and equipped Soviet reinforcements had arrived from Asia but did not appreciate the importance of this information. The Soviets were already considerably stronger than the Germans realized, and they had the benefit of extensive earthworks around the capital, built with the help of Moscow's citizens.

On November 15, having some 760,000 men against 1.1 million Soviet troops in the front or in reserve, the Germans attacked Zhukov's West Front and the neighboring Kalinin and Southwest Fronts. Siberian reinforcements were streaming in, as well as troops from the Transcaucasus and Central Asia, and the Soviets enjoyed a short supply line. The German plan was the usual scheme of a double envelopment. On the German right, Guderian's command, now renamed the Second Panzer Army, was to drive northeast past Tula, isolating Moscow from the south, while the Fourth Army and the Fourth Panzer Group attacked from the west. The latter was to swing northeast around Moscow in coordination with the Third Panzer Group, attacking farther north and passing through the front of the Ninth Army. They were to reach, at least, the Moscow-Volga Canal.

At first the weather was favorable. The mild cold actually helped the Germans. Frost enabled their tanks to move over open countryside as though it were a paved road. They did well, reaching the Moscow-Volga Canal and even seizing a bridgehead over it on November 28. Meanwhile, on November 23, the northern panzer groups had begun to slow down. They nevertheless tore a gap in the Soviet front, and the Soviets perceived a major crisis by November 27. They hastily sent in reserves and plugged the gap, however. In the south, the Germans were unable to finish encircling Tula. The Second Army halted entirely on December 1. From that day the offensive bogged down both in the north and south.

The Soviets, meanwhile, were preparing a major counteroffensive aimed at throwing back the enveloping panzer groups, with the main blow falling on the Third Panzer Group. Whether by accident or design, it began on December 6, right after the temperature, which had already been falling gradually, had begun to drop sharply. Heavy snow crippled the Germans. Exhausted, they lacked winter clothing and other gear, lubricants for machinery and weapons, and even proper food. Frostbite, often resulting in amputations, was common. Tanks and other vehicles often would not start, and machine guns and cannon would not fire (the lubricants had congealed.) Even when tracked vehicles could run, their treads were too narrow for deep snow. The supply situation collapsed as German locomotive boilers burst in the cold. Indeed, locomotive losses were so enormous, and the number needed in the east so great, that the German railroad system was in desperate straits. The Germans could rely only on the few captured Soviet locomotives, which were on as yet unconverted stretches of track. Belatedly ordered winter clothing was on trains halted dozens or hundreds of miles from the men who desperately needed it. The effects of the cold on the already weakened German forces, the arrival of masses of well-supplied Soviet troops operating close to their Moscow base, and even the loss of air superiority to the Soviet Air Force led to catastrophe. The German commanders were taken aback as their radio-monitoring stations picked up messages from newly arrived Soviet units of which the Germans had previously been unaware.

Soviet soldiers did not enjoy the cold, but they were at least properly dressed. (The Germans were especially impressed by how well the Siberians were clothed.) They had sleds to haul supplies and often used skis or snowshoes or rode horses. The Red Army's excessive investment in horse cavalry units was now a help. The fighting became a bitter struggle to keep open the few roads not blocked by snow and, at the lowest level, to take and hold villages and gain some shelter from the cold. The few hours of daylight and poor visibility probably hampered the Germans more so than their opponents. The Luftwaffe kept flying but did not have much effect.

The German central front and then much of the rest of the army in the east teetered on the brink of collapse. Bock had ordered a defensive line prepared, but except in the Fourth Army's area, little had been done to build one. Elsewhere, there were no prepared positions to fall back on. The danger of a panicky retreat, in which all heavy equipment would be lost because it could not be moved, was considerable. Indeed, signs indicated panic was rising.

On December 16, Hitler forbade further withdrawals (although in a few cases he later issued special permission for movements back). Whether his order was correct has always been regarded as highly controversial; but even many German commanders who otherwise had no use for Hitler's military leadership thought that in the peculiar conditions on the Russian front in 1941–1942, it proved justified, preventing an early and complete German defeat in the east.

Hitler now intervened more often in the conduct of the campaign. Brauchitsch who was ill and had done little for some time, resigned. Hitler himself became the army's commander in chief. Over the next few months, he replaced all three army group commanders in the east (although he would recall Bock and Rundstedt in 1942) and many lower-echelon commanders.

By the latter part of December, the Soviets had eliminated the German spearheads threatening Moscow. The extent of their success, and the condition of the Germans, surprised them a bit. The "local" Moscow counteroffensive grew larger, into an offensive against the whole of Army Group Center. In the first week of January, Stalin decided on a vast program to destroy not only Army Group Center but also Army Group North, to relieve Leningrad, and, in the south, to retake the Donetz Basin and the Crimea. (The latter operation, an amphibious landing on the Kerch Peninsula, was already under way.) The nine Soviet armies still in reserve were parceled out among no less than six different fronts. This move went against the advice of Zhukov, who proposed concentrating on destroying the Army Group Center. Zhukov proved correct. As it was, the dispersed Soviet attacks almost all came tantalizingly near complete success. A prudent concentration on one, or even two of these objectives, would almost certainly have inflicted a titanic defeat on the Germans.

The Soviets did make their main effort against Army Group Center. The Kalinin Front drove from Kalinin toward the Smolensk-Vyazma area, while the left wing of the West Front and the newly reformed Bryansk Front drove northwest on Vyazma. Running parallel with the Kalinin Front, the Northwest Front tried to break through the German line at the boundary between Army Groups Center and North. The Germans were gradually pushed back, losing tremendous amounts of equipment. The Soviets nearly closed a pocket around the German Ninth and Fourth Panzer Armies, which held the huge Rzhev salient pointing toward Moscow, but the German Fourth Army barely held open the base of the salient. The Soviets mounted an airborne operation, supported by local partisans, to close the pocket, but in the end the Germans trapped and destroyed the enveloping force.

By mid-February, the greatest danger to the Army Group Center had passed. It had been shoved back, however, a hundred to two hundred miles, and the Northwest Front's Third and Fourth Shock Armies had torn a hundred-mile gap between Army Groups Center and North. The Soviets could not exploit the gap, though, because they needed to maintain the siege of German forces encircled at Demyansk and Kholm south of Leningrad. At Demyansk, two Soviet armies surrounded six divisions and 95,000 men of the German II Corps from February 9 to April 21. The Germans held out thanks to an airlift, which was massive by the standards of the time. Hitler, particularly, was influenced by the airlift's success. He did not realize that that the Soviets could have disrupted it easily had they bombed the German air bases; the endeavor had disrupted the Luftwaffe's training effort as schools were stripped to provide crews and planes. In the end, the Soviet attempt to relieve Leningrad not only failed but led to a local disaster. Similarly, by a narrow margin, the Soviet attacks on the Donetz and Crimean fronts were blocked.

Apart from their lack of strategic concentration, the Soviets often failed to concentrate tactically. Winter conditions hampered them too, and they could not keep their forces supplied when they advanced over long distances. The Soviets also suffered from the huge losses of the summer and fall. Many units were only partially trained, lacked transport and communications, and above all fire support. Usually a strong point of Russian and Soviet armies, the artillery pieces lost in the earlier campaigns had not been replaced. But even if they had not destroyed the German Army in the east, the Soviets had weakened it permanently.[15]

# 5

## The Mediterranean and the Middle East I

*From the Fall of France to December 1941*

With defeat in western Europe and Italy's entry into the war, the British faced a whole new front in the Mediterranean and the Middle East, even while they were defending their homeland. Middle East Command was in a desperate situation. Its small forces were stretched from the outpost of Malta, formerly the main base of the Mediterranean Fleet; through Egypt, nominally independent but effectively under British control; through the restive League of Nations mandates of Palestine and Transjordan; and the independent but unreliable ally Iraq. Sudan and Kenya, as with the British in Egypt, faced overwhelming numbers of Italians in East Africa. The Mediterranean was largely closed to sea traffic; only some long-range planes and a costly sea route stretching twelve thousand miles around Africa connected the British forces with home. Late in August 1940, the British inaugurated a six-week cycle of regular "Winston's Special" (WS) military convoys to the Middle East. The Italians seemed perilously near the lifeline of the British forces in the Red Sea, a problem that perhaps overly influenced British strategy. The precious "monster" liners, such as the *Queen Mary* and *Queen Elizabeth*, then shuttling men from Australia, unloaded passengers at Bombay. The men transferred to smaller ships for the last, most dangerous stage of the trip to the Middle East Command. The British developed the Takoradi air route across Africa to shorten the trip for air reinforcements. Planes were delivered in crates, or sometimes flown off aircraft carriers, to Takoradi on the Gold Coast (now Ghana), assembled, and flown across the continent.

Since 1939, Gen. Archibald Wavell, the commander in chief of the Middle Eastern theater, had been building a major base in Egypt and at Basra,

Iraq, to support a force of 15 divisions, or 300,000 men, and air and naval forces, although the combat units were not even in sight. Handicapped by shortages, the British undertook frantic efforts to develop ports, airfields, oil storage, and transport facilities. Fortunately for Britain and the Allied cause, Wavell was extremely capable. Some, indeed, have argued that he was the greatest British commander of the war. One of the most modern and original thinkers among the British senior officers, his judgment in some strategic matters would prove extremely questionable in 1940–1941 and later in Southeast Asia after the Japanese struck; but he was probably the best man available for the job of creating a base in a huge underdeveloped area and for directing a far-flung command with many non-British units engaged on several fronts. (At one point, in 1941, he ran five campaigns at the same time.) Very popular, he dealt effectively with local political problems and some prickly Commonwealth partners, and at Britain's lowest point, he inspired morale among men far from home.

Of Wavell's 80,000 troops, 36,000 were stationed in Egypt and 27,500 in Palestine. His British troops were well-trained regulars, joined by Australians and New Zealanders. The Royal Air Force in the Middle East, under Air Chief Marshal Arthur Longmore, had no modern fighters at all. It was equipped with seventy-five obsolete biplanes, only ninety-six obsolete bombers or "bomber transports," and a handful of other planes, mostly of dubious value and all short of spare parts. The Italians, meanwhile, had half a million men in Libya and East Africa and an air force of more than fifteen hundred planes. With Malta unusable, at least as a major fleet base, Adm. Andrew Cunningham's Mediterranean Fleet fell back on an inadequately equipped base at Alexandria. When Italy entered the war, less than 4,000 men held Malta. They had food for only five weeks, one operational airfield, and four biplane fighters in crates. But Malta would soon play an extremely important role in the Mediterranean struggle.

The British commanders in the Middle East had not expected the French armistice. Wavell had planned to fight on even if Britain was overrun. Iran and Vichy Syria and Lebanon were at best unfriendly, while most Arabs were restive if not hostile to Britain. Many foolishly imagined that the Axis would "liberate" them from British domination. To placate the Arabs, the British made little use of the most pro-Allied local element, the Jewish settlements in Palestine. The British did have one card that enabled them to dominate the Arab Near East, the Arab Legion. A British officer, Lt. Gen. John Glubb, had built the small army of Transjordan into the only effective military force in the Arab world. Unlike the Egyptian and Iraqi forces, on which the British had lavished far more aid, the Arab Legion was willing to fight and fight well alongside the Allies rather than against them.[1]

Despite their weakness, the British played a bad hand well. Instead of concentrating against the threat to Britain itself, they maintained their fleet in the Mediterranean and sent ground and air forces around the Cape of Good Hope as the Battle of Britain raged. Admiral Cunningham, backed by Churchill, reinforced Malta. The British went from victory to victory over the Italians, and finally the Germans had to intervene.

The Mediterranean–Middle East theater was vital mainly for its oil, even though the world did not yet depend on the Middle East for fuel. If the Axis captured the Middle East oil fields, their scarce fuel supplies would enormously increase. Especially after the Japanese took Southeast Asia, losing the Persian Gulf oil fields would have paralyzed Allied activity around the Indian Ocean. Until late in the war, the refinery at Abadan, Iran—one of the three largest in the world—was the only source of 100-octane aviation gasoline in the whole area from Africa to Indonesia. After the Japanese seized Indonesia, Abadan was the sole source of aviation fuel between Britain and the West Coast of the United States. Moreover, its peculiar construction rendered it vulnerable to bombs, and it was poorly defended against air attack even in 1942. The British concluded in 1941 that if the Iranian oil fields and Abadan were lost, carrying on the war in the Middle East would be quite difficult. Indeed, the British Chiefs of Staff stipulated in July 1942 that Abadan must be held even at the cost of losing Egypt. Maj. Gen. Dwight Eisenhower reported in April 1942 that given the shortage of tankers, losing the Near Eastern oil fields would make it impossible to carry on the war in the Middle East, India, and China.[2]

In their defensive aspect, the North African campaigns would be fought to end the threat to the oil fields from the west. But the threat of a German attack from the north through Turkey or the Caucasus (and, until June 1941, of a Soviet assault) was a major concern, one later historians often underestimated. This fear often shaped British decision making and caused London to insist on early efforts to defeat or at least drive away Gen. Erwin Rommel's forces so the British could counter a northern attack. There would also be a complex interplay between the British fighting in North Africa and their defense of Malta. The latter threatened the enemy's supply lines across the Mediterranean, and an early British advance in the desert could provide forward air bases that would aid efforts to supply the island.

Offensively, once they developed their strength, the Mediterranean and Middle Eastern positions would let the Western powers reach behind their enemies in Europe, bring France back into the war, and knock Italy out of it. Further, the Allies would open a land front in southern Europe from which they could bomb critical targets, especially the European Axis powers' main natural source of oil at Ploesti, that were difficult to strike from Britain.

The Axis lacked detailed plans or preparations for a Mediterranean campaign. Hitler and other Germans, expecting an early peace with Britain, did not think a strategy was needed, although Hitler early pondered attacking Gibraltar to "encourage" Britain to surrender or negotiate. General Jodl, outlining Germany's course if Britain fought on, envisaged helping Spain and Italy seize Gibraltar and the Suez Canal but with Germany merely acting in a supporting capacity. (Gen. Francisco Franco, right after the fall of France, had seemed ready to join the Axis in the war.) After the British attacked the French fleet at Oran, Hitler showed more interest in the region, suggesting to the Italians on July 7 that they consider seizing Crete and Cyprus with German air support. The General Staff gradually came to agree with Jodl, should it prove impossible to conquer Britain, although it became more pessimistic about the Italians' capabilities. It also revived an earlier idea of pushing Stalin to advance south. Although Hitler did not initially welcome sending a German armored force to North Africa, he eventually accepted dispatching two panzer divisions and air units to Libya and made plans to attack Gibraltar. The Third Panzer Division also prepared for a move to Africa. But Hitler's willingness to intervene in the Mediterranean at an early date fell afoul of two developments—the Italians' reluctance to accept Germany's help, although they badly needed it, and Franco's growing reluctance to join the Axis. German historians doubt, however, that Franco had wanted to do so in the first place.

The Italians had not planned or prepared intelligently for war. Right off, they lost 130,000 tons of shipping to capture, scuttling, or internment because they failed to recall their ships to safe ports, although they had expected to join the war for months. In the armistice negotiations with the French, which were poorly coordinated with the Germans, they failed even to demand the use of Tunis and Bizerte as supply ports for their forces in Libya. They did not arrange to take Malta, although since 1938 Italian planners had warned that its capture was a vital prerequisite to successful operations in North Africa. They lackadaisically prepared to attack Egypt, hoping it would coincide with a German landing in Britain. Partly because of fears of revolt, they did not give their forces in East Africa a serious offensive mission. Their only offensive move was a foolish and strategically useless conquest of British Somaliland. At an early stage, the Italians passed up any chance to seize important positions in the Sudan, which might have caused the British serious trouble. They played for time, hoping for relief when Egypt was taken.

For prestige reasons and to keep Germany out of the Italian sphere, Mussolini refused the request of Marshal Italo Balbo, his first commander in Libya, that he secure some German weapons, especially tanks, for the Italian forces. Mussolini did not want close cooperation with Germany. In his mind, Italy's relationship with Germany was implicitly competitive. Italy's compensation for and safeguard against German aggrandizement was to grab what it could. By contrast, Hitler remained loyal to Mussolini. Italy's failures caused Hitler to lose interest in helping the Italians, but later forced him to intervene in the south.[3]

## The Italian Armed Forces

The Italian armed forces proved far less effective than expected, a product of the blustering incompetence of Mussolini's regime and the low-grade leadership of the armed services. They had limited economic backing. While Italian industry manufactured high-quality goods, its productive capacity was limited, notably in aircraft, electronics, and shipbuilding.

Admiral Cunningham judged that the Italian fleet was no more advanced than the British were at the Battle of Jutland a quarter of a century earlier. Designed to fight France rather than Britain, the Italian Royal Navy's bases, except for Taranto, were poorly placed and defended. Inadequately trained, with extreme differences between officers and men, it neglected night fighting and antisubmarine warfare. It appeared to have considerable superiority over the British in battleships and an even greater one in cruisers, destroyers, and submarines. But, though its surface ships were sleek and fast, they were not well armed or armored. None had radar and few had sonar. As noted earlier, Italian submarines were poor. To some extent, the small escort ships—destroyers and torpedo boats—redeemed the Italian Navy's record, doing most of the fighting and shepherding convoys to Africa. Unlike the commanders of the big ships, who showed a notable ability to fumble things, the escorts' commanders and crews made the most of their equipment. The navy's smallest units, the motor torpedo boats and especially certain special weapons—such as the manned torpedoes that frogmen rode into British-held harbors to plant delayed-action charges under ships—were effective.

Poor air support seriously hampered the Italian navy. It had no aircraft carriers, which need not have been fatal in a narrow inland sea ringed with airfields; but it also lacked any air arm or adequate cooperation with the independent air force. The latter had recently received torpedo bombers and depended mainly on level bombing from fairly high altitudes to hit ships and land targets. Although the British thought Italian high-level bombing was more accurate than the Germans' and rated some Italian air units as more determined than their German counterparts, this form of attack was not effective against fast-moving ships. The Italians had well-trained pilots but few good leaders above squadron level and were behind other major powers in tactics and technology. Their planes were obsolete, although the British aircraft they faced early in the war were even more so. Italian bombers were perhaps adequate, but their fighters were two or three years behind those of other air forces. Many were still biplanes, while even newer monoplanes were underpowered and underarmed and their short range made it hard to cover convoys.

Italy's army, meanwhile, was a mess. Its generals, with few exceptions, were poor. The Germans did not think much of the junior officers and noncommissioned officers, either. Relations between officers and enlisted men were bad; the latter were even meagerly fed. The army was ill equipped, and although its artillery units fought well, most of their guns were short ranged. Italian armored divisions were, the Germans held, "in name only." When Italy entered the war, it did not have any armored divisions in Libya. Italian tanks were too light, and unreliable, most being armed only with machine guns. British antitank rifles, otherwise useless, easily penetrated them. The Germans even described the Italians' few modern tanks, which lacked radios, as "self-propelled coffins." Apart from the artillery, some Italian units fought well in 1940 and 1941, putting up an impressive defense by any standards at Keren, Eritrea. At Sidi Barrani, Egypt, some Italians attacked British tanks with just machine guns and grenades. Later, under German influence, the Italian Army showed some improvement. In general, however, it was no match for the British. Although certainly not totally incompetent and much less cowardly as often portrayed, the Italian forces at best performed unevenly. They proved mostly ineffective in offensive warfare without close German support. But many Germans, even when disenchanted with their reluctant allies, conceded that the Italians often understood "overseas warfare" and the strategic situation in the Mediterranean better than the German leaders did.[4]

The Italians' weaknesses, however, were soon exposed. Ignoring their earlier thoughts on the subject, they convinced themselves that they could eliminate Malta as a base by bombing it and making its supply difficult. They had passed up any early chance—which probably would not have been very good—to invade Malta, whose terrain presented formidable obstacles to an attacker, while it was still weakly held. Now, the few obsolete British fighters drove Italian bombers to heights from which they could not bomb accurately. The barren, rocky island and its limestone buildings proved resistant to air attack, while the Maltese, who were loyal to the British, demonstrated powers of endurance more modern and violent societies might envy. The Maltese played a big part in Malta's effectiveness as a base.

Along the direct route from Italy to Libya, Malta served as a base for aircraft, submarines, and, sometimes, surface ships attacking the Axis supply lines to Africa and finally as an advanced base to support the invasion of Sicily. Malta's fate was closely interwoven with the course of the North African fighting. While the British could sometimes maintain an effective defense in the desert campaign even when Axis supply lines were safe, as in July 1942, the Axis forces could not launch an offensive unless Malta's threat to their supply lines had been at least temporarily suppressed, as it sometimes was. For long intervals, Malta had only potential value. Early in the war, for instance, no important available forces could use it. Later, in early 1941 and for the first seven months of 1942, intense German air attacks neutralized it as an effective base, and the Axis came close in 1942 to starving it out. But when those attacks ended and just enough supplies got through, Malta sprang back into action. The Germans could not maintain a major air effort against Malta and support a land offensive in Africa at the same time.

## Naval Operations

Operations to support Malta led to the first major naval action in the Mediterranean. Early in July 1940, both the British and Italian fleets were at sea; the Italians were guarding a convoy to Benghazi, Libya, while the British fleet conducted two convoys from Alexandria to Malta. Cunningham, alerted by air reconnaissance to the Italian movements, sought battle even though in some respects the Italian force was superior to his own. He had one aircraft carrier, the old, small HMS *Eagle*, with eighteen Swordfish biplane torpedo bombers and no fighters at all. The two modernized Italian battleships outranged two of the three British battleships, and the Italian cruisers and destroyers outnumbered their British counterparts. Italian high-level bombers in "Bomb Alley," south of Crete on the way to Malta, heavily attacked the British. Evasive action was usually effective against such attacks, although the British found their antiaircraft fire ineffective. Constant near misses did damage the *Eagle*. The British encountered the Italian fleet off Calabria on July 9. The small force of Swordfish failed to score any hits, while the battleships closed within firing range, a rare event in World War II, and the British damaged an Italian battleship. The Italians then withdrew. Since one virtue of their ships was speed, they were hard to catch, and fearing he would run into Italian submarines, Cunningham turned away. After this incident, the Italians, to the Germans' disgust, became even more cautious about engaging in a major fleet action. The battle had taken place in artificial conditions. Neither side had fighter cover, and the British had too few torpedo bombers to be effective. Despite the inaccuracy of high-level bombing against maneuvering warships, a bit of bad luck might have led to a hit on their only carrier. Fortunately for the British, the Italians remained remarkably reluctant to send in their bombers at low level or even coordinate high-level attacks with torpedo bombers when those aircraft became available. Cunningham asked for and got a large modern carrier, HMS *Illustrious*, with an armored flight deck, air defense radar, and some Fulmar fighters, along with another modern battleship and an antiaircraft cruiser.

Calabria and subsequent actions showed that until the Germans' arrival, the British fleet, covered by a few carrier-based fighters, could enter the central Mediterranean and see convoys to Malta. But the fleet could not stay there or block the route to Africa; and while it could supply Malta, doing so would always require a major operation. Thus, despite their weaknesses, the Italians still dominated the central Mediterranean and closed it to regular British traffic. It was up to the forces based on Malta, not the British Mediterranean Fleet, to threaten the Axis supply lines.[5]

## The Desert and Greece

The markedly less competent Rodolfo Graziani replaced Balbo as commander in Libya, who was accidentally killed in June 1940. The Italians, short of vehicles and overburdened by unnecessary paraphernalia, were unable to start the long-expected invasion of Egypt until September 13. They then made a limited advance to Sidi Barrani. The British, keeping the bulk of their forces well east at Mersa Matruh, withdrew and suffered few losses. They were a bit surprised and even disappointed that the Italians did not move on to Mersa Matruh, as the British were sure they would whip the Italians in a model defensive battle. Instead, Wavell prepared to launch a counterstroke against Sidi Barrani. As it was, the Italian advance may have made the British task easier. So did Mussolini's next move and his continued rejection of German offers of an armored force for Africa.[6]

The Germans had given him a free hand with Greece and Yugoslavia, but they never expected the Italians to take on a new commitment so recklessly or so soon. Even Mussolini had not expected to attack Greece at such an early date, but he was upset and embarrassed after the German forces moved into Romania and offended the Italian public. Mussolini reacted by invading Greece on October 28, giving this campaign a higher priority than that in North Africa. Hitler, astonished and angry, subsequently was less willing to back the Italians in the Mediterranean. The Greek war proved a spectacular folly. The Greeks not only held the Italians but threw them back into Albania with very heavy losses. By the spring of 1941, no less than twenty-nine Italian divisions were tied down in the Balkans.[7]

Another disaster followed. Long before the war, the British had planned a surprise carrier air strike on the Italian fleet at Taranto. *Illustrious* provided the forces. In a night attack on November 11, 1940, twenty-one Swordfish, using specially modified torpedoes that could be dropped in shallow water, knocked out half the Italian battle fleet for the loss of just two planes. This was a remarkable feat in some ways more impressive than the Pearl Harbor attack, for which it served as a model; it was carried out against an alert enemy already at war with far greater economy of means. Taranto dealt a terrific blow to Italian morale and a corresponding boost for the British, who felt free to take some battleships from the Mediterranean. But overall, it had surprisingly little strategic result, as did the Italian manned torpedoes that disabled two British battleships at Alexandria in December 1941. The great battleships destroyed or damaged in these famous attacks (and indeed the Pearl Harbor attack). were simply not as important as had been supposed. Their presence or loss was ultimately not crucial to the course of the war.[8]

## Hitler and the Mediterranean

In late September, with invading England no longer a prospect, Hitler had shown some interest in large-scale plans that Admiral Raeder had advocated for the Mediterranean, including seizing Gibraltar and the Suez Canal. Raeder initially regarded these operations as a substitute for the attack on the Soviet Union, but later he came to view them as only a prelude to it. He and others urged Hitler to make efforts to befriend Vichy

France and bring it into the war on the Axis side. Hitler pondered the idea, although it was contrary to his deepest beliefs and could not be easily reconciled with Spanish and Italian demands. Hitler himself recognized that solving the problem would require a "gigantic fraud." His dilemma—apart from the self-imposed limitations on the time and resources that he could devote to the Mediterranean theater, if he was to attack the Soviet Union in 1941—was a complex one. The Italians were reluctant to accept aid. They needed Spanish help to take Gibraltar and close the western Mediterranean, but Franco was reluctant to enter the war unless Britain was on the verge of final defeat and then only for a very steep price. Hitler neither liked nor trusted Franco—a "Jesuit swine"—nor respected the Spanish regime. Supporting Spain, if it joined the Axis, would be an economic burden. Although Spain's armed forces were unimpressive, Hitler did not want to occupy Spain by force. Thinking of what had happened to Napoleon, he respected the Spanish people's ability to wage a guerrilla war. He might have been able to reconcile Franco's demands for annexations in French North Africa with Mussolini's ambitions, but Hitler thought it would cause the whole French colonial empire to join the Free French and the Allies. At the same time, he had no faith in long-term collaboration with Vichy. No Frenchman, he thought, could be a real ally of Germany. The basic premise of his policy toward France was never to allow it to regain its strength. Any short-term collaboration was not worth risking that possibility or endangering German relations with Italy.

Conceivably, Hitler could have sent German forces to the Spanish border and tried to bluff or force Franco into joining the Axis even without fulfilling Franco's demands at French expense—the British were sure that Franco would cave in—but Hitler had neither the time nor the inclination for such a gamble before the Russian campaign. So he limited his efforts to bring Spain into the war to uncharacteristically diplomatic ones. (For a time he may have also hoped that the Soviets could be gulled into striking the Middle East from the north, averting the need for Germany to act in the Mediterranean.) Britain's survival and victories in the Mediterranean did not make dealing with Spain or Vichy France easier. On December 8, Franco made clear that he would not willingly enter the war unless Britain was about to fall, so his help would not be needed, while a week later political changes at Vichy temporarily weakened the more extreme collaborationists there. Hitler continued to seek Spain's entry into the war but without success.[9] Defeats in Greece, at sea, and in the desert, however, made Italy more cooperative.

## The Desert Campaign against the Italians

Led by Maj. Gen. Richard O'Connor, and backed by the British commander in Egypt, Lt. Gen. Maitland Wilson, the British force in the Western Desert of Egypt was numerically inferior but technically and tactically superior to the Italians. Although the RAF was outnumbered in the air, its two Hurricane squadrons provided air superiority. Western Desert Force comprised the Seventh Armored Division and the Fourth Indian Division, both well-trained regular units. Although it was short of trucks and its tanks were already badly worn, the British force had one great advantage, forty-eight heavily armored Matilda II infantry (I) tanks that no Italian antitank weapon could counter. They were virtually immune to everything except some heavy antiaircraft guns. (Even they do not seem to have penetrated their armor, but hits in the right spot could jam their turrets.) In relation to the opposition, they were as fearsome as the German Tiger tanks later in the war.

On December 9, after careful preparation, the British took the Italians' chain of fortified camps at Sidi Barrani by surprise. The Italians had not expected any attack. While a small British infantry force held the Italians' attention to their front, the armored and Indian divisions penetrated, remarkably undetected, between the fortified camps to hit them from behind. The Italians fought bravely but were quickly overcome. The Allies captured 40,000 men.

O'Connor was ready to go on, but Wavell insisted on withdrawing the Indian Division for transfer to the East African campaign, a move probably costly in transport and time. He was forced into this step partly by political factors (the need to placate the South Africans, many of whom opposed participation in the war) and by severe time constraints. The move to the Sudan depended on ships slated to return soon to Britain. The Sixth Australian Division, which was not yet completely trained or equipped, replaced the Indians. O'Connor later calculated that this changeover cost him three weeks, probably preventing a complete Axis defeat in North Africa at an earlier date.

The Australians were still not quite ready when O'Connor tackled the formidable Italian fortified position at Bardia early in January, but the Allies took it with relative ease. On January 21, the Western Desert Force captured the fortified port of Tobruk. O'Connor planned to resume his offensive and take western Cyrenaica on February 10, but on February 1–2, it became clear that the Italians were evacuating the area. O'Connor decided to catch them, although the Seventh Armored Division's tanks were worn out and his air support was stretched; indeed, the RAF only kept going on fuel that the Italians had abandoned. As the Italians withdrew along the long coastal road, a small British column struggled through Cyrenaica's interior to beat them to the "corner" where it bordered on Tripolitania. A ridiculously small force crossed the Italians' line of retreat at Beda Fomm and barely stopped them from escaping. The Beda Fomm battle completed the destruction of the Italian Tenth Army. The British had eliminated ten Italian divisions and captured 130,000 prisoners, 380 tanks, and 845 guns for a loss of less than 2,000 men.

Although his tanks were in poor shape, O'Connor was prepared to resume his advance on February 20 and take Tripoli. But he was not given a chance to do so. The British shut down the desert campaign, so a British force could go to Greece. Later critics overwhelmingly condemned the decision, when its consequences should have been obvious at the time to all: the Greek expedition was doomed to failure, while the halt in Libya let the Axis keep a secure base there from which they could attack the British in Egypt. Even had the British been able to hold a beachhead in Greece, they could not have made use of it, while the Axis could exploit their position in Libya.[10]

The failure to take Tripoli exposed the Allies to great danger in 1941–1942. Holding the Middle East against an attack that would have been impossible had Tripoli been captured also diverted British naval efforts from the Battle of the Atlantic and helped ensure that the Far East would be left poorly defended against Japan. In the long run, continuing the desert campaign, given the ultimate British victory there, wrecked the Italians, pulled German forces into a theater where the Allies were able to learn how to fight the German Army effectively (which they would have found hard to do anywhere else), eventually tied down German forces in an area where they could not be properly supplied and were ultimately trapped, and left southern Europe poorly defended. That outcome, however, was a narrow one. Had the Axis taken the Middle East or even Egypt in 1942, the decision to halt in early 1941 would appear in a much grimmer light.

Early, final victory in Libya had been partly sacrificed for the sake of conquering Italian East Africa, which the British regarded as necessary to protect the Red Sea route. Churchill and many later critics thought this focus was a mistake, holding that the Italians there were weak and could have been left to wither in the face of blockade and rebellion. Churchill would have preferred to bring the British and South African forces north to Egypt. (Characteristically, the campaign having been decided on, he then lashed Wavell into starting it as early as possible, or even sooner.) Necessary or not, the campaign was a remarkable success at low cost; the Italians were largely defeated in the spring of 1941.[11]

## The Germans Intervene in the Mediterranean

Italian defeats in the Mediterranean forced Hitler to intervene. But it was now too late for a campaign on a grand scale to smash the British there before the attack on the USSR. In early December 1940, he decided to transfer strong air forces to Sicily and attack the British fleet and Malta. On January 9, he told his military chiefs that he wanted an armored force sent to Tripoli as a "blocking unit," whose mission, for the near future at any rate, would be defensive rather than conquering Egypt. This force was the nucleus of the Afrika Korps. Rommel, who had proved an outstanding commander of a panzer division in France, was given command of the force. Rommel was an extremely capable man whose view of the world was broader than most of his colleagues'. Given German priorities and the difficulty of supplying the Axis forces in Africa, he achieved much more than could have been reasonably expected.

The Luftwaffe began attacks in the Mediterranean in January. The Mediterranean Fleet, covering a Malta convoy, was hit hard. The Luftwaffe also sank a cruiser and damaged the precious carrier *Illustrious* so severely that it was out of action for many months. The attacks on Malta were so heavy that it could not function as an effective base for months, allowing the Axis to reinforce Libya with little loss. The Luftwaffe made it harder for the British to supply their forces in Cyrenaica, and mined the Suez Canal.

The Afrika Korps, along with the Ariete Armored Division and the Trento Motorized Division, perhaps the best units in the Italian Army, reached Libya intact. The first German units, an antitank battalion and a reconnaissance battalion, landed in Libya on February 14 and were hustled to the front. The Germans assembled small ships to improve the supply of the forward Axis forces, and the Italians granted Rommel control of the Ariete Division on March 7. The British quickly detected the arrival of German air units—they read Luftwaffe but not German Army ciphers—but were slow to recognize that the Germans were sending ground troops to Libya. They had suspected an attack on Malta or Tunisia, instead. They realized that the Germans were present only after their armored cars encountered their more formidable German counterparts, and they continued to have little knowledge about the Germans at the tactical level, while the Germans were kept well informed by reading low-level British ciphers. That ability and, later on, their breaking of the cipher that the American military observer in Egypt used considerably helped Rommel up to the summer of 1942.

Underestimating Rommel's daring and overestimating the Axis powers' logistical difficulties, Wavell did not expect a major attack before the end of April. He also seems to have thought that the terrain south of Benghazi afforded the British better defensive positions than it did. Berlin officials, for that matter, assumed that Rommel would wait until the complete Fifteenth Panzer Division joined his Fifth Light Division (later reinforced to become the Twenty-first Panzer Division) in mid-May before he undertook offensive action. Wavell's intelligence chief suspected that the Germans would be able to strike as early as April 1, but no one heeded his warning. By focusing on Greece, Wavell had taken experienced units from Libya, broken up the Western Desert Force–XIII Corps headquarters, and replaced it with a static Cyrenaica Command under Gen. Philip Neame, a courageous man but not a suitable commander. His command had little transport, and the Luftwaffe made it impossible to use the forward port of Benghazi. Neame had only the incomplete Second Armored Division (half of which was en route to Greece), whose poorly equipped Third Armored Brigade had one regiment of nearly worn-out British "cruiser" medium tanks, one regiment of light tanks, and one regiment equipped with miserably inadequate, captured Italian medium tanks. The Ninth Australian Division, not completely trained, and the Third Indian Motor Brigade were Neame's only other combat units. Wavell did not like Neame's dispositions but, being fantastically overburdened, did not intervene. In the event of a major attack, Neame was to pull back to, and possibly even give up, Benghazi.

Rommel, attacking before his force was complete, nevertheless had more medium tanks in the forward area than the British did (150 to 70) when he struck on March 31. This was the only battle in the desert where the Germans seriously outnumbered the Allies at the start, but, as in other desert battles, numbers were not critical. The British supply and communications systems functioned poorly, as did Neame and the commander of the Second Armored Division, which disintegrated. Between failures to connect with fuel supplies and mechanical breakdowns, the Allied force lost all its tanks—practically none to German guns. Initially planning a limited advance, Rommel was emboldened to recapture all of Cyrenaica. O'Connor, hastily sent back to take command, was captured along with Neame. Thus the British lost the only man who could then have dealt with Rommel on equal terms.

The British were lucky not to suffer more serious losses. They fell back to the Egyptian frontier, except for the Australian division, which held out in Tobruk. Rommel then showed the reckless aspect of his character, as he tried to overwhelm the determined defenders of Tobruk with several poorly prepared attacks that were costly failures. The British were encouraged when they learned, on April 5, that Rommel had exceeded his orders and that the German High Command had no intention of launching him on the conquest of Egypt (although Rommel was planning just that). The General Staff, in fact, was angry at his actions and his request for additional forces. Tobruk remained a thorn in Rommel's side for the rest of 1941. He could not prudently advance farther east without dealing with it, and he wanted to use it as a supply port.[12]

## THE CONQUEST OF THE BALKANS

Hitler felt forced to launch a Balkan campaign in the spring of 1941 to bail out the Italians; to protect Germany's only important natural source of oil, the Romanian oil fields and refineries; and to secure his southern flank for the invasion of the USSR. He had been quite willing to leave the region to the Italians; other than the Romanian oil, it did not interest the Nazis. He only reluctantly sanctioned occupying all of Greece. However, in March 1941, a pro-Allied coup in Yugoslavia, whose importance he may have overrated, led him to include that country in the Balkan campaign, too. He ordered his troops not merely to conquer it but to destroy it.

The British had vaguely hoped to forge a Balkan front, including Greece, Yugoslavia, and Turkey. None had modern forces, however, and all of them together, supported by all available British forces, could not have held out against Field Marshal Wilhelm List's Twelfth Army. Neither the Turks nor the Yugoslavs would depart from their positions of neutrality (although in the Turkish case, it was a pro-British neutrality.)

Despite considerable misgivings (especially on the part of the Chiefs of Staff) and wavering by Churchill himself (generally one of the most important proponents of the idea), the British government favored sending British ground forces to Greece. Indeed, the dictator and prime minister Ioannis Metaxas, who welcomed RAF support but feared that the arrival of British ground forces would guarantee German intervention, initially stopped the British from sending troops. Metaxas's death in early 1941 reopened the issue, for the Greeks were now willing to accept British ground troops. Strong political pressure moved the Chiefs of Staff and Wavell to sanction a commitment they had opposed previously, for which Churchill himself and Foreign Secretary Anthony Eden were most responsible. (Wavell's reversal in early February was striking, although perhaps it was a reversion to an earlier conviction, dating from even before the war, that a Balkan campaign was inevitable.)

The decision strikingly ignored the real balance of forces, especially in the air, for the RAF in the Middle East was hopelessly outnumbered and qualitatively inferior, having only a few Hurricane fighters, to Axis airpower. The British, however, felt committed for moral and political reasons. They had guaranteed Greece against German attack in 1939 and believed that they had to be seen, especially in American eyes, as supporting a weak victim of Axis aggression. President Roosevelt's special representative on the scene, William Donovan, encouraged their view, although it did not represent the considered policy of the U.S. government, which accepted that the Balkan situation was hopeless.

Wavell was reluctant to cut back the commitment even when it became apparent that the Greeks would not preemptively withdraw their troops to the "Aliakmon line," a defensive line running from the Aegean coast to the Yugoslav border that the British had stipulated was necessary for taking a defensive stand. Only part of General Wilson's "W Force," comprised of the Second New Zealand and Sixth Australian Divisions and an armored brigade, arrived before the Germans struck on April 6.[13]

### CAPE MATAPAN

The Germans had pushed a reluctant Italian High Command into aggressive action at sea. The Italian Navy was going to try to catch the British convoys to Greece.

In late March, the British learned from reading Luftwaffe and Italian ciphers that a major fleet operation was imminent, although they did not know the details of the Axis plan. Admiral Cunningham halted convoys to and from Greece and took his fleet to sea. A new carrier, HMS *Formidable*, had replaced the crippled *Illustrious*, and he now had three battleships. As in the hunt for the *Bismarck* some weeks later, the carrier would win the day, enabling the big-gun ships to close with the enemy.

On March 28, the Italians found and engaged a force of British cruisers, not realizing the main British force was near. A running battle ended when British torpedo bombers attacked, hitting and slowing the battleship *Vittorio Veneto* and halting a cruiser. The Italians were still unprepared for night actions; that evening the British overtook and destroyed the crippled cruiser, two other cruisers, and a pair of destroyers but missed *Vittorio Veneto*.

This battle of Cape Matapan was the first important operation in the Mediterranean based on communications intelligence, which probably saved at least one convoy from destruction. The Italians, blundering badly at several levels, were lucky not to suffer greater losses. Matapan discouraged the Italian fleet from interfering with further convoys to Greece and the evacuation of Greece and Crete.[14]

## GREECE

The British had hardly entered Greece when they had to retreat. Superior German mechanized forces cut far behind the stretched Allied front, while the RAF was outmatched in the air. The Yugoslav army disintegrated as the disaffected Croats simply gave up. Further, on the night of April 6–7, the Luftwaffe quickly wrecked the Piraeus, the main Allied supply port, when it blew up an ammunition ship.

The campaign was a desperate rearguard action from the start, notable for its well-timed withdrawals, for which Ultra's information may have been largely responsible. By April 19, it was obvious that the British could not hold any position in Greece; for that matter, they could not feed the Greek population behind their front. They decided to leave, with the Greek government's consent. The Royal Navy carried out a difficult and dangerous evacuation, with little air cover, and mostly at night. Most of the British force of 58,000 men escaped, but 12,000 troops were lost, along with almost all the equipment sent to Greece.[15]

## CRETE

The Germans had had a long-standing interest in taking Crete, the navy and the Luftwaffe seeing it as a key base for air attacks on the British fleet and the Suez Canal. Early in the Greek campaign, the Germans had championed an Italian landing on the island, but clearly the Italians could not do the job. The Army General Staff and elements of the OKW preferred attacking Malta, but Hitler thought that a Malta operation should await the end of the Russian campaign. He believed that Crete should be taken to round out and secure the Axis position in the Balkans. Halder and the Italians also came down in favor of Crete. The job was assigned to the Luftwaffe's airborne units under Gen. Kurt Student.

The British had perceived the importance of Crete early and decided in the fall of 1940 to hold it even if mainland Greece was lost. They stationed a weak brigade group and a few antiaircraft guns there but little else, while the Greek regular forces on Crete left for the mainland. But Crete would be hard to hold. Apart from the grave British weakness in the air, the island's geography did not favor the defenders. All ports and airfields and the only east–west highway were on the exposed north shore. Other roads and communications were bad, so the defenders were divided into several poorly connected sectors and could make little use of reserves. There were just a few small fishing towns on the rugged south coast, and they were linked only by trails with the north. Despite ample Cretan and Italian prisoner labor, the British did not develop the southern harbors and roads to the north or move airfields to better locations.

On April 17, London directed that at least part of the force evacuated from Greece be dropped off on Crete. There, Maj. Gen. Bernard Freyberg of New Zealand took command of his battered Second New Zealand Division, the Sixth Australian Division, and the British forces that had been on Crete, totaling about 32,000 Commonwealth troops, along with 7,000–10,000 Greeks. But only light weapons had been brought from Greece. He had few tanks, which were in bad shape, scant artillery pieces, and limited communications gear. Even a few more working tanks might have made a big difference. He tried to arm the Cretans but had little to give them.

The Allies might have been easily overcome but for the Germans' poor planning. General Student's plan was most un-German in its lack of concentration; instead, he envisaged a dispersed airborne attack against four points—Maleme, Heraklion, Retimo, and Khania—with no particular weight of attack against any of them. He did not arrange to keep a significant reserve and wound up with a small one only because the troop carrier planes could not carry all his men on the first day. He was reluctantly persuaded to include a seaborne move as well. The Italians would shepherd small convoys carrying German mountain troops, Italian Marines, and heavy weapons to back up the airborne force. The Germans underestimated the British force, thinking 5,000 troops might be on Crete. At first, they even anticipated the British might abandon Crete. They also believed, wrongly, that the Cretans would be passive or would welcome the Germans.

The British, meanwhile, had detected preparations for an Axis airborne operation. Reading Luftwaffe ciphers, on April 26 they saw clear evidence that Crete was the objective. In early May they developed an unusually clear and complete picture of the German plan and order of battle, although they thought that the seaborne element of the scheme was bigger than it really was, leading Freyberg to overrate the threat from the sea. This information was conveyed to Freyberg personally and attributed to a British agent in Athens. Freyberg was expressly forbidden to strengthen the New Zealanders holding the key Maleme sector, as he wished to do, a step that would almost certainly have led to an Allied victory. He and others also mistakenly supposed that not only gliders but troop carrier planes could land on almost any open space; thus, the fight for the few airfields looked less crucial than it was.

Enjoying complete air superiority, the Germans drove the RAF off Crete, and the last seven planes left on May 19. The RAF would be strained to mount a few night bomber missions to support the defenders. A few Hurricanes with long-range tanks reached the Heraklion area; otherwise, the Allied ground force had little air support. Holding back its battleships and one carrier (which never had more than twelve fighters) to deter an Italian fleet operation south of Crete, the Royal Navy sent cruisers and destroyers north of the island at night to try to stop Axis sea traffic.

On May 20, the airborne attack began. The German glider and paratroop forces suffered heavy losses, especially at Maleme, and failed to take any of their objectives. The Cretans fought fiercely, and the Royal Navy sank or delayed the enemy convoys. Almost at the last minute, the Germans did what they should have done from the first and concentrated on reinforcing at Maleme. After a terrific battle, they secured an airhead there, whose expansion the Allies could not stop. Freyberg, recognizing that the battle was lost, began a timely retreat over the mountains to the south coast. The Allied force barely evaded the German mountain troops' efforts to cut it off, and the Royal Navy evacuated it at a high cost: three cruisers and six destroyers sunk and the only carrier, three battleships, six cruisers, and seven destroyers damaged. The British force suffered more than 15,000 casualties (12,000 captured), while the narrow victory at Crete had blunted the German airborne forces. Germans never used paratroopers again in a major airborne operation.

Losing Crete was a lesser evil than the loss of Malta. It was not an especially effective German base and was not the key position that the Luftwaffe and German Navy had supposed. But the loss of Crete did make the Allies' supplying Malta harder and forced the British to commit an entire division to hold Cyprus, which they feared might be the next target in a step-by-step airborne drive aimed at the Middle East. In the long run, however, holding Crete would have given the Allies a useful base for air attacks on the Romanian oil industry and increased German apprehensions about an invasion of the Balkans, tying down additional enemy forces there.[16]

With defeat in Africa and the Aegean, the British were in desperate straits. Had the Germans concentrated on a serious offensive in the Mediterranean and Middle East, instead of attacking the Soviets, they would have overrun the region. That option was not a serious alternative given Hitler's basic ideas. His earlier excessive trust in and later disillusionment with Mussolini and his inability to resolve the problems with Spain and Vichy France caused Hitler to miss a chance to administer a serious blow to the British. Had he acted promptly after he realized that Britain could not be invaded, the Axis powers might have seized Malta and sent a sufficient German armored force to Libya to drive the British out of Egypt. Further, the Germans could have withdrawn their forces in time so as not to interfere with the invasion of the Soviet Union. Thus the invasion and occupation of the Balkans, which proved costly, would have been unnecessary. One can even argue that continuing a secondary offensive in the Middle East, at some cost to the Russian campaign, would have been justifiable to secure valuable oil supplies, although even the greatest possible success there could not have won the war for the Axis.

The British did not realize that the Germans themselves would terminate the threat to the Middle East. In April London forced a reluctant Admiral Cunningham to undertake a dangerous bombardment of Tripoli instead of expending one of his battleships as a blockship to shut its harbor. The attack, requiring the fleet to go deep into waters dominated by enemy airpower, was only moderately successful. Cunningham was astonished that he got away without serious losses. Early in May, the British rushed a special convoy of five fast cargo ships carrying desperately needed tanks and fighter planes right through the Mediterranean to Egypt. One ship struck a mine and sank, but 238 tanks and 43 crated Hurricanes arrived—a success due to the cover of unusually bad weather and a healthy dose of luck. The tanks, however, proved less useful than expected. Poorly stowed, they were damaged by seawater and showed signs of slipshod workmanship. Evidence even indicated that some had been sabotaged.

Wavell had his hands full. Apart from the desperate situation in Greece, Crete, and the desert, he was still supervising the liberation of Italian East Africa and faced trouble in the north with a pro-Axis takeover in Iraq that the Axis supported through Vichy-held Syria. Not realizing that the Iraqis had moved too soon and that their actions did not fit in with German plans, London overestimated the immediate danger. Wavell had to send forces to Iraq and occupy Syria—with insufficient ground forces, no tanks, and little airpower—at the same time that London insisted on a premature attack in the Western Desert. The Syrian campaign, launched on June 8, proved tougher than expected and took five weeks. It was a costly diversion although not decisive in causing the next British effort in the desert to fail.[17]

## Operation Battleaxe

The British offensive of June 1941, code-named Battleaxe, was a larger version of a failed counterattack that the British had launched in mid-May against the Germans in Libya. Wavell attempted it under pressure from London, which did not realize the effects of the unreliability of the newly arrived Crusader tanks and the inexperience of the British tank crews.

The British hoped to use a temporary superiority of strength in the forward area to overcome the enemy frontier defenses, rout the German armor, and relieve Tobruk. They were not well informed about German dispositions, but German intercept and deciphering units warned Rommel of all British movements and intentions. The Germans reacted much faster than anticipated. In sheer numbers, both sides were about evenly matched with about two hundred tanks each. On June 15, while infantry units and I tanks attacked the frontier defenses in the coastal sector, the Seventh Armored Division protected its desert flank. The attack on the frontier defenses was partially successful, but the armored division's tanks were not well coordinated with artillery support and suffered severely from screens of well-camouflaged antitank guns, which the Germans employed offensively and skillfully coordinated with their tanks and artillery. The British mistakenly attributed their tank losses to German tank fire; they also thought, mistakenly, that the two-pounder guns of their tanks were inferior to the 50mm guns of the German Mark III tanks.

Rommel brought up the Fifth Light Division to join the Fifteenth Panzer Division in the forward area, and on June 16, both sides attacked. Neither achieved a decisive success, but the following day Rommel's attacks forced the British to break off the action lest their line of retreat be cut. The British suffered major tank losses, and the Germans, dominating the battlefield, recovered most of their own damaged tanks and some British ones. The British decided that their problems resulted from poor preparation, the unreliability of their tanks, and the alleged inferiority of their guns and armor compared to the Germans' weapons. Neglecting the lesson of the German antitank screens and cooperation of all arms, the British continued to think in terms of a simple tank versus tank battle.

The operation's failure finished Wavell, who the British thought must be burned out. In July, he was ordered to exchange places with Sir Claude Auchinleck, the commander in India. Being an Indian Army officer, the capable Auchinleck was unfamiliar with armored warfare and the senior officers of the British Army. When he took direct control of the British forces in the desert, he did well but chose a succession of inadequate men to take charge there. He benefited, however, from a changed situation. The immediate threat to the Middle East had ebbed, and he was not distracted by multiple campaigns as Wavell had been. The forces in Iraq and Iran were then separated from the Middle East Command, and the occupation of Iran, which the British and Soviets undertook in August 1941, was not his problem. (He was later saddled with Iraq and Iran.) Nevertheless, although Churchill was skeptical about the danger in 1941, during the next year Auchinleck would spend much time monitoring the region lest the Germans defeat the Soviets and strike the Middle East from the north.

Auchinleck made clear that he would not be rushed into an attack in the desert. He would finish the Syrian campaign and garrison Cyprus first. Then he would insist on having two properly prepared armored divisions, with a 50 percent reserve of tanks, before launching a decisive offensive, which could not take place before September. (It did not take place until November.) Churchill was angry but could not very well fire another general so soon after getting rid of Wavell. The British hoped to follow victory in Cyrenaica by capturing the rest of Libya. Then they planned to enter French North Africa, possibly with American help, and perhaps land in Sicily.[18]

The Nazis had not finished with the Mediterranean and Middle East. On June 11 Hitler issued Directive 32, which covered the period after the expected Soviet defeat and envisaged forcing Spain into the war, with a concentric attack on the Middle East from Libya, Turkey, and possibly the Transcaucasus. For a brief period in July, the General Staff fleshed out the overall scheme: forces would drive from Libya through Egypt and from Bulgaria through Turkey in the spring of 1942, and an offensive would be launched from the Transcaucasus as well to reach the Persian Gulf in October 1942. Preliminary operations would reduce Malta and Tobruk, with reinforcements bringing Rommel to four mechanized divisions. This program was soon set aside.

Rommel believed that with the reinforcements he could repel a British attack, reach the Suez Canal in the spring of 1942, and then drive for Iraq, even without a supporting attack from the north. Once the eastern Mediterranean coast was taken, he could shift his base to Syria. He believed—wrongly, for it could not handle enough cargo—that if Germany captured

Tobruk, his supply problems would be solved. Achieving this goal became the focus of his endeavors for the rest of 1941.[19]

## The Assault on Axis Shipping

Axis supply problems in Africa became worse and worse. The diversion of German aircraft from Malta, and the arrival of Hurricane fighters, let the British use Malta as an offensive base for planes, submarines, and even surface ships. The Allies were enormously aided by their ability to read the Luftwaffe cipher and, from late June 1941, the Italian convoy cipher, which disclosed departure times and often cargoes. (They had read Italian Air Force ciphers fairly steadily since September 1940 but rarely had intercepted the signals, which went mostly by landline.) From July 1941, deciphered messages disclosed almost every German convoy to Africa. Reading the enemy's messages guided the preliminary reconnaissance flights sent out to "find" the enemy convoys and disguise the fact that the British already knew about them.

During the summer and fall of 1941, ground and air units steadily reinforced Malta, and the Allies built up stocks of supplies. While Wellington bombers hit Italian and Libyan ports at night, Blenheim light bombers attacked Axis convoys by day and Swordfish torpedo bombers hunted them at night. The main killers, however, were British submarines. Intercepted messages helped them sink three of the biggest Italian ocean liners converted to troopships in August and September. From mid-October, the Italians almost always ferried their soldiers to North Africa in destroyers, a costly practice. In late October, the British based a force of cruisers and destroyers on Malta that, on November 9, wiped out a whole German convoy. From July through October 1941, the British sank 20 percent of the Axis supplies to North Africa and 62 percent in November. Maintaining Malta as an Allied base was costly. Beginning in July 1941 the Italians finally tried coordinated high-level bombing and torpedo attacks. Nevertheless, after the convoy of late September, stocks of most supplies—except coal, kerosene, and animal feed—were deemed sufficient for four to five months or more.[20]

## The Crusader Offensive

The British fall offensive, code-named Crusader, was delayed far longer than Auchinleck had wanted. It barely beat Rommel's planned attack on Tobruk. Rommel was so focused on Tobruk that he failed to react properly to the British attack. Against the advice of the Italians and some of his own officers, he didn't believe a British offensive was imminent; indeed, he anticipated at most a British "reconnaissance in force" designed to disturb his preparations against Tobruk. This assumption might have been fatal had the British done better.

Although his supply situation was deteriorating, Rommel's Panzer Group Afrika (renamed Panzer Army Afrika during the battle) had been reinforced. His panzer divisions had never received all their tank companies, but he was assigned a third German division, the Afrika Motorized Infantry Division (later named the Ninetieth Light Division), which was unusually strong in firepower. Formed especially for the African campaign, it included German veterans of the French Foreign Legion. The Germans had added "face-hardened" sheets of armor plate to many Panzer III and IV tanks, making them almost immune to uncapped armor-piercing shells from British two-pounder tanks and antitank guns. Rommel's tanks were now qualitatively better and more reliable than his enemies' Crusader tanks; moreover, the British had neither face-hardened armor nor the capped shells needed to pierce it. Rommel's artillery also had been built up for the attack on Tobruk, and he had 88mm and 50mm antitank guns, which were greatly superior to their British counterparts. Finally, the Me 109F was more effective than the British fighters were, although they were badly outnumbered.

Auchinleck's buildup, meanwhile, had been badly delayed. He had one and a half armored divisions as only the Twenty-second Armored Brigade of the First Armored Division had arrived. Its tanks were in poor shape and required much work before the brigade could begin training. Luckily, the British now had some American M3 Stuart tanks. Fast and reliable but not well armed, these gas-guzzlers had a short radius of action. The British still lacked good antitank guns. Possibly for good reasons, they did not use their counterpart of the excellent German 88, the 3.7-inch antiaircraft gun, in an antitank role; further, they also ignored the possibility of using obsolete 3-inch antiaircraft guns for that purpose.

The defects of their equipment, however, were less serious than the British poor tactics and command. Auchinleck had made Lt. Gen. Alan Cunningham the commander of Eighth Army, as the desert force was now designated. Cunningham had done well leading the British advance from Kenya into Italian East Africa, but Auchinleck had promoted him above his level of competence. He knew little about armored warfare, had never commanded such large forces, was indecisive, and was in poor health.

British armored tactics were poor, and cooperation between tanks and infantry bad. The British did not properly coordinate their excellent artillery with tanks, infantry, and antitank guns, as the Germans did routinely. The British remained addicted to dispersing their forces. That would bring them close to disaster in the Crusader offensive and in several later campaigns. Their considerably greater quantity of equipment and sheer determination saved them as 118,000 British, with 610 tanks in the Eighth Army's main body, another 101 in Tobruk, and a fair number in reserve, faced 119,000 Axis troops. The Desert Air Force, with 530 aircraft, maintained control of the air against 342 Axis planes. The RAF and excellent security precautions gave the British the element of surprise, for although many on the Axis side expected an attack, they never had any proof.

Cunningham's poor plan was a scaled-up version of the failed Battleaxe offensive. While Lt. Gen. Alfred Godwin-Austen's infantry-heavy XIII Corps dealt with the Axis defenses on the Libyan frontier, Lt. Gen. Willoughby Norrie's XXX Corps, with the main weight of the armor, would swing wide through the desert, hopefully engage and destroy the German panzer divisions, and eventually break through to Tobruk. But, in fact, the initial plan was for Norrie simply to advance to Gabr Saleh in the desert well southeast of Tobruk and wait for Rommel to react. Norrie favored going farther, at least to Sidi Rezegh, a major air base and a much more direct threat to the force besieging Tobruk, but Cunningham did not concur. Cunningham committed the basic blunder of simply going out on a limb and depending on the enemy to react in a certain way, a bad idea at any time but a worse one in dealing with Erwin Rommel. In addition, heeding the complaints of Godwin-Austen, he tied the Fourth Armored Brigade, though part of Norrie's command, close to XIII Corps to ensure flank protection for the latter. Cunningham also poorly distributed the divisions between the two corps, giving the strong and experienced Fourth Indian Division to Godwin-Austen, while the relatively weak and new First South African Division formed the main infantry component of XXX Corps.

On November 18, the British advance began, starting a complicated battle in which fortunes changed rapidly. Heading straight to Gabr Saleh, XXX Corps stopped there as planned to wait for Rommel to react.

Rommel took no notice. Not at his best in this battle, he insisted on continuing preparations against Tobruk. "Mercifully for us," as his staff officer, Gen. Friedrich von Mellenthin put it, the British then recklessly dispersed their armor. Holding one armored brigade at Gabr Saleh, they sent another to Sidi Rezegh and one against the Italian Ariete Division dug in at Bir el

Gubi, where, attacking without supporting infantry, the brigade suffered heavy losses.

Although reacting slowly—Rommel may have accepted that he faced a major offensive only after the BBC announced it on November 20—the Germans were able to concentrate their forces against relatively weak and isolated British units. The battle came to focus on the British forces' thrust to Sidi Rezegh that threatened to join up with a breakout from Tobruk. On November 22–23, a panzer division of the Afrika Korps, joined by the Ariete Division, inflicted heavy losses on the British and South Africans at Sidi Rezegh. The latter were so shocked by their great losses that they were never entirely dependable thereafter. The Germans suffered heavily themselves, so it was perhaps a pyrrhic victory.

Meanwhile, the overconfident Rommel broke off action in the Tobruk area and drove toward the frontier to relieve the Axis garrisons there. He hoped that the thrust into the rear of XXX Corps and the New Zealand Division, now advancing west, would panic the British. Lt. Gen. Ludwig Crüwell, the able commander of the Afrika Korps, and Rommel's staff thought this idea a mistake. They believed that if the Axis armor continued the battle southeast of Tobruk, it would finish off the British there. Although the Germans narrowly failed to cripple the British offensive, the "dash to the wire," as Rommel's raid became known, on top of the heavy losses the Germans experienced on November 23, cost them the battle. The Germans' move east was disorganized and guided by erroneous information on British positions; it luckily missed Eighth Army's well-camouflaged supply dumps. Although disorganizing the British rear, it accomplished nothing decisive. The Axis garrisons on the frontier remained trapped.

The dash to the wire allowed XXX Corps to reorganize and recover. New tanks were brought up and damaged ones repaired. Meanwhile, Auchinleck replaced Cunningham, who had been inclined to break off the British offensive, with the former's deputy chief of staff, Maj. Gen. Neil Ritchie.

The battle resumed near Tobruk, where the New Zealanders and the breakout from Tobruk were threatening to join up. The Germans were successful in cutting off Tobruk again and inflicted serious losses on the elite New Zealand Division, but they were worn down in the process. Rommel tried to keep the initiative, but the British were equally as stubborn. The Axis did not have enough strength left, and in early December their supply system clearly was breaking down. On December 4, Rommel had to order a retreat. On Pearl Harbor day, he decided to withdraw from Cyrenaica completely, back to the line he had left in the spring. The British could not repeat the success of Beda Fomm and did not cut off the Axis forces as German rearguards gave them a lot of trouble.

Through sheer stubbornness, the weight of resources, and Rommel's uncharacteristic mistakes, the British had won their first serious land victory over the Germans and Italians in World War II. They also inflicted heavy losses on the Axis (comparable to those at El Alamein in the fall of 1942)—38,300 men, with nearly 30,000 captured—while the British had suffered 17,700 casualties, with the New Zealanders and South Africans particularly hit. But the offensive had taken far longer and cost far more than expected. Their forces were exhausted. Despite that the world situation had greatly improved, thanks to America's entry into the war and the disasters the Germans were suffering in the USSR, the strategic situation in the Mediterranean was turning against the Allies.[21]

# 6

## The Hinge

*American Intervention*

The conquests of 1940 had made Nazi Germany the dominant power in Europe. Although it had no prospect of invading Britain in 1940 or starving it into submission with a quick victory in the Atlantic, Germany had achieved a position and sufficient freedom of action to make British defeat in the long run inevitable, even if not quick and easy. Against the enormously greater resources of Nazi-controlled Europe, on its own Britain's position was hopeless.

But the British were never entirely alone. They counted on considerable American help, even as the Nazis' own compulsions forced an unwilling Soviet Union onto the Allied side. Effective American intervention, however, required considerable time. When World War II began, the United States had a powerful navy but a tiny army and air force (the latter, until June 1941, was just the "Air Corps" of the army). The U.S. Army Air Corps was a fraction of the Luftwaffe's size and had no fighters comparable to the Spitfire or the Me 109. It had concentrated on developing a small, prototype heavy bomber force and gaining experience in the techniques of strategic bombing. As late as the attack on Pearl Harbor in December 1941, the U.S. Army Air Force had only sixty-nine P-38 fighters that would have been considered up-to-date in Europe.

The Nazis had always looked forward to global domination and expected eventual war with the United States, but Hitler wished to delay that battle until he securely controlled Europe, including the Soviet Union, and had built up Germany's air and naval power. He may not have expected to live to see a final struggle with the Americans (he always worried that he would not live long), and in a way, he did not regard that clash as truly crucial. As he told Joseph Goebbels as late as May 1943, the conquest of Europe *meant* the conquest of the rest of the world. Once Germany had Europe, Hitler felt nothing could stop it. Moreover, he was basically contemptuous of the United States, although he sometimes exaggerated his disdain to bolster the courage of those who rightly feared American intervention in the current war. He regarded the United States as a Jewish-dominated mongrel country weakened by Negro influence and privately described President Roosevelt as a "tortuous, pettifogging Jew." But while he justifiably regarded the existing American military forces as weak, he did not wish to add the United States, with its industrial capacity, to the list of his active enemies.

Thus, facing more important tasks and lacking the necessary forces, he did not formulate concrete long-range plans to deal with the United States, although, according to Hermann Rauschning, as far back as 1934 Hitler had speculated about how he might do so. Despite more pressing matters, even in the late 1930s, he also was interested in building long-range bombers capable of striking the United States at least from the Azores. The Germans developed the Me 264 bomber for this purpose despite other priorities and a lack of manufacturing capacity. In 1940, as American intervention became a more immediate danger, Hitler wanted to obtain bases in the Atlantic islands and Morocco to deal with the Americans.[1]

Nazi intentions did not go unnoticed in the United States, where they were always regarded as evil. Early on, Roosevelt was convinced that Nazi Germany was a deadly threat and aimed at nothing less than world domination. He did not care for Germans in general. Unlike most Americans, he never regarded American intervention in World War I as a mistake, although, until the latter part of World War II, he was not as bitterly anti-German as has been supposed. By 1938, if not long before, he expected war with Germany; he had foreseen war with Japan since 1933. Indeed, important elements of his early foreign policies—establishing diplomatic relations with the Soviets and improving relations with Latin America—were partly motivated by the dangers posed by Germany and Japan. Roosevelt and most Americans who agreed with him—called interventionists or internationalists, in the jargon of the day—tended to think that the Germans and Japanese worked together more closely than they actually did. (They saw the Italians as little more than German puppets.) They also tended to assume that if Hitler disposed of Britain, he was likely to seek quick conquests in the Western Hemisphere, perhaps acting in Latin America if not striking directly against the United States, rather than tackling the USSR. The danger would be especially great if the Germans secured the French and/or British fleets more or less intact, an unlikely but especially perilous development.[2]

In mid-1940, these ideas became popular and largely replaced a different set of ideas that persisted, albeit in somewhat modified form, among the anti-interventionist, or isolationist, opponents of Roosevelt's policies. Since this crucial change, and indeed the whole political struggle in the United States, was arguably the point on which the fate of the world turned, it is worthwhile to explore these ideas.

To a considerable degree, the isolationism of the period between the world wars was simply a continuation of American tradition. During most of its history, the United States had avoided political involvement outside the Western Hemisphere. Americans had always been isolationists. Much of the rest of interwar isolationism was a reaction to the seeming anomaly of American intervention in World War I and its disappointing results. A remarkable proportion of isolationist leaders—notably Senators Robert Taft, Arthur Vandenberg, and Gerald Nye and former president Herbert Hoover—had been ardent supporters of war in 1917, only to be disgusted later. They reacted, like many Europeans, as historian Trumbull Higgins put it, by taking refuge in the "embittered illusion, usually considered disillusionment, that since war was an evil, it was therefore unnecessary."

Bitterness at the war's results and the curious assumption that any future war would simply be a repetition of World War I are the keys to understanding the isolationists' mentality in the 1930s and 1940s. Although most isolationists were not pacifists, outright pacifism was widespread in the 1930s; indeed, genuine opposition to all wars was probably more popular then than ever, before or since. The constant recital of the horrors of war numbed people's minds, and some assumed that if people in the democratic countries were scared out of their wits, peace would triumph.

The isolationist mentality cut across other political, social, and economic lines. The political lineup of the 1930s differed vastly from that of the late twentieth and early twenty-first centuries. Compared to modern America, with its rigid, predictable ideologies, the political world of the 1930s might seem exceedingly complex and almost chaotic.

First, in the 1930s and 1940s, the major political parties were not clearly divided along ideological lines. Both Democrats and Republicans had conservative and liberal wings; only the balance within the parties differed. The Democrats were not the liberal or left-wing party but only the "more liberal" party, extending both to the left and right of the Republicans. In fact, the situation in which the Democrats' center of gravity was to the left of the Republicans' was relatively new. It dated from the Wilson administration and may not have been fully formed until the 1930s. Even then, many Democrats and especially, but not only, Southerners were far to the right of any Republicans.

Next, the meaning of "liberal" and "conservative" in American politics were more limited in scope. The divide between them was defined by a relatively restricted number of domestic issues. Liberals favored the New Deal, the labor movement, and certain social and economic reforms; conservatives opposed these causes. Of course, many other issues, ideas, and attitudes were loosely associated with being liberal or conservative, but individuals could stray broadly on other matters and not compromise their basic alignment.

Finally, in the 1930s, a "liberal" or "conservative" stand on foreign policy, which was not usually a live issue in American politics, did not exist. Liberals and conservatives could be either internationalists or isolationists, with the balance squarely in the isolationists' favor until 1940. Isolationism appealed to all ethnic groups. (Later explanations of isolationism as a product of Irish or German-American resentments were absurd. Hardly any isolationist leaders belonged to those groups.) The South was the least isolationist section, followed by the Northeast and West Coast. The Midwest and the prairie and mountain states were the most isolationist of all.

Many important isolationist leaders, perhaps the core of isolationism in Congress, belonged to the western progressive wing of the Republican Party, which was based in those states and the West Coast, or were Democrats of similar background, like Senator Burton Wheeler of Montana. This political force, now extinct, was an important ally of Roosevelt's in domestic matters. Indeed, Roosevelt perhaps had more in common with such people than he did with urban liberals. Some foreign policy moves of the 1930s that later seemed strange were due to FDR's desire to placate this group, which included some of his personal friends, such as George Norris of Nebraska, perhaps the most admired man in the Senate. Later, many western progressive isolationists became Roosevelt's bitterest enemies, more bitter than the conservative mainstream Republicans who had never liked him at all but whose isolationism tended to be more moderate in tone. During 1940–1941, those northern conservative Democrats who were isolationists, notably Ambassador Joseph Kennedy, also tended to be more extreme than the typical Taft Republicans were.

While many isolationists were conservatives, such of their ideas as were not simply traditional were of liberal and leftist origin. Their isolationism was built on six principal concepts. First, they felt the outcome of any war in Europe or Asia could not vitally affect the United States, because they thought it was not possible for European or Asian enemies to conquer the United States, which could render the whole Western Hemisphere invulnerable to attack without much effort. Isolationists tended to be proponents of the "Pan-American" illusion, which absurdly imagined that the United States had more in common with Latin America than it did with the western European democracies. The United States to avoid entanglements outside the Western Hemisphere and subordinate virtually all other considerations to avoiding war. Unilateralism, not forging alliances, was desirable.

Third, to a large extent, isolationists thought war could be avoided by unilateral decision. The isolationist "model" of war, it cannot be too strongly stressed, was World War I, or the then prevailing image of that war, which was seen as a tragic and unnecessary conflict. (It is no coincidence that neither Churchill nor Roosevelt shared this view and always regarded World War I as just and necessary.) Any future war, it was believed, would be a repetition of that war. Isolationists tended to assume that there would be no real difference between the two sides, or the moral issues involved, and that war would take much the same form: an exhausting trench deadlock in which victory for one side or another would take a long time. Further, if the United States entered such a war, it would have an even worse impact on domestic life than World War I had. War hysteria and intrusions on civil liberties would recur in worse form. Many isolationists were sure that intervening in the next war would end American democracy. As the Socialist leader Norman Thomas put in 1937, "America's entry into a new war means Fascism at home without corresponding benefit anywhere." Senator Taft declared that "a war to preserve democracy . . . would almost certainly destroy democracy in the United States." Many went even further, saying it would wreck civilization.

Many believed in a fourth precept: that America's unnecessary participation in the earlier war had been caused by the machinations of foreign propagandists (mainly British) and evil munitions makers known as "merchants of death." This was a forerunner of the later obsession with the "military-industrial complex." Although the idea tended to contradict their faith in "hemisphere defense," many believed that an arms buildup must lead to war, just as the pre-1914 arms race was believed to have led to war.

Although most isolationists were not pacifists, they shared the anti-military feeling and posturing common in the 1920s and 1930s, which saw such oddities as a nationwide "student strike against war" in 1935 directed not against the Axis powers but against the Reserve Officers' Training Corps and President Roosevelt's efforts to build up the navy. In a gesture characteristic of the era, the Girl Scouts changed their uniforms from the "militaristic" khaki to, as unkind critics noted, a gray color that was close to the color of German Army uniforms.

Fifth, the isolationists felt that war, even against an evil aggressor, would be futile. As the *New Republic* noted in October 1937, "You cannot defeat fascism by waging war. On the contrary, nothing is more likely than that the United States would go fascist through the very process of organizing to defeat the fascist nations." In a popular cliché of the era, they maintained that the United States "could not solve Europe's problems."

Finally, any cause for which the United States or the other democracies would fight must be morally tainted. There was a dogmatic conviction that all wars were fought for cynical political purposes or economic gain. The Versailles Treaty and the Nine-Power Treaty in Asia, they said, were wicked attempts by "have powers" to preserve an evil status quo; force should not be used to stop "have nots" — such as Germany, Italy, and Japan, which were supposed to be desperate for raw materials — even though their aggressive actions were bad. Many liberals and pacifists blamed Japanese aggression in China on America's unjust immigration laws, tariffs, and limited rearmament measures.

Such isolationist ideas were so widespread that while few Americans could accurately be called pro-Axis, their lack of reaction to the aggressors' initial moves was remarkable. This passivity was particularly true of liberals. One can read through issues of the *New Republic* and *The Nation* in 1935 and 1936 without finding condemnation of the Italians' attack on Ethiopia or the Germans' march into the Rhineland, while finding sharp attacks on President Roosevelt for his naval buildup and many expressions of hostility toward the British and French "ruling classes" and especially toward British imperialism. (British concessions to nationalists in India, Ceylon, and Burma bounced off their consciousness.) Curiously the main event turning liberal opinion against the Axis powers was not their overt or strategically important aggressions but their intervention in the Spanish Civil War, a comparatively minor episode on the road to war.

Contrary to later belief, intervention in Asia was, if anything, even less popular than intervention in Europe. Few who were isolationists in relation to Europe opposed Japan. Some of the more extreme isolationist organs, such as the *Chicago Tribune* and the Hearst papers, were open apologists for Japanese aggression. Ironically, after Pearl Harbor, they would revile the Japanese in the most extreme terms of all.

During 1937, distaste for Nazism, German and Italian actions in Spain, and Japan's one-sided and nasty assault on China ended "moral" neutrality for the vast majority of Americans. Polls suggested that only 2 percent of Americans were pro-German. It cannot be stressed too strongly that few had any use for the Axis powers, as the far-sighted German ambassador in Washington Hans Dieckhoff warned his government. Moreover, Dieckhoff forecast, the jump from isolation to intervention would not be very great, especially if Britain's survival was threatened.[3] So it proved. The fall of France reduced isolationists to a desperate, even unpopular minority.

The prevailing current of opinion made Roosevelt's attempts to prepare the United States more difficult but did not prevent them. As early as 1933, he diverted some economic recovery expenditures into building up the military, especially the navy. By 1939, he had launched several important programs—stockpiling raw materials, reviving the construction of merchant ships, and expanding civilian pilot training. As historian Basil Rauch pointed out in 1950, these long-range preparations "could not be completed swiftly no matter how large the appropriations. Without them the holding operations after Pearl Harbor and the rapid shift to the offensive in both the Mediterranean and the Pacific within a year could not have been achieved." From 1938 he favored building up the air corps over the army and the navy. The latter established a separate Atlantic squadron (before this there had only one fleet, in the Pacific), and in 1939 this force undertook maneuvers simulating an operation to intercept a German fleet supporting a fascist revolt in Brazil. Avoiding invoking the Neutrality Acts, Roosevelt also made it possible for China to buy arms while preventing their sale to Japan and the European Axis. He expedited orders for weapons, especially planes, from Britain and France to encourage the expansion of America's aircraft industry. Not least important, he promoted the rise of able figures—above all, the brilliant Gen. George C. Marshall—to the top echelons of the army and navy.[4]

Apart from isolationism, relations between the United States and Britain had not been particularly close before World War II. Their military forces had no consultations until 1938. While the British were not hostile to Americans, they were often astonishingly ignorant about the United States (despite—or because of?—the enormous impact of Hollywood). Some of the British elite, notably Neville Chamberlain, regarded Americans as un-reliable blowhards. Churchill, whose mother was an American, was an ex-ception to these generalizations. Americans were even more ignorant of the British, often nursing antiquated notions of what contemporary Britain was like. Even among those who otherwise liked the British, many Ameri-cans had much hostility toward their imperialism, while others, including the president, nursed wholly unreal conceptions of British power before World War II. Relations and attitudes improved, however, in 1939–1940, with Roosevelt and Churchill establishing a personal channel of communi-cation even before the latter became prime minister.

The fall of France led to a revolution in American opinion, of which Roosevelt took quick advantage. Indeed, a near panicky reaction resulted, and he had to calm public opinion. The American people readily accepted his push for an enormous military buildup, including a two-ocean navy, and his policy of "all-out aid short of war" to the remaining Allies. The U.S. Army's strength increased from the absurdly low level of 267,767 men in June 1940 to 1,460,998 a year later.

Most Americans favored aiding Britain even at the risk of war because they believed that if victorious in Europe, Germany would intervene in South America or attack the United States directly. But, while all of Roos-evelt's actions up to December 1941 received majority support, most peo-ple opposed deliberately entering the war. This somewhat schizoid state of mind persisted right up to Pearl Harbor.

In the frantic atmosphere of the French defeat, the Americans' first mil-itary plans were not to intervene in Europe but to move troops into Brazil in case the Nazis attempted to support the overthrow of the Brazilian gov-ernment and to forestall the Nazis or local allies in taking the British and Dutch possessions in the West Indies. Later in 1940 and 1941, much atten-tion focused on planning operations to hinder German attempts to occupy the Atlantic islands and West Africa.

### Short of War

After Dunkirk, overcoming the understandable reluctance of the small U.S. Army to part with much of its modest reserve of equipment and am-munition, Roosevelt shipped much of the stockpile and many of the few available planes to Britain and France. He based planning on the expecta-tion that with American help, they would repel invasion. In addition to the military buildup and aid to Britain, Roosevelt worked to keep the Latin

American countries on the American-Allied side and deter Japan from exploiting the situation. The Pacific Fleet thus stayed at Pearl Harbor, formerly a little-used advance base, instead of returning to its usual home on the West Coast.

The most dramatic step in the president's short of war policy was the "Destroyer Deal" of August 1940, in which he swapped fifty obsolete World War I destroyers for the American acquisition of bases in British territories in the Caribbean, Bermuda, and Newfoundland (not yet part of Canada.) The British, desperate for anything to combat the U-boats, welcomed the deal although the ships were not good ones. As the semi-official historians William Langer and S. Everett Gleason noted, "After the Destroyer Deal, American neutrality was hardly more than a technicality. . . ." Britain's financial resources were becoming exhausted; after his reelection, proclaiming that the United States must become the "arsenal of democracy," Roosevelt developed the Lend-Lease aid program to ensure the continued flow of matériel to the British and remaining Allies. In January 1941 the British and Americans began formal staff conversations to explore the strategy they would follow against Germany, Japan, and Italy. They agreed on a policy of "Germany first." War with Germany would receive first priority in any multifront conflict.[5]

Hitler had not initially worried much about American intervention. He had expected that Britain would make peace, or be beaten, before the Americans could intervene, while German Army intelligence estimated in July 1940 that American armaments production would not increase much before mid-1942. As the summer and fall of 1940 wore on, Hitler became more anxious to head off American intervention. He consequently formed an alliance with Japan and took further moves to establish a "Eurasian bloc," including Spain, Vichy France, and perhaps the Soviets, although he much preferred an early conquest of the USSR, which, he thought, would also deter the Americans. On September 27, 1940, the Germans, Italians, and Japanese signed the Tripartite Pact, a formally defensive alliance, in which the three powers threatened to fight any country—meaning the United States—that entered either the current or a future war against them. It was characteristic of the Axis powers' superficial relations that the authoritative text of the Tripartite Pact was in English. Americans were not impressed. Even isolationists resented Axis threats, so the Tripartite Pact was more of a provocation than a deterrent. Hitler soon suspected that it was a failure as far as its immediate aims were concerned. Although Hitler indicated to General Halder by November 4 that he thought the United

States would stay out of the war until 1942, he evidently did not count on its remaining out of it much longer. Hitler and the German military leaders continued to assume that they would have a year or so after Americans' entry before the latter move had serious effects.

By the end of 1940, the German leaders thought whatever hope remained of keeping the Americans out of the European conflict now lay in defeating the Soviets and in Japanese actions to divert the Americans. From February 1941, the Germans strongly urged Japan to attack Britain, even at the risk of bringing the United States into the war at an early date. Later, in March and April, they implied that Germany would join Japan if it went to war with either the United States or the Soviet Union and not simply if either attacked Japan. To be sure, Hitler did not want war with the United States and, as we shall see, continued to enforce caution upon the reckless German Navy in dealing with American intervention in the Atlantic. But he was willing to take certain risks because he was afraid of going to war with the United States without Japan as an ally. The Nazis fully appreciated the importance of delaying war as long as possible and promoted U.S. domestic opposition to Roosevelt's policies. Using intermediaries and unknown to their leaders, the Nazis subsidized isolationist organizations and publications.[6]

## The Battle against Intervention

The fall of France reduced isolationists to a large, although noisy, minority in the United States. To combat the tide turning against them, isolationists formed what became their main organization, the America First Committee. Ironically, in view of the later slant given isolationism, liberal Republicans formed the group in late 1940, while conservatives started the chief interventionist organizations, the Committee to Defend America by Aiding the Allies and the Century Group. Isolationism gained a more conservative hue as more and more liberals switched to the interventionist side.

The main arguments used from the fall of France to Pearl Harbor were stated in America First's Declaration of Principles:

- The United States must build an impregnable defense for America.
- No foreign power or group of foreign powers can successfully attack a prepared America.
- American democracy can be preserved only by keeping out of the war.
- "Aid short of war" weakens national defense at home and threatens to involve America in war abroad.

The second of these arguments, which the advance of technology most discredited, was the core of the isolationist position. The pseudo-moralistic arguments, popular earlier, were less common but not rare in 1940–1941. Not absent was an edge of ethnic resentment, more acute among Irish Americans than among German Americans, although most generally regarded it with disgust. In May 1941, Roosevelt, usually the most tactful of men, snarled at one isolationist Irish-American congressman, "When will you Irish ever get over hating England?" America Firsters quickly took up the point that since Hitler had been unable to invade Britain, he could not take on the United States. A few, like aviator Charles Lindbergh, generally considered the isolationists' most effective spokesman, argued that even outright American intervention would not enable the Allies to defeat Germany. In testifying against the Lend-Lease bill early in 1941, Lindbergh remarked, "We are strong enough to maintain our own way of life regardless of what the attitude is on the other side. I do not believe that we are strong enough to impose our way of life on Europe and on Asia." The president's policies would lead to "failure in war and conditions in our own country as bad or worse than those we desire to destroy in Germany."

Many isolationists argued that war could not preserve civilization or defeat fascism. Congressional isolationists often indulged in even more unreasonable and less dignified arguments than America First, suggesting that even actions far short of war—such as instituting a military draft—could destroy democracy. Some maintained that joining the war or even implementing the Lend-Lease program would lead to dictatorship; indeed, some said Roosevelt wanted such a government (or already was a dictator). Congressman Clare Hoffman moaned that the Roosevelt administration was forcing a "tyranny as ruthless as that employed by Hitler on Americans." Much abuse of the British as evil imperialists and cries that the United States would be fighting Britain's war were heard in Congress. (These examples by no means exhaust the category of spectacularly silly arguments.) Even as the isolationists' strength waned, attitudes became more extreme on both sides. Some accused the isolationists and especially Lindbergh of being pro-Nazi. Indeed, President Roosevelt genuinely thought that Lindbergh was a Nazi. Such was the bitterness of the debate in 1940–1941 that many repeated the false assertion long afterward.

Attitudes on either side were not particularly affected when the Nazis attacked the Soviet Union, since they had already been settled when the Nazis had been fighting only against the Western powers with the Soviets as silent partners. For the isolationists, the Soviet-German war bolstered their argument for not getting involved. Their points usually were moral ones: The Soviets were as bad as the Nazis—some said they were worse—and that erased any difference between the Allies and the Axis. Many insisted that the Soviets were too evil to help, and some interventionists agreed with that point. The *New York Times*, for example, initially opposed giving the Soviets Lend-Lease aid. While some suggested letting the Nazis and Communists destroy each other, not many expected it would happen. As with most people, including the American and British military leaders, the vast majority of isolationists thought the Nazis would beat the Soviets and probably quickly. So one argument against aiding the Soviets was that the equipment would be wasted or, even worse, that Stalin would make peace and change sides. Given the immediate Axis menace and those general beliefs, a possible future Soviet military and political threat was not a major factor in anyone's thoughts, although isolationists occasionally invoked it to bolster "futilitarian" arguments against American intervention. As the isolationist publicist John T. Flynn put it, "If Germany wins, Russia will go fascist. If Russia wins, Germany will go Communist. There is no chance for us at all. The question now is, are we going to fight to make Europe safe for Communism?"

Bitter as the conflict became, the isolationists were steadily beaten back. They could not even get one of their number nominated as the Republican presidnetial candidate in 1940. Wendell Wilkie was even more outspokenly an interventionist than Roosevelt himself. Congress passed the Lend-Lease Act on March 11, 1941, handing the isolationists a decisive defeat. Isolationist illusions and obstructionism frightened more far-sighted people, but as historian Manfred Jonas commented, "however difficult the struggle [against isolationism] may have seemed, there was, in fact a continuous and relatively rapid retreat from isolationism after the start of the Second World War."[7]

### The Atlantic Conflict

In the spring of 1941, with Lend-Lease safely under way, the Allies hard pressed in the Atlantic and the Mediterranean, the British increasingly anxious for American intervention, and the provocation of a German extension of their declared "combat zone" in the Atlantic, Roosevelt undertook new steps. Late in March, British warships went to American ports for repairs, and Roosevelt ordered the seizure of Axis and Danish ships interned in the United States. On April 10, he incorporated Greenland in the American defense zone and sent American forces to occupy it. Ten Lake class Coast

Guard cutters were transferred to the British. American ships were allowed to enter the Red Sea, and fifty American tankers were assigned to shuttle oil products between the Caribbean and American East Coast ports, where their cargoes were transshipped to British tankers for the transatlantic run. Other cargo ships, of Norwegian and Panamanian registry, were turned over to the British. Some aid to the British went over the narrow line between assistance and involvement in the war. American pilots attached to the RAF to introduce the Catalina flying boat to the British participated in the hunt for the *Bismarck*. After its sinking, U.S. Navy ships helped search for its supply ships. In May, British airmen began training in the United States and Americans helped ferry aircraft to Canada and Britain. During the rest of 1941, the Americans' role in the ferry service grew, and they developed new ferry and transport routes to Britain and Africa.

Roosevelt also extended aid to China. In March, he let American military pilots resign from the service to join Claire Chennault's First American Volunteer Group, which was formed to fight in China. In May, China received Lend-Lease assistance.

The question of when the United States would openly enter the war or at least intervene decisively in the Atlantic battle by escorting convoys remained. On March 24, the president indicated to some of his closest (and most interventionist) associates that he hoped that Germany would make a "blunder," which Secretary of the Interior Harold Ickes interpreted as his hoping for an incident that would justify a declaration of war or at least an outright escort of convoys. Roosevelt mentioned to the British ambassador early in May the possibility of simple "patrolling" in the Atlantic leading to an incident. And it is likely that in the spring of 1941, if not before, he decided that the United States would have to enter the war. He did not take drastic action, however, after an incident in April between the destroyer USS *Niblack* and a U-boat or after the sinking of the American merchant ship *Robin Moor* in the South Atlantic on May 21. He refrained from ordering convoy escort partly because the Atlantic Fleet was unready; several of its major ships were being overhauled. On May 13, he had ordered a large-scale transfer of ships from the Pacific to the Atlantic. Anxiety over public support was also a factor in not ordering the escorts. On May 23, Hitler warned that escorts meant war, albeit through a private interview with the isolationist and former diplomat John Cudahy rather than in a public statement.

Even if Roosevelt could persuade Congress to declare war, he knew it would only be after a bitter fight, and the country might enter the struggle painfully split. And, knowing that Hitler was about to attack the Soviets, Roosevelt may have wished to avoid doing anything that might divert him from that action. An attempt to secure an early declaration of war might have led Hitler to cancel the attack, leaving the USSR a hostile neutral, but waiting ensured that the Soviets would be forced onto the Allied side. If that possibility was a factor in his thinking, his view was well taken, for even Hitler might have found it hard to work up the nerve to go to war with both the United States and the USSR at the same time.

In his reluctance to take the final plunge, Roosevelt differed from his closest advisers. Secretary of War Henry Stimson, Secretary of the Navy Frank Knox, and Secretary Ickes, joined in mid-May by Treasury Secretary Henry Morgenthau—the president's friend and a far more important figure in the administration, and especially in foreign policy matters, than his position would suggest—all favored entering the war. Stimson, Chief of Naval Operations Adm. Harold Stark, and many others felt that only a declaration of war would make it possible to mobilize the economy properly. Weapons deliveries were sluggish, although military production already conflicted with production for civilian purposes. Roosevelt's reluctance to make some hard decisions about organization and priorities exacerbated this situation. The administration should have insisted on severely cutting car production and stopping car model changes to free resources for war production, but it did not. Shortages of aluminum and railroad cars and a failure to push oil pipeline production were particularly serious.

Stimson, other cabinet members, and many later observers believed that the president underestimated the public's readiness to follow his lead in 1940–1941. On May 27, he declared in a radio address an "unlimited national emergency" expounding the strategic issues, the Nazi threat, and what was at stake in the most complete exposition he ever gave before Pearl Harbor. Hitler aimed at world domination, and the United States was already in serious danger; the security of Britain and control of the seas were critical. He warned that the Nazis were sinking ships at more than twice the rate that they could be replaced and admitted that the rearmament program was not going well. He did not call for convoys but said that "all additional measures necessary to deliver the goods [to the Allies] will be taken." His intent was to move the public further toward intervention and economic mobilization and lay the groundwork for the occupation of Iceland, and for conducting future convoys in particular. The public's overwhelmingly favorable response to his speech surprised him.[8]

The excellent reception of the speech emboldened Roosevelt to occupy Iceland. That would place American forces farther east on the North Atlantic convoy route, relieve the strained British escort force (particularly stretched since starting the end-to-end escorts all the way across the Atlantic), release some heavy British ships from the Atlantic so they could replace losses in the Mediterranean or face Japan, and might relieve the British garrison already on the island. With reinforcements reaching the U.S. Atlantic Fleet and negotiations with the Icelanders completed on July 1, American forces landed on Iceland on July 7. The president remained reluctant to authorize clear-cut escort of convoys, other than for American and Icelandic ships going to Iceland, although Stark strongly him urged to do so. He delayed a decision on this point until the famous Atlantic Conference of August 9–12, where Roosevelt, Churchill, and their staffs met aboard warships anchored at Argentia, Newfoundland. There, the two agreed on war aims, which were embodied in the so-called Atlantic Charter—itself a rather pointed comment on American "neutrality"—and policies aimed at deterring Japan. They also exchanged views on many subjects, although not much was definitely resolved.

Roosevelt, however, decided to convoy British ships as far as Iceland. In conversations otherwise not recorded, Roosevelt apparently indicated to Churchill that he would become still more "provocative" and naval incidents would develop that would bring the United States into the war. Some have claimed that this was an effort by Roosevelt, or Churchill, to string along British opinion, for the British people were disappointed with Americans' actions and uneasy about whether the Americans would enter the war. But what happened later suggests that Churchill's account of what Roosevelt said corresponded quite well with the latter's policy. Meanwhile, many British had expected the Atlantic conference to produce the Americans' entry into the war, and Roosevelt for once was disheartened with public reaction to the meeting. Also, the president and others were shaken that an important but extremely unpopular measure to extend the term of service for draftees for another year had passed Congress by only one vote. Evidently many congressmen who favored it estimated that it would pass by a good margin, so they could afford to evade personal responsibility for it by not voting for it.[9]

Hitler reacted to the Americans' moves with a most unaccustomed moderation, although they seriously interfered with the Atlantic campaign. In March 1941, he had pondered a completely different and rather more characteristic policy—that is, starting the war himself with a massive, surprise U-boat attack on the U.S. Atlantic Fleet at its bases. He discarded the idea because his naval staff did not think a workable plan could be produced for the operation, although Admiral Dönitz thought such an attack quite practical. The outcome might have been different had the German Navy, as had the Italians and Japanese, developed frogmen, manned torpedoes, or midget submarines for attacks on harbors, something requiring modest investments with potentially big payoffs—but it did not bother with such ideas until much later.

The naval high command's view did not come from basic caution. Playing the unusual role of the voice of reason, Hitler often had to restrain the navy, whose attitude toward war with the United States was as reckless as that of Hitler, and most other German leaders, toward war with the Soviets. As American Adm. Walter Ansel later wrote, the Germany navy's views were based on "appalling ignorance and wishful thinking." (Göring seems to have been in rare agreement with the navy.) Hitler repeatedly rejected the navy's demands for operations in the Pan-American Neutrality Zone and for attacks on American ships. He ordered that incidents with the United States must be avoided. In June and July Hitler especially cautioned Admiral Raeder and even considered, but rejected, halting U-boat operations completely for a time. He told Raeder on June 21 that he hoped that after he defeated the Soviets, the Americans would be less inclined to enter the war. On July 9, after the U.S. occupation of Iceland and further complaints from the navy, Hitler was far more pessimistic, explaining that he was still "most anxious to postpone the United States entry into the war for another one or two months" and to avoid incidents with the Americans. Even warships in the combat zone were not to be attacked unless they were definitely not American. He alluded only slightly to the possibility of keeping the Americans completely out of the war.

On July 14, Hitler remarked to the Japanese ambassador, "If we can keep the United States out of the war at all, we will be able to do so by destroying Russia, and only if Japan and Germany act simultaneously and unequivocally." On July 25 he told Raeder that while he wished to avoid having the United States declare war during the eastern campaign, he would not punish a U-boat commander who torpedoed an American ship by mistake. Further, after the eastern campaign, he reserved "the right to take severe action against the USA."[10] He was evidently resigned to war with the United States in the near future. He still wished to delay it, but it was only a matter of time and not much, at that.

## Undeclared War

The incidents Roosevelt expected and Hitler dreaded soon led to an unde-clared shooting war with Germany. On September 4, 1941, a British plane warned the American destroyer *Greer*, sailing alone to Iceland, that a U-boat was some miles ahead of it. As the plane and the *Greer* both searched for the submarine, the plane dropped depth charges. Assuming that the destroyer, whose nationality he did not know, had made the attack, *U-652's* commander fired two torpedoes at the *Greer*. They missed. The *Greer* then dropped depth charges, which also missed, and made it safely to Iceland.

Five days after the *Greer* incident, German planes sank the American merchant ship *Steel Seafarer* in the Red Sea. After a slight delay, caused by the death of his mother, and consultation with congressional leaders, Roo-sevelt gave an important speech on September 11. He recounted the *Greer* and *U-652* incident in a not entirely candid manner, omitting some facts known to him and giving the impression that the Germans had deliber-ately attacked what they knew full well to be an American ship. But he stressed the context of the overall struggle at sea. While not specifically mentioning convoys, he clearly stated that the United States would protect all ships in the American neutrality zone and would attack German and Italian forces on sight. Full-blown convoy escorts began with convoy HX 150 on September 16.

This "shoot on sight" order marked the true entry of the United States into World War II. The chief of naval operations and Maj. Gen. Henry H. Arnold, the chief of staff of the U.S. Army Air Force, agreed that for practi-cal purposes, a state of de facto war existed from this time—and they, if anyone, should have known.[11] The German Naval War Staff, in a throat-clearing manner, characterized it as a "locally limited declaration of war." Under the traditional rules governing such matters, the Germans would have been legally justified in responding with a declaration of war. Hit-ler, however, still rejected lifting the restrictions on the U-boats; as late as November 17 the disguised merchant cruisers were specifically warned to avoid incidents with American ships.

Belligerent actions nevertheless continued thick and fast. Americans overwhelmingly supported the president, even after isolationists showed that he had distorted the facts in reporting the *Greer* incident. Although interventionists were unhappy at the public's continued unwillingness to back a declaration of war, some isolationists, notably the influential Republican congressman Everett Dirksen, switched sides. As Wayne Cole, the leading student of the anti-interventionist movement concluded, the remaining isolationists were "beaten and discredited." In despair, some America Firsters favored disbanding the organization. Indeed, if they had not, their problems would have gotten even worse. A government investigation of America First's funding would probably have uncovered the Nazis' financial support for the organization had Pearl Harbor and the dissolution of America First not overtaken the probe.

On October 17, the destroyer USS *Kearney*, sent to reinforce the escort of SC 48, was hit by a torpedo from *U-568*. Some days later, a U-boat sank an American merchant ship off West Africa. On October 30, the naval oiler *Salinas* was damaged by *U-106*. The day after, *U-552* sank the destroyer USS *Reuben James*, escorting HX 156, with the loss of 115 men. The Germans were a bit surprised that Roosevelt did not use these incidents to declare outright war. Roosevelt may still have hoped to limit American participation in war to air and naval action, although the armed forces held no such view. In an important joint estimate on September 25, the latter reported that Germany could not be defeated by the powers now fighting it; that required American entry into the war. Similarly, the British and Dutch could not withstand a Japanese attack without American help. It concluded that the United States must plan for war with both Germany and Japan. The estimate warned that a compromise ("inconclusive") peace would probably give the Germans an opportunity to reorganize continental Europe and replenish their strength. "Even though the British Commonwealth and Russia were completely defeated, there would be important reasons for the United States to continue the war against Germany, in spite of the greatly increased difficulty of attaining victory."

The undeclared war went on as Congress repealed important parts of the Neutrality Acts, the last restrictions on American support of the Allies. On November 6, American ships captured the German blockade-runner *Odenwald* in the South Atlantic, and American forces rounded up German weather-reporting forces in Greenland. The British Eighteenth Infantry Division crossed the Atlantic, embarked in American military transports, and in convoy WS 12X sailed around the cape to the Middle East.[12]

In view of these facts, it is really remarkable that many people still suppose that America's entry into World War II only took place with the Pearl Harbor attack. Events in the Pacific determined, at most, the timing of a *declared* war in the West.

## The Way to Pearl Harbor

Even before they blundered into war with China, which they had not originally planned, Japan's leaders had envisaged a gradual advance toward
the South Seas. Most Japanese military leaders expected eventual war
with the Western powers but did not want one in the near future. In the
1930s, the Japanese had been more than willing for an alliance with Germany against the USSR but not one against the Western powers as well.
Meanwhile, the Nazis were unenthusiastic about Japanese aggression
against China. Paralleling their earlier attitude toward Italy's attack on
Ethiopia, they viewed it as a morally irreproachable but unfortunate diversion of forces better employed against the Western powers and the Soviets.
For their part, the Germans surprised and alienated Japan with the Nazi-
Soviet Nonaggression Pact, which the Japanese regarded as a betrayal.

As Japan bogged down in China, its relations with the Western powers
deteriorated. The United States clearly disapproved of Japanese aggression
but did little to oppose it, merely terminating its trade treaty with Japan
and giving loans to the Chinese government.

When the Germans conquered western Europe, Japanese-German relations improved, and the Japanese moved to exploit the situation. Emboldened, they were now ready for an alliance against the West, and the focus
of their interest switched to Southeast Asia. Japan's leaders were sure that
the Nazis would defeat Britain and continued to expect this into 1942. The
Imperial Japanese Army, which had earlier favored concentrating on defeating China, became convinced in 1940 that a move into Southeast Asia
was a way to end the stalemate. It would encircle the Chinese and cut off
their supplies. The navy had long wanted an advance into Southeast Asia
and had secured preliminary moves toward this possibility even in 1939,
but it had been unenthusiastic about close ties with Germany and generally
more cautious than the army was. The navy now supported alliance with
Germany and occupying Indochina as a base for operations against the rest
of Southeast Asia.

Fortunately for the Western powers, the Japanese, while aggressive,
were slow to make decisions and failed to strike while the Western powers
were most vulnerable. In 1940, the British and Americans might have felt
too weak to oppose the seizure of the French and Dutch colonies, while the
Americans might not have fought even had the Japanese attacked the British as well.

The Japanese brought pressure to bear on the French and Dutch. They
tried to force the Netherlands East Indies into satellite status, but the Dutch

skillfully played for time and spun out negotiations that ended in failure for the Japanese in June 1941. The Vichy French, in a hopeless position, caved, and the Japanese occupied northern Indochina in September 1940. The Americans responded by halting shipments of strategic materials to Japan, especially aviation gasoline and scrap metal. Japan heavily depended on imported raw materials, especially petroleum and bauxite. A complete halt to all oil shipments by the United States, the British, and the Dutch would strangle Japan. In a complete embargo, the Japanese would only be able to obtain fuel by seizing the oil fields of Southeast Asia. Any Japanese move that provoked such an embargo meant a major crisis and probably war.

Renewed efforts at Japanese-American negotiations in the spring of 1941 failed, as well as Japan's attempts to gain control of the Dutch East Indies. The Japanese-American negotiations frightened the Germans, who feared such an arrangement would prevent the Japanese from attacking the British, as the Germans were urging, and pinning down the Americans. In fact, however, the two sides were never close to agreement. The talks were confused by the efforts of pro-Japanese "fixers" and the Japanese ambassador in Washington, who neither fully reported the statements of Secretary of State Cordell Hull to his government nor conveyed Tokyo's position properly to the Americans. The Americans backed China more strongly. As noted earlier, they provided Lend-Lease aid and helped with the formation of the American Volunteer Group, better known as the Flying Tigers (which did not actually fight until after Pearl Harbor). The Americans had a seeming advantage in that they could read the Japanese diplomatic cipher, but it proved less helpful than might be supposed.

Meanwhile, the Japanese secured their rear for a move against the Western powers by concluding a neutrality pact with the Soviets in April 1941. In June, the Japanese military agreed on occupying southern Indochina, which would serve as a base for attacking Malaya and the Dutch East Indies. They calculated that they could take Indochina and Thailand, already under strong Japanese influence, without going to war or incurring a too drastic American reaction. It was the biggest step south that all involved deemed safe. The army thought that an attack on the British and Dutch colonies need not mean war with the United States, but the navy leaders, with few exceptions, disagreed. They were sure that the Americans would fight if Japan attacked the British and Dutch. At the navy's insistence, trying to tackle the Western powers separately was rejected.

For a time, it was uncertain whether Japan would make the move south. After the Germans attacked the Soviets, some Japanese leaders favored joining them. Many army leaders wanted to use the opportunity to finish off a traditional enemy, as did Foreign Minister Yosuke Matsuoka, who had signed the Japanese-Soviet Neutrality Pact only three months earlier. But in the last resort, grabbing weakly defended Western colonies was more appealing than a showdown with the Soviets, and the raw materials the Japanese wanted were in the south, not the north. Nor did the Japanese find close cooperation with the Nazis, who had been repeatedly dishonest in their dealings with Japan, attractive. Some Japanese leaders suspected that a common border with the Nazis would not be a good idea. On July 2, 1941, the Japanese government decided to occupy southern Indochina and reinforce their forces in Manchuria in case a German victory presented a favorable opportunity to finish off the Soviets.

Having miscalculated the Americans' reaction, the Japanese takeover of southern Indochina began the final crisis. For more than a year, the Roosevelt administration had bitterly argued over whether to stop all oil shipments to Japan. Stimson, Knox, Morgenthau, and Ickes had long favored this, believing that an all-out embargo would cause Japan to reverse course. On the other hand, the secretary of state, the ambassador in Tokyo, most State Department officials, and the chiefs of staff of the armed forces opposed it as too dangerous. The president, despite his personal inclinations toward a hard line, came down on the side of caution until the occupation of southern Indochina; then many favored a complete embargo. Only the navy continued to oppose it, but it was overruled.

The Americans, British, and Dutch froze Japanese assets and ended all oil shipments. The general conviction was that the Japanese would back down, partly because the Allies were far too confident that they would defeat the Japanese easily if they did fight. Although for many years American military planners had assumed that in the event of a war most if not all of the Philippines would be lost quickly, the Americans now hoped that the creation of a Philippine Army and, still more, assembling a strong air force in the islands would allow an all-out defense of the Philippines and even an early air counterattack on Japan itself. Churchill and the British leaders were even more optimistic about avoiding war than Roosevelt, who rather doubted that negotiations would succeed. The British favored taking a harder line, although they had more to lose.

The embargo, which most Japanese leaders had not expected, did force them to reconsider. Many civilian leaders were ready for a change in course, and even the military was ready to retreat a little in Indochina, but Japan would not give up its conquests in China. On September 6, the military forced through a decision to fight if no diplomatic settlement was reached by the end of October. The nominally civilian government of Prince Fumimaro Konoye fell, and as few at the very top were truly eager for war, the new prime minister, Gen. Hideki Tojo, extended the negotiations for another month. Despite their belated caution, however, the military leaders were fundamentally confident, believing that they could take Southeast Asia with acceptable losses in six months. They still thought Germany would defeat the British and Soviets, and the United States, a decadent democracy faced with serious threats elsewhere, would not endure the heavy losses required to defeat Japan.

In the final talks with the United States, the Americans had rejected a summit conference with Konoye unless a preliminary agreement was reached. China was clearly the main issue. The Japanese were reluctantly willing to pull back in Indochina, although not evacuate it completely, and effectively drop their alliance with Germany. In return, they demanded an end to American aid to China and would not back down there. The Americans, having finally put on the pressure, would not abandon China.

Both sides considered attempts at a modus vivendi, or a temporary stopgap agreement, to gain time. But the next Japanese proposal, presented on November 20, seemed to involve the United States abandoning China and stopping the reinforcement of the southwest Pacific. The Japanese offered to leave southern Indochina right away, but they insisted on staying in the north until the war in China ended. In late November, the Americans decided not to present their modus vivendi. They had never had much confidence that it would be accepted, intercepted Japanese messages suggested the offer would be futile, and the British and Chinese strongly objected to it.

Rejecting a summit conference and failing to present the modus vivendi may have been mistakes. The Americans would not have resolved the issue of China, but they might have delayed war and won time for Allied military preparations. They might even have averted war, since events would soon have shown the Japanese that Germany was much weaker than they supposed. But the Japanese were basically unwilling to give up their new empire, as long as they thought they had a chance to win. After late November, war was a matter of time, and both sides, as well as the Germans, knew it. The Americans expected a Japanese attack, probably without warning, on Southeast Asia. Contrary to the later myth that the war came as a "bolt from the blue," the imminence of war with Japan was well known, as most newspapers from New York to Honolulu warned their readers.[13]

## Open War

The Japanese-American negotiations made the German leaders nervous. The shoot on sight order and subsequent developments convinced them that open war with the United States was near. They felt having Japan as an active ally was vital to prevent the Americans and British solely concentrating on Europe. Hitler evidently now thought that any slight delay in preventing the Americans' open entry into the European war was not worth alienating Japan and risking its staying out of the war or feeling free to make an early peace with the Western powers. Hence, on November 21, Foreign Minister Ribbentrop told the Japanese that Berlin considered it self-evident that in the event of war with the United States, neither Germany nor Japan should sign a separate peace. On November 28, Ribbentrop also indicated to the Japanese ambassador that Germany would join Japan immediately if it went to war with the United States. This accord went beyond the obligations assumed under the Tripartite Pact. The Japanese were receptive and wanted a written agreement to this effect. Hitler evidently decided, not later than December 4, that he would not only agree to it in writing but also would take the initiative in declaring war on the United States.

On that day, a new tripartite agreement was drafted committing Germany, Italy, and Japan to join in a war with the United States if any of those powers found itself at war with the United States and not make a separate peace. It was not yet signed when Japan attacked the Western powers on December 7.

Hitler and others at Wehrmacht headquarters were pleased and relieved by the Pearl Harbor attack. Hitler decided to include a declaration of war on the United States as part of a long-planned speech to the Reichstag. On the night of December 8–9, he ordered U-boats immediately to attack American ships, before formally declaring war. He thought Germany should declare war before the Americans did to maintain good relations with Japan and avoid any impression that Germany feared the United States.

Although Hitler's explanations of his actions are always suspect, some remarks he made on May 17, 1942, may cast some light on his thinking in late 1941. Speaking to his intimates, he said,

The Japanese alliance has been of exceptional value to us, if only because of the date chosen by Japan for her entry into the war. It was, in effect, at the moment when the surprises of the Russian winter were pressing most heavily on the morale of our people, and when everybody in Germany was oppressed by the certainty that, sooner or later, the United States would come into the conflict. Japanese intervention, therefore, was from our point of view, most opportune.[14]

Hitler did not act out of reckless overconfidence (though he remained overconfident) but rather, as Shakespeare writes, in the spirit that "it is better to leap in ourselves than tarry until they push us."

His actions were not as irrational as often alleged, but they did make President Roosevelt's life simpler. Despite the advice of Secretaries Hull and Stimson, FDR did not mention Germany specifically in his "Day of Infamy" speech on December 8, calling for Congress to declare that a state of war already existed with Japan. Stimson urged declaring war on Germany as well. The president probably estimated that it was best to concentrate on the most immediate and hardly controversial issue of Japan and not complicate it by bringing in the problem of Germany. Indeed, the reading of intercepted Japanese messages strongly suggested that he could sit back and let Hitler take the initiative.

Meanwhile, Roosevelt did prepare the way for any necessary action. In his Fireside Chat radio address of December 9, he made clear to his listeners that he not only regarded Germany, as well as Japan, as being guilty of the Pearl Harbor attack and also that he would not divert current U.S. forces from the Atlantic. Further action on his part was not needed. On December 11, Hitler declared war.

Churchill's reaction to this news was, "So we had won after all. . . . Hitler's fate was sealed. Mussolini's fate was sealed. As for the Japanese, they would be ground to powder. All the rest was the merely the proper application of overwhelming force."[15]

### After America's Entry

One week after Pearl Harbor, the OKW Operations Staff submitted its appraisal of the consequences of America's entry into the war. It was cautiously optimistic, despite the power of the coalition now arrayed against the Axis and its recognition that Germany would probably lose the initiative in the foreseeable future. Pondering the choices facing the Western powers—allotting priority to Europe or to the Pacific, or simply assuming the strategic defensive everywhere until their strength had been built up—the OKW staff prudently assumed that the Allies would give priority to Europe, but the Japanese would tie down considerable Allied resources. Further, the Allies could not launch a decisive offensive in the west in 1942. And whatever they did, the Western powers could not defeat Japan nor could the United States wage offensives in both the Atlantic and Pacific for the foreseeable future.

It became apparent that even as Hitler ushered America's entry into World War II, the Germans were in a vastly worse situation than they had supposed in the east. The prime points of danger for Germany would be the Atlantic coast of Africa and its offshore islands, reinforcement of the Middle East and/or stiffening of the Soviets in the Caucasus, and Norway. Meanwhile, in 1942, Germany could still secure a decision in the east by capturing Murmansk and Archangel in the north, by cutting off the Soviets from Western aid via the north Russian convoys, and above all, by seizing the Caucasus oil fields. Germany should advance to the Suez Canal and the Persian Gulf, but the main attack would be through the Caucasus.

With these operations completed, Germany would be set for the strategic defensive. A defensive front could be formed against the Western powers by securing North Africa; bringing Spain, Portugal, Vichy France, and Sweden into the war on the Axis side; and eliminating Gibraltar. How the Allies would actually be beaten was left unexplained. The OKW's overview vaguely referred to the effect of destroying both the British position in the Middle East and Anglo-American shipping.

Despite some realistic premises, the OKW wrongly assumed that the Germans could reach their objectives in the Soviet Union and the Mediterranean before the Americans fully mobilized. In addition to underestimating the Soviets once again, it also miscalculated the American buildup, which took place faster than the Germans expected. The OKW staff did not explain how the diplomatic miracle of dragging several unwilling and mutually hostile countries into the war could be performed. The Germans also overestimated Japan's power in relation to the Americans, who ended up holding the Japanese and taking the offensive much faster than the Germans expected.

The view of the Army General Staff was markedly less optimistic, but focused on the crisis in Russia, it had little original thinking to offer. The Naval War Staff belatedly (in late February 1942) advanced a scheme for true coalition warfare, with a German thrust into the Middle East to link up with a Japanese drive west. Hitler rejected this plan as unrealistic "for the time being" and beyond Germany's resources, although he nursed hopes that such a strategy would be possible eventually. To plan for it, before the Caucasus oil fields had been taken, was premature; that was the precondition for any global strategy.

Hitler still had high expectations of victory. He hoped that once the Soviets were beaten and India was seriously threatened, the British would surrender. (He seemed surprised and disappointed when they did not turn against Churchill's government after Singapore fell in February 1942.) He may still have hoped that the Japanese would attack the Soviets once they took Southeast Asia, and he may have preferred that option to other possible strategies involving Japan. For Hitler, Germany had to concentrate on Russia, although a secondary effort might be possible in Egypt. Going against the OKW's advocacy of launching an attack in the Arctic, which had not proved successful in 1941, Hitler preferred to take Leningrad, for it would have the same effect as taking Murmansk and Archangel. He was also anxious about an early attack on Norway. Defeating the Soviets and taking the Caucasus, however, was his prime concern. Other Germans, too, recognized that capturing the Caucasus was "the last chance."[16]

Some Germans already suspected the war was lost. Notably one of the most intelligent Nazis, Dr. Fritz Todt had already told Hitler, on November 29, that the war could no longer be won militarily. Others, such as the pessimistic officers on Admiral Dönitz's staff, suspected that the war was not going well. But while many Germans had feared war with the United States and were shocked at the crisis on the eastern front, the Nazis handled the propaganda problems skillfully and capitalized on Japan's early victories. Encouraged by renewed success on the eastern front, in North Africa, and in the Atlantic and by the Japanese advances, German morale rebounded in 1942 and remained surprisingly high for much of that year.[17]

## THE GERMAN WAR EFFORT

The shock of defeat in the east was probably the main reason for several belated improvements in the German war effort that did much to prolong the war. During 1941, Dr. Todt, with Hitler's backing, had rationalized the war economy, reducing the excessive number of types of equipment being made and instituting proper controls of scarce resources that eliminated much of the waste and low return on investment that had marked the production effort up to then. In December, Hitler issued a decree on "Simplification and Increased Efficiency in Armaments Production."

After Todt's death in a plane crash on February 8, 1942, Albert Speer replaced him. Hitler's selection of his architect to supervise the armament effort might have seemed an odd choice, but it was a brilliant move that greatly prolonged the life of the Nazi regime. Speer's originality and achievements may have been exaggerated, but he carried on Todt's work with even greater success. Contrary to later myth, they did not increase the level of mobilization of the German economy, which was already high, but made it run far more efficiently. Speer also benefited from the completion of important projects that had taken a long time to pay off, notably in synthetic oil and aluminum production. Only the jump in synthetic oil production and tighter controls on civilian use of petroleum products averted a crisis in fuel consumption.

The war economy also undertook a major switch in priorities. In July 1941, Hitler, expecting early victory over the Soviets, had changed production priorities from the army to the Luftwaffe and the navy. In January 1942, he reversed priorities again and in time to reequip, although not entirely, the army in the east. Yet the rationalization effort also greatly increased aircraft production. Although Speer did not control aircraft production until 1944, he cooperated successfully with Field Marshal Milch, whose domination of the Luftwaffe was less hampered after the suicide of his rival Ernst Udet in November 1941 and Göring's increasing withdrawal from active work. Further, a major reorganization and increased effort during the winter of 1941–1942 overcame the near collapse of the railroad system in the east.[18]

German shipping (of surprising importance to the economy) was also in bad shape. Nearly a quarter of the German merchant marine had been lost since the start of the war (largely to air-laid British mines) with little replacement, and the rest was used in a wasteful manner. In May 1942, Karl Kaufmann, the able gauleiter of Hamburg, assumed the task of overcoming the shipping crisis. He started a major shipbuilding program, largely in the occupied countries, and began using ships more efficiently, perhaps just in time. Had the Allies realized the critical state of German shipping, a modest increase in their efforts directed against it might have paid off handsomely. Even the inaccurate night-bombing force available in 1942 might have been more effectively directed against German ports and naval bases along with those few industrial targets that could then be found and attacked at night. As it was, even in 1942, the attacks of the RAF's Bomber and Coastal Commands tied down German forces in an increasing defensive effort.[19]

## The Allies' War Effort

Japan's entry into the war, a surge in German war production, and the re-organization of Germany's transportation system proved no compensation for American intervention. At the end of 1941, however, the U.S. armed forces were still relatively weak, weaker than their numbers would have suggested, and the economy had not yet fully converted to war production. The United States had a powerful navy, although early experience against the Germans and Japanese showed that its training and doctrine—especially for night battles and submarine and antisubmarine operations—required more work. Further, important items of equipment—notably its carrier fighters and torpedo bombers and, above all, its torpedoes—were inadequate.

The army and the army air force were still in the early phases of expansion. Neither was as remotely powerful as their British or German counterparts were. The army had just thirty infantry, five armored, and two cavalry divisions, but their men were in mostly recently activated units and still in the early stages of training. The USAAF nominally had fourteen heavy bomber groups, nine medium bomber groups, five light bomber groups, twenty-five fighter groups, eleven observation groups, and six transport groups; but many were only cadres and few had suitable aircraft. General Arnold estimated that of his 3,000 aircraft, only 1,157 were combat worthy. Of these planes, only 159 were heavy bombers. The U.S. armed forces, except in the Pacific, were in no position to exert decisive influence on a world war. Even critical points in the Western Hemisphere such as the Panama Canal were weakly defended. Meanwhile, the armed forces were stretched hastily to reinforce the West Coast and Hawaii and build up a line of defense for the island chain stretching from Hawaii to Australia, where, on December 17, the Americans decided to build a major base.[20]

The course for the war as a whole was set at the first major Anglo-American conference after Pearl Harbor, held in Washington in December and January. En route to the meeting, Churchill outlined his ideas for how to win the war, and, with some qualifications, they proved surprisingly close to the course followed by the Allies. In Washington, the British were relieved to learn that despite the Pacific emergency, the Americans were determined to uphold their prior agreements making Germany the prime enemy and that supplies to Britain would not be disturbed. The conference worked out further supply arrangements and set up machinery for Anglo-American military coordination by creating the Combined Chiefs of Staff. A British mission, acting as deputies for the British Chiefs of Staff

Committee, sitting with the American Joint Chiefs of Staff would coordinate the two countries' military efforts. As far as issues of grand strategy were concerned, the American leaders were so preoccupied with the Pacific that they generally let the British take the lead. The Americans did secure the formation of the short-lived and ineffective American-British-Dutch-Australian (ABDA) Command to supervise the defense of Southeast Asia.

The British feared possible German moves into Spain and North Africa and a major threat to the Middle East from the north should the Soviets be defeated in 1942 (although Churchill personally discounted this danger). Still underestimating Japan, the British believed, at least in the early stages of the campaign, that they could hold Burma, Singapore, Sumatra, and Java.

The Allies' top priorities were to maintain the security of Britain, the American West Coast, and vital sea routes; to support the Soviets and ensure that they could hold on to Moscow, Leningrad, and the Caucasus; and hold Australia, New Zealand, and India. If the immediate dangers could be overcome, and a "ring" closed around Germany, the Allies looked forward to major landings in Europe in 1943. They did not envision one concentrated blow but a series of landings, primarily by armored forces, on both the Mediterranean and western coasts. American military leaders did not find these ideas convincing, but they did not offer an alternative of their own. The U.S. Navy estimated at that point that the available shipping could support sending only forty-five American divisions to Europe through 1943.

For 1942, the British proposed, the Americans should send four divisions to Britain, mostly to Northern Ireland, and a strategic air force to join the RAF in the bombing of Germany. If possible, the western Allies also should land a force of several divisions in French northwest Africa perhaps as early as March. That operation, however, was premised on an Allied success in Libya and an invitation of some sort from the French. Although many American officers did not particularly like it, Roosevelt welcomed this idea, but the date on which the operation could be mounted was steadily postponed. Early in 1942, the British suffered a serious defeat in Libya, and it became apparent that neither a French invitation nor sufficient shipping for the operation would be available.[21]

But it would be revived.

# 7

## The Battle of the Atlantic II

*December 1941–May 1943*

The British could reasonably have supposed that with the United States fully in the war, the situation in the Atlantic would improve, but the Americans were far less ready for war than expected. So, as disastrous as war with the United States proved in the long run, it actually simplified the German Navy's immediate problems.

As noted earlier, Hitler ordered attacks on American ships even before declaring war on the United States, but the concentration of U-boats in the south and the Arctic left the Germans in a poor position to strike along the American coast. Because Hitler became exceptionally nervous about a British attack on Norway, he ordered more U-boats north in early 1942. In December 1941, Dönitz wanted all possible U-boats—twelve—to go to the American Eastern Seaboard at once. The Naval Staff let him send just five Type IXs. At this point the navy believed that the Type VII U-boats' range was so short that they could not operate south of Nova Scotia.

The force spread out between the Gulf of St. Lawrence and Cape Hatteras, North Carolina. In mid-January, the U-boats would strike only when all were in position (unless they could attack ships of more than 10,000 tons) to attempt to take advantage of whatever surprise was still possible. They assumed that the attack on the American East Coast would be a temporary diversion from the main battle in the mid-Atlantic and that the Americans would soon organize convoys, making long patrols to their coastal waters unprofitable. This was not the case.

A month had passed since Pearl Harbor, but the Americans took longer to react than expected. As John Waters wrote, had the Germans been fully aware of the Pearl Harbor attack in advance and pre-positioned twenty to thirty U-boats, including minelayers, off the Eastern Seaboard, they would probably have shut down traffic there completely.[1] As it was, the Allies suffered a major disaster. Apart from the fact that ships carrying supplies to Britain usually departed U.S. East Coast ports before joining transatlantic convoys, the American economy depended far more on coastal shipping than was generally realized. No less than 260 of the United States' 350 large tankers hauled oil from Texas to the East Coast. Other goods also traveled by sea rather than overburden the railroads, which were in bad shape after decades of bad regulation and the Depression.

The astonished Germans found the American coastline well lit, with shipping proceeding in an unorganized, normal peacetime fashion, silhouetted by the lights of towns. They gained useful information from listening to the chatter of the ships' radios. Cape Hatteras proved an especially good hunting ground. In two weeks after the first attack on January 12, the U-boats sank thirteen ships of 95,000 tons, nearly three-quarters of them tankers. To their astonishment, the massacre went on and on, eliciting only a slight reaction. Dönitz soon reinforced the U-boats off the East Coast and, in mid-February, sent some to the Caribbean. The Type VII boats began pushing farther southwest. By using the most efficient method of cruising and carefully conserving supplies, they could reach the Eastern Seaboard. But the Germans rarely had more than a dozen U-boats there at any one time. Wolf pack tactics were temporarily discarded. The U-boats operated individually, usually on the surface at night, right offshore. American defenses were so poor that they attacked by day as well, sometimes on the surface, and found it possible to use their deck guns, which were normally of little value in World War II.

The Germans did not encounter any convoys, and the American forces were almost totally ineffective. The Americans' only defensive preparations against the U-boats were minefields in the approaches to New York, Boston, and the Chesapeake Bay, and booms and nets to keep submarines from actually entering New York and some other harbors. Adm. Adolphus Andrews's Eastern Sea Frontier started the campaign with only seven Coast Guard cutters; three unreliable Ford Eagle boats (poorly built World War I–era antisubmarine patrol craft); four wooden subchasers also left over from the earlier war; two gunboats; and four converted yachts.

The new chief of naval operations, Adm. Ernest King, poorly supported Andrews's efforts. Able enough in directing the Pacific War, King's disinterest in the Atlantic struggle and Anglophobia made him a dubious asset in the war against Germany. (General Eisenhower once speculated in the privacy of his journal that if somebody shot King, it would help win the war.) King only belatedly let Andrews shift the regular shipping lanes sixty miles out to sea to make it harder for the enemy to find targets, and King rejected a blackout. Meanwhile, the U.S. Navy showed little interest in British and Canadian experience or the ciphers and procedures the latter had prepared for the Americans' use. King disallowed an early start of coastal convoys, wrongly believing that poorly escorted convoys were worse than none. Instead of shepherding shipping, Andrews sent the few available destroyers that he occasionally borrowed from other duties out on offensive patrols to hunt U-boats. This tactic proved as useless as it always had against submarines and that led to *U-578* sinking the destroyer *Jacob Jones* on February 28. The navy and U.S. Army Air Force (USAAF) did not collaborate well in providing air cover, and the few aircrews available were poorly trained for work over the sea. (Civilian fliers, acting on their own, had organized the Civil Air Patrol before Pearl Harbor.) King also failed to act on proposals to mobilize small civilian craft in a Coastal Picket Patrol until June 17, after the crisis was largely past. The small craft would have seriously interfered with German operations near the shore. Except around Cape Hatteras, East Coast waters were so shallow that the Germans would not have dared attack near the coast had the defenses not been so incredibly weak. Even less forgivably, the navy broadcast many claims of U-boat kills it knew were false.

Effort and lives were wasted on Q-ships, or converted freighters and trawlers armed with hidden guns to act as U-boat traps. Q-ships had enjoyed some success in World War I. British attempts to revive the idea in the second war had already failed, however; the Germans were too alert for it to work again. The Q-ship *Atik* was lost with all 161 men aboard. The president had pushed using the Q-ships, but King did not resist the idea. King seems to have been waiting for the arrival of new 110-foot subchasers and 173-foot patrol craft, but the program to build them received priority only in April 1942.

Meanwhile, the shipping losses had caused an adverse public reaction and alarm within the armed forces. The army grew increasingly concerned and angry, and the AAF launched a rival antisubmarine effort that lasted into 1943. The British were furious at losing precious ships in waters that should have been relatively safe. They had to send some of their own escorts to the Caribbean to guard tanker convoys, and King reluctantly accepted the loan of twenty-four British antisubmarine trawlers and later a

Coastal Command squadron. The trawlers were mostly slow coal burners that required high-grade coal, were in poor condition, and were unsuited for the Atlantic crossing—one was lost en route to the United States—but as they became operational in March 1942, they proved welcome. By April, the strength of the Eastern Sea Frontier had grown to eighty-four army and eighty-six navy planes, sixty-five Coast Guard cutters, three 173-foot patrol craft, a dozen Eagle boats and converted yachts, and fourteen British trawlers. This larger fleet and the greater caution of merchant ship captains complicated the U-boats' work. On April 1, the Americans finally started a semi-convoy system, the so-called Bucket Brigades, along the coast. During the day, locally based escort craft herded gaggles of ships close inshore, and the ships halted for the night in protected anchorages—regular harbors or specially mined and protected sites.

Losses, especially of tankers, however, remained so horrendous that the oil industry warned that the United States would run out of tankers by the end of 1942. Finally the disaster became so obvious that on April 16, all tankers were ordered to stay in port until further notice, although a few had special permission to move via Bucket Brigade. Frantic efforts were made to reduce dependence on oil moved by sea. Industries converted many oil-burning plants to coal or natural gas, and disused railroad tank cars and barges were rehabilitated.

By the end of April, ships passed Cape Hatteras only by day and at varying distances from the coast. The Germans perceived that U.S. defenses were at last hardening. They concluded that it was no longer safe to attack near the coast, except on dark nights. On April 14 the destroyer USS *Roper* sank *U-85*, the first U-boat destroyed by American forces off the East Coast.

By May, the Germans had eighteen U-boats operating from Newfoundland to Florida and seven more in or near the Caribbean, but in mid-May a true convoy system finally went into effect. That made patrolling the Eastern Seaboard unprofitable. Dönitz shifted the effort to the Gulf of Mexico and the Caribbean, where the opposition remained weak for three more months. The Germans were assisted by the introduction of the first Type XIV supply U-boats—known as the milch cows or U-tankers, they could refuel other U-boats—although only three were available during the American campaign. Italian submarines, which proved surprisingly effective, also joined the Germans. Eventually, however, convoys started in southern waters too, ending the campaign.

In the first seven months of 1942, the U-boats had sunk 609 ships of 3.1 million tons, including 143 tankers, mostly in the Americas. The Allies had lost another 45 tankers to other causes. (By comparison, at the start of the Pacific War, the Japanese merchant marine had 94 tankers and 1,609 passenger and dry cargo ships.) The peak month of June saw the U-boats sink 136 ships of 637,000 tons. Some sources give a slightly higher total of 144 ships of 700,000 tons, which, if correct, made June 1942 one of the few months of the war in which Dönitz attained his self-set target for destroying the Allied merchant marine. All Axis submarines in the months of January through July 1942 had sunk 757 merchant ships and auxiliary naval vessels of 3,773,469 gross registered tons. The Allies had lost 1,120 ships of 4.8 million tons to all causes. Most of these losses were suffered in American waters and, even given the limits of Allied resources, quite unnecessary.[2]

## Allied Shipbuilding

These fantastic losses were only bearable because of the growing success of the American and Canadian shipbuilding efforts, without which the Allies could not have sustained Britain, much less won the war. In 1941, the United States and Canada had begun mass-producing standardized freighters, often in entirely new shipyards using new workers. The American industrialist Henry Kaiser became especially effective and prominent at this effort. He was so successful that, against the navy's opposition, he persuaded President Roosevelt to let him build escort carriers in the same way with good results.

Most new cargo ships were based on an older British design, the steam-powered Sunderland tramp steamer, which the British had standardized as the Empire Liberty type. The British had had some built as the Ocean class in American and Canadian yards in 1940. The U.S. Maritime Commission altered this design to make it easier both to mass-produce and for inexperienced crews to operate by modifying its engines, rudder, and crew accommodations and specifying all-welded construction, then a novelty. The result was the EC-2 Liberty ship of 7,176 gross registered tons. Usually named for famous Americans, Liberty ships were ugly but effective. They were powered by old-fashioned reciprocating steam engines when turbines and diesels were needed elsewhere. The first of 2,710 Liberty ships, the SS *Patrick Henry*, was launched on September 27, 1941. Kaiser's organization built Liberty ships in fantastically short times, and by 1944 it completed Liberties in an average of forty-two days each. In that year, the industry also began to build faster and slightly bigger Victory ships.

During 1942, the American ship construction effort took off, building 646 freighters (597 Liberties) plus 62 tankers and 33 miscellaneous types. In

December 1942 alone, American industry produced as many ships as it had in the entire preceding year. In the first six months of 1943, the Americans built 711 ships of 5.7 million tons.

A concurrent Canadian shipbuilding drive was in some ways even more remarkable given the lack of industrial base The Canadians concentrated on their own variant of the Ocean type, the Fort class. Unlike Liberties, they were originally coal burners, although a later version was oil fueled. The first of these ships, *Fort Ville Marie*, was launched on October 10, 1941, and in all, the Canadians built some 300 vessels.

The shipbuilding effort made it possible for the Allies to replace a good portion of their losses, even in the worst period of the war. From January to August 1942, for instance, 357 new ships of 2,634,000 tons came into existence.[3]

## German Doubts

As noted earlier, by the end of 1941, some Germans, including members of Dönitz's staff, doubted the viability of the U-boat campaign in its present form. The relatively disappointing development of the Atlantic campaign since mid-1941, culminating in the disaster of convoy HG 76, suggested that the Allies already had the counter to the U-boat, and it was only a matter of time until they used it properly. The success in the Americas, never expected to be more than a temporary diversion, lasted longer than they had dared to hope. Dönitz, to be sure, remained optimistic and still thought that enough of the existing U-boat types could compete with the Allied shipbuilding program. That effort impressed even the Germans, although they underestimated its scope.

As he explained to Hitler on May 14, Dönitz thought that sinking 700,000 tons of shipping a month would offset Allied new construction, which he believed would reach 8.1 million tons in 1942 and 10.3 million tons in 1943. (It was a slight overestimate for 1942 but a gross underestimate of the 14.39 million tons that would be built in 1943.) But Dönitz overestimated Allied losses by a great margin. Hitler backed his call for concentrating all shipyard resources on U-boats rather than the more balanced program Admiral Raeder wanted.

The Naval War Staff continued to doubt that Dönitz's integral tonnage strategy would work, if the rate of sinking (then high) remained the same and the Allied shipbuilding plans succeeded. The staff pointed out that success as had been attained so far in 1942 came from surprise attacks in weakly defended areas, and the rate of success against convoys was expected to fall. It would be necessary to sink not 700,000 tons but 1.3 million tons a month; however, that target was not in prospect. The staff suggested that the U-boats' aim should be not on destroying tonnage but eliminating cargoes and sinking ships headed to Britain, both immediately around Britain and in the South Atlantic, although it did not fully explain how to accomplish this mission. Cmdr. Kurt Assmann of the Naval Operations Department even suggested that they could not expect victory in the U-boat war, but this conclusion was cut from the Naval War Staff's final assessment, which it submitted on October 20.[4]

## New Submarines

Even Dönitz must have had private doubts about winning with the conventional U-boats. He and others looked for a technical breakthrough. An engineer working in the German Naval High Command, Adolph Schneeweisse, suggested building "underwater assault boats" to attack convoys. He envisioned that Type XB and Type XI U-boats would carry these superfast midget submarines, capable of speeds of 30 knots and armed with two or three torpedoes, to the battle area. But even had the midgets been developed in time to affect the outcome of the war, Germany did not have enough big submarines to serve as "mother ships" for a major campaign. Although these subs might have posed a difficult problem for the Allies, Dönitz had to look for a different solution.

Since the early 1930s the German Navy had backed work on closed-cycle propulsion systems that required no external air supply and would let submarines with radical new hull forms run faster while submerged than on the surface and with speeds comparable to those of surface ships. Such systems used diesel or turbine engines supplied either with oxygen in high-pressure bottles or in liquid form or with a fuel carrying its own, or not needing, an oxidizer. Dönitz was especially fascinated by the work of Dr. Hellmuth Walter, who developed a high-speed submarine powered by the decomposition of highly concentrated hydrogen peroxide. The Walter U-boats would use three different modes of propulsion: diesels on the surface, battery power for most submerged operations, and the Walter turbine to provide bursts of very high speed when attacking convoys. They could outrun most escorts. On June 24, 1942, Dönitz resolved to build a fleet of them; Hitler approved his plans on September 28. But the Walter boats were not a good choice. Apart from the problem that they would not appear in force until 1946, hydrogen peroxide, which could probably not be made in sufficient quantity, was very costly, hard to handle, and dangerous.

Postwar British attempts to develop submarines of this sort strongly suggest that the Walter boats were a mistake. Dönitz would have been better advised to concentrate on a less radical closed-cycle system such as diesel engines fed with bottled or liquid oxygen, which conceivably might have been ready in time for the war. A system of this type, when tested, provided better range than the Walter boat.

As the situation in the Atlantic became more desperate, it became apparent that the Germans could not wait for the Walter boats. In March 1943, one of Walter's engineers, Heinrich Heep, suggested to the director of naval construction that a modified version of the hull designed for the large Type XVIII Walter boat could carry an improved diesel-electric propulsion system that used new diesels, bigger electric motors, and a battery capacity triple that of a conventional submarine. Although not promising as much performance as hydrogen peroxide boats, it would be much faster than current U-boats when submerged. It at least could stay with slow convoys, escape from attacks, and run faster than some of the slower escorts, such as corvettes. It could also be built much sooner than the Walter boats.

Walter himself, at about the same time, suggested using a device the Germans had found years earlier on captured Dutch submarines, the *schnorkel* (snorkel), which was basically a breathing tube that enabled a submarine at periscope depth to run, albeit slowly and uncomfortably, on diesel power. The Germans incorporated the snorkel in their new designs and added them to conventional U-boats in 1944. The design of the large Type XXI "electro-boat," as the Germans called it, was finished by June 1943; Dönitz approved the idea, and while work continued on Walter boats, they had lower priority. The new project was such an obviously better alternative that Dönitz, Speer, and others wondered why they had not initiated it a year or more earlier. Being a large craft of about twice the size of the Type VII, however, its manufacture involved a huge effort that seriously taxed German industry. The Germans also planned a much smaller electro-boat, the Type XXIII, for short-range operations in the North Sea and the Mediterranean. Considering its limited armament—only two torpedoes, or as many as the Seehund (Seal) midget submarine carried—it was a poor investment.

In July 1943, shortly after approving the Type XXI's development and anxious to speed its construction, Dönitz accepted proposals from car manufacturer Otto Merker to build the new types in a radically different way. They would be prefabricated in eight different sections at inland factories. Only the final assembly would take place in conventional shipyards on the coast. The Germans hoped this process would minimize the effects of Allied bombing. The system resembled Kaiser's construction of Liberty ships and the Germans themselves had built some U-boats this way in World War I, but German naval construction firms rightly suspected that it would not work well with such sophisticated craft. Some U.S. Navy submarines were prefabricated in sections, but this method was applied only to an already standard design by experienced builders such as the Manitowoc Company, which built all the sections in-house and at one site.

The Type XXI and XXIII submarines and the new construction system proved overrated. Apart from the "bugs" to be expected in any new type of equipment, the Type XXI's diesel engines were less powerful than expected. Their hydraulic systems were vulnerable and unreliable. Further, the sections were often not properly made and were hard to "mate." The finished U-boats performed far less well than projected. The first ones built were relegated to training. Defects and Allied bombing also delayed the new U-boats considerably; eventually the bombing of the inland water transportation system stopped the sections from reaching the final assembly points. Only a few Type XXIIIs and one Type XXI were ready in time to make war patrols. They seem to have been more effective at escaping Allied antisubmarine measures than at increasing sinkings. While it is difficult to say what would have happened had the new submarines become available years earlier, it seems unlikely that they could have won the war at sea.[5]

## Intelligence and Technology

As costly as it was to the Allies in other respects, the U-boat campaign in the Americas did minimize the impact of their losing access to U-boat messages in February 1942. The individualistic nature of U-boat operations in the Western Hemisphere made reading their transmissions much less important for a time. And the British were not quite as badly off for intelligence as they had been before they had started to read the German naval ciphers in May 1941. They had much better photoreconnaissance than before of German ports and observed U-boats being built and readied, and they had a more extensive network of direction finders. Moreover, the Germans' shift to a separate cipher for communications in the main theater in the Atlantic left the British able to read the ciphers used for U-boats training in the Baltic or based in Norway; and they still read the Home Waters cipher that the surface craft used while escorting U-boats going in and out on war patrols in the Atlantic. So the arrival and departure even of U-boats employing the Triton cipher could be tracked. British estimates of the number of U-boats at sea remained accurate, and they continued to try to plot the positions of individual U-boats at sea. Their main failure was their inability, for some months, to recognize the deployment of the U-tankers, which they mistook at first for a new class of mine-laying submarine.

The Allies, meanwhile, were developing a whole new set of devices and weapons to deal with the U-boats. Early in 1942, they introduced special rescue ships—in effect, small hospital ships specially equipped to pick up survivors—but most Atlantic convoys did not have them. In June 1942, the British began refueling convoy escorts from tankers in the convoys themselves, a process requiring special gear and training for the tanker crews. This ability greatly simplified escort organization and eventually made it easier to spread convoy routes over a larger sea area. The Allies also introduced heavier airborne depth charges, better camouflage for planes, 10cm radars (at first only on surface ships), high-speed direction finders for the escorts, and the Hedgehog ahead-throwing weapon. This spigot mortar fired contact-fused projectiles ahead of an attacking escort. Unlike depth charges, which could only be dropped after passing the U-boat being attacked, these projectiles only went off when they hit something and did not interfere with maintaining sonar contact with the target.

Another successful device was the Leigh Light, a searchlight carried on an aircraft's wing. While attacking at night, a pilot who spotted a surfaced U-boat on radar used the light to illuminate his target. The Leigh Lights, introduced in June 1942, made offensive patrols over the Bay of Biscay far more effective until the Germans introduced a radar search receiver that could pick up the metric wavelengths that the older airborne radars still used.

Other devices made aircraft more effective against submerged submarines. The sonobuoys (an air-dropped sonar set) and magnetic anomaly detectors (MAD) enabled planes to detect submerged submarines, although the latter was useful only at close ranges. As they overflew their targets, the pilots of the MAD-equipped planes dropped retro-bombs, which were slowed by small rockets, and air-to-surface rockets. When dropped by an aircraft, "Fido"—an especially secret, small acoustic homing torpedo given the misleading designation Mark 24 mine—stood an excellent chance of destroying a submerged submarine.[6]

## Return to the Transatlantic Routes
As the convoy system developed in the Western Hemisphere, Dönitz shifted attacks to the main route between Britain and America, although he contin-

ued to devote more of the U-boat effort than before to distant operations, mostly in the South Atlantic. The the U-tankers and the new long-range Type IXD2 "U-cruiser," which could reach Cape Town without refueling, made it possible to extend operations to South Africa in September–October 1942 and, later on, into the Indian Ocean.

Some U-boats continued to work near North America and off Newfoundland. There was a bottleneck of sorts, where all convoys going to and from North America had to pass, at least if they were to stay within range of air cover from Newfoundland. Moreover, some small ships did not have enough fuel to let their convoys deviate very far south. In this area, the concentration of Allied ships, the poor visibility from the air, and the fact that planes based on Newfoundland had older and less effective radars made it profitable for Dönitz to keep at least one group of U-boats operating within range of air patrols there and for wolf packs to pursue westbound convoys coming under air cover, something they avoided elsewhere.

In the Atlantic, the Allies continued to be hampered by several factors. (From this point, the escort of the northern Atlantic convoys was almost entirely a British and Canadian job, while the Americans guarded convoys to North Africa.) They were strained to support operations in many areas, while the Canadians were, through no fault of their own, a weak link. The hastily expanded Royal Canadian Navy was at the end of the line for equipment, and its ships had been in continuous action with little chance to rest or refit. Two new types of American aircraft committed to the struggle in 1942, the PV-1 Ventura and PBM Mariner — replacements for the Hudson and Catalina, respectively — proved to be duds or so full of bugs that they were of little value at first. A reduction in the number of convoys and a shortage of tankers forced transatlantic and Sierra Leone convoys to use the most direct routes. And with the success of the German Navy's B-Dienst at decrypting the British Naval Cypher No. 3, convoys became easier to find. Finally most U-boat operations took place in a big "air gap" in the mid-Atlantic, where convoys did not yet enjoy air cover.

By August 1942, the U-boat fleet had risen to 339 submarines, of which 149 were considered frontline vessels. In late July, convoy ON 113 ran into a wolf pack, lost three of its thirty-three ships, and sank *U-90*. The Canadian escort had lacked up-to-date radar. ON 115, also with a poorly equipped but skilled Canadian escort group, lost a pair of ships and had another damaged, but it destroyed *U-558* and damaged two more U-boats. These battles represented successes for the Allies, particularly considering what the Canadians had to work with, and the Germans could not afford to trade

U-boats for merchant ships on anything like that basis. When SC 94 was caught on the Grand Banks heading out for Britain, its escorts again lacked good radar, although two modern British destroyers reinforced the convoy in the middle of a running battle. The convoy lost eleven of thirty-six ships, while the escort sank two U-boats. The Germans, in this case, had reversed their usual tactics, running ahead of the convoy and making successful submerged attacks by day. A wolf pack chewed up SL 118 using the same methods a week later. In late August, ONS 122 with modern escorts, including a group of well-equipped and trained Norwegian corvettes, lost four ships while damaging two out of a pack of nine U-boats.

Against less well-equipped or handled escort groups, however, the Germans scored heavily. Beginning on September 10, ON 127, hitting a submerged day ambush, lost three ships in the first attack plus four more and the Canadian destroyer HMCS *Ottawa* later. In late September, SC 100 lost four of its twenty-four ships despite bad weather of a sort that usually hampered U-boats. Even with a well-equipped escort, SC 104 lost eight ships from October 12 to October 17, but the escort sank two U-boats. Shortly afterward, HX 212, with a poorly equipped escort group, lost nine ships.

Thereafter, the escort of the North Atlantic convoys was reduced to release ships for the North African invasion. SC 107 and SL 125, running with poor escort groups, suffered particularly heavily. Despite a Canadian plane sinking two U-boats at the start of a weeklong battle between seven escorts (mostly poorly equipped Canadian corvettes) joined by an eighth ship en route and a huge pack of U-boats, SC 107 lost fifteen ships, and the Germans lost three U-boats, all to air attack. This battle led to a belated local reinforcement of escorts near Newfoundland. At about the same time, SL 125 lost eleven ships.

To concentrate the remaining escort resources for Atlantic convoys—for the North African invasion was not a brief, one-shot commitment—the Allies terminated all SL and nonmilitary Gibraltar convoys, inbound and outbound, for six months. Ships headed to Britain from southern waters sailed to North America and joined transatlantic convoys there. This entailed long, roundabout voyages and a further strain on Allied shipping. A fuel shortage toward the end of 1942 also forced opening the convoy cycle from eight to ten days.[7]

The North African invasion seriously handicapped those fighting the Atlantic battle. It diverted escort resources and delayed the deployment of support groups, whose formation had begun in September. The latter were designed not to take individual convoys from one side of the ocean to the other but to serve as mobile reserves and reinforce the escort groups of convoys under threat. Even worse, perhaps, the North African invasion's requirement for air support tied down the already delayed escort carriers. Most escort carriers had gone to the Pacific (where they mostly ferried planes), and the British were reluctant to use American-built escort carriers in the state in which they were delivered. They regarded them as unstable, requiring the addition of considerable ballast for safety, and thought their aviation fuel systems were dangerous. The last design flaw led to the loss in combat of HMS *Avenger* with nearly the entire crew in November 1942 and an accidental explosion that destroyed HMS *Dasher* with heavy losses in March 1943. The modifications the British deemed necessary further delayed the escort carriers' service. For their part, the Americans complained that the British escort carriers were not commanded by air officers, had inadequate deck crews (a result of the Royal Navy's shortage of manpower), and lacked onboard repair facilities. In any case, making the changes meant scheduling setbacks.

## Hard Fall and Winter

November 1942 saw the Allies' heaviest monthly losses to all Axis submarines, or 128 ships of 824,644 gross registered tons. The Germans sank all but 10 of them; however, many were stragglers or independents. The North African invasion itself broke the Germans' train of success, as they diverted many U-boats against the invasion forces. They arrived too late to have a serious impact, apart from the usual ineffectiveness of submarines against amphibious operations. On December 9, the German command relented and let some U-boats return to the Atlantic convoy routes, but they ran into exceptionally awful winter weather, the worst so far of the war. It made attacks difficult, although it also caused the Allies to lose a ship a day from "maritime casualties." Sinkings fell, although storms tended to cause merchant ships to straggle from convoys, producing easy targets. In late December the Germans did score a victory over ONS 154, which had relatively old escorts and was routed far south. The U-boats sank 13 ships, including the convoy's refueling tanker, which forced most of its escort to leave. In January the weather was even worse. Sinkings fell to 29 ships, 14 of them independents. The Germans did attain a spectacular victory over a special tanker convoy running from Trinidad to Gibraltar, TM 1, and virtually wiped it out, with 7 of 9 tankers sunk.[8]

That winter, another factor aided the Allies: they regained the ability to read the Germans' most important messages. The British had recovered documents from *U-559* in the Mediterranean, right before it sank on October 30, 1942, in a feat that cost the lives of two men of the boarding party. Although *U-559* used a different operational cipher (Medusa) from that employed in the Atlantic, its weather cipher provided clues that helped the British break the Triton cipher on December 13. After some difficulties, they began reading it, with delays running from less than a day to 72 hours, and with occasional lapses. Triton was unreadable for ten days in January 1943 and from February 10 to 17, and the British usually suffered a full day's delay in reading it for most of the rest of February. The British were gratified to learn that their U-boat tracking had been basically accurate even during the blackout from February to December, but reading Triton assisted their evasive routing.

A curious situation then developed because the Germans' reading of Naval Cipher No. 3 was also at peak efficiency. They read the messages in which the British ordered convoys to change course to evade the wolf packs, while the British read the messages in which Dönitz directed the wolf packs to counter those changes. Curiously, both sides' security precautions in formulating their own messages were such that the fact that they read the other's ciphers was not obvious. After some months the Allies recognized what was going on, but the Germans never did. In February 1943, once again, Dönitz did suspect that the Enigma cipher had been compromised, but his chief of communications convinced him otherwise.[9]

Evasive routing proved helpful, but as Triton was being cracked, operational researchers made discoveries that, if acted on promptly, would alone have turned the tide in the Atlantic; moreover, the Germans could have done nothing to counter them. The physicist P. M. S. Blackett, now working for the Admiralty, produced a report demonstrating the importance of closing the mid-Atlantic air gap. Had air cover been provided in the mid-ocean area, he showed, two-thirds of the losses there could have been avoided in the previous year.

He also showed that had the average size of an escort group been enlarged from six to nine ships, losses would have been reduced by yet another quarter. That finding was interwoven with another discovery—or rather a rediscovery, since the British officer Rollo Appleyard had worked it out in 1918—of the "law of convoy size." It would be much more effective, Blackett determined, to have only moderately larger escort groups defend far bigger convoys of eighty to a hundred ships instead of the thirty- to forty-ship standard up to then. The decisive problem in defending a convoy was not the ratio of escorts to either attackers or ships to be protected but the length of the perimeter the escorts had to screen. Doubling or tri-pling the number of ships in a convoy only modestly expanded the area it covered and the perimeter that the escorts had to defend, while a big-ger convoy was only slightly easier for the enemy to find. And increasing the number of targets would make little difference. If an escort screen was penetrated, the average U-boat still would probably sink only one ship, so even a successful U-boat attack would achieve the same number of sinkings out of a much larger group of ships. Blackett estimated that in 1942 alone using bigger convoys would have saved two hundred ships. Enlarging convoys, however, seemed to pose more problems in loading, unloading, and moving their cargoes, and many officers feared that bigger convoys would be harder to control and more exposed to head-on attacks. The Al-lies did not successfully implement Blackett's discoveries until late March.[10]

As events showed, most of the Allies' problems resulted from the air gap, which could easily have been closed much earlier. The failure to deal with it was the result of a remarkable maldistribution of effort at several levels. Adding merely forty more very long-range (VLR) shore-based anti-submarine planes or committing six additional escort carriers could have closed the gap. The latter were not yet available, but plenty of four-engine heavy bombers—B-24 Liberators or Halifaxes—could have been converted into VLR patrol planes with a cruising range of more than 2,000 nautical miles, allowing them to stay over a convoy for four hours at a thousand miles from base. (Long-range planes, such as unmodified Liberators or Halifaxes, B-17s, PBY Catalinas, PBM Mariners, and PV-1 Venturas, had an effective radius of 400 to 600 miles, while medium-range planes, such as Hudsons or B-18s, could patrol up to 400 miles.)

The standard B-24 Liberator required extensive changes to become a VLR type, including the removal of self-sealing fuel tanks to provide more fuel capacity, most armor, belly turrets, and turbo-superchargers. Although the value of the VLR Liberator was well known, only RAF 120 Squadron, based in Iceland, had them. It averaged eleven serviceable planes at the start of March 1943. 86 Squadron, based in Northern Ireland, had twelve planes but was not yet fully operational. The Allies had no VLR planes in Newfoundland, although the Canadians begged for them as the few planes assigned to the east could not cover the gap. They tried desperate impro-visations to substitute for VLR planes. In January 1943, the British Coastal Command tried to base Hudsons at Bluie West 1, Narsarssuak Air Base, on the west coast of Greenland, but flying out of the place was difficult. Command lost two Hudsons and their crews covering one convoy. The

Canadian 5 Squadron stripped Cansos (the Canadian version of the PBY Catalina) of everything that could be dispensed with, including guns, so they could reach 700 miles out from Newfoundland.

Many later blamed the lack of VLR aircraft solely on the devotion of too many planes to the strategic bombing offensive against Germany. Subtracting the small number of planes needed to close the gap from the strategic bombing campaign would certainly have been justified and made a much greater contribution to the Allied war effort than those planes could have made over Germany. The strategic air war against Germany, however, was not the immediate cause of the problem in the Atlantic. Plenty of aircraft already assigned to naval tasks could have been converted to VLR work. The U.S. Navy alone had 52 Liberators by the end of 1942. On March 19, 1943, when Roosevelt began asking awkward questions, the navy had 112 Liberators—70 in the Pacific and the rest on the U.S. East Coast, which had no pressing demand for such long-range planes. The USAAF had deployed its two B-24 antisubmarine squadrons first with the RAF over the Bay of Biscay and in March 1943 mistakenly moved them to Morocco to defend the lifeline of the North African campaign, which was not seriously endangered. Meanwhile, RAF Coastal Command had not converted all possible Liberators to VLR standards and had some over the Bay of Biscay, patrolling the German transit routes to and from the Atlantic battle. Occasionally paying off in terms of killing U-boats, it was a reasonable use of moderate-range planes but not a good way to use planes that could have been modified to cover the Atlantic air gap.

The Allied strategic air forces' attempt to deal with the U-boats with airpower was an even bigger failure. Although the RAF had failed to bomb the huge concrete bunkers that protected the U-boat pens and all important supporting activities when they were under construction in 1940–1941 and might have been vulnerable, from October 1942, the U.S. Eighth Air Force tried for six months to smash the U-boat bases in France and, later and less intensively, the U-boat shipbuilding yards in the north German ports. The American daylight attacks damaged only one U-boat, caught moving between pens, and were at most a small nuisance. In January 1943, even with the situation in the Atlantic seemingly desperate and over the strong opposition of the not-too-finicky head of Bomber Command Sir Arthur Harris, the RAF launched the only area attacks made on cities outside Germany and bombed the French towns in which U-boat bases were located. After wrecking several French cities with no effect on U-boat operations, the operation stopped.[11]

## The Climax: January to March 1943

The Allies found the serious losses suffered in the fall of 1942 disquieting, although, even then, a disproportionate number of ships sunk were independents, stragglers, or lost from convoys whose escort was unusually thin or inexperienced. Dönitz's replacement of Raeder as the head of the German Navy on January 30, 1943—Hitler had finally become fed up with Raeder—rightly portended an all-out struggle in which the enemy would stake everything on submarines. Indeed, Dönitz promptly shifted dockyard workers from working on surface ships to U-boats. Germany had more U-boats than ever, 415 at the beginning of February, of which 221 were already in the front line.

Even then, some on the Allied side understood that this move was not likely to succeed and that it was the enemy's last throw. The Casablanca Conference in January had given the war against the U-boats "first charge" on Allied resources, although implementing that decision was not simple.

With the weather improving, a pack of five U-boats caught HX 224 on the Grand Banks on January 29. They sank three ships. The five-day running battle ended when a plane from Iceland sank *U-265*. Although three ships for one U-boat was a poor exchange for the Germans, the Allied loss was heavy considering that HX 224 had enjoyed an unusually strong surface escort. The Germans concentrated an even bigger force against an exceptionally big (sixty-one ships), slow convoy coming up behind HX 224, SC 118, which had an escort group containing many new personnel and ships. In a terrific battle from February 4 to February 8, three U-boats were sunk for eleven ships, two of the submarines being destroyed by surface ships and one by an RAF plane. This exchange was again really unfavorable for the enemy, but the Allies were conscious of the heavy loss of ships and those aboard, who stood little chance of surviving a sinking in a North Atlantic winter. Moreover, one ship lost from SC 118 was the troop transport USS *Henry Mallory*, a fast ship wrongly assigned to a slow convoy and not given the safest spot within it. Many soldiers died when it sank. A U.S. Army transport ship, the *Dorchester*, was sunk out of a small convoy headed for Iceland. Together, the sinkings of the *Mallory* and the *Dorchester* cost almost a thousand lives. ONS 166, slowed by violent gales, ran into wolf packs in the air gap on February 20. During another terrific six-day battle, three U-boats went down for fourteen ships, although the convoy's last stages saw support from stripped Canadian Cansos staggering a hundred miles beyond their usual limit. The Cansos damaged two U-boats and saved the convoy from worse losses. The next westbound convoy, ONS 167, was more fortunate and lost only two ships.

German officers, other than Dönitz, were not that pleased with how the war was going. They noted that they were running into more and more surface escorts with good radars, making it hard to gain a good position ahead of a convoy unless a wolf pack had the luck to be well ahead of it on its line of advance. Dönitz felt compelled on March 5 to order all U-boats to dive and stay submerged for half an hour on picking up a radar transmission. (The Germans did not realize that the Allies now often used 10cm wavelengths, and their search receivers could not detect them.) Some German officers suspected that their run of success was owed largely to the unusually good intelligence that the B-Dienst supplied. Although they did not know it, the blackout of the Allied decryption effort during a good part of the coming month would accentuate B-Dienst's success temporarily.

SC 121, from February 27 to March 11, had a bad time. Bad weather damaged escort ships' radars, prevented the convoy from assuming a normally tight formation, and caused many stragglers to drop out. The convoy actually wriggled through one U-boat patrol line, but the U-boats pursued and caught it, sinking thirteen ships without losing one U-boat. HX 228, following it, was the first transatlantic convoy to enjoy some support from an escort carrier, the USS *Bogue*, but it could only stay with it for five days. After it left, the wolf packs closed in, sinking four ships and a British destroyer and causing a heavy loss of life, although a French corvette destroyed two U-boats, a remarkable feat. Between March 12 and March 18, the Germans made submerged attacks before sunset on UGS 6, a central Atlantic convoy en route to Casablanca. It lost four of its forty-five ships in return for sinking *U-130*. On March 16 Dönitz broadcast a general order that the U-boats should try to maintain contact with convoys at a maximum distance and attain a position ahead of them from which to attack underwater.

The situation seemed desperate to many on the Allied side. Practically every North Atlantic convoy was now sighted, and half were attacked, a rate of success for the enemy at finding and attacking convoys without precedent. And worse was to come. SC 122, closely followed by HX 229, set out across the Atlantic from New York. (The terminus for slow convoys had not yet been moved to Halifax.) HX 229 was organized oddly. Instead of being crammed into one convoy, as was routine later, its eighty ships were split into two halves. HX 229A, consisting of the faster and more valuable ships, went ahead. It escaped attack while losing a ship to an iceberg. The slower half, designated simply HX 229, was not so lucky. It gradually overtook SC 122's sixty-four ships, and after some days, the Germans realized that they were attacking two adjacent convoys instead of a big, disorganized one. They sent no less than forty U-boats against the two convoys, an unprecedented concentration exceeded only once later in the war. The result was a massacre, and the U-boats hung on until they came under Iceland-based air cover. From March 15 to March 20, they sank twenty-one ships, losing only *U-384* to an RAF Sunderland flying boat. Next, a German plane on a mission supporting a blockade-runner spotted the relatively weakly escorted SL 126, the first Sierra Leone convoy since the fall of 1942. U-boats guided to the convoy sank four ships and damaged another.

German officers analyzing the HX 229 and SC 122 battle were not that pleased with the results, noting that most of the sinkings occurred during a surprise attack on the first night. During tough fighting afterward, the U-boats had taken a heavy pounding from the surface escort, even though no submarines were actually sunk. For the Germans, neither the exchange rate of less than eight merchant ships for each U-boat lost nor the number of sinkings achieved per U-boat per patrol was particularly spectacular. The Allies, however, were extremely worried, having lost 108 ships of 627,377 tons to submarines in March, mostly from convoys, while sinking only fourteen U-boats. Such heavy losses to convoys with strong surface escorts—comparable to those inflicted steadily earlier only on ships going it alone—caused some planners to fear that the convoy strategy was becoming unviable. And no one had a substitute for it. Evasive routing, although not useless, seemed to be losing much of its effectiveness. With so many U-boats at sea, it was hard to get around them. In a famous remark, repeated by the British official historian Stephen Roskill, the Germans "never came so near as to disrupting communications between the New World and the Old as in the first twenty days of March 1943."

But the Allies were finally acting to solve the problem. At the Atlantic Convoy Conference that month, they rearranged command boundaries in the Atlantic that lasted the rest of the war. Giving the Canadians a more satisfactory position, they left the northern route entirely to the British and Canadians. The Americans took over tanker traffic between the Caribbean and Britain and the Mediterranean. The conference increased the convoy cycle and allotted enough VLR aircraft so that the Canadians at last would have enough planes for a squadron based in Newfoundland. It doubled 120 Squadron in strength, finally put support groups into action, and assigned more escort ships.

HX 229, SC 122, and SL 126 were about the last convoy battles the Germans could rate as successes.[12] Those victories had occurred because the Allies' normal communications intelligence had been handicapped and the overwhelming concentrations of U-boat wolf packs in the air gap had reduced the chances for evasive routing. Those conditions were about to change. The Allies allocated more resources, especially surface escorts and VLR aircraft equipped with 10cm wavelength radars, and recovered, most of the time, the reading of Enigma traffic.

The Allies enjoyed a brief, relative lull, as many U-boats that had fought in the big battles of March returned home. HX 230, covered by an escort carrier and a support group, got through while losing only one straggler. The British had the impression that German morale might be shaky and that the U-boats approaching HX 230 were not trying very hard. Dönitz, for his part, then threw in every resource. He ordered the Type IXC boats, usually reserved for more distant waters, against the northern Atlantic route. It was not a good idea. They were too big, clumsy, slow diving, and susceptible to bomb damage to be suitable for the northern theater.

HX 231, the first regular "supersize" convoy, ran into a real battle from April 4 though April 7. It lost six ships, but the Germans lost one U-boat to the surface escort and one to a plane, and another was damaged. In all, it was a defeat for the Germans. ON 176, leaving Britain and picking up some ships from Iceland, took advantage of direction finder fixes on U-boats and deciphered messages to change course. The U-boats nevertheless finally caught it, sinking a British destroyer and a merchant ship on April 11, but air cover severely hampered them. HX 232, heading for Britain at the same time, lost three ships on April 12 to a surprise night attack, but air cover forced the U-boats away. HX 233 ran into a patrol line on April 17 and lost one ship but sank a U-boat in return. Several other convoys in mid-April escaped attack entirely thanks to evasive routing far to the north, or, if they were sighted, air cover prevented the Germans closing to attack or maintaining contact. The Germans did catch a small convoy, ONS 3 (the Allies had started renumbering slow westbound convoys over again). *U-415* sank two of its ships on April 21, but it broke away. The Germans decided not to pursue it and concentrated against bigger prizes.

On April 21, HX 234, running right along the edge of the ice pack, hit a concentration of nineteen U-boats. They sank three ships, two of whom were stragglers, but air cover forced the U-boats to leave. The Germans rediscovered the convoy and sank another ship, but a supporting plane sank *U-189*. Two days later, the Germans hit ONS 4, a slow convoy that crept along because it included some very slow ships that the escort leader thought were coasters and unsuited for ocean crossings. It did have, however, an escort that included the carrier HMS *Biter*. *Biter* was mistakenly stationed too far from the convoy, but despite these handicaps, the escort ships and planes, reinforced by a support group, sank two U-boats. The convoy lost not one ship.

ONS 5 set out from Britain with forty-three ships on April 22, guarded by the same escort group that had won the battle around HX 231, with a pair of destroyers, a frigate, four corvettes, and two trawlers. It was routed far north in very bad weather, which severely hampered the British. Several ships dropped out as the weather damaged some ships (two collided), scattered the rest, and made it impossible for others to refuel. U-boats found, then lost, then found the convoy again, while a support group of four destroyers reinforced its escort, with another joining the convoy en route. The weather also hampered the air support; one Canadian Canso was lost and others could not find the convoy. The defenders faced a fantastic concentration of forty-one U-boats, the greatest ever against an Atlantic convoy. During a running battle, which peaked from May 4 to May 6, yet another support group arrived. The convoy lost thirteen ships, but at least six U-boats were sunk, a loss as unprecedented as the U-boat concentration. Other U-boats were badly damaged.

Even Dönitz recognized it as a defeat. He ordered Type IX U-boats withdrawn from the North Atlantic on May 5, after their losses proved too great. Between May 7 and May 14, HX 237, running east with carrier support, lost three ships for three U-boats sunk and five damaged, while SC 129 lost two ships for one U-boat sunk and another damaged. (The Germans also sank a nearby Irish neutral, which they mistakenly supposed was part of the convoy.) The Germans found themselves increasingly unable to close to attack range or to maintain contact with a convoy. Making attempts to do so were becoming suicidal, while most of the few sinkings they achieved were of stragglers or ships in slow convoys hit by bad weather. After a few more tries, even Dönitz saw the futility in continuing. On May 24, he pulled all U-boats out of the North Atlantic. An incredible total of forty-one U-boats were lost to all causes in May. (By contrast, the American lost fifty-two submarines during the whole war.)

Dönitz then concentrated farther south against convoys between North America and North Africa, which he thought were still weakly defended. They were supported, however, by American escort carriers in a region where the weather was far more favorable for carrier operations than in the north. With Enigma traffic revealing the refueling rendezvous between attack submarines and U-tankers, American carrier planes inflicted severe losses. The Allies also finally realized that Naval Cipher No. 3 had been compromised, so the Germans lost their main source of intelligence.

While the main battle in the Atlantic continued, the Germans had also sustained heavy casualties in transit to their operational areas in the Bay of Biscay. There, the British had only occasionally destroyed U-boats, although they slowed and harassed their movements. In March, however, they began to kill many U-boats at night thanks to the combination of the Leigh Light with the 10cm radars that the Germans could not detect. Dönitz, on April 27, ordered the U-boats to receive more antiaircraft armament and to go through the bay by surface, not submerging, during the day and to fight their way through. In June, they began doing so in groups, sometimes with German air support, but the losses were disastrous. After two weeks, only especially heavily armed "flak trap" submarines continued to fight it out on the surface. Finally, on August 3, after losing nine U-boats in six days, Dönitz relented. The U-boats henceforth went out individually and surfaced in the Bay of Biscay at night only when it was absolutely necessary to recharge batteries. He had lost twenty-six U-boats in the bay—most of which would have survived had they surfaced only in the dark while hugging the shore.[13]

The U-boats, in their present form, were obsolete. The new equipment that they gained in 1943—search receivers for microwave radar, radar decoys, and acoustic homing torpedoes—did not work well, and the Allies had countermeasures. Some U-boat captains were scared of the homing torpedo, suspecting it would come back at them. The Germans did not even recognize some of the devices the Allies were using against them, notably the high-speed direction-finder and the Fido homing torpedo, which was much more successful than its U-boat counterpart. A return to the main transatlantic routes also failed. Dönitz had to continue the U-boat war in distant areas where the Allies were not yet strong and wait for the newer model U-boats.

The nature of the crisis in the Atlantic in March 1943 has often been misunderstood. The losses in 1942–1943, although serious, did not threaten Britain with starvation and immediate defeat. More than enough shipping was available to support the British people and war production; instead, what was at stake was the Allies having enough shipping to support future offensives. Losses of Allied merchant ships to all enemy agents in 1942 only slightly exceeded total construction during that year, and the curve of merchant shipbuilding had surpassed that of U-boat sinkings alone in 1942.[14]

The crisis of 1943 was neither a narrow escape from catastrophe nor the culmination of a situation worsening steadily throughout the war. As Donald Macintyre wrote, "A setback on one part of the battlefield was being unreasonably looked upon as a herald of general defeat." Nor were the losses absolutely unbearable, as even the convoys that were attacked suffered losses of 11 percent. Further, the Germans found that only strong concentrations of U-boats were successful and then only in the air gap. Those men immediately responsible for the fight against the U-boats did not share the pessimistic assessment that Roskill attributed to the Admiralty staff. Macintyre, an escort commander, remarked that "those closer to the fighting, however, such as the C-in-C [commander in chief] Western Approaches, and his staff at Liverpool, the captains commanding the escort bases and the escort commanders themselves were by no means dismayed." They understood that the Allies were taking the measure of the U-boat threat. The staff of the Admiralty's operational intelligence effort was also confident of eventual success.[15]

The unnecessary crisis arose during the enemy's last desperate effort before the Allies closed the air gap. It was partly the result of the Allies taking a chance with their supply lines to support their early offensive efforts and of their maldistribution of available planes. The surface escort forces often comprised not the latest and best-equipped ships but "cast-offs and surplus ships," as historian Martin Middlebrook said.[16]

Closing the air gap and the new microwave radars were the most important elements in the Atlantic victory. Given the density of the U-boat concentrations and the Germans' own intelligence successes, recovering the ability to read German ciphers was probably not decisive. Knowing where the U-boats operated aided evasive routing. Although still useful, this information was not that crucial, as too many U-boats were now at sea. The vital issue was the tactical location of the U-boats in actual contact with the convoys. Planes and radar were the main factor in solving this problem. Ultra did help the Allies rush reinforcements to threatened convoys and later helped escort carrier groups massacre U-boats by guiding the Allies to their refueling rendezvous.

Germany's chances to win the Battle of the Atlantic, if any, had been slim. As noted earlier, whatever chance of victory for the Germans had probably existed only in the first two years of the war. It seems doubtful whether, even given higher priority, the U-boat fleet could have been built up fast enough. Defeat in the Atlantic seems to have been largely pre-determined by Germany's limited resources and by the navy's prewar mistakes in planning. Hitler had had little to do with these decisions. There is a parallel here with the fate of the Luftwaffe.

# 8

## The Russian Campaign II

*To the Caucasus and Stalingrad*

The Nazis had long planned on seizing the oil fields of the Caucasus after defeating the Soviets and following up their conquest of the area with a push into Iran and Iraq in 1942. Disregarding the problem of moving the oil after it had been secured, the Germans had formed Oil Detachment Caucasus to exploit it before the war with the Soviets began. But detailed military planning for the Caucasus waited until October 1941.

A move into the Caucasus would not take place until 1942 and depended on German forces reaching the lower Volga to provide a secure flank. On November 19, Hitler made clear that the Caucasus would be his primary objective in 1942, but still expecting to take Moscow, he anticipated that the Caucasus offensive would be accompanied by one on the main eastern front toward Gorki (Nizhni Novgorod) or Vologda.

The Soviet counteroffensive caused planning for the Caucasus to lapse. When it resumed in February 1942, instead of following up the defeat of the Red Army on the main eastern front, it became a substitute for it. While apparently avoiding a showdown with the Red Army, which the Germans no longer thought that they could win, that seemed a way to paralyze the Soviets by depriving them of fuel and to acquire resources Germany desperately needed. Hitler was still bent on achieving a decision in the war as a whole by defeating the Soviets, and he believed, with good reason given the advice he received, that Germany could not win without the oil of the Caucasus. Access to it was a precondition for a true global strategy; without it Germany could not effectively wage war against the Western powers. Hitler believed, based perhaps on the OKW's overview of December 14,

195

1941, that he still had a year in which to defeat the Soviets before the Western powers could seriously act against Germany, and he may have thought that Japan—and perhaps Turkey—still might join the war against the USSR.

Germany's oil situation was desperate and getting worse. As Hitler told the officers of Army Group South on June 1, "Either we get the oil of Maikop and Grozny, or we shall have to end this war." The German forces, especially the Luftwaffe, had cut heavily into fuel reserves in 1941; the German and Italian navies were also extremely short of fuel oil. While synthetic fuel production was rising, it had not offset a decline in Romanian oil production. Fuel, apart from anything else, was not available for an air offensive in the West comparable to the Battle of Britain. As it turned out, the oil situation would improve enough for Germany to wage a formidable defensive effort for several years without Caucasian oil, but this situation was not apparent in 1942.

Hitler combined the new strategy with a comforting ideological "reinterpretation" of the war. (For a time in the winter, as he later admitted to Goebbels and others, he had been extremely worried.) As he explained to his intimates on July 22, 1942, at a moment when he imagined the summer campaign was going well, what had taken place during the Nazis' "period of struggle" among the political parties in Germany itself was now occurring in the whole world as a struggle among nations. As the German Communist Party had been the "battering ram" then, the Soviets were acting the part now, and as the "bourgeois" parties had in Germany, the capitalist states were making their debut on the outer edge.

Hitler and most of the leaders of the armed forces became more optimistic, once the winter crisis in the east had passed, even if it was tacitly accepted that the Germans were not strong enough to capture Moscow. Hitler's approach violated Carl von Clausewitz's fundamental rule: the proper objective of a military campaign was the defeat of the enemy's military forces, and seizing political and economic objectives must follow, not precede, this. In southern Russia in 1942, the course Hitler chose should have seemed dubious even from a narrowly pragmatic standpoint. To reach the main Soviet oil fields the Germans had to advance nearly a thousand miles over a rugged mountain range, while the Soviet fleet dominated the Black Sea. Their chances of crossing the main Caucasus range would not be good unless the Soviet forces were thoroughly smashed before they could fall back on the mountains. The Germans' lines of communication, which were likely to be inadequate, would run through a vulnerable bottleneck at Rostov-on-Don and would be exposed to an attack by the undefeated mass of the Red Army from the northeast. Precisely because Hitler was evading a confrontation with the bulk of the Soviet forces, they would be in a position to launch a counteroffensive and force a decisive battle when it would be least convenient for the Germans. Hitler's decision to make the Caucasus the objective was thus fundamentally bad strategy.

But what would have been a good strategy? General Halder, after the war, and some other critics argued that Germany should not have attacked at all in the east in 1942; instead, Germany should have remained on the defensive, shortening the eastern front and reorganizing, refitting, and conserving its forces to repel Allied attacks. Many critics later argued that the Germans should have resumed the offensive against Moscow (as the Soviets expected), but Germany no longer had the strength for that. To stay on the defensive would have been totally alien to Hitler's mentality and unpleasantly reminiscent of Germany's strategic errors in World War I. In terms of a major offensive, the Germans had to take the Caucasus or nothing. Even those who doubted it would work saw no other choice. As historian Geoffrey Megargee later characterized the 1942 offensive, it was not Germany's last gasp but the "last grasp." However, the Germans would come close to an even bigger disaster than the one they would suffer at Stalingrad (Volgograd), so it might well have been a "last gasp" as well.

Field Marshals Gerd von Rundstedt and Wilhelm von Leeb had favored retreat to the old Polish border, but Hitler had fired them. Some skeptics remained, notably Quartermaster General Wagner and Gen. Friedrich Fromm, the commander of the Replacement Army and chief of the army's Armament Office, while the General Staff's Operations Department warned that it would not be possible to reach beyond a line running from Tuapse in the northwest Caucasus to Stalingrad, far from the main oil fields. But these doubters were not vocal. Indeed, the Germans were probably right in believing that the Soviets could not carry on the war without Caucasian oil, although British intelligence thought Soviets reserves were big enough to prevent their being seriously impaired until well into 1943.[1]

### Underestimating the Enemy

The Germans still gravely underestimated the Soviets. Although the new edition of their handbook on the Red Army was far more sober than the 1941 edition, the Germans underrated the Soviets at the strategic level and vastly underestimated the growing Soviet war production, which already considerably exceeded theirs. The chief of the General Staff agreed with Hitler that the Soviets were at the limit of their strength. Intelligence estimated that the Soviets could form no more than 60 new rifle divisions and a dozen new tank brigades during the coming year, and that they could not take defeats of the magnitude they had suffered earlier. The existing Soviet forces were thought, in June 1942, to comprise 270 rifle divisions, 2 tank divisions, and 115 rifle brigades and 69 tank brigades. In fact, despite losing more than four million men in 1941, in early 1942 the Soviets already had 293 rifle divisions, 34 cavalry divisions, and 121 rifle and 56 tank brigades. They had formed more units by summer.[2]

Field Marshal Fedor von Bock, whom Hitler had returned to command and put in charge of Army Group South, largely devised the ultimate plan. Hitler then broadly described it in his Directive 41 on April 5. Hitler added the reduction of Leningrad to the offensive, although it would only be undertaken if circumstances were favorable. After clearing the Crimea and several other preliminary operations, the German forces in southern Russia would drive east to the Don, and over it in the south, in a succession of three phased offensives from north to south. The directive prescribed small, tight encircling movements to prevent the Soviet forces from escaping. The Germans would form a defensive flank along most of the course of the Don and secure the land bridge between the Don and the Volga near Stalingrad. The directive was ambiguous about whether the army would actually capture Stalingrad, stating that "every effort will be made to reach Stalingrad itself or at least bring the city under fire from heavy artillery so that it may no longer be of any use as an industrial or communications center." The Germans overestimated the city's importance as a transportation hub. Not knowing that the Baku-Astrakhan railroad existed, they thought that taking Stalingrad or eliminating it as a rail center would interrupt rail connections with the Caucasus.

In Bock's plan, Stalingrad was not a primary objective and its capture was not definitely stipulated. The evident assumption was that the Don flank would be formed and the vicinity of Stalingrad reached before a drive south to the Caucasus was launched. Although the last push was not described in detail, the Axis allies, with strong German supporting forces, largely would hold the long defensive front on the Don. Dependence on the weak Axis forces, however, would lead to disaster.

One aspect of this planning process was novel. The Germans abandoned their traditional practice of running as a war game first. If not a guarantee of success, that had saved the Germans from mistakes in the past. Whether this change merely reflected Hitler's growing overconfidence in his own judgment or a subconscious suspicion that a "fair" war game would show that an offensive was unlikely to reach the oil fields is, of course, unknown.[3]

## Rehabilitating the German Army in the East

The Germans' dependence on their weak allies, and their inability to resume an offensive on the scale of 1941, was the product of the heavy losses of the previous year, especially during the winter in which they had lost 900,000 men—376,000 to battle casualties and more than 500,000 to illness, mostly from frostbite. Despite enormous replacements, the army in the East was still short 625,000 men. Equipment losses had been huge, also. From October 15 to March 7, the Germans had lost 74,000 motor vehicles and 2,300 tanks but received only 7,500 vehicles and 1,800 tanks. They had lost more than 7,000 artillery pieces, and production could not replace them. Of the 180,000 horses that had been killed, the army only replaced 20,000. The sixteen panzer divisions had only 140 working tanks among them. By the end of March 1942, only 8 of 162 divisions in the east were classed as fully capable of any action.

The Germans took desperate measures to rebuild the shattered eastern army. After the worst crisis was over in February, three panzer and six infantry divisions were withdrawn, without their equipment, and sent to occupied western Europe for rehabilitation and complete reequipment. Later, ten divisions were swapped from the east for eight from the west. It was extremely hard to get replacement tanks and trucks, and only part of the army could be rehabilitated. Army Group South happened to be the best off of the three army groups in the east, ending the winter at 50 percent of its strength compared to 35 percent for the other two, and it was the only group to be more or less restored. The panzer divisions of Army Groups North and Center transferred experienced men to the south, leaving them only one tank battalion each instead of three. Infantry divisions were left with six battalions apiece instead of nine, and artillery batteries were reduced from four guns apiece to three. The shortage of trucks led to their removal from ordinary, as opposed to motorized infantry divisions. Even in Army Group South, rehabilitated infantry divisions each had to be filled out with a thousand replacements who had only two months' training. Panzer and motorized divisions, far more lavishly supported than the rest, finally received only 80 percent of their normal complement of motor vehicles. The German Army began the 1942 summer offensive with 360 fewer tanks in the east than a year earlier. Its tanks had been up-gunned, but they were still not as good as the Russians' T-34 tanks.

Some other limited improvements in equipment took place. The Germans now had a heavier 75mm antitank gun and shaped-charge antitank ammunition available, while three companies of infantry in each panzer division had half-tracked carriers rather than trucks. Army flak units were distributed to some panzer and motorized divisions. The army built up the elite Grossdeutschland Regiment into a full motorized division and strengthened the Waffen SS, now comprising motorized infantry divisions with tank complements. The Luftwaffe in the east was numerically as strong as in 1941, but heavy losses of transport and twin-engine bomber crews and the disruption of flight training had left it qualitatively weaker. The Luftwaffe in southern Russia, however, would be well led by the ablest German air commander, Field Marshal Wolfram von Richthofen.

Drastic measures had been taken to repair the transportation situation. The German rail system overall had not functioned well in the winter of 1941–1942, quite aside from the disaster in Russia; so its administration had been shaken up. It overcame the crisis by bringing locomotives from western occupied countries to Germany to release German locomotives for the east. Still, they had been short of locomotives; so mass-production of a standard type of "winterized" locomotive was under way. The Germans also increased their preparations to exploit the Caucasus and expanded the Oil Detachment Caucasus. The Germans planned to bring French and Italian tankers from the Mediterranean (where they were already desperately short) into the Black Sea, salvage and repair damaged ships there, and build concrete tankers and more Danube River–type tankers in the hope that they would solve the oil transportation problem. To support the summer offensive, the Germans also brought small Type II U-boats and motor torpedo boats to the Black Sea. The Italians sent motor torpedo boats and midget submarines to join the German naval contingent. German naval forces in the Black Sea, however, achieved little. In this case the Italians outperformed them.

The Nazis did not neglect another part of their program. Although short of manpower, they reinforced the Einsatzgruppen with several police battalions to destroy Jews and other targets in the occupied areas and those lands they expected to take in the coming campaign.[4]

## The Axis Allies' Contribution

The Germans pressed their allies to increase their forces in the east. Only Mussolini responded willingly against the advice of the commander of the existing Italian contingent, and reinforced the Italian force to an army of six divisions. Mussolini evidently believed that an advance through and south from the Caucasus would help the Italian forces in the Mediterranean. This move was not popular in Italy, where even many Fascists were horrified by reports of what was going on in the German-occupied USSR.

The Germans persuaded the Romanians to reinforce their forces to twelve divisions and the Hungarians to ten. Nearly all of these units were poorly equipped infantry. The Romanians and Hungarians also had one armored division each, with obsolete tanks. The Germans told the Hungarians that their forces would be rearmed with German weapons, a promise the Germans knew they could not honor. The Germans' Slovak puppet state contributed a motorized infantry division. In all, the Axis contingent was expected to grow to forty-four divisions during the campaign, in which it played a crucial and disastrous role.

## First Victories

The Germans considered it necessary to take Sevastopol, a Black Sea port. To do so, they eliminated the strong Crimean Front, now with three armies, holding the Kerch Peninsula. The Soviet defenders considerably outnumbered the attacking force and held a short and formidable line, but their commanders were incompetent. Erich von Manstein, the ablest German general, brilliantly planned the German attack, which enjoyed strong air support. The attack began on the night of May 7–8. By May 19, the Germans overran the peninsula, largely destroyed the Crimean Front, and took 170,000 prisoners.

The Germans would have been better advised to have sealed off the Kerch position and, indeed, Sevastopol and concentrated on the offensive on the mainland. Once the Germans had proceeded far enough, they would have either forced the Soviets to evacuate the Crimean Front or trapped it as the Germans drove south and past it through the Kuban, east of the Kerch Strait. There was little to be said for capturing Sevastopol. Even Hitler may have had doubts about whether it was really necessary to storm one of the most heavily fortified places in the world, held by strong Soviet field forces in the Independent Maritime Army. The Soviets enjoyed reinforcements and supplies throughout the siege. Meanwhile, Manstein insisted that it was necessary to take Sevastopol; otherwise, half his Eleventh Army, including three or four German divisions as well as Romanian units, would be pinned down containing the Soviets there. This argument was not much justification for a long and costly campaign. With the help of massive superheavy artillery and extremely strong air support, the Germans and Romanians needed almost a month, from June 7 to July 4, to take Sevastopol and more than 90,000 prisoners. Given that the Axis ground force hardly outnumbered the determined defenders, this victory was remarkable, and Manstein was promoted to field marshal.

Shortly afterward, Hitler decided that instead of transferring the Eleventh Army to the southern wing of the main front, he would send it across the Kerch Strait and into the Kuban Peninsula to drive east and south to intercept any Soviet forces that escaped over the Don. But this potentially useful operation was eventually cut down in size and delayed until it was of little value.[5]

When Sevastopol fell, the German offensive was well under way on the main front. Stalin had inadvertently made a considerable contribution to what success it had. He and his generals had initially expected a renewed German offensive against Moscow, as did the western Allies. Despite growing evidence from Soviet intelligence and the West that the Germans would strike in the south, Stalin stubbornly insisted long after his generals had been convinced otherwise, that Hitler's main objective would be Moscow.

He also favored striking first, launching a major spoiling offensive in the south in the spring. He approved a modified version of a plan proposed by Marshal Semyon Timoshenko, now commanding the Southwest Front, in which strong forces would encircle most of the German Sixth Army and recapture Kharkov. Unfortunately for the Soviets, the Germans had been preparing one of their own preliminary operations, which was designed to cut off the Soviets' Izyum salient. Thus they had far stronger panzer and motorized forces nearby than the Soviets expected.

The Soviets struck on May 12. The Germans launched a major counter-offensive on May 17 and encircled the Sixth, Fifty-seventh, and parts of the Ninth and Thirty-eighth Soviet Armies. By May 29 the Germans had cleared the resulting pocket. The Soviets lost 240,000 men and 1,200 tanks. This battle and the Kerch disaster left them gravely weakened.[6]

### The Summer Offensive

Next, the Germans planned to strike on a 350-mile front but not all at one time. Bock had to command no less than seven armies (two allied), and more would join him later. (Normally, an army group would never control more than four armies at once. In 1944–1945, the Western democracies hardly ever had an army group command controlling more than three armies on their whole front of no more than 600 miles.)

To control the growing force and increasingly widespread operations, another headquarters, Army Group A, under Field Marshal List would take over Army Group South's southern wing and conduct the advance south to the Caucasus. Army Group South, redesignated Army Group B, would handle the Don-Stalingrad flank.

The left wing of Army Group B, or "Group Weichs," comprised Maximilian von Weichs's Second German Army, the Second Hungarian Army, and the Fourth Panzer Army. According to plans, it would strike from east of Kursk to the Don and, probably, over the Don to Voronezh, an important road and rail hub five miles east of the river, while the German Sixth Army drove north and east from Belgorod to meet it and form a pocket around Stary Oskol. While the Sixth Army and the Hungarians cleared the pocket, the Fourth Panzer Army would turn south along the west side of the Don with Sixth Army on its right. The First Panzer Army would then strike east from the Artemovsk-Izyum area to meet the Fourth Panzer Army between the Don and Donetz Rivers. This strategy was a late and not promising alteration of the original plan. Originally the main thrust on the right was to have been based in the Taganrog area by the Sea of Azov, but the Germans decided that First Panzer Army was too weak to operate so far from the other enveloping force and had insufficient bridging equipment. The change shifted the right pincer almost 150 miles north, close to the center rather than the right of Bock's front, and reduced the chance of cutting off the Soviet forces before they escaped over the Don.

Farther south, Group Ruoff, comprising the German Seventeenth Army and the Eighth Italian Army, would pin down the Soviets in the coastal region. Right before the First Panzer Army jumped off, Army Group A would take over Group Ruoff and the Eleventh Army, which by that point was expected to have come up from the Crimea to take over a sector of the main front. The Italians and the Seventeenth Army would advance on Rostov and the lower Don from the west and converge with the two panzer armies, which would then come under Army Group A. Then they would drive on Stalingrad, along with Army Group B's Sixth Army. The northern flank secured, Army Group A could safely head south for the Caucasus and the oil fields.

This complex, step-by-step plan would come apart fairly quickly. The Soviets did not play into the Germans' hands this time, while logistics problems and command conflicts hampered the Germans.

The attack of Group Weichs on June 28 tore a hole right through the Soviets' Bryansk Front, and the Sixth Army attacked on June 30. On July 2 the Sixth and Fourth Panzer Armies met, encircling parts of the Soviets' Twenty-first and Fortieth Armies. The Soviets desperately tried to block the road to Voronezh, believing that the Germans wanted it as a jumping off point for a deep encirclement of Moscow from the southeast. Hitler, however, could not decide whether to take Voronezh, as Bock wished. Hitler finally let Bock go ahead as long as he did not waste time or entangle panzer and motorized divisions in city fighting. On July 6, the city fell without much of a fight. Although the move helped confuse the Soviets, it may have been a costly diversion of effort at a critical moment. In a more serious development—which Bock perceived as early as July 3, but most Germans, including Hitler, missed—not many Soviet units were caught west of the Don. On July 6, while hastily reinforcing around Voronezh to block the threat from there, the Soviets had ordered the Southwest and South Fronts to start a strategic retreat farther south.

Bock's tying up of forces around Voronezh helped prevent the encirclement of the Twenty-first and Twenty-eighth Soviet Armies. Army Group A now officially took over its sector and received control of the First Panzer Army, which attacked eastward that same day, July 7. But it was too late to destroy the Soviet forces west of the Don. First Panzer Army and Group Ruoff encircled only rearguards of the withdrawing Soviets.

On July 9 and 10 the Fourth Panzer Army's drive south was spasmodic and hampered by fuel shortages. The first phase of the German plan had been completed, but they had taken only 30,000 prisoners. Any chance the Germans had had of success in the 1942 summer campaign was probably already gone.

Hitler, fast losing confidence in Bock, began intervening in the conduct of operations and issued orders affecting even the movement of the corps. His ideas were frequently erratic. Over the next few months, Hitler's actions in the eastern campaign were often so odd that they constitute probably the best evidence for the otherwise highly improbable thesis, occasionally advanced (notably by Robert Waite in *The Psychopathic God*), that he subconsciously sought defeat.

On July 9, he decided to have the Eleventh Army cross from the Crimea to the Kuban in early August and drive east to the Maikop oil fields instead of taking up a front on the mainland north of the Sea of Azov. It was a good idea, but he aborted its execution. On July 12, Hitler again intervened. He ordered the First Panzer Army to attack toward Millerovo and Kamenets-Shakhtinsky (the first place on the main north–south railroad in the Donetz Basin and the latter, a crossing of the Donetz), while the Fourth Panzer

Army headed for the same places to trap the Soviets. While Hitler and the General Staff expected the Soviets to stand and fight for those objectives, Bock did not, warning that this move would pile up armor uselessly around Millerovo. The Fourth Panzer Army should be directed much farther east, instead, at Morozovsk on the Rostov–Stalingrad rail line. Hitler may have begun to suspect that Bock was right, but he was fed up with him, blaming him for earlier mistakes. On July 13, he ordered the Fourth Panzer Army transferred from Army Group B to Army Group A and fired Bock, replacing him with Weichs. As Bock had predicted, however, the two panzer armies largely "hit air," taking only a modest number of prisoners and producing a traffic jam. Hitler believed that the Soviets in force were still present north of the lower Don but were farther west around Rostov. He belatedly and partially adopted Bock's plan. He ordered the First Panzer Army to turn south, cross the Donetz, and drive on Rostov from the north, while the Fourth Panzer Army should drive south to Morozovsk, to and across the Don, and attack west, parallel with the First Panzer Army north of the Don.

On July 14 Hitler moved his headquarters from East Prussia to Vinnitsa in western Ukraine, indicating his intention to take even closer control of the fighting. Bad weather and difficulties in transporting fuel delayed the Panzer armies' move down the Don, while the Soviet South Front and Southwest Front were fast retreating out of danger. (The new Stalingrad Front replaced the Southwest Front on July 12. Three reserve armies, which were not in good shape, reinforced the new front.)

On July 17, Hitler changed his mind. He ordered the Fourth Panzer Army to stop crossing the Don and instead follow the north bank, and sent the Seventeenth Army to attack farther south than planned, a move that involved lengthy regrouping. On July 19, he belatedly decided to follow Halder's advice and ordered part of the Fourth Panzer Army, four divisions, to cross the Don after all. He also ordered the Sixth Army to resume its advance on Stalingrad and transferred some units to it from Fourth Panzer Army. All this was unusually erratic even for Hitler. He may have suspected that the Soviets had already retreated out of range. On July 20–21, the Seventeenth Army and First Panzer Army found Soviet resistance around Rostov weakening and took the city, a place nearly as large as Stalingrad, on July 23. In a remarkable feat, the Second Battalion of the Brandenburg Regiment (the German Army's special force) and the SS Viking Division took the main bridge over the Don intact, making possible a quick drive for the Caucasus. But the Soviet forces had escaped south of the Don, largely unscathed.

Hitler's Directive 45, issued the same day, probably ended any remaining chance of reaching the Caucasus oil fields. Although the Germans had only taken slightly more than a tenth of the 700,000–800,000 prisoners they had expected to capture west and north of the Don, Hitler had convinced himself that they had actually smashed the Soviets. In view of the small number of prisoners taken, he must have assumed that the Soviets had all along been much weaker than anyone had dared hope; he had already ventured to suggest that possibility as early as June 25. He seems to have clung to this idea for at least another six weeks. Directive 45 declared that "only weak enemy forces have succeeded in escaping encirclement and reaching the south bank of the Don." Army Group A would now encircle them south and southeast of Rostov and then clear the Black Sea coast while, at the same time, driving on Maikop. Then an advance would take place toward Grozny and the most important oil fields at Baku. Wildly overconfident, Hitler had cancelled the plan to send the Eleventh Army into the Kuban, opting instead for a much smaller, delayed crossing of the Kerch Strait. The Eleventh Army and most of its German divisions, with the superheavy artillery, would go north to eliminate Leningrad and its population. (Only the German Navy dared to differ with this idea, squawking about the destruction of Leningrad's shipyards.) The Eighth Italian Army was also switched from Army Group A to take over part of the defensive front along the Don south of the Hungarian Army. This transfer denied the Caucasus drive Alpine divisions, which would have been invaluable in the mountains. While Army Group A struck into the Caucasus, Army Group B would take Stalingrad, with which Hitler became increasingly fatally fascinated. (As late as July 17, however, he had not insisted on capturing it.)

The Germans had split their forces and sent them against two different objectives at right angles to each other. It would have been hard to supply either advance or give them sufficient air support. Moreover, the southward advance, originally supposed to be the main one, was itself split between two objectives—the Black Sea coast and the oil fields. In practice, the Caucasus advance would become more and more subordinate to capturing Stalingrad. Aside from other diversions, Hitler transferred the Grossdeutschland Division to the west, where he feared an Allied landing. in France. Directive 45 has much claim as the death warrant for Germany's last chances of success in the east.[7]

## The Caucasus

A decreasing fraction of the Axis forces in the east carried out the drive for the oil fields, supposedly the objective of the whole campaign; but it might not have been possible to supply stronger forces even had they been available. Already, in late July, as it started south of the Don, Army Group A was not well supplied and suffered serious fuel shortages. Just one railroad running south from Rostov supported the German advance, and only airlifts were able to get fuel to the spearhead divisions.

The Soviets were worried. On July 28, Stalin issued his "not a step back" order, which, with surprising frankness, recounted the loss of territory and resources the Soviets had suffered. He forbade further retreats, backing this command with horrendous threats of punishment. The order, however, does not seem to have applied in the great isthmus between the Black and Caspian Seas. There, the Soviets fell back, often in disorder, but evaded the planned encirclement south of the Don. On July 29, Field Marshal List had urged canceling the planned move, for the Soviets were retreating too quickly to be trapped.

At this stage, the Germans were in the rare position of actually outnumbering the Soviet troops in both men and equipment. The battered Soviet Southern Front was absorbed by Marshal Budyonny's North Caucasus Front, which was backed up, to the south and east, by Gen. Ivan Tyulenev's Transcaucasus Front. The North Caucasus Front numbered no less than eighteen divisions, but some were in bad shape. The Soviets frantically mobilized local resources, forming new units in the Transcaucasus, where they thought the population was relatively dependable, while ruthlessly rounding up and deporting Muslim Caucasian mountaineers like the Chechens. Although the Germans supposed that the Caucasus had been cut off from the rest of the USSR, the Soviets had made the region self-supporting except for tanks and planes. Contact was maintained by sea, and between August 6 and September the Soviets shipped two guards corps and eleven separate infantry brigades to the Caucasus from Astrakhan.

The drive to the Caucasus steadily lost resources and priority. On July 31, Hitler transferred the Fourth Panzer Army and most of its units to Army Group B, which drove northeast on Stalingrad. Army Group A also had to cede a Romanian corps; nevertheless, it made surprising progress at first. Field Marshal List, despite the failure of the encirclement south of the Don, was quite optimistic in early August about reaching Baku, 700 miles from Rostov. But Army Group A was badly spread out, with twenty divisions on a front growing to a length of more than 500 miles, and operating on two divergent axes—the Seventeenth Army south through Krasnodar to the coast and the First Panzer Army southeast toward Grozny and Baku. The Seventeenth Army itself was split between an effort toward Novorossisk in the northeast and an attack toward Sukhumi-Batum in the southwest over the higher mountains. The first German penetration into the mountains on August 12 struck lightly guarded passes and took the Soviets by surprise, but they soon pulled back to a shortened front in incredibly rugged terrain. The Germans found themselves inching along narrow mountain trails through dense forests. Their clothing and equipment were unsuitable. Only mules, caterpillar-tracked motorcycles, and Schwimmwagens (amphibious Volkswagens) could get up the trails. The First Panzer Army also lost momentum. The Army Group steadily lost more units and air support to Army Group B. Three Italian mountain divisions were diverted to join Eighth Italian Army on the Don, while a panzer division, a flak division, and two rocket launcher brigades left for Stalingrad, along with most of Richthofen's supporting planes.

Supplying even the remaining units was difficult. Moving fuel to the front was especially arduous. The Germans even used camels. The truck columns bringing up supplies themselves ran out of gas. The Germans resorted to the expedient of running trains over short stretches of open track, loading the trains from trucks at one end and shifting the cargo back to trucks at the other.

By mid-August, the First Panzer Army was pessimistic, and both German armies were slowing to a halt. The Germans took the least important oil field at Maikop only to find it thoroughly demolished. As early as August 26, List warned that his forces would have to take up winter positions soon and that he needed reinforcements and more air support.

The First Panzer Army tried to cross the Terek River, which the Transcaucasus Front's Northern Group held. The Terek was a formidable obstacle, being both wide (500 meters) and fast, and bordered by swampy ground. In a difficult operation, the Germans crossed the river and seized a confined bridgehead, but they could not exploit it. Soviet night bombers then smashed their newly constructed bridge. They shifted their effort farther west but were soon stopped. On October 1, the First Panzer Army called a halt until reinforcements could arrive.

On September 6, the Seventeenth Army had finally taken most of Novorossisk against heavy resistance by the Soviet Forty-seventh Army but did not get much farther. The weather became worse and worse. Hitler had become increasingly irritated at List, who he thought had picked the wrong mountain passes to attack, and there was some confusion about what he wanted List to do. On September 9, he fired List for supposedly not following orders, but he did not name a successor, in effect, acting as commander of Army Group A himself. The Seventeenth Army ultimately stalled on the Maikop-Tuapse road in early October. By then, even Hitler accepted that the advance was over until reinforcements could arrive, that is, after Stalingrad fell.

The First Panzer Army did launch a local offensive on October 25, biting out a Soviet salient around Nalchik that had threatened its rear. At first it was successful, making a surprising advance, but it was stopped on November 4. The leading panzer division had to fight its way back out of a trap.

What was supposed to be the advance intended to decide the whole war had stalled at Novorossisk, on the Terek, and in the mountains. There are indications that by early September, Hitler realized that the objectives in the east could not be attained and even that the war was lost.[8] This defeat was the result of failure in the Caucasus and not Stalingrad, where he still hoped for at least a local victory.

## Stalingrad: The Fight for the City

While the Caucasus drive petered out, the battle for Stalingrad, a large industrial city on the lower Volga, became the focus of the fighting on the eastern front. Hitler became more obsessed with capturing it, partly for the political propaganda value of taking a city named after his nemesis, who had usurped credit for defending then named Tsaritsyn against the Don Cossacks in 1918 during the Russian Civil War. Hitler also seems to have genuinely believed that taking Stalingrad would cut the Soviets off from the Caucasus, even if the oil fields remained out of reach, and that they would be compelled to commit the Red Army to a decisive battle there, where it could be bled white.

Although the Soviets had not suffered the overwhelming defeat that Hitler supposed, they were in bad shape. Their forces west of the Volga and in the Don bend were disorganized and had huge gaps in the front. On July 12, remnants of the Southwest Front, with three newly arrived armies—the Sixty-second, Sixty-third, and Sixty-fourth—were concentrated in the Stalingrad Front. (On July 28, the Stalingrad Front split into the Stalingrad Front and the Southeastern Front. Just to confuse historians, on September 28, the Stalingrad Front would be renamed the Don Front while Southeastern Front was redesignated Stalingrad Front.)

The German advance east, however, was slow to start. The Sixth Army stalled entirely for ten days for lack of fuel, as supplies had been diverted to the Caucasus. When the advance resumed, the Fourth Panzer Army drove up from the southwest below the Don, but the advance was still intermittent because of fuel and ammunition shortages. On August 7, the Sixth Army began a decisive attack on the long troublesome Kalach bridgehead in the Don bend directly west of Stalingrad, where the Soviets had concentrated powerful armored forces. The Germans succeeded in trapping the Soviet defenders. When the pocket was cleared on August 11, they had taken more than 50,000 prisoners and claimed destroying or capturing eleven hundred tanks. It took still more time to clear most of the rest of the Don bend, but they never entirely succeeded. Soviet counterattacks on the northern side of the Don bend had gained new bridgeheads and prevented the Germans from concentrating sufficient forces for a successful encirclement between the Don and the Volga. The Sixth Army finally crossed the Don on August 21. The Soviets were badly disorganized, and though the Germans quickly reached the Volga on a five-mile stretch of the riverbank north of Stalingrad, they did not trap large Soviet forces. On August 23 and 24, unusually strong air attacks largely wrecked Stalingrad, but the Germans still hit stiff opposition.

The city stretched for twenty miles or more along the Volga but was only two and a half miles across at its widest point. When wrecked by bombs or shells, its many large, strongly built industrial plants became even more formidable obstacles than they had been when intact. The Soviet Sixty-second and Sixty-fourth Armies held a large bridgehead encompassing the city and the area south of it. When the Germans broke into Stalingrad on September 4, Stalin undoubtedly was inclined to insist that "his" city be held for propaganda reasons, but he probably still thought that holding Stalingrad blocked a German move to outflank Moscow from the south. Even after that idea dissipated, it became apparent that a continuing fight there tied up strong German forces under conditions that discounted their mobility, air support, tanks, and tactical skills and favored the Red Army. Moreover, the battle kept the Sixth and Fourth Panzer Armies pinned down at the tip of a long, awkward salient, which the Soviets hoped to sever.

On September 12–13, the Soviet military leaders began planning a major counteroffensive to be launched in the fall. The Sixty-second Army, as historian John Erickson put it, now served as "live bait" to keep the German forces tied up at the eastern end of the Don-Volga corridor. The Soviets felt keeping the battle in the city going was essential because if the

Germans took the whole city, they would be free to redistribute their forces to hold the long front on either side. The Soviets' problem therefore was to feed in enough reinforcements to the bridgehead west of the Volga to keep the Germans in play (in itself an expensive business) and maintain enough pressure on the flanks of the German salient to discourage them from concentrating entirely on the fight for the city itself. The fighting on the flanks was also costly.

Although the Germans' attempts to take Stalingrad were often not well managed, they seriously threatened the Sixty-second Army. On September 14 the Germans split the Soviet bridgehead in two. They took the city center and cleared the southern part of Stalingrad. That day, the Soviets committed their Thirteenth Guards Rifle Division (rated the best in their army), and only desperate efforts prevented the Germans from driving them into the Volga. Through the end of the month, the Soviets sent in nine rifle divisions, two tank brigades, and a rifle brigade to reinforce the Sixty-second Army. The fighting increasingly revolved around the ruins of three huge factories in the northern half of Stalingrad—the Stalingrad Tractor Factory, the Barrikady Ordnance Plant, and the Krasny Oktyabr (Red October) Metallurgical Plant—and the Mamayev Kurgan (Hill 102), a Tatar burial ground that was so heavily worked over by shells and rockets that sometimes neither side could stay on it. The Soviets, while suffering heavy losses, became expert at city fighting.

The struggle was by no means limited to the city, as the Soviets attacked the long German defensive front on either side of Stalingrad. A serious attack on the Eighth Italian Army on August 20 was stopped only with great difficulty. Early in September, the Soviets repeatedly attacked the German XIV Panzer Corps, which held the northern face of the land bridge between the Don and the Volga, and subjected the Germans to heavy artillery fire and tank and infantry attacks. Despite this, the Germans continued to bring in the Third Romanian Army to release their forces from defensive tasks along the Don so they could be used in the city. They also planned to bring in the Fourth Romanian Army to hold the long flank south of Stalingrad. The Third Romanian Army would hold a 105-mile front with sixty-nine battalions, and the Fourth Army's thirty-three battalions would hold an unwieldy stretch of 250 miles. The Romanian dictator Marshal Ion Antonescu would command a new Army Group Don, controlling the German Sixth Army and both Romanian armies, once Stalingrad fell.

In a hopeful attempt to chop off the whole German salient, a Soviet counteroffensive on September 18 launched between the rivers failed, but the Soviets struck successfully against the Romanians later in the month. On September 28, a relatively small attack on Romanian forces under the command of the Fourth Panzer Army south of Stalingrad led to a panicky retreat, forcing the commitment of a German panzer division. Gen. Hermann Hoth, the commander of the Fourth Panzer Army, acidly commented that "German commands which have Romanian troops serving under them must reconcile themselves to the fact that moderately heavy fire, even without an enemy attack will be enough to cause these troops to fall back and that the reports they submit concerning their own situation are worthless since they never know where their units are and their estimates of enemy strength are vastly exaggerated." Hoth recommended allotting the Romanians very narrow sectors, with a German division as a backup for every four Romanian divisions. The Romanians themselves protested their weakness. They pointed out that the Soviets still held bridgeheads on the Don's west bank in the Third Romanian Army sector. Its commander, Petre Dumitrescu, requested forces so he could eliminate them, but this was denied.

By September 20, Gen. Friedrich Paulus, the Sixth Army's commander, Weichs, and Richthofen had all noted the Germans' awkward position at the tip of a salient, sticking out from an overextended front. The XIV Panzer Corps commander Gen. Gustav von Wietersheim lost his command for his too-insistent warnings and, worse, his suggesting a withdrawal from Stalingrad to avert disaster. Hitler saw the danger but insisted on taking all of Stalingrad before doing what was necessary to deal with the problem. Capturing the city, the goal to which he had become publicly committed, was liable to be the only "prize of victory" obtainable from the 1942 campaign. As noted earlier, he had begun to realize by early September that the German Army would not take the oil fields, that the USSR campaign would be a failure, and even that the war would be lost. He had quarreled not only with List but also with the normally pliable Jodl. He had also fired General Halder, although the latter may have deliberately provoked his relief, having concluded himself that defeat was inevitable. Halder was replaced by an out-and-out Nazi, Kurt Zeitzler. Although not an especially able chief of staff, General Zietzler did exhibit some courage in standing up to Hitler. Eventually Zietzler grew to hate him even more than Halder did and became involved in the July 1944 plot against the führer.

The Soviets nevertheless suffered heavily. The Germans made considerable gains in late September and October, reducing the Soviets' position to four separate, shallow bridgeheads. Getting reinforcements and supplies into the city, and getting wounded men out, was costly, as Luftflotte 4 attacked the ferries and small boats on the Volga and rail traffic east of the river. On September 28, the Luftwaffe sank five of the six large ferries that reached the Krasny Oktyabr factory's landing stage. The Soviets feared a landing on the islands in the river or even on the east bank, which would have been a more sensible course of action than the one the Germans chose of chewing up the Soviets in Stalingrad block by block, and committed strong forces to defend those places as a precaution. A renewed German offensive was particularly dangerous on October 14 and 15. On one day the Soviets evacuated thirty-five hundred wounded men across the Volga. On October 15 German guns and planes stopped traffic on the river entirely.

The Germans' advance slowly tapered off, however. In launching a final effort on November 11, they were reduced to bringing engineer battalions from divisions outside the battle area to take the city's last ruins. By mid-November, they were exhausted and short of supplies, although the Soviet Sixty-second Army was also in poor shape, now trying to hold three separate bridgeheads. With the Volga freezing, it was hard to get even small boats across. Moreover, Axis operations in the Mediterranean had drawn off much of their air support. Between mid-August and early November, $4\frac{2}{3}$ bomber groups (140 planes) and $5\frac{1}{3}$ fighter groups (160 planes) had gone south. After El Alamein and the North African landing, $3\frac{1}{3}$ bomber groups (100 planes) and $1\frac{1}{3}$ fighter groups (40 planes) had followed. Defeats in the Mediterranean were a considerable distraction for the German leaders, as the Soviets prepared to strike.[9]

## The Soviet Counteroffensive

Hitler recognized the threat to the German forces on the long Don front. In fact, he showed more awareness of the problem than either Halder or Zeitzler had. Since mid-August, he had spoken several times of the threat of a major attack across the Don on Rostov, through which ran the lines of communication not only for the Sixth and Fourth Panzer Armies but also Army Group A. Given his fixation on taking Stalingrad, however, he would not allow, much less order, a preemptive retirement from the Don-Volga salient that would allow redistributing the German forces to provide a firm defensive front.

The Germans anticipated a much smaller, less well conducted, less ambitious, and later offensive than the one they confronted. By mid-October, the movement of Soviet troops to the Don front opposite the Third Romanian Army had been reported, but thanks to Soviet security precautions, air reconnaissance could not confirm the account. Hitler nevertheless ordered some Luftwaffe field divisions to back up the Axis allies, a characteristically disastrous idea of Göring's, designed to avoid transferring men from his overstrength service to the army. Army Group B—saddled with the impossible burden of controlling seven armies, four of which were not German—tried to increase the strength of the German "bolsters" and backed up the Romanians in other ways. It also attempted radio deception measures to try and convince the Soviets that the Don front was stronger than it really was.

Foreign Armies East (German military intelligence) gradually came to admit that an attack was imminent but believed that it would be a limited, local effort. It estimated that the Soviets were capable of launching only one major offensive aimed at Army Group Center. For many years after the war, the Soviets successfully hid that their primary aim in 1942 had not been to trap the Germans at Stalingrad but to destroy the German Ninth Army in the Rzhev salient and, if possible, drive as far west as Smolensk. Foreign Armies East, however, not only underestimated the Soviets' overall strength and assumed that any attack on the Don front would only be secondary but also thought that it would take place only after the expected offensive against Army Group Center.

Hitler was not so sure. On November 2, he ordered that the bridges the Soviets were building to their long-standing bridgeheads on the Don's right bank be bombed. On November 3 he ordered the Sixth Panzer Division and two infantry divisions sent from western Europe to take up reserve positions behind the Romanians and Italians. They were still en route when the Soviets struck. Hitler did not expect the Soviets to attack as early as they did. Foreign Armies East slowly and reluctantly increased its estimate of the threat. On November 12, it predicted an attack on the Third Romanian Army but believed that it would be merely a "salient cut" designed to sever the railroad to Stalingrad and force the Germans to leave the city and not be part of a double envelopment to trap them.

The Soviet buildup had been far more massive than the Germans supposed. A huge force was assembled under the Southwest, Don, and Stalingrad Fronts: 1,050,000 men, 900 tanks, 13,500 guns (not counting antiaircraft guns or 50mm infantry mortars), and 1,114 planes. They outnumbered the German and Romanian forces at least two to one in planes, tanks, guns, and men and far more in the attack sectors. On November 19, the Soviets struck, coordinating tanks, infantry, and artillery far more smoothly than the Germans had seen before. Along most of the front, the Soviets hit the thinly spread, poorly armed Romanian Third and Fourth Armies, which had weak artillery and few effective antitank weapons. The Third Army was supported only by a German close-support group that comprised a Panzergrenadier battalion, an antitank company, and a few heavy artillery pieces. Many Romanians fled after the preliminary bombardment, even before the Soviet tanks and infantry advanced. The only reserve nearby, XLVIII Panzer Corps, consisted of two weak divisions—the Twenty-second Panzer Division and the First Romanian Armored Division (the latter had only obsolete Czech tanks.) Worse, many of their tanks were immobilized after mice had eaten their electrical insulation.

On November 23, the Soviet spearheads met in the Axis rear, cutting the Sixth Army's supply line and line of retreat. On the one hand, the Soviets vastly underestimated their success. They thought that they had trapped a force of 85,000–95,000 men; instead, more than 250,000 men were caught. On the other hand, the Soviets overestimated the mobility and striking power of the encircled German units.

Hitler realized the situation was serious. On November 20, he ordered the immediate formation of Army Group Don to take over the threatened portion of Army Group B's front. Instead of awarding command to Antonescu, Manstein took command, and his Eleventh Army headquarters, pieced out with some German-Romanian liaison staffs, supplied his head-quarters staff. Manstein was Hitler's best general but not his favorite. He was an icy Junker, whose personality and social class did not appeal to the führer; and—worse—Hitler was almost certainly aware that the field marshal's great-grandfather was Jewish. He was respected but not liked by men of his own background. Nevertheless, Manstein, who had played the central role in devising the plan that had brought victory in the west in 1940, also played a central role in greatly prolonging the life of Hitler's empire.

But it took nearly a week for Manstein's command apparatus to move from the Leningrad area (where it had been stymied in an attempt to take the city) to the south. The following day, Hitler finally appointed a commander for Army Group A, Kleist, who had commanded First Panzer Army. He and Manstein would be fired on the same day in March 1944. Meanwhile, Hitler rejected having the Sixth Army retreat, regardless of the danger of a "temporary" encirclement in its present position. Weichs and Paulus concluded on November 23 that the Sixth Army must break out quickly. Richthofen concurred. He stressed that the army could not be supplied by air. Weichs specifically declared that the Luftwaffe could not provide even a tenth of the Sixth Army's needs. Zeitzler backed their assertions. Some evidence indicates that Hitler briefly wavered and nearly authorized a breakout, but the pandering of the OKW generals Keitel and Jodl undermined any reconsideration on his part. Further, the Luftwaffe chief of staff Gen. Hans Jeschonnek appears to have assured Hitler on November 20 that Stalingrad could be adequately supplied by air if and when it was cut off, although he may have meant to refer to only a temporarily brief encirclement. Worse, Göring backed Jeschonnek without any qualifications whatever. When the conscience-stricken Luftwaffe chief of staff realized that he had blundered in his assurances, Göring forbade him to warn Hitler. He even stopped Jeschonnek from pointing out that the Luftwaffe's standard 250- and 1,000-kilogram air supply containers were named after the size of the bombs they replaced, not the weight of their own contents, and that they carried only two-thirds of the weight of those bombs.

Manstein also undermined the united front of the ground commanders. Reaching south Russia on November 24, he disagreed with Weichs's pessimism. Apparently arrogantly confident in his own ability, he may have actually believed that he could relieve the Sixth Army while it remained in place and could restore the front completely; however, he soon became more realistic, especially after conferring with Richthofen. Manstein rejected an immediate breakout, though, in favor of a relief operation to start in early December. His decision played straight into Hitler's hands, and the latter fixedly determined that the Sixth Army should stay in place for relief.

Writer Alan Clark suggested an alternative interpretation: the field marshal had privately concluded that Hitler would not allow an immediate breakout in any case, but in the context of a planned relief effort, a breakout might be arranged later. Moreover, Manstein may have actually recognized, as his colleagues did not, that an early breakout attempt would probably lead to disaster. It was not simply the Sixth Army but the whole German southern front—particularly Army Group A, out on a limb in the Caucasus—that was at stake. Further, the Soviet ring around the Sixth Army was so tight, and Sixth Army was in such bad shape, that an immediate breakout attempt would probably lead to its being largely destroyed. Even if part of the panzer and motorized elements reached the German lines, that would not compensate for releasing the besieging Soviet forces, which would quickly finish off the German southern wing. The Sixth Army must stay at Stalingrad to pin down the Soviets, even at the grave risk of total destruction. Its only hope was to hold out as long as possible so that an orderly relief effort and breakout might be prepared. If Manstein thought this way at the time, however, he never directly admitted it, although he alluded to these ideas in his memoir. Such an admission would have been unpopular in postwar Germany, where Stalingrad had become an emotional symbol and many were anxious to heap all responsibility for the destruction of the Sixth Army on Hitler alone.

The chance of a successful early breakout in November 1942 was slight. The Sixth Army's supply situation had been so dire even before the Soviets attacked that it hardly could have stayed on the Volga during the winter. Living a hand-to-mouth existence at the end of its long supply line, it had hardly any fuel on hand and not enough to support a desperate effort to crash through the Soviet ring. Paulus's vacillations, and his submission to Hitler's will despite the urging of several subordinates, suggest that he realized this situation.

Fortunately for the Germans, the Soviets cautiously concentrated an overwhelming portion of their forces on insuring against the overestimated threat of a breakout. They were determined to destroy the encircled German force, whatever prizes beckoned elsewhere, and did not exploit the Stalingrad breakthrough to the southwest as much as they might have. The Germans were able to form a defensive front west of the Don on the Chir River while preparing a relief effort. Manstein thought that the Soviets, by better coordinating their forces, could have smashed the Chir front.

Meanwhile, the Soviets readied a second major offensive in the south. In Operation Saturn the Southwest and Voronezh Fronts would attack the Italians. In its original form, the plan was to encircle the Italian Army and the whole Army Group Don, reach Rostov, and cut off Army Group A.

In the meantime, the Germans' airlift and relief attempt for Stalingrad failed. Richthofen, saddled with the responsibility for the air supply effort, calculated that delivering the estimated absolute minimum of 300 tons of supplies a day—although the Sixth Army really needed 500 tons daily—required 150 Junkers 52 transports landing in Stalingrad each day. But because bad weather would often prevent all operations and many planes would not be working at any given time, he really needed 800. The whole Luftwaffe had only 750 Junkers 52s and half of them were in the Mediterranean. Using some civilian airliners and converting some bombers and long-range reconnaissance planes enabled Richthofen to assemble a fleet of 500 planes; however, many were unsuitable for the job. Moreover, Stalingrad had only one fully equipped airfield, with five more barely usable landing strips. The terrible weather and Soviet fighters took a steady toll on the transports. Some space was wasted on unnecessary supplies, and the airlift never approached the minimum level of deliveries needed.

The relief effort by LVII Panzer Corps was seriously delayed from an original starting date of December 8 to December 11, and it was never strong enough on the ground or had sufficient air support. Two of the three panzer divisions allotted to it were weak. Manstein decided that an attack across the Chir, the point nearest the Sixth Army, was too obvious, so the Germans launched the attack from south of the Don. It took the Soviets by surprise, but it meant that the panzers had a longer way to go. A huge truck convoy hauling 3,000 tons of supplies and some tractors slated to pull Sixth Army's otherwise immobilized artillery trailed the panzers. The attack made slow progress. It reached the Myshkova River thirty-five miles from the pocket and stuck. Only Soviet overcaution may have prevented its envelopment and destruction.

Hitler still refused to let the Sixth Army break out if that meant giving up its position. Paulus again refused to act without Hitler's authority, and the Sixth Army was perhaps too weak to strike out successfully. When the Soviets pushed the relief force back, the Sixth Army was doomed.

Despite its failure, the relief attempt—along with the disastrous misfire of the Soviets' Mars offensive against Army Group Center (begun November 25, it petered out in early December after the Red Army suffered enormous losses)—may have led the Soviet command on December 13 to curtail its plans for the next offensive in the south. Operation Saturn was scaled down to Little Saturn and involved a shallower envelopment whose pincers would meet well north of the Black Sea coast. Rostov would have to be reached in two bites, not one. The offensive began on December 16 and crashed through the Italians, who were supported only by one German infantry division, two battalions from another, and a weak panzer division in reserve. The Soviets failed to break through the sector to the south, but the Germans' situation was soon desperate. The forward fields for the airlift were overrun, and it became obvious that the issue was now how to get the German forces out of the Caucasus before they were isolated.

Had the Soviets reached Rostov or the coast further west, the early defeat of Germany would have been likely. On December 28, Hitler, barely in time, allowed a (gradual) withdrawal from the Caucasus. He insisted, however, that part of Army Group A fall back into a bridgehead on the Kuban Peninsula, and from there, he hoped, a new offensive against the Caucasus oil fields would be launched in 1943. By then, the Soviets planned Operation Don, or a bigger Saturn—involving the South Front (the renamed Stalingrad Front), Southwest Front, and Transcaucasus Front—to reach Rostov and trap the Fourth Panzer Army and Army Group A.

The Germans were helped by the fact that the Stalingrad garrison continued to pin down considerable Soviet forces, and the Soviets insisted on attacking into the perimeter. The Sixth Army did not surrender completely until February 2. Only a few thousand men survived to return to Germany.

Meanwhile, Manstein directed a skillful retreat and delaying action. In a great "castling movement," as his aide described it, the First Panzer Army fell back behind the Fourth Panzer Army and was switched around to face north and northwest. He was hampered not only by Army Group A's late start but also by the sluggishness of its commander Kleist. The Germans blocked multiple threats to the Rostov bottleneck through which they had to retreat. In the last stages, the route was so crowded that some German units marched over the frozen Sea of Azov instead of lining up to cross the Don bridges at Rostov. The Germans fell back to the line of the Mius River in the south while the Voronezh Front, supported by Bryansk and Southwest Fronts, attacked the remaining parts of Army Group B's front on the northern Don—the Hungarian Second Army and the German Second Army—on January 14. The Soviets tore a 200-mile wide gap in the front and retook Kharkov and the Donetz industrial area. They then advanced steadily toward the Dnieper crossings and the isthmus to the Crimea.

The Soviets, however, were too widespread, exhausted, and at the end of a lengthy supply line. Manstein, meanwhile, had skillfully assembled strong forces on either side of the gap. On February 14, with effective support from Richthofen's Luftflotte 4, Manstein launched a counteroffensive that smashed four Soviet armies, recaptured Kharkov, and by March 18, largely restored the line from which the German armies had departed in June 1942.

Nevertheless, the Germans in the east had been permanently lamed. The Sixth Army, or more than 250,000 men, had been lost, and with it four allied Axis armies.[10]

The Stalingrad disaster was a particular shock to German morale. The Nazis had already noted, with disquiet, the public's willingness for a compromise peace with Stalin (although some of the Nazis shared that inclination). For most of 1943, German morale was low. Paradoxically it recovered a bit after the Germans rode out Italy's surrender without a spectacular disaster. The Axis allies proceeded to look for the exits. Mussolini already wanted a separate peace with the Soviets. Other Italians, Fascist or not, and all but a few people in the Axis satellites wanted peace with the West.[11]

The Stalingrad-Caucasus campaign was the military turning point of the war in the east. Yet that campaign had had little, if any, chance of success in the first place. Even had the Germans taken the Caucasus oil fields intact, they would not have been able to ship their products back to Germany. The campaign itself demonstrated that German hopes had no foundation in logistics. As George Blau observed, the Germans' problem of transporting supplies could only have been solved had they complemented the few railroad lines in southern Russia with a tremendous trucking and airlift effort. But the Germans lacked the necessary trucks, transport planes, and gasoline, and their repair facilities were inadequate. "From the outset, there was actually not the slightest hope that the supply services would be capable of keeping up with an advance to the Volga and beyond the Caucasus." Thus Williamson Murray concluded that the 1942 campaigns in both Russia and the Mediterranean were the "last spasmodic advances of Nazi military power, there was no prospect of achieving a decisive strategic victory."[12]

Indeed, the Germans could not have held Stalingrad even had they captured it. The lack of supplies for the Sixth Army hopelessly prejudiced its chances for survival even if Hitler had been more reasonable about its withdrawal. That the Germans enjoyed such an initial success as they did was mainly owed to Soviet blunders in the spring.

# 9

# The Mediterranean and the Middle East II

*From Pearl Harbor to the Invasion of Northwest Africa*

Even as the British took eastern Libya, the balance in the Mediterranean turned against them. The Axis recovery in the air and on the sea, their easing supply problem, and Japan's entry into the war outweighed, in the short run, the impact of America's entry. The Allies had to drop the tentative plans for Africa that they had agreed on at the Washington conference. Soon they lost all their gains and for much of 1942 were in a desperate struggle to hold Malta and Egypt.

Hitler's concentration of U-boats in the Mediterranean, however unwise in relation to the Atlantic, cost the British heavily. On November 12, 1941, *U-331* destroyed the battleship HMS *Barham* and most of its crew in the eastern Mediterranean. On November 13–14, *U-81* sank Force H's carrier HMS *Ark Royal*. Other losses followed.

In early December, the Luftwaffe transferred Luftflotte 2 from Russia to the Mediterranean. Hitler also ordered antisubmarine equipment and technicians there. The Allies soon found it harder to supply Malta and attack the Axis supply route to Libya. On December 19, Force K, the Malta-based force of cruisers and destroyers, suffered terrible losses in a minefield, and its remaining ships fled. The same day, Italian frogmen rode manned torpedoes into Alexandria's harbor and disabled the Mediterranean fleet's last two battleships. Sunk at anchor in shallow water, they were out of action for a long time, although the Axis did not seem to have realized this until the end of January. As with Taranto for the Italians, this disaster was not as big as it seemed, but it shook the British.

With the air situation improved, the Italians restarted their supply runs. Their first attempt to do so misfired horribly. A pair of cruisers rushing to Libya, carrying aviation gasoline in drums on their decks, and escorted only by a torpedo boat ran into four destroyers from Gibraltar on December 13. Both cruisers went down in flames. The Italians rammed an unusually large, heavily escorted convoy across on December 19. Another convoy reached Tripoli on January 6, giving Rommel equipment and supplies that drastically changed the situation in Libya.

Meanwhile, the Japanese attack forced Middle East Command to part with large forces for the Far East, although this was not a direct cause of the reverses the British were to suffer in the Mediterranean in early 1942. At first, the British government resolved to take no units from the Middle East and merely divert some en route. The British redirected two infantry divisions, the Eighteenth British and Seventeenth Indian, and no less than seven fighter squadrons to the Far East. Commander in chief of the Middle East Sir Claude Auchinleck, however, had to give up fifty light tanks and antiaircraft batteries and, by the end of 1941, the entire Seventh Armored Brigade. He lost a light tank squadron, two of his three Australian divisions, two Hurricane squadrons, four complete light bomber squadrons, and a dozen additional light bombers. In February 1942, he had to give up the Seventieth British Division.

The British position in western Cyrenaica was largely a bluff. Their units were scattered and poorly supplied. Demolitions and mines delayed their using Benghazi harbor, with the first British convoy entering it only on January 7. The inexperienced, badly trained First Armored Division had replaced their experienced armored units. Rommel's staff recognized the weakness of the British position and calculated that the tanks delivered in early January should give the Axis superiority in the forward area. Rommel, initially doubtful about the adequacy of his supplies, finally decided on a counterattack without telling his German or Italian superiors. He suspected that the British somehow knew Axis secrets and thought the Italians might interfere with his plans. The British, however, did not think a serious attack in the desert was possible yet. Misinterpreting data from intercepts, they underestimated the deliveries of Rommel's replacement tanks and, hence, Panzer Group Afrika's actual armored strength.

Rommel's brilliant attack of January 21 took the British unaware and badly deployed. Auchinleck mistakenly had left General Ritchie in command of the Eighth Army. The battered British pulled back to the Gazala Line in the middle of Cyrenaica, losing Benghazi and valuable air bases for the support of Malta. The able XIII Corps commander Gen. Alfred Godwin-Austen, who had prevented a worse disaster, resigned in protest against Ritchie's habit of bypassing him and issuing wrong-headed orders to his divisional commanders.[1]

## Axis Plans for 1942

As of December 14, 1941, the Oberkommando der Wehrmacht was optimistic about the Axis powers' ability to advance into the Middle East, but the OKW clearly stressed a drive from the north, via the Caucasus, while the army, given the desperate situation in Russia, even set that operation aside for a time. General Halder and the army's High Command had never liked the North African campaign or, indeed, Erwin Rommel. The German Navy talked of making an early thrust to the Persian Gulf and linking with a westward drive by the Japanese, giving this push priority over everything but the capture of the Caucasus. The navy did not, however, have a definite plan or even an assessment of what forces would be needed for this. Indeed, by the time the navy formulated a memorandum for Hitler expounding its approach in late February, it was already too late to influence the Japanese in favor of such ideas. (Per the reports of the naval attaché in Tokyo, the navy and probably the German leaders in general seem to have assumed that the Japanese were more interested in a westward drive and joining up with the Germans than they really were.)

Hitler did not reject such ideas, but he saw them as grossly premature. The Caucasus must come first. He pondered a lesser operation to capture Suez, but in the end he simply hoped that Rommel would conquer Egypt for the Axis. Hitler did not issue any numbered formal directives dealing with the Mediterranean after November 1941. With German forces in Russia at full stretch, he allotted no important new units to the Mediterranean. However, Rommel did get a small, specialized force, Special Command 288, originally formed for operations in Iraq, and the tank companies of his panzer divisions that had long been waiting in Europe finally reached Libya. More important, he received major help to confront the threat to his supply line—Malta. Massive air operations by Luftflotte 2 and the Italians would neutralize Malta, softening it up for an invasion.

The Germans and Italians planned a large-scale operation, code-named Herkules, to take Malta. Some thirty thousand airborne troops—one German and one Italian paratroop division and an Italian glider-borne division—would seize a beachhead at Marsa Scirocco for a follow-up force of no less than seventy thousand men in five Italian divisions and some supporting German units. Originally scheduled for May or June, the operation was to precede a major offensive in North Africa. Hitler and Jodl, however, were skeptical that the Italians would go through with the plan, which Hitler feared would fail. Jodl favored having Rommel attack in the desert first. Field Marshal Kesselring, the German commander in chief south, and Rommel originally were happy to take Malta first, before anything else. By March the Italians were inclined to postpone the operation until July, but the Germans did not want to wait until far into the summer before striking on land. Rommel feared that the British were building up their strength too quickly to be left alone, and, like Hitler, he may have wondered if the Italians actually would carry out the plan. In April, he and Kesselring, to whom Hitler had disclosed his doubts, changed their minds. They now urged capturing Tobruk, then tackling Malta, before turning back to take Egypt. Hitler readily agreed. At the end of April, Mussolini was easily persuaded to go along.

Yet, since Crete, Hitler had been uncomfortable with airborne operations. On May 21, he told General Student, who was to command the airborne phase of the Malta invasion, that he feared that the British fleet would intervene when it began, and the Italian fleet would flee, leaving the airborne force in the lurch.[2] The invasion never happened. The Axis came perilously close to finishing off Malta without it.

## Malta

It had been estimated at the end of 1941 that Malta had enough flour to last until May, coal until the end of March, kerosene and benzene until the end of April, and aviation gasoline until well into the summer. In January, though, the Maltese began suffering one of the great ordeals of the war. They and the British garrison endured a concentrated pounding by bombs and suffered near starvation, almost unique on the Western democratic side of the war. The war at Malta saw none of the chivalry said to have characterized the North African fighting. The usually well-behaved Maltese wound up killing downed German and Italian airmen when they got their hands on them.

More than four hundred planes attacked the island, day after day. A small, three-ship convoy from Alexandria reached the island, but thereafter regular supply efforts failed. In February, a convoy bound for Malta never made it; two ships were lost, and the rest turned back. With western Cyrenaican airfields back in Axis hands, supporting planes could no longer aid convoys. Malta's obsolete Hurricanes found it harder and harder to attack enemy bombers given the superiority of their Me 109 escorts. Skillfully concerted fighter sweeps and bomber attacks caught many British planes while landing, and the British bomber force was eliminated. Offensive air operations practically ended. Submarines also found it increasingly difficult to use the Malta base. The Italians no longer took the elaborate evasive route and did not bother to sail more than fifty miles from Malta. In March, a British convoy of four ships left Alexandria. A far stronger Italian surface force, built around the battleship *Littorio*, came out to intercept it, but Adm. Philip Vian's covering force of light cruisers and destroyers laid a smokescreen to hide the convoy and vigorously counterattacked, damaging *Littorio*. When the cargo ships reached Malta, the Axis bombed and sank them before they could be completely unloaded. The inefficiency of the unloading process led London to replace Governor-General William Dobbie with Lord Gort.

The Germans' concentration on bombing the Malta dockyards gave the remnants of the RAF a breathing space. By March 23, few RAF fighters were left. Dockyard work virtually stopped except in underground shops. Malta desperately needed more Spitfires. (A few had arrived in March.) As no British carrier capable of carrying enough Spitfires was available, President Roosevelt loaned the carrier USS *Wasp* to do the job. On April 20, forty-six Spitfires flew off the *Wasp*, but the fighters were in poor condition, and no proper reception had been prepared. Before the Spitfires could refuel, they were caught on the ground by a carefully timed Axis air attack. Within two days, most were destroyed or damaged. The bombing went on, paralyzing the submarine base. One Greek and three British submarines were sunk, the remaining submarines hid on the harbor bottom by day. Because of the bombing, mines could no longer be swept. Mines laid by Axis motor torpedo boats finally rendered the base untenable. Beginning April 26, the last submarines fled, two being lost in the process. By then, only four torpedo planes were left on Malta. On April 23, the British had decided that no further convoys could be run until June. But more Spitfires flew in, while the fast minelayer HMS *Welshman* ran in some supplies.

Fortuitously, the German air effort fell off after April 28 as planes left for Russia and North Africa. On May 9, the *Wasp* returned and flew off sixty-four Spitfires. Having been carefully prepared at home (although, in another incredible blunder, some of their pilots were so inexperienced that some had to be returned to Britain), the Spitfires experienced no nonsense at the Malta end this time. Their reception, dispersal, and refueling were ably planned. This new force turned the tide in the air, but supplying Malta remained difficult and dangerous. The Germans had neutralized it as an offensive base. In April and the first half of May, Axis ships were safer than at any other time during the war in the Mediterranean. Almost all of the few Axis sinkings were victims of submarines sailing on long patrols from remote bases.[3] Rommel was able to prepare his offensive with little difficulty.

## The British Dilemma

Auchinleck was anxious about both his northern front, should the Soviets be beaten, and about the Japanese; moreover, his troops were nowhere near ready for an offensive in Libya. The British knew nothing about German plans, which were communicated by landline, but in late March they began to fear the Germans were preparing to invade Malta. As Malta's position grew dire, London resumed pressure for an offensive. Churchill and the chiefs of staff were not impressed when Auchinleck suggested putting off an attack still longer to release forces for the Far East. Nor were they persuaded when the Middle East Defence Committee suggested, on May 9, that Malta's fall would not necessarily be fatal for holding Egypt (it pointed out that Malta was already effectively neutralized) and that it might be to the Allies' advantage if Rommel struck first in the desert. London disagreed and forced Auchinleck to prepare for an attack in June. But the Axis struck first. Enigma decryption efforts provided some advance warning, although they revealed nothing else of the enemy's plan.[4]

## Gazala to Tobruk

As the British official history of World War II noted, the Axis attack of May 27 offered the British "a chance of winning a really great victory, but they did not succeed in taking it." Instead, after a close call with disaster, Rommel inflicted one of the most spectacular defeats of the war on the western Allies.

The British had built a curious defensive line in the middle of Cyrenaica, constructing a series of "boxes," with all-around defenses, held by infantry brigade groups dug in behind minefields and supported by artillery and in some cases by I tanks. With wide gaps between the boxes, the line stretched south from Gazala on the coast down to Bir Hacheim, which a Free French brigade held. The wisdom of deploying infantry units along a long line that could be bypassed to the south was doubtful, but individually the boxes were strong. The British were anxious about the big supply dumps built up for the coming offensive around Tobruk and other places near the front.

Lt. Gen. William Gott's XIII Corps controlled most of the Gazala Line, with the First South African and Fiftieth British Divisions in the line, the new Second South African Division behind in Tobruk, and two army tank brigades with no less than 276 I tanks. Lieutenant General Norrie's XXX Corps controlled the armored divisions in reserve and Bir Hacheim. It had 573 tanks in the three armored brigades of the First and Seventh Armored Divisions. Most were still unreliable British Crusaders, but 177 were American-made, reliable, well-armored General Grant tanks. For the time, the Grant was a formidable tank, with a 37mm gun in a fully revolving turret and a 75mm gun; however, since American industry could not yet cast big enough turrets, the tank's big gun was mounted in a sponson on one side of the tank. Thus the 75mm had a limited traverse, and the tank was very high and easily seen. Still, it was a big addition to the Eighth Army's strength and gave the Allies overall superiority in armor in this battle. The British also had a much better antitank gun, the 6-pounder, although they had limited numbers and a small supply of ammunition.

Auchinleck and others expected the Germans to hit the center or northern part of the Gazala Line. Ritchie disagreed, foreseeing correctly that the Germans would sweep around the south end of the Line. On every other matter, however, he proved disastrously wrong. He ignored Auchinleck's advice to keep his armored divisions concentrated and remained consistently overoptimistic throughout the coming battle, although not only his own reactions but those at all levels of command were slow, indecisive, and uncoordinated.

Rommel never considered a frontal attack. Instead, while his immobile Italian infantry divisions with some German support feinted in the north, the Afrika Korps, the Ninetieth Light Division, and the Ariete Armored Division and Trieste Motorized Division of the Italian XX Mobile Corps would go around the line. Ariete would take Bir Hacheim while the Germans drove northeast to the Acroma area, defeated the British armor, and cut off the infantry in the Gazala Line before taking Tobruk. Materially, the odds were not in his favor. He had roughly 580 tanks: 228–229 Italian, 242 older Panzer IIIs, 19 new Panzer III Specials mounting long 50mm guns, 40 Panzer IVs, and 50 German light tanks. The German tanks had heavy, face-hardened armor resistant to the British 2-pounder guns, but were inferior to the Grants. The Germans did have a considerable superiority in antitank guns, including not only their own 88mm guns but also captured Soviet 76.2mm guns. The Axis had some 460 planes to 320 British in the forward area and a degree of air superiority over the battle area. Rommel somewhat underestimated British strength and still more their determination, and he overestimated the ease with which Bir Hacheim could be captured. Contemptuous of the British command, he tended to underrate the British and French soldiers.

The Axis moved around the Gazala Line on the night of May 26–27. The Ariete Division was unable to take Bir Hacheim. The Germans quickly overran the Third Indian Motor Brigade but found the British tanks more formidable even though the British were slow to coordinate their reactions. Then the Germans hit the Fourth Armored Brigade and overran Seventh Armored Division's headquarters, but the Grants inflicted heavy losses on the German tanks. Other Allied units were slow to support the Fourth Armored Brigade and could be tackled separately, some taking severe losses themselves.

The Germans resumed the battle on May 28, but accomplished little. Their supply line, running all the way around Bir Hacheim, was long and exposed to attack, and much of their armored force ran out of fuel. The British, however, failed to exploit the situation. With supplies dwindling, Rommel retired to a defensive position east of the Gazala Line known as the Cauldron. There, the Italian Mobile Corps had found paths, though not very safe ones, through the minefields over which supplies could be brought, but they were under artillery fire. The Germans then concentrated on destroying the Sidi Muftah (or, to the Germans, Got el Ualeb) box, which the British 150th Brigade occupied and which overlooked and menaced the supply line. Rommel may not have known of the Sidi Muftah position before the offensive began, and apparently he did not realize its strength until May 30. For their part, the British had misread his retirement west as a preliminary to breaking off the whole battle and still reacted slowly when it became clear that they were wrong.

Rommel's position was in fact desperate. He was almost encircled, and a concentrated attack on the Cauldron at any point over the next few days might well have destroyed the core of Panzer Army Afrika at one blow, even after the Sidi Muftah box was taken. Before it fell, he was near catastrophe; overcoming the 150th Brigade was vital. Until late on May 30, he received no food, water, or gasoline. When a captured British officer, Major Archer-Shee, complained that the men of the Third Indian Motor Brigade were dying of thirst, Rommel told him that they were getting the same water ration as his own men, half a cup a day. He admitted, "We cannot go on like this." If he did not get a convoy of supplies through, he would have to ask General Ritchie for terms. At the last minute, enough supplies arrived, and antitank guns stopped a British tank attack. On June 1, Rommel, personally leading the attack, captured the Sidi Muftah box and the entire defending force. Now his rear was free, and he could count on a safe supply line.

He then turned, perhaps unnecessarily, to eliminate the French at Bir Hacheim, a move delayed by dust storms and minefields. Meanwhile, after poorly reconnoitering the Axis positions and with only half the available troops, the British finally attacked the Cauldron. They struck on a too-extended front, with poor coordination between widely separated blows and between tanks and infantry. Their preliminary shelling fell on an outpost line instead of the main Axis line of resistance, and the attack failed with heavy losses. Rommel then struck out of the Cauldron, overrunning an Indian infantry brigade and four artillery regiments. Bir Hacheim proved tougher than Rommel expected, and most of the French broke out on the night of June 10–11. Even now, the British were still stronger in numbers, but Rommel was free to concentrate his forces and drive northeast. In a series of battles on June 12–13, the German armor, closely supported by antitank guns, smashed the British armored units in succession. Although the Germans themselves were tired and worn down, they now actually outnumbered the British in tanks. On June 14, Ritchie ordered a withdrawal from the Gazala Line. Only the exhaustion of the Afrika Korps, perhaps, allowed XIII Corps to pull back.

The Allies had decided, as far back as February, that in the event of a retreat, Tobruk would not be held in isolation. They had allowed its defenses to run down and lifted much of the minefields to supply mines for the Gazala Line. Auchinleck wished, if possible, to hold a line west of Tobruk. Ritchie, who was more willing to see Tobruk invested, led him to believe that it was possible; however, his XIII Corps was not able, nor its commander willing, to do so. Churchill now intervened, insisting that Tobruk be held, even in isolation, evidently assuming that it was a still a viable fortress whose retention would prevent the Axis driving into Egypt. A force built around the Second South African Division stayed in Tobruk as the army fell back. Rommel now carried out the attack originally planned for late 1941 with his whole army rapidly breaking through poorly organized defenses. Tobruk fell with thirty-three thousand men, enormous supply dumps, and a port that Rommel supposed would enable him to overrun Egypt if he promptly exploited the victory. A grateful Hitler made him a field marshal.[5] He was encouraged when intelligence disclosed the heavy losses and discouragement of the British.

Putting off the Malta invasion indefinitely, Hitler let Rommel pursue the British into Egypt. The Italians, who were short of oil fuel for the fleet in the Malta operation, agreed to this change remarkably readily, which tended to justify Hitler's earlier suspicions. The decision in favor of Rommel was often later criticized as a blunder. Had Rommel halted in accordance with previous plans, however, it is far from clear that the Axis would actually have launched the Malta operation. On the one hand, the Axis had starved nearly it into submission. On the other hand, its success was not likely since Malta was well defended against direct assault.[6]

The British broke contact with the enemy and retreated to Mersa Matruh. There, Ritchie planned a stand, although his main subordinate, Gott, had misgivings, and Ritchie had sent XXX Corps farther east to prepare defenses at El Alamein. Having come up with the New Zealand and Fifth Indian Divisions, X Corps held the Mersa Matruh defenses. After Ritchie made peculiar dispositions, apparently designed to draw the Germans into a trap, Auchinleck relieved him and took command of the Eighth Army. In a battle in which both sides were extraordinarily confused about the others' dispositions and strengths and in which British communications were appalling, the British were routed again and lost another eight thousand men.[7]

## First Battle of El Alamein

Whatever the wisdom of the decision to drive east instead of attacking Malta, some of Rommel's staff thought that he should have stopped for a few days after Mersa Matruh to rest his men, repair tanks, and bring up supplies. But he drove the already exhausted Panzer Army Afrika on, although supply lines and air cover were already stretched. The Italians lagged behind, and in fights during the confused retreat from Mersa Matruh, the British Seventh Armored Division destroyed most of the newly arrived Littorio Armored Division's tanks and artillery. The largely intact British Desert Air Force covered the retreat skillfully, but enormous losses of equipment, especially tanks and artillery, and supplies left the British ground forces weakened.

The British planned a stand on the Alamein position, sixty miles west of Alexandria. At this point, the Qattara Depression, a vast dead lake bed, whose bottom was a salt marsh, narrowed the front to barely forty miles. It was apparently the only place in the desert that could not be outflanked by a move through the interior. Boxes similar to those in the Gazala Line had been laid out since 1941 for up to two infantry and two armored divisions, but Auchinleck no longer had the forces to hold the whole "neck" between the Qattara Depression and the sea. His main line of resistance had a refused left flank along ridges running west to east. (Ironically, the narrowing of the battlefront by the Qattara Depression ultimately helped the Axis more than the Allies.)

With morale low—actually a semi panic gripped the British rear, although not the Eighth Army itself—not everyone favored a stand there. Gott and the commander of the First South African Division wanted to retreat farther and stand behind the Suez Canal. Norrie of XXX Corps and the New Zealanders, however, were unfazed. Auchinleck himself did not plan to take a last stand at El Alamein. Should the Eighth Army be beaten again, most of it would retreat up the Nile, using Port Sudan as a base, and prevent Rommel from crossing the canal by threatening his flank. But it is questionable whether the British forces in the Middle East could have functioned after losing the bases along the lower Nile.

Whether Auchinleck wanted it or not, the coming battle would be decisive. He arranged important changes of tactics and put the Eighth Army's artillery under direct, centralized control, playing up one of the great strengths of the British Army. The situation was not as bad as it looked. He would be fighting close to his bases and with effective air cover. The British were also getting better intelligence. During June, they had broken a new Luftwaffe-Army cooperation key, which provided a more complete picture of the enemy's order of battle, supply situation, and intentions. In mid-July, they would break the German Army's supply cipher.

At El Alamein, XXX Corps, with the First South African Division on the coast, held Auchinleck's northern front in and by the Alamein box. Norrie had almost all of the armor committed in the First Armored Division and concentrated southeast of the South Africans, and the Fiftieth British Division backstopped the South Africans to the east. The Eighteenth Indian Infantry Brigade, newly arrived from Syria, held a new box at Deir el Shein and west of a critical terrain feature, the Ruweisat Ridge. The XIII Corps held the southern sector with the New Zealand Division, Seventh Armored Division (which controlled only the Seventh Motor Infantry Brigade and a South African armored car regiment), and the Fifth Indian Infantry Division. The latter had one brigade left and manned a box right on the rim of the Qattara Depression. The New Zealand Division had its fresh Sixth Brigade in the Bab el Qattara, or Kaponga box. The rest of the division was stationed to its east.

As weak as the Allied forces seemed, the Axis forces were in terrible shape, reaching El Alamein with fifty-five German medium tanks (fifteen were Panzer III Specials), thirty Italian tanks, and fifteen hundred German and five thousand Italian infantry. Only the artillery remained strong. Fortunately for the British, Rommel attacked without proper reconnaissance, and his picture of the British position was badly mistaken. Had it been more accurate, he might have defeated them on July 1 and overrun Egypt. His plan was quite similar to the one that had worked at Mersa Matruh. The Ninetieth Light Division and Italian infantry were to thrust around the Alamein box to the coast, and the Afrika Korps, followed by the Italian mobile force, were supposed to overrun a box believed to be at Deir el Abayad and then thrust southeast into the rear of XIII Corps. Rommel thought that the whole Fiftieth British Division and an Indian brigade were crammed into the Alamein box, but only one South African brigade was there. The rest, with the Fourth Armored Brigade, held positions in the open desert.

Navigational errors led the Ninetieth Light Division to blunder right into the Alamein box; a later attempt to bypass it failed under intense artillery fire, leading to a near panic. The Afrika Korps did not find a box at Deir el Abayad and only discovered the Deir el Shein box by running into it. An attempt to outflank it must run into another strongpoint on the Ruweisat Ridge, so the Germans attacked the Eighteenth Indian Brigade. British armor moving to support it stuck in soft sand, but it was overcome only after a daylong heroic defense that cost the Germans eighteen precious tanks. Gen. F. W. von Mellenthin later wrote, "Our prospects of victory were hopelessly prejudiced on 1 July." An attempt to renew the drive on July 2 by attacking Ruweisat Ridge was stopped by British armor. On July 3, with only twenty-six German tanks fit to fight, Rommel changed plans and concentrated his whole mobile force in an effort to get around the Alamein box to the sea. He was stopped, and the New Zealanders counterattacked and wrecked the Ariete Division.

After a lull on July 4 and 5, Auchinleck went over to the attack, concentrating on hitting the Italians and forcing the Germans to rush about to prop up their allies. One of these attacks destroyed Rommel's radio-intercept unit. Violent fighting raged until July 27, with both sides bringing up reinforcements. The British inflicted but also suffered heavy losses. Several times they nearly broke through, while Rommel was on the verge of pulling back to the Libyan frontier. But no one attained a decisive success. Both sides remained on the line of July 1, temporarily exhausted.[8]

Auchinleck's excessive prolonging of his offensive was largely caused by fear for his northern front, which, if the Soviets were defeated, would face German attack. On July 9, the Middle East Defence Committee estimated that in the worst case the Germans could attack northern Iran by October 15. A move through Anatolia and Syria, although less likely, might be possible in September. Churchill and the Inter-Service Intelligence Committee in London doubted that the Germans could reach Iran so soon, but the chiefs of staff were still concerned. They warned Auchinleck that the six infantry divisions and one armored division needed to stop such a move could not be sent from Britain or North America in time, although if battles went well in the desert, two infantry divisions (the Forty-fourth and Fifty-first) that were en route to him might go to the Persian Gulf. One more division, and possibly others, might be provided from Britain and India. The chiefs of staff agreed that in the last resort the Abadan area must be held at the risk of losing Egypt, but the only way the Allies could provide a force to hold it against a northern attack was to destroy Rommel's army or at least drive it to a safe distance. Auchinleck tried, and narrowly failed, to do that. Only in October 1942 did the British chiefs of staff decide that the Germans could not attack Iran until the spring of 1943.[9]

## Malta

The British had stopped the Axis in the desert at a time when their seaborne supply lines were as secure as ever and when Malta was being starved into surrender. Even as the battle raged in Libya, the struggle to supply the island continued. Relieved of air attack for a time precisely because of that battle, Malta began to recover as an offensive base.

The British prepared a pair of convoys, one from each end of the Mediterranean. Six ships—one was a tanker—came via Gibraltar, covered by only twenty-two fighters based on the small, old carriers HMS *Argus* and HMS *Eagle* and, once they were close enough, Spitfires from Malta. (The small force of Beaufort day and Wellington night torpedo bombers at Malta operated in support of the eastern convoy.) Despite its weakness, the convoy did relatively well against massed air attacks by coordinated high-level and torpedo bombers, losing one freighter sunk and a cruiser damaged. The main escort force, with the carriers, finally turned back. Only a close escort with the antiaircraft cruiser HMS *Cairo* and nine destroyers accompanied the convoy on the last stage of the voyage to Malta.

On the morning of June 15, it was surprised to meet an Italian force with two cruisers that outranged *Cairo*'s guns. The Allies had detected the

Italian ships' departure from Palermo, but had then lost track of them, and assumed they would join the main Italian fleet against the convoy coming from the eastern Mediterranean. The *Cairo* and four Hunt class destroyers laid a smoke screen while five large destroyers attacked the Italians. The *Cairo* was hit. The Italians broke off the action, thinking they would catch the British again when they would pass through a gap between a minefield and the island of Pantellaria. The Italian surface attack did enable German and Italian planes to get at the convoy, which lost a tanker and two freighters. Vice Adm. Alberto da Zara's squadron, returning to action, finished off only a pair of crippled ships the British had been about to sink themselves. Only two freighters actually reached Malta. Fortunately, they were unusually large and heavily laden.

Although much bigger, the June eastern convoy failed. The whole Mediterranean Fleet, which did not have any carriers or any real battleships, escorted the convoy. The old battleship HMS *Centurion*, a radio-controlled target ship, sailed as a dummy, and the British fleet received considerable air support, even at the expense of the land battle. The main Italian surface fleet, with two modern battleships, came out to attack the convoy, which turned away to let Allied air and submarine attacks weaken it. The British had to avoid confronting it by day, although hoping they might have some chance against it in a night action. But the Italian fleet was not seriously hurt, while Axis planes and motor torpedo boats got at the convoy, which suffered some losses. It finally used up so much antiaircraft ammunition that it had to turn back.

The June convoy delivered barely enough food for Malta to stagger to the end of September. But fuel was short. Air strikes from Malta were limited to promising nearby targets. Submarines ran in aviation gasoline, ammunition, and special equipment, while *Eagle* launched more Spitfires during July. In late July, submarines were able to resume using the Malta base. But a new convoy was needed. The Maltese were on a diet that spelled slow starvation. They had eaten their last pets long ago. Illness was common, medical supplies short, and electric power gone.

No convoy could come from the east. All possible strength was assembled to ram through one big convoy from the west—fourteen ships, including the big tanker SS *Ohio*, hauling a precious cargo of oil. Aviation gasoline, a dangerous cargo not usually mixed with other items, formed part of the load for all freighters. While the Allies faced a huge Axis force of 784 aircraft, 20 submarines, and 23 motor torpedo boats, the main Italian fleet was held back. Its formidable force of cruisers and destroyers would attack only if conditions were right. The British had a total of 256 planes on ships and Malta itself. They had two modern carriers, HMS *Indomitable* and HMS *Victorious*, and the *Eagle*, with 72 fighters and 28 strike aircraft.

Passing Gibraltar on August 10, the convoy embarked on one of the great air-sea battles of the war. On August 11, *U-73* sank the *Eagle*. Motor torpedo boats and special weapons supported furious air attacks. The latter included a new circling torpedo, a crude guided missile—a radio-controlled drone plane packed with a huge bomb load fortunately went out of control and crashed in Algeria—and two Italian fighter-bombers camouflaged to resemble British planes and carrying special heavy bombs designed to wreck the planes on the carriers' decks. On August 12, they sneaked into the landing pattern of the *Victorious* and scored a hit. Luckily the bomb was a dud. Conventional air attack damaged *Indomitable* and left it unable to operate planes. During August 12 and the early hours of August 13, constant attack by planes, subs, and motor torpedo boats whittled down the convoy. An attack by the Italian cruisers on August 13 would probably have finished it off, but the Italians would not send them into action without strong fighter cover. The Axis air leaders preferred to use their fighters to escort bombers, instead. On August 13–14, the convoy's last five ships reached Malta. All were damaged. The *Ohio*, carrying a cargo worth far more than its weight in gold, arrived at the end of a towrope. After being bombed and torpedoed, it rode barely above the water with two crashed bombers on its deck. Malta was saved. It could hold out until December 1942. The August convoy was a great victory, although in any other situation, such losses would have been catastrophic.[10]

Malta revived as an offensive base. Allied forces there and in Egypt hacked away at the Axis supply line. Small forces of Beauforts (rarely were more than 20 available), escorted by no more than a dozen Beaufighters and occasionally by Spitfires when attacking convoys close to Malta, struck during the day, while Swordfish and Albacore biplanes and Wellingtons operated at night. Wellingtons and American B-24s based in Egypt bombed Libyan ports at night, nullifying much of the advantage the Axis had gained in taking Tobruk. The RAF destroyed the fuel storage facilities there in July, and a particularly effective attack on August 6 reduced Tobruk's capacity permanently. Sinkings of Axis supply ships were only modest in July and the first half of August, but in the last half of August targeting became far more effective. In August, a third of Rommel's supplies and 41 percent of his fuel were lost en route to Africa. Rommel thought that much of what did make it through was mismanaged and wasted. He complained that the

Italians allotted much more than their share of cargo space to their own forces, shorting the more effective Germans. He eventually secured a reorganization of the supply effort, although it was too late to make a difference.[11]

Meanwhile, he decided to take one last gamble in Egypt.

## Alam Halfa

During August, both sides received reinforcements. Many of Rommel's were flown in by air, although his force was increasingly difficult to supply. If not for the vast supplies he had captured earlier, his position would have been impossible. He estimated that he was short 210 tanks, 175 troop carriers, and at least 1,500 other vehicles; many were available but stuck in Italy. Meanwhile, the British sent substantial reinforcements around Africa, although the most important additions to their equipment arrived only in September.

British command experienced a major shake-up. It was generally thought in London, and especially Churchill, that Auchinleck must go. He was replaced by Gen. Harold Alexander, who had enjoyed more success than most British generals had, albeit in conducting retreats. Well liked and respected, Alexander chose good subordinates, although some doubted his personal intelligence. Next, General Gott, a dubious choice, was originally supposed to take command of the Eighth Army. However, Gott's death when his plane was shot down led to the selection of Lt. Gen. Bernard Montgomery, a competent although cautious man whose forte was the tightly controlled, set-piece battle that could be planned in advance. Unlike many of his fellow generals, he was lucky enough to command in circumstances where he could play from his strengths. He was the exact opposite of Rommel. Montgomery became enormously popular with the British lower ranks, the British people, and the Dominion units under him, but unfortunately he was an egomaniac who would become harder and harder for others to deal with. He also found it hard to deal with Allies, especially the Americans. Finally, on Churchill's insistence and over the objections of the War Cabinet and most of the chiefs of staff, Alexander's tasks were simplified by putting Iran and Iraq in a separate Persia and Iraq Command under Gen. Maitland Wilson. The new organization was generally considered unsound. Fortunately it was never tested by an attack from the north.

Rommel, a sick man, faced an extremely unpromising situation. Hitler rejected his suggestion that General Guderian should replace him. He had ruled out a retreat to Libya, which Hitler would probably have vetoed in any case. OKW officers had already indicated that in view of the situation in the Caucasus, they wanted his army to stay where it was. But he did not want to wait to be hit, so he would attack during the full moon period at the end of August and before the British could build up further. He knew a major convoy would reach Suez early in September. (It was even more important than he thought, for it carried 300 Sherman tanks and 100 self-propelled guns.) Attacking was a desperate gamble that might well lead to the destruction of Panzer Army Afrika, but if he could bring about a mobile battle, the Axis might end up taking Egypt. He did not even consider striking the northern part of the British front. Italian infantry units and the newly arrived German 164th Light Division and Parachute Brigade would feint there while the Afrika Korps, the Ninetieth Light Division, and the Italian XX Corps broke though the relatively weak XIII Corps line in the south. It would strike the eastern end of the Alam Halfa ridge, a key position; take the ridge; and drive up to the sea. In the event of success, the Twenty-first Panzer Division would move on Alexandria, and the Fifteenth Panzer and Ninetieth Light Divisions would drive on to Cairo and eventually Suez. He had no pontoon bridges, so he hoped to seize a Nile bridge intact.

Rommel knew the odds were against success. He remarked to his doctor, "The decision to attack today is the hardest I have ever taken. Either the army in Russia succeeds in getting through to Grozny and we in Africa manage to reach the Suez Canal, or—" He made a gesture of defeat. His only remote chance was that the British again would make a gross blunder that would give him an opening. But Montgomery, whatever his other limitations, was unlikely to do that. Still, while the decision to attack was a gamble, as with the campaign in southern Russia, it was the best chance Germany had left.

However, the British already had anticipated what Rommel would do even before decrypted messages revealed the enemy plan more completely than in almost any other battle of the war. Montgomery planned a closely controlled static defense. He occupied the crucial Alam Halfa ridge with two brigades of the Forty-fourth Infantry Division, dug in tanks of the Twenty-second Armored Brigade, and had two other armored brigades, one on either side, in close support. In all, he had more than 700 tanks, including 164 Grants, and plenty of 6-pounder antitank guns. The RAF had air superiority. On the other side, Rommel had about 500 tanks, including 70 Panzer IIIs and 27 Panzer IVF2 Specials. The latter were superior to the Grants but not enough to make up for their scarcity.

The Axis attacked on the night of August 30–31. Rommel's plan went awry from the start. Penetrating the minefields on the XIII Corps front, which were covered by elements of the Seventh Armored Division, took longer than expected. They were deeper than the Germans had anticipated, and the mine-lifting parties suffered heavy losses. They were still stuck in the minefields at dawn, long after they had expected to be in open country. The British had already bombed the assembly areas by night as well as day and continued to do so throughout the battle. (At a late stage they even dropped two-ton blockbusters on the Axis troops.) The Axis had not attained surprise, and fuel consumption was far higher than expected, thanks to bombing and soft sand. Sandstorms were also a problem, although they did interrupt the air attacks.

Rommel had serious doubts about continuing the offensive. Because of the fuel shortage, he had to turn north far short of the originally planned point and assault Alam Halfa directly. The attack was delayed until late on August 31. The effectiveness of the Panzer IV Specials shocked the British, but their defenses were too strong. On September 1, the Germans had only enough fuel for one panzer division to renew the attack; it failed. On September 2 Rommel decided to withdraw. Fuel was so short that he had to execute his retreat slowly.

The Germans were surprised that the British did not drive south from the Ruweisat area and cut off their whole mobile force. Montgomery's belated, small-scale counterattack failed, and the British may have lacked the necessary training and cooperation between armor and infantry. As it was, the Axis loss was not great—1,859 Germans and 1,051 Italians killed, wounded, or missing and 49 tanks—while the British had 1,750 casualties and lost 67 tanks, mostly in their failed attack of September 3. The Axis defeat resulted from a lack of fuel, overwhelming Allied air superiority over the battle area, and Montgomery's able handling of his numerically superior armor. Had more fuel been available or the situation in the air been even, Rommel might have been able to force a battle of maneuver on Montgomery, and he might have won.[12]

### Second Battle of El Alamein

Rommel rejected Kesselring's advice to retreat to Fuka, or even the Libyan frontier. Kesselring thought Hitler might have allowed it at that point. Even after Alam Halfa, though, Rommel may have hoped to defeat a British attack and launch a counteroffensive "on the backhand" that might secure Egypt. But, being ill, he outlined a defensive plan and turned over command temporarily to Russian front veteran Gen. Georg Stumme. Expecting to fight under a sky controlled by the Allies, the Axis developed a defensive system unlike anything used earlier in the desert. They built a continuous web of deep defenses from the Qattara Depression to the sea, behind thick minefields. To compensate for the Italians' weakness, a system of "corseting," or sandwiching, put the Germans and Italians in adjacent sectors all along the front. Mobile reserves, instead of being tightly concentrated and held well back, were kept close behind the front and split up in mixed German-Italian battle groups.

Montgomery rejected the closest plan to the usual desert pattern, a breakthrough in the southern sector designed to force a big tank battle, after which the British would round up the Axis infantry. That was his deception plan, which sought to lead the enemy to expect an attack in south at the end of the first week of November, with the help of outstanding security precautions and the use of cleverly designed dummy equipment. Instead, he would strike in the northern sector relatively near the coast, emphasizing defensive tactics. The British infantry divisions of XXX Corps would attack, closely followed by the two armored divisions of X Corps, to seize bridgeheads beyond the Axis minefields. The armor then would attract and defeat enemy counterattacks while the British gradually "crumbled" away the Axis infantry.

The British forces were carefully trained and reorganized, improving air-ground and tank-infantry cooperation. Montgomery made many command changes and replaced as many old desert hands as possible with newer men who had been closely associated with him in Britain. He had plenty of new equipment, notably some Scorpion mine-clearing tanks and American Sherman tanks with 75mm guns in fully revolving turrets that were superior to any Axis tank except the Panzer IV Special. The Sherman had several bad features that would later lead many to curse it—it was too high, burned too easily (early models used a modified airplane engine using high-octane gasoline), and carried ammunition at a vulnerable spot in the turret—but in 1942 it was a vast improvement on anything else available. He also received a new Mark III model of the Crusader tank armed with a 6-pounder gun. But no capped armor-piercing shells for it had arrived, and it was still prone to break down.

The British strangled the Axis supply line. The Axis forces in Africa had lost 20 percent of their supplies at sea in September and 44 percent in October. On October 17, the British decrypted the entire program for tanker shipments for the rest of the month. No fuel at all reached the Axis in Libya that first week of October, thanks to torpedo bombers and submarines. Practically all significant shipments during the Alamein battle were destroyed at sea.

The British attacked on October 23. They did not want to wait any longer so they could ensure air cover for the next Malta convoy and beat the landings in Northwest Africa. In all, 195,000 British and Allied troops faced 104,000 Axis troops. The former had 1,029 tanks ready for action (252 Shermans) with plenty in reserve against 496 Axis medium tanks with no immediate reserves. The Desert Air Force had 750 aircraft (530 operational) versus 625 Axis planes in the desert, only 350 serviceable. Also, the British had roughly a two-to-one superiority in artillery and antitank guns, although the Germans had some heavier guns than their British counterparts. The British fooled the Germans into expecting the attack in the Ruweisat Ridge sector, about ten miles south of the actual point of concentration, but Stumme and his staff—although not the OKW—expected the blow to fall when, if not where, it did.

A tremendous British bombardment silenced the Axis guns almost entirely for some hours, and nearly continuous bombing plagued them throughout the battle. But the British attack did not go well. The XXX Corps advanced, but clearing routes through the minefields and getting tanks forward on the jammed tracks proved far harder than expected. The XXX and X Corps commanders both wanted to break off the attack, at least to regroup, but Montgomery refused. Some crumbling of the Axis position took place, but on October 26, Montgomery tacitly admitted that events had not gone according to plan. He changed the direction of the attack, shifting the main effort north toward the coast in the Australian sector. The Tenth Armored and New Zealand Divisions went back into reserve. The New Zealanders' sector was allotted to XIII Corps, whose Seventh Armored Division also went into reserve. The change worked.

Stumme had died of a heart attack at the start of the battle. Rommel hastily returned from Europe. His counterattacks failed and played into Montgomery's hands, and the major effort on October 27 cost him a third of his tanks. After delays in moving the necessary forces, Montgomery launched his final breakthrough on November 2. It cost many tanks—90 of 94 in the leading Ninth Armored Brigade—but he fractured Rommel's final defense line. The biggest tank battle of the campaign followed, costing Rommel more than 100 tanks.

Meanwhile, on October 26, British torpedo bombers sank the tanker *Proserpina* and the freighter *Tergesta*, which was also carrying a major load of fuel. They also sank the *Luisiano* on October 28. It was likely the last shipment to be sent to the Axis forces while they were still at El Alamein.

Rommel ordered a retreat, only to be countermanded by Hitler on November 3. Hitler ordered Rommel to make a last stand at El Alamein. Stupefied, Rommel obeyed but finally reversed himself the following afternoon. But it does not seem to have made much difference. Rommel's order to stop the retreat had never reached some units, and apparently others ignored it. The British pressure was so tremendous that the Axis units kept falling back. Unfortunately, after defeating the opposing force, Montgomery failed to exploit his victory. Attempts to cut off Rommel's retreat failed, thanks to poor planning, the disorganization of some units assigned to the task, skillful rearguard actions, and rain that turned the desert into a morass. The Desert Air Force does not seem to have done well despite being presented good targets on the crowded coastal road. Nevertheless, Rommel had lost nearly all his tanks (450) and most of his guns (1,000), and the British took 30,000 prisoners and inflicted about 25,000 other casualties. The British had lost 13,500 men, 500 tanks (only 150 permanent losses that could not be repaired), and 100 guns.

Although its advance was rapid by normal standards, Rommel stayed ahead of the Eighth Army all the way to Tunisia. He never had more than 54 tanks against at least 200 in the Eighth Army's vanguard, but he had saved his army from destruction. Renamed the German-Italian Panzer Army and finally First Italian Army, it joined the Axis forces that had secured a bridgehead in northern Tunisia after the Allies had invaded French Northwest Africa. The British official history, meanwhile, considered the failure of the Allied pursuit "remarkable."[13]

## Origins of the Invasion of Northwest Africa

The Americans and the British had wished to take the offensive against the European enemy at an early date. They had planned to invade French North Africa at the first Washington conference in December 1941. Capturing Northwest Africa would forestall any enemy move there, put the Axis forces in Africa in a hopeless position, and provide a base for later operations against southern Europe. The lack of prospects for French cooperation, the demands of the Pacific, and the shipping shortage led to the operation being cancelled. It was revived and executed, however, in a curious, complicated way.

American military leaders had never liked the North African scheme. The navy wished to concentrate on the Pacific, and the army favored a different strategy against the European Axis. The army held that the best way to defeat Germany was by striking through western Europe. An offensive there offered the shortest route to the heart of German industry. It had the best transportation network in the world, and the sea routes to it were shorter than to any other theater. Those routes had to be guarded in any case, and Britain had plenty of ports and air bases. Only an offensive based there could employ most of Britain's strength. Even before an invasion of western Europe could be launched, the buildup for it would threaten the Germans and prevent their concentrating completely against the Soviets.

Conversely, American military leaders rejected an attack through the Mediterranean. Defeating Italy would not decisively harm Germany, and the Alps would block an attack on Germany from the south. A campaign in the Mediterranean would require a separate, longer supply line and encounter poorer communications and worse terrain. Even if an offensive there could start earlier, it would waste time and tie up forces needed for a decisive blow in the west. The British never contested the idea that a decisive offensive must be launched through western Europe, but they did not believe that it could be done soon or, perhaps, without a preliminary, diversionary blow in the south.

In the spring of 1942, Maj. Gen. Dwight Eisenhower, then head of the U.S. Army's planning division, devised a plan far more congenial than the North African scheme to the U.S. Army and Secretary of War Henry Stimson. After an all-out buildup in Britain, forty-eight American and British divisions would invade France in Operation Roundup in 1943. If possible, no other actions would take place on land against the European Axis before then. The planners assumed that the Japanese would be contained and that the Soviets would continue to engage most of the German Army. However, Eisenhower also drew up an alternative plan called Sledgehammer for a small landing in France in 1942 either to divert German forces from the east if the Soviets seemed on the verge of defeat or (far less likely) to exploit an unexpected German collapse. Gen. Omar Bradley later acidly observed that, given the available forces, Sledgehammer would have been better named Tackhammer. The unwanted, unexpected emergency operation for 1942 would cause much argument and confusion.

The British quickly agreed to Roundup. Churchill and others wanted to land in France in 1943 and did not want to do anything that might lead the Americans to change their minds about defeating Germany first. However, Chief of the Imperial General Staff Alan Brooke did not really believe that Roundup could be successful in 1943. And, while the other British leaders were more optimistic, none had any use for Sledgehammer. They rightly estimated that it would be a suicidal endeavor that would not help the Soviets, would not divert any German forces, and would end in catastrophe. They were, however, also readier to entertain launching an offensive in the Mediterranean—not as a substitute for invading France, for they agreed with the American arguments for its necessity—but as a preliminary, subsidiary attack to pave the way for a main attack across the Channel.

The Soviets demanded a second front in western Europe in 1942; and by May 1942, both Roosevelt and Churchill felt that they dared not wait until 1943 to launch some sort of major operation against the European Axis. In June, the British clearly opposed Sledgehammer. Meeting President Roosevelt on June 9, Vice-Adm. Louis Mountbatten, the head of Combined Operations (the British directorate for amphibious and raiding operations), insisted that no landing in 1942 could draw German forces from the east. Roosevelt seemed receptive to reviving the plan to invade Northwest Africa, or Operation Gymnast, which Churchill was trying to resell to the Americans. Churchill was sure that it need not prevent a landing in France in 1943, and Roosevelt agreed.

At first, Churchill had trouble getting his own military leaders in line. They wished to postpone a final decision for North Africa, as it would tie up vital naval forces and divert reinforcements otherwise available for operations in the Middle East. The U.S. Army and Secretary Stimson were also strongly opposed. They were convinced, correctly, that a North African invasion in 1942 would render a major invasion of western Europe in 1943 impossible.

When Churchill went to Washington for a major conference in June 1942, he could not obtain the Americans' agreement to the North African plan. While he was there, Tobruk fell. In a decision Churchill regarded as exceptionally generous, Roosevelt immediately took 300 Sherman tanks and 100 self-propelled guns from U.S. Army units so they could go to the Middle East. This session, if not the meeting with Mountbatten, may have been the point at which Roosevelt privately decided in favor of a North African invasion. But wishing to avoid a quarrel with Stimson and Gen. George Marshall, men whose advice and support he deemed invaluable even if he disagreed with them, he arranged a final agreement in an indirect manner. So, in July, the president sent his military leaders to London with orders to agree on some operation against the European enemy in 1942 that would use American ground troops. That instruction forced the American military leaders to advocate Sledgehammer, which they did not really believe in themselves (Eisenhower estimated its chance of success at one in five), in the hope of maintaining the strategic emphasis on Western Europe. The British, as before, adamantly rejected Sledgehammer. The Americans finally, reluctantly, agreed to invade North Africa, since they thought it better than the only remaining alternatives—invading Norway or sending American ground forces to the Middle East. The British and American chiefs of staff warned Roosevelt and Churchill that the decision meant that no landing could occur in France until 1944.[14]

In this roundabout way, the Western powers made their most important strategic decision of the war. The North African invasion led to a continuing campaign in the Mediterranean area and postponed any attempt to invade western Europe until 1944. Some have questioned the wisdom of this decision, for a successful invasion of France in 1943 probably would have meant a much earlier defeat of Germany. When and if the Allied armies were safely established ashore, France was a far better place to fight than the Mediterranean. But as Eisenhower had begun to fear by the summer of 1942, the chances were excellent that Roundup could not have been launched in 1943, whether or not the Allies invaded North Africa, for various reasons. The plan, he realized, had been predicated on the British being stronger than they really were. The U-boat campaign, not fully defeated until 1943, would probably have prevented an adequate buildup. Enough landing craft—they had underestimated the number needed in 1942—could not have been built or their crews trained in time; furthermore, landing craft production directly competed with that of vital antisubmarine craft and could not have been easily expedited. Finally, carrying out Roundup would have meant committing inexperienced American forces to a landing on a defended coast, the toughest of all operations. The history of the North African campaign does not inspire confidence in the outcome.[15]

## Preparing the North African Invasion

Planning and preparing the North African invasion, or Operation Torch, proved difficult, both militarily and politically. Northwest Africa was a huge underdeveloped area with a poor road and railroad network, and it was essential to bring the French over to the Allies as soon and as cheaply as possible. With eight divisions and 500 (largely obsolete) aircraft, they could either be a major asset or a serious threat. The Americans thought that the French would receive their forces better than they would the British. The British doubted that, but they agreed to an American commander, Eisenhower, who earlier had bitterly opposed the invasion. American consular officials also had contacts with pro-Allied officers and underground groups in North Africa. The former were hostile to General de Gaulle's Free French, so the Americans, who did not especially like de Gaulle, insisted on excluding the Free French from a role in the invasion. As a substitute leader, they brought in another French general, Henri Giraud, who they expected to rally the French when the Allies landed. That idea proved highly optimistic.

Deciding where to land was a contentious issue. The Allies expected the Axis to react to an invasion by rushing forces to Tunisia, although they gravely underestimated the strength and speed of the enemy's response. To finish the campaign as fast as possible, it was desirable to land in, or as close as possible, to the major Tunisian ports of Tunis and Bizerte. Given that they were near Axis bases, and the invasion force would have only limited carrier-based air support, a landing in Tunisia would be very dangerous. Admiral Cunningham, now the naval commander for the North African invasion, nevertheless favored landing at Bizerte, but he was overruled. Adm. Lumley Lyster, who commanded the British carrier force, suggested readying a force of 5,000 troops on Malta and rushing them to Tunis in stripped-down bombers as soon as possible after the Allies landed in Algeria, but this idea was not pursued either.

The British and Americans also differed on timing. The British wanted a target date in October, but the Americans argued for more time. U.S. Navy leaders insisted on a target date of November 7 in order to gather shipping (some ships required conversion) and finish training, while the U.S. Army felt the Second Armored Division needed more time to get acquainted with its new Sherman tanks.

With a landing in Tunisia ruled out, four possible targets were left. Bône, a small port in eastern Algeria, had a valuable airfield and would be a good starting point for an advance into Tunisia, but it was not suited for a major landing. Algiers, the Algerian capital, was the center of French power and should be taken as soon as possible. Oran, farther west, had to be taken quickly so that short-ranged planes could reach North Africa from Gibraltar. The U.S. Army and General Brooke felt that landing on the Atlantic coast of Morocco was necessary in order to secure Casablanca and its railroad running to the Mediterranean. While the Americans were more optimistic about French reactions than the British (who were more apt to emphasize the desirability of an early move into Tunisia and wanted an early landing at Bône), the Americans were more afraid of General Franco's reaction. They feared that the Spanish would agree to German pressures to close the Straits of Gibraltar and let the Germans cross Spain, trapping the Allied forces in the Mediterranean. That strategy would have been the logical Axis counterstroke to Torch, had the Germans had the strength for such a move and had Franco agreed to it. Landing in Morocco, however, would deter the Spaniards from joining or caving into the Axis and ensure a lifeline of sorts for the forces landing inside the Mediterranean.

While the landings in the Mediterranean would be mounted from Britain by mixed Anglo-American forces, an all-American force would carry out the Moroccan attack. Eisenhower's friend Lt. Gen. George Patton, sailing directly from the United States, would command the force.

Eisenhower and many of the British, however, did not like the Moroccan operation. Although designed as a safety measure, it would actually be the riskiest part of the invasion. Casablanca was too strongly defended to attack directly, while sea conditions prevented landing on the open coast four days out of five. Those limitations alone would have made Eisenhower dislike the Moroccan operation, and on strategic grounds he and most of the British preferred putting all available forces inside the Mediterranean, where the weather was less of a problem. That would aid an early move east. If the French in Morocco held out or the Spanish attacked, a force could be sent back down the railroad from Oran to Casablanca.

The first plan for Torch called for simultaneous landings on November 5 at Casablanca, Oran, Algiers, and Bône, with only one regiment going ashore at Bône. But the Combined Chiefs of Staff thought that scheme would spread the Allied forces too thin. The planners then designed a Mediterranean-only plan, to be implemented earlier. Patton's force from the United States would attack Oran on October 15, while British-based forces landed at Algiers and Bône. But the Americans, Brooke, and Cunningham deemed a Moroccan landing a necessary precaution.

On September 5, the parties agreed on the final plan, which was actually a reduced version of the first plan. While mixed forces, with the Americans in the lead to placate the French, went ashore at Oran and Algiers, Patton would land at three places in Morocco and then march overland on Casablanca. If the surf was too high, his force would wait at sea for better conditions. If conditions seemed unpromising, it would pass through the Straits of Gibraltar, land on the Mediterranean coast of Morocco, and move southwest on Casablanca. The Allies expected to take northern Tunisia by mid-December, the rest of Tunisia by January 1943, and Libya by mid-March, unless the Eighth Army took it first—as it actually did.

The limited time in which Torch had to be planned and prepared, and the time and energy consumed in deciding where to land, distracted the planners from the real problems of how to get to Tunis, what to do if the Allies did not take Tunis quickly, and where to go once North Africa was taken. Intelligence arrangements, and the plans for air organization and operations, were poor.[16]

## The Invasion

In late October the assault convoys set sail. Eisenhower supervised the operation from a headquarters on Gibraltar, a vital base jammed with 350 planes, parked wingtip to wingtip, and enormous amounts of gasoline. Although far from enemy bases, it was terribly vulnerable to a small, well-conducted air strike. Eisenhower was anxious. His forces were not well trained, preparations had been hasty, and the weather and French and Spanish reactions were all uncertain. Secrecy was hard to maintain. He recalled that at no time during the war did he feel more relieved than on hearing that the Moroccan landing had succeeded. But the Allied convoys reached their targets without interference.

The Axis had been fooled narrowly but sufficiently. The Germans had much information pointing toward a North African landing, but they had ignored it. They had thought that an attack on Dakar was possible, while the Italians had rated a Moroccan landing more likely, but neither expected a landing inside the Mediterranean before 1943. If such an attack transpired, the Germans thought, it would probably be a descent on Rommel's rear in Libya or even a landing in southern Europe rather than in North Africa. The Italians were a bit more worried. They held some ground forces and small transports, originally slated for the Malta invasion, for a move into Tunisia. When naval movements were detected around Gibraltar, the Germans believed they were for another Malta convoy. The Italians and their German liaison officers began to suspect a landing in Algeria or Tunisia, but those men and Mussolini, who agreed with this view on November 7, could not convince Berlin. By November 6, the German leaders conceded that an invasion was imminent, but they had expected it to hit Libya or southern Europe. The Vichy government seems to have had some advance indication of an invasion, but they did little. Admiral Darlan, the Vichy commander in chief, was visiting Algeria, where his son was ill. He seems to have put himself in a position to work with the Allies, but he was reluctant to actually join them.

The main landings went well and encountered little Axis interference. Although attempts to storm Algiers and Oran harbors misfired, the Allies quickly took Algiers and Oran. The French resisted but not enthusiastically or effectively. The Allies' political arrangements and forecasts of French reactions proved badly miscalculated. The Americans had been correct in thinking that de Gaulle had no following in North Africa but neither did Giraud. Furthermore, the toughest resistance took place against the all-American landing in Morocco. Fighting ended only on November 11, after the Allies dealt with Darlan, an arrangement both parties had hoped to avoid. Indeed, genuine patriots such as Gen. Alphonse Juin pressed Darlan into acting. The Allies finally accepted Darlan as "high commissioner" in North Africa, causing widespread outrage in the democracies.

Despite their earlier blunders, the Axis reacted promptly and decisively once the invasion began. The Germans had belatedly ordered U-boats against the invasion forces. They had considerably reinforced their air forces in the Mediterranean since September, transferring units from Norway and Russia and causing a heavy drain on the Luftwaffe's strength. While occupying Vichy France, the Axis leaders—despite Rommel's advice to cut their losses in Africa—automatically assumed that they must secure a bridgehead in Tunisia. Hitler and Mussolini, as usual, were not solely to blame. Admiral Raeder, in a typical misjudgment, particularly stressed the desirability of holding Tunisia to keep the enemy forces in Africa divided, prevent the Allies from opening the Mediterranean to their shipping, and tie down the Allies in Africa to keep them from invading southern Europe. Despite the problems of supplying Libya earlier, Raeder and Kesselring were remarkably optimistic about supplying Tunisia, pointing out that the route between Sicily and Tunisia was only one-third as long as that to Libya. This argument, of course, ignored the developing balance of forces that would make it harder to get supplies over even that stretch of sea.

In the short run, however, the Axis was successful in Tunisia. The Vichy authorities accepted the Germans' plan of landing at Tunis on November 9. (The French Tunis Division, initially passive, withdrew westward and belatedly joined the Allies.) Strong German and Italian air and ground forces poured into Tunis and Bizerte. By November 25, 15,575 German and 9,000 Italian troops were in Tunisia, with strong air support and the formidable new Tiger tanks. By the end of the month, the whole Tenth Panzer Division had arrived. Gen. Walter Nehring capably led the Axis force and faced a jumble of Allied units. The British First Army, under the command of the not particularly distinguished Lt. Gen. Kenneth Anderson, amounted to little more than an armored division with obsolete tanks and a reinforced infantry division. The First Army was short of transportation and antiaircraft protection and operated over poor lines of communication under local Axis air superiority. Eisenhower and Anderson knew they were unlikely to win the "race for Tunis." The Allies demonstrated their inexperience, and their operations, even given the difficulty of their situation, were not well planned. On Christmas Day 1942, the Germans' successful defense and bad weather led Eisenhower to halt operations.

But the Axis powers' tactical success guaranteed a long-term disaster. Strategically, in the long run, their position was hopeless. They had plunged into a prolonged Tunisian campaign. Holding on there would require pouring more and more forces across the Mediterranean, their supply lines exposed to air and submarine attacks that would become more intense. They tied down much of their air transport fleet when it was needed at Stalingrad. As the Allied air forces received reinforcements and established more and better forward bases, they outnumbered the Axis air forces and dominated the sky not only over Tunisia but also over the sea and southern Italy. Ultimately, the Allies would shut down supplies to Tunisia and make it difficult for the Axis forces to evacuate. The struggle to cut the Axis supply line was not short or easy—both Germans and Italians fought stubbornly to get convoys through, and it took time for the Allies to bring their forces to bear—but it could only end one way. Thus the decision to fight for Tunisia proved a fatal mistake, accentuated by the Axis rulers' stubborn refusal to admit the obvious and cease wasting their resources. They sent in reinforcements long after it was clear that they would merely crowd Allied prison camps.

The Allies would be amply compensated for the delay in clearing North Africa. There, their ground forces gained invaluable experience in fighting the Germans in relatively favorable circumstances. Inflicting heavy losses on the Luftwaffe and the Italian fleet and merchant marine, they destroyed an entire enemy army group and captured 240,000 prisoners (130,000 German) at the cost of 70,000 Allied casualties. Southern Europe was left poorly defended against the next Allied attack, and German forces were tied down, weakening the defense of the west. At a time when the Western powers could not have effectively struck the European Axis on land anywhere else, the North African campaign proved a wise move. "Fortress Europe" began to crumble.[17]

# 10

## The Pacific

*Pearl Harbor to Midway*

Within six months the Japanese expected to capture Southeast Asia and attain a defensive perimeter that would enable them to stand off an American counteroffensive. They hoped that the Americans, despite their immensely greater war potential, would settle for a negotiated peace while the Germans finished off the British and the Soviets.

Japan's army, although not up to the standard of equipment of the West, was well trained. The force allotted to take Southeast Asia was more than equal to overcoming the jumble of colonial forces it faced.

Some of the more reckless members of the pro-Axis "battleship" faction in the Imperial Japanese Navy imagined that the gigantic *Yamato* and *Musashi*, the greatest battleships ever built, would ensure supremacy at sea. The navy was superbly trained and especially skilled at night operations. Its technical branches were staffed with top graduates of Tokyo Imperial University. Its surface ships were fast and heavily armed, emphasizing torpedoes, while Western fleets relied more on guns. The Japanese had effective air, submarine, and surface torpedoes that were faster and with heavier warheads than those of their Western counterparts. Moreover, unlike American torpedoes, they were reliable. Better optical instruments, flares, and star shells also compensated to some extent for Japan's backwardness in radar.

But, above all, the Japanese depended on their naval air force. They had more aircraft carriers than the U.S. Navy had and were far stronger in the Pacific when the war began. Japan had six well-equipped fleet carriers in the First Air Fleet (also known in the first months of the war as the First

250

Carrier Fleet, the Striking Force, and Mobile Force), three light carriers, and one escort carrier versus the Americans' seven fleet carriers—some of which were in the Atlantic, others being repaired or obsolete—and one escort carrier. The navy also had a strong land-based air arm, the Eleventh Air Fleet. Prewar Japanese aircrews, which were superbly trained and outstandingly accurate in bombing and torpedo attacks, averaged many more flying hours than their American counterparts. Their planes—especially the Zero, the first strategic escort fighter—were good to excellent.

Flying from both carriers and land bases, the Zero was the key to Japan's early victories. Although the Japanese lacked powerful aircraft engines, the brilliant designer Jiro Horikoshi had developed a light, fast, and agile fighter with fantastic range. That made it possible to dispense with carrier support in Southeast Asia, helping make the Pearl Harbor attack feasible. Horikoshi cut the plane's weight through his clever design and by using new, lightweight materials. The Zero outclimbed and outmaneuvered all Allied fighters early in the war and outran all but the American P-40 in level flight. Armed with 20mm cannon, it had good vision through a bubble canopy, which was ahead of most Western planes. Only later did the plane's weaknesses become apparent. It was not strong; it lacked a good radio, armor, and self-sealing tanks; and almost any Allied fighter could outdive it. The Imperial Japanese Navy, however, failed to develop an adequate replacement for the Zero until almost the end of the war or a training program to reinforce the carefully developed, prewar aircrew elite.

Japan's numerous submarines were heavily armed with fine torpedoes, fast on the surface, and began the war with better optical instruments than their American counterparts had. But they dived slowly, were slow and unmaneuverable when submerged, and could not go very deep. Like the American submarine force before Pearl Harbor, it was oriented to waging a war of attrition on the enemy fleet, not attacking enemy supply lines. Moreover, unlike the Americans, the Japanese did not alter this policy much. While inflicting serious losses in the first year of the war—sinking the carriers USS *Yorktown* and USS *Wasp* and twice knocking a third, USS *Saratoga*, out of action for several months—over time, Japanese submarines achieved little for heavy losses.

Other weaknesses mattered more in the long run than in the first months of the war. The orientation of the Japanese toward the offensive, and their neglect of defense, proved most costly in antisubmarine warfare, which they almost entirely overlooked. The armed forces wasted Japan's too small shipping pool. They only rationalized and centralized its control in May 1945, after most of its ships had been sunk. The failure to cope with American submarine attacks on their merchant shipping doomed Japan's economy, which was insufficient from the start, despite a vast increase in heavy industry and armaments production in the 1930s and intensified efforts after 1941. Japan never produced more than a tenth of America's war output and, despite the remarkable Zero, still lagged behind the West in aeronautical engineering as well as electronics.[1]

## Allied Preparations

The Western powers did not prepare well for the coming war. Generally they greatly underestimated Japan's power. Some believed right up to the attack on Pearl Harbor that Japan would back down and refrain from war.

Coordination between the Western powers was imperfect at best. They did consult one another, but they did not engage in any effective joint planning, much less establish an inter-Allied command. Instead, the British and Americans hoped that a buildup of their respective positions in Malaya and the Philippines might deter Japan.

It had been apparent for many years that in the first stages of a war, Japan, with its strong fleet and control of the League of Nations–"mandated islands" of the Marshalls, Carolines, and Marianas, would dominate the western Pacific and largely overrun the Philippines. The Americans' strategy in the Philippines was to fight for central Luzon, but if this effort failed, American and Filipino forces would try to hold the Bataan Peninsula and the fortified islands controlling the entrance to Manila Bay while the American fleet fought its way across the Pacific. American leaders, however, had little conviction that the garrison could last long enough to be relieved. During the latter part of 1941, the United States undertook a major effort to strengthen the forces in the Philippines, especially in airpower, so that they could hold the whole archipelago, bar the Japanese from moving south, and even bomb Japan itself. Lt. Gen. Douglas MacArthur, who had commanded the Philippine Army since 1935 and had been recalled to command the American forces in the islands, hoped that if war was delayed until March or April 1942 to be in a stronger position. The U.S. government hoped, although without much conviction, that the buildup might deter the Japanese from war.

British strategy in the Far East revolved around the naval base of Singapore. The British accepted that they could not afford a two-ocean navy capable of fighting a major European foe and Japan at the same time. In the event of war with Japan, the fortified Singapore base was supposed to hold out until Britain's main fleet arrived to relieve it. The doubtful basis of this strategy was not news in the 1940s. Long before World War II, Britain had considered that war with Japan was unlikely unless Britain was fighting in Europe, so its main fleet would probably be tied down in the West. Further, by the late 1930s, it could not hold Singapore as an isolated position; much of the mainland of Malaya had to be held to protect it. As the war went on, the time frame for the fleet's arrival in the East was lengthened, and the British conceded to the Pacific Dominions, that Britain would probably not send its main fleet.

Churchill and many other British and Americans underestimated the quantitative and qualitative strength of the Japanese, especially in the air, and until late in the day tended to think that they would not fight. Many ignored or dismissed accurate accounts of the Zero fighter and Japanese torpedoes. It should be emphasized that this tendency to underestimate the Japanese forces was spotty. In some cases, particularly among the British in the Far East and some American admirals, it reached grotesque proportions, especially when racial preconceptions were involved; but others, notably some American naval aviators, were fairly immune to it. Lt. Cdr. John Thach, the U.S. Navy's top fighter tactician, had no patience with such notions.

Several elements compounded the tendency to underestimate Japan. Racial prejudice was an important factor, but so was a general inclination to underrate "late industrializers." Before June 1941, for instance, Westerners had regarded the Soviets in a similar fashion. Further, especially among liberals, many in the West engaged in wishful thinking and hoped that Japan had been exhausted by its war with the Chinese, whose abilities had been overestimated.[2]

### Opening Disasters: Pearl Harbor

Japan's main objective was obtaining the vital resources of Southeast Asia, especially oil and bauxite. Japanese strategists had pondered an attack on Pearl Harbor for many years but always wound up rejecting it as impractical. In the spring of 1940, Adm. Isoroku Yamamoto, commander of the Combined Fleet, the navy's principal operational force, revived the idea. To him, it became more important than the Southeast Asia drive. His chief planner, Cmdr. Minoru Genda, also favored following up a Pearl Harbor attack with an early invasion of Hawaii.

The Imperial Naval General Staff initially opposed the Pearl Harbor attack, wanting to concentrate all resources on the Southeast Asian campaign and believing that its carriers would be needed there. It favored a surprise submarine attack on Hawaii but looked forward to a later decisive battle with the American fleet when it tried to cross the Pacific. Yamamoto argued that it was sounder to knock out the American fleet at the outset to prevent its interfering with vital attack on Southeast Asia. He won his point by threatening to resign. He discounted the effect of a sneak attack on the Americans' morale.

On November 27, the War and Navy Departments had sent formal war warnings to all commands. Contrary to later myth, the American government expected war with Japan, and anyone reading the daily newspapers, including those of Honolulu, would have known that war was likely. Despite this notice, the fleet under Adm. Husband Kimmel had granted personnel normal peacetime liberty and only took routine precautions. Thus, the attack of Vice Adm. Chuichi Nagumo's First Air Fleet—the carriers *Kaga*, *Akagi*, *Shokaku*, *Zuikaku*, *Hiryu*, and *Soryu*, preceded by five midget submarines, which entered Pearl Harbor the morning of the main attack— found the Americans unalert.

Under Lt. Gen. Walter Short, the army's Hawaii command used the six available radar stations only for training and did not have ready ammunition at its antiaircraft guns. Further, not all of the guns had been installed (since some of their wartime positions were on private property). Although many planes were being overhauled or modified, the USAAF had enough fighters on hand to have given the Japanese a serious fight and plenty of revetments to protect them from bombing and strafing. But its planes and those of the Marines were jammed together and emptied of fuel and ammunition to protect against sabotage. Along with submarine attack, sabotage was the only threat taken seriously. Navy planes were also neatly lined up. The command ignored the detection and then the sinking of a midget submarine. When radar detected Japanese reconnaissance planes and the attacking force, the command mistook them for American planes en route from California.

So the Japanese, despite what should have been ample warning, took the Americans by surprise. They sank five of the eight U.S. battleships in the harbor and slightly damaged the rest. They also sank an old battleship used as a target ship, two destroyers, and a minelayer, and damaged several other ships. Of the nominal air strength of 394 planes, many obsolete or unflyable, 165 were completely destroyed, but few others were usable. More than twenty-four hundred Americans lay dead, and the United States was enraged, making the Japanese goal of a negotiated peace impossible. Japanese losses—twenty-nine planes, one large submarine, and five midget subs—were small and far fewer than they had feared.

But the attack fell far short of the truly catastrophic blow it might have been and that the Americans widely supposed that it was. Even the battle fleet was not entirely destroyed. A brilliant salvage effort returned to service three of the sunken battleships, although some doubted that the effort expended on these old ships was worth it. The two other Pearl Harbor–based carriers USS *Enterprise* and USS *Lexington*, off delivering fighter planes to outlying bases at Wake and Midway Islands, narrowly escaped destruction. An attack forty-eight hours before or later would have caught at least one carrier in port. Indeed, had bad weather and difficulties refueling not delayed the *Enterprise*, it would have been caught entering Pearl Harbor that Sunday morning and almost certainly sunk.

Fortunately for the Americans, Nagumo rejected another strike at Pearl Harbor. The aboveground and vulnerable oil tank farms, whose destruction would have forced the Pacific Fleet back to the West Coast for months, were left intact, as were the dockyards, power plant, and submarine base. Nor did Nagumo hunt down the American carriers, as Genda and others urged. Had he encountered them—and they were recklessly seeking him, although luckily, in the wrong direction—he almost certainly would have sunk them. In a curious way, the Pearl Harbor attack was based on a misunderstanding. Genda had largely aimed and succeeded at eliminating the traditional battle line of the American fleet, but those battleships were no longer the critical element of U.S. seapower. Last, Genda and some others proposed quickly returning to take Hawaii or at least to seize the outlying bases at Midway and Johnston Islands but were overruled. Although no one could know it then, the Americans would be lucky in one more respect: never again, in the critical period of the war, did the Japanese properly concentrate all their fleet carriers in one task force against a strategic target.

The Pearl Harbor attack generated a controversy that never ended as some charged that President Roosevelt had plotted to bring the United States into the war against Germany by the "back door," that is, by deliberately provoking war with Japan and exposing the fleet to attack. The absurdity of these charges will perhaps be obvious after the discussion in chapter 6 of the actual situation in the Atlantic in the fall of 1941. And the administration had already decided that fall that even if Japan attacked only the British and Dutch, it would ask Congress for a declaration of war against Japan.

The American contribution to Pearl Harbor was the product of failures at several levels from Washington to Hawaii. Clues from decrypted diplomatic messages were ignored. Fundamentally, however, all levels of command had assumed that the Japanese would use their fleet to support a main effort in Southeast Asia. Others thought the Japanese would go north and help finish off the Soviets; indeed, President Roosevelt himself believed that possibility as late as mid-October.

Despite the breakdown of Japanese-American negotiations and the ignored warnings, some at high levels—notably Vice Adm. William Pye, the Pacific Fleet battleship commander, and Rear Adm. Claude Bloch, commander of the Hawaiian naval district, and perhaps even Kimmel himself—deemed war unlikely, because they thought the Japanese would lose. Such attitudes were far from universal in the fleet. Vice Adm. William Halsey, taking the *Enterprise* to deliver planes to Wake Island, had fully expected war. And he intended to attack any Japanese ships or planes he encountered.

On the one hand, many people had predicted a Japanese carrier attack on Pearl Harbor, and American carriers had practiced such an attack. The Martin-Bellinger Report of March 1941 and the Farthing Report of August 1941 had closely outlined what the Japanese would do and recommended a far-ranging, 360-degree air search to prevent a surprise attack. The planes for such sweeps, however, did not exist. On the other hand, others doubted that the enemy could carry out such an attack. As Admiral Kimmel admitted to the postwar congressional investigation, "I never thought the little yellow sons of bitches could pull off such an attack so far from Japan." Contributing to overconfidence were the beliefs that Pearl Harbor was so shallow that torpedo attack, the deadliest sort, would be impossible (thus anti-torpedo nets were not used inside the harbor) and that high-level bombing alone would not inflict enough damage to be worthwhile for an enemy. Other people had pet theories that made the danger seem small. For one, Rear Adm. Richmond Kelly Turner, the head of the U.S. Navy's War Plans Division, was sure that the Japanese would attack the Soviets first.

Washington did not check Kimmel and Short's preparations, which would have shown that they were not making ready. Despite the November 27 warnings, which no other commanders misinterpreted, they had concentrated on training rather than defense and had discounted the dangers of attack except by submarines and saboteurs.

Short, especially, was obsessed with sabotage. He distrusted the Japanese American minority on the island, although his predecessor and others in Hawaii were certain they were overwhelmingly loyal. Short's obsession with sabotage was not merely a diversion but also led to his neutralizing of the American air defenses.

Had Kimmel tried to prepare for an attack, he would have faced serious difficulties. His forces badly needed training, and he lacked enough patrol planes for a prolonged search effort. The limited searches he did launch were confined to areas west and south of Oahu, facing the nearest Japanese bases in the Marshalls, rather than to the northwest, although air officers had warned that that approach was the likeliest route for an attack.

Thanks to Kimmel's and Short's misjudgments, American planes were jammed together unready for action, torpedo nets were not in place, no real use was made of radar, peacetime routines were followed, and most anti-aircraft guns were unmanned. They allowed such a state of laxity that even the sighting of Japanese submarines and planes did not evoke a response. It was wrong to pile all the blame on them, but it is hardly surprising that they were relieved of their commands after a disaster that, had the Japanese been more adept, might have become a true catastrophe.[3]

## The Critical Balance

Adm. Chester Nimitz, a submariner, replaced Kimmel. One of the great commanders of the war, he faced an extremely difficult problem: preserving his fleet until it could be reinforced, defending Hawaii and its outlying outposts of Midway and Johnston, and maintaining the line of communications between the United States and Australia and New Zealand. Right after Pearl Harbor, the United States feared that the Japanese would invade Hawaii or even the West Coast. Air and ground reinforcements rushed to both. By the end of 1941, however, the enemy clearly was concentrating on Southeast Asia.

The balance of carrier strength was vital for the course of the war and critical for 1942. For the first few months, Nimitz had three or four carriers in operation against six large Japanese carriers and three light carriers. The inferiority was unnecessary; but the U.S. Navy's backward-looking General Board, from 1935 to 1940, poured money into battleships and (reluctantly and under congressional pressure) had bought only one new carrier. The navy had seven large carriers: *Enterprise, Lexington, Saratoga, Yorktown, Hornet, Wasp,* and *Ranger.* The last four were in the Atlantic on December 7; the new *Hornet* was in the process of working up, or training. The *Ranger,* a slow, poorly designed ship, was vulnerable to bomb and torpedo hits, unsuited for Pacific service, and rarely in combat at all. The *Ranger* was mainly used for training, and ferrying planes. The *Wasp* too was tied down in the Atlantic for months, and a submarine torpedo would shortly knock the *Saratoga* out of action. The new Essex class fleet carriers and light carriers built on cruiser hulls (ordered only after Pearl Harbor) would not arrive until 1943.

Moreover, Nimitz, at first overoptimistic, did not realize that his carrier force was qualitatively inferior in most respects to the Japanese force. (The Americans also underestimated the size of the Japanese carriers *Hiryu* and *Soryu* and their air groups.) Japanese airmen were better trained and equipped, with one vital exception: U.S. Navy air gunnery and fighter tactics were superior to those of the Japanese. Naval airmen, especially Lieutenant Commander Thach, were aware of the Zero's threat and devised new, well-designed tactics to counter it. Unlike the Japanese, the U.S. Navy used the superior finger-four formation. These maneuvers enabled American fighter pilots to survive and even triumph, although the standard carrier-based fighter, the Grumman F4F Wildcat, which also equipped Marine units, was inferior to the Zero in speed, acceleration, climb, maneuverability, and range. Only its rugged construction, armor, self-sealing tanks (added only after the war began), heavy armament, and ability to outdive the Zero were saving graces. At first, the carriers carried too few fighters, and the navy was desperately short of Wildcats for much of 1942.

At the time of Pearl Harbor, some U.S. Navy and Marine units and the British and Dutch in Southeast Asia still flew the Wildcat's predecessor, the Brewster F2A Buffalo. Among other faults, its landing gear was too weak for carrier work. British pilots bitterly described it as a "sick old cow." Their Japanese counterparts thought that Allied pilots in Buffalo flew suicide missions.

Thach described the first American torpedo bomber, the Douglas TBD Devastator, as a "firetrap." It was so slow and short ranged that it was of little use. Torpedo squadrons awaited its replacement, the Grumman TBF Avenger, which reached the carriers only after the battle of Midway. Even good torpedo bombers, however, would not have been effective, for American aerial torpedoes had small warheads and were slow and unreliable. Critics like Harold Buell thought that the TBD's should have been either confined to antisubmarine patrols and bombing ill-defended land targets or replaced by dive-bombers. The Douglas SBD Dauntless dive-bomber was the only first-class American carrier plane available when the war began.

Despite radar, which the Japanese acquired only belatedly, the U.S. Navy fleet's antiaircraft defenses were inadequate, consisting early in the war of

1.1-inch "pom-poms" that frequently jammed and short-ranged .50-caliber machine guns. During 1942, the navy replaced them with far better 20mm Oerlikon and 40mm Bofors guns. The heavy, 5-inch, dual-purpose guns were not effective, however, until the arrival of the proximity fuse. The Americans also lacked an adequate "train" to supply the fleet. Further, a shortage of oilers dogged American carrier operations during much of 1942. Given these difficulties, Nimitz could only raid the perimeter of the expanding Japanese sphere and cover the establishment of a line of bases to protect the route between America and Australia.[4]

## Wake Island

After Pearl Harbor, the Japanese in the central Pacific did little except occupy the undefended Gilbert Islands (Kiribati) and attack Wake Island. Their first attempt to take Wake, poorly conducted, failed in the face of a determined defense.

The Japanese returned with a stronger force, detaching *Soryu* and *Hiryu* from Nagumo's fleet to support it. This was an early display of Yamamoto's tendency to scatter his forces. (The Americans would also disperse their forces on occasion.)

The second attack on Wake Island nearly produced the first carrier battle of the war. Still underestimating the Japanese, Kimmel devised an elaborate plan to relieve Wake. While the *Lexington* would raid a Japanese base in the Marshalls, the *Saratoga*, arriving from the West Coast, would fly off a Marine fighter squadron to Wake and cover a seaplane tender carrying reinforcements and supplies to the island. The *Enterprise* would stay back to cover Hawaii and support the other forces. A poor plan, it dangerously scattered the carriers. (Kimmel had kept them cruising around Hawaii, exposed to submarine attack, apparently to keep them out of Pearl Harbor.)

Kimmel was relieved before he could carry out his plan. Admiral Pye, a cautious and conservative battleship man, assumed command until Nimitz arrived. Pye knew that the chief of naval operations wanted Wake evacuated and not held. Rear Adm. Frank Jack Fletcher, a cruiser officer rather than a flier, led the *Saratoga* task force. He would be the principal American commander in several of the great battles of 1942 and was a controversial figure. Popular and a man of undoubted personal courage who had won the Medal of Honor in 1914, Fletcher was later widely damned as overcautious. He was one of the few Americans who might have "lost the war in an afternoon," to coin Winston Churchill's characterization of the British First World War admiral Sir John Jellicoe, but Fletcher often had better reasons for his actions than his critics supposed. He did not deserve much of the criticism later heaped on him. He may not have been a great admiral, but he was more competent than widely supposed.

The *Saratoga* relief force was repeatedly delayed. After it finally left Pearl Harbor, an old, slow, and poorly equipped oiler held it to a crawl. The Americans already had found that estimates of fuel consumption based on peacetime exercises were overoptimistic, and refueling at sea was much less efficient than it would be later. Passing up a chance to refuel his destroyers in good weather on December 21, Fletcher did so in bad conditions the next day, although they were in no immediate danger of running out of fuel. Had he left the oiler behind and run in at top speed, he might have delivered the reinforcements on December 21. Instead, that day Japanese carrier planes hit Wake. On December 23, the Japanese landed. On learning of this, Pye, who had harassed Fletcher with conflicting orders and knew that Washington deemed Wake a liability, decided that the risk of losing a precious carrier was too great. And it was now unlikely that the force could rescue the men on Wake. He ordered Fletcher, still 425 miles from Wake, and the *Lexington* force back to Hawaii.

The fleet reacted with shock and anger. This moment, not Pearl Harbor, was the nadir of morale in the U.S. Navy. Had Fletcher pressed on—some had wanted him to disobey orders and head for Wake—he might have inflicted heavy losses on the invasion force off Wake. Had he been earlier, he might have relieved Wake, and the American carriers might have found and destroyed the two Japanese carriers. But given the Americans' equipment and level of readiness, the outcome of such a battle even between all three American carriers and *Soryu* and *Hiryu* would not have been certain. Moreover, *Saratoga's* fighter squadron was at half strength, while the *Lexington's* still flew the unreliable Buffalo. The ifs of the Wake relief operation may always be argued. Had it gone well, it might have meant the early and vital truncation of Japanese carrier strength that took place months later in the battle of the Coral Sea. Had it not gone well—which seems the more likely case—it might have led to a disaster the Allies could not afford.[5]

## Southeast Asia

Japan's main objectives were Malaya, Singapore, the Netherlands East Indies (Indonesia), and British Borneo. Economically, Burma and the Philippines were not that important, but they had to be secured for strategic reasons. The Philippines held the strongest Allied concentration of modern planes, but that was not saying much. A lack of adequate airfields crippled the Americans in the Philippines. While the British and Dutch had good bases, they lacked antiaircraft defenses and had few planes and hardly any modern ones. Their airfields aided the Japanese more than they did the Allies. The Japanese allotted eleven army divisions and seven hundred army planes, as well as most of the navy's land-based Eleventh Air Fleet, to the Southeast Asian theater. Moving under land-based air cover, they used the extraordinary range of the Zeros, which quickly flew into captured bases, to cover the next amphibious hop. They carried out a huge pincer movement based on Indochina and Taiwan converging on Java. As the assault on Southeast Asia got under way, they took Hong Kong. The British had stationed six infantry battalions and a motor torpedo boat squadron there, although it was deep in enemy territory and utterly indefensible.

The Japanese would conquer Southeast Asia with far fewer losses than they feared, losses the official British historian Roskill would describe as almost trivial. Meanwhile, the Allies lost almost all their forces committed there, damages aggravated by a tendency to reinforce hopeless situations, especially in Malaya and Singapore and the East Indies. The Americans might have done the same in the Philippines, but the Japanese had largely cut off their forces at the start of the war. The Allies maintained a tenuous connection with the Philippines only by aircraft, submarine, and almost entirely unsuccessful blockade-running operations with small freighters.

Curiously, as historian H. P. Willmott noted, both the major Western powers, although they had not coordinated their efforts,

> employed policies of forward defense against an enemy with air superiority and superiority of numbers on the ground at the point of contact. This enemy possessed a sound and carefully developed battle doctrine based on mass firepower and armor, the latter being used in both reconnaissance and strike roles. British and American doctrines were based on infantry and their infantry lacked an effective antitank weapon. The ground on which battles were fought was known to the defense, which had had years in which to conduct proper reconnaissance and prepare proper defensive positions.

The British and Americans had suffered defeat. Little was behind them to stop the Japanese. Reinforcements could not come in time, and the Dutch were even weaker than their allies were. Their largely obsolete air and sea forces fought hard, but their army was little more than a backup for the police and their widely hated rule.

A feeble inter-Allied command was improvised at the first Washington conference only after the war began. There Field Marshal Wavell was appointed head of the American-British-Dutch-Australian Command. On hearing of this, Wavell remarked that he had heard of being handed the baby, but this post involved twins. Later, he admitted that he had gravely underestimated the Japanese. He planned to hold a line of bases from Sumatra through Singapore, Java, Bali, Timor, and Darwin in northwest Australia. Evidently he rightly wrote off the Philippines at an early date. His plan was not realistic, although it is hard to say what a realistic plan would have been or whether the Allied leaders, perhaps, would have been able to accept one.

The Allies believed Singapore was the only really good base in the region and hoped they could hold it for a prolonged time. While they sent considerable ground and air reinforcements to Southeast Asia—after the war began, however, when it was too late—they had little prospect of arriving in time to affect the outcome except perhaps in Burma. But the British wrongly estimated that the Japanese could not launch a major drive there until the offensive in the archipelago was completed. That mistaken appreciation, along with the obsession with Singapore, prevented an early decision to write off the rest of Southeast Asia and concentrate on holding Burma, probably the only course available after the war began, which might have salvaged part of the region.[6]

The Japanese attack on December 8 interrupted a buildup that might have enabled the Americans to hold the Philippines. The Japanese had a superior air force of 590 planes on Taiwan, although range limitations prevented their using many army planes until they had bases in the Philippines. Meanwhile, 108 Navy Zeroes and 144 bombers were ready to strike from Taiwan.

The Americans had a nominal total of 277 planes in the Philippines, but most were obsolete, unflyable, or otherwise useless. On Luzon, 35 modern bombers and 90 operational fighters—some obsolete, others newly issued to units and not combat ready—were jammed on four poorly defended fields, with little dispersal, too few revetments, and inadequate supporting services. Aided by weather and command confusion, the Japanese smashed much of the force on the ground on December 8. They cut its strength in half the first day of the war. On December 10, they further reduced the force to 30 fighters and 18 bombers. The remaining bombers soon left for Australia.

The disastrous air losses in the Philippines had largely occurred on Pearl Harbor Day, although mistakes and accidents exacerbated the situation. Much was later made of the mistakes, but even had the USAAF survived the first day it would soon have been defeated. If it had somehow held out against the Eleventh Air Fleet's attacks, the Japanese would have sent Nagumo's carrier force in if necessary.

The small U.S. Army and Philippine Scout units, supported by a mass of recently formed, almost untrained, and poorly equipped Philippine Army divisions, could not stop the Japanese. After an unnecessary delay, MacArthur belatedly reverted to the older plan to retreat to Bataan, where the Filipinos fought well; but the struggle could end in only one way. The other arm of the great Japanese pincer went ashore easily in Malaya. The Japanese immediately gained control of the air and sank the battleship HMS *Prince of Wales* and battle cruiser HMS *Repulse*, which, with Force Z, had gone east in an attempt to deter Japan. Although the Japanese did not have greater numbers of land forces, their ably led troops did have tanks, which the British did not have. They hustled the British forces, which were largely ill-trained Indian units that been committed piecemeal and held overstretched fronts, out of successive positions.

British reinforcements arrived too late and merely swelled the enormous total of prisoners (130,000) taken when Singapore fell on February 15. The Japanese then overran the Netherlands East Indies, where they sank the defending fleet in the Battle of the Java Sea and its aftermath. On March 8, the Dutch surrendered. Afterward, the Japanese only had to complete the conquest of Burma and finish off the American pockets, far behind the Japanese front lines, in the Philippines. In Burma, while again holding an overstretched line too far forward, the British suffered disastrous losses at the start of the campaign and quickly lost the vital port of Rangoon (Yangon). They and the Chinese forces belatedly arriving in central Burma were steadily pushed back and retreated in horrible conditions to India.

With the loss of Burma and the surrender in the Philippines on May 6, the defense of Southeast Asia ended in total defeat. Many years of wishful thinking about Japan had helped produce this disaster, along with Britain's failure to rush as many reinforcements as possible to the region when it became clear that war was near. The Philippines, nearly surrounded by Japanese-held territory, and most of the Dutch East Indies were indefensible. MacArthur erred in abandoning the traditional plan of defense before the forces were actually available to hold the whole archipelago, but his forces were probably built up as fast, or faster, than possible. Indeed, the air buildup outstripped the development of the necessary bases. While Churchill's insistence that the Mediterranean and Middle East must have priority was correct—without Middle Eastern oil, holding the Far East or even India would have been impossible—it is hard to excuse the delay in reinforcing Southeast Asia once war was inevitable. Had the British written off Hong Kong instead of reinforcing it, and had they sent the forces that were rushed east after Japan attacked to Malaya and Sumatra, they might have held those territories. After Pearl Harbor, though, it was too late to save anything but Burma. Had the Eighteenth Division and the other reinforcements wasted at Singapore been assigned to Burma, the Allies might have been able to defend it.[7]

## Japanese Second Phase Planning

By early 1942, the Japanese knew that they would soon secure their original objectives in Southeast Asia and the western Pacific and at a lower cost than they had feared. As early as November, Imperial General Headquarters had mentioned future operations against eastern New Guinea, Fiji, Samoa, the Aleutians, Midway, and "strategic points in the Australian area," but the Japanese had not developed any plans. The Japanese now explored advancing beyond the perimeter. The navy strongly favored a decisive drive but did not agree in what direction it should go. Rear Adm. Ryunosuke Kusaka, Nagumo's chief of staff, was practically alone in wanting to go on the defensive. The army was more cautious about further expansion against the Western powers, probably because it still hoped that Germany would defeat the Soviets and that Japan could join in for the finish.

In late January, the Japanese had easily seized Rabaul on New Britain, which became their main base in the South Pacific and supported operations in both New Guinea and the Solomon Islands. In early February, Imperial General Headquarters decided on a further advance. The Japanese planned to take Lae and Salamaua in northeast New Guinea in March, and in early April Port Moresby, the main Allied base on the southeast coast of New Guinea, along with the island of Tulagi, right off the larger island of Guadalcanal in the Solomons. These operations did not seem to require any more than the small forces already assigned to the region.

The Naval General Staff wanted to push even farther. In January, it strongly argued for the outright conquest of Australia to eliminate it as a base for a future Allied counteroffensive. Vice Adm. Shigeyoshi Inoue, who commanded the Fourth Fleet (South Seas Force), the operational command in the region, strongly supported this idea. Although some army men—notably Gen. Tomoyuki Yamashita, the victor at Singapore—liked the idea, the army high command adamantly rejected it. Such an operation would take ten to twelve divisions, which the army did not have, and an impossible amount of shipping (1.5 million tons). It recognized, however, the danger of an Allied counteroffensive based on Australia and was open to a compromise—that is, cutting off Australia by capturing New Caledonia, Fiji, and Samoa. This plan was agreed on in mid-March, although the staff never formally rejected invading Australia itself.

Admiral Yamamoto had different ideas. Although as Combined Fleet commander he was nominally subordinate to the Naval General Staff, in Japanese military affairs nominal subordinates often overrode or outmaneuvered those supposedly above them in the hierarchy. Yamamoto had done so before Pearl Harbor, with results that had bolstered his influence. He and his staff preferred a drive east.

As early as December 9, he had urged taking Hawaii as a bargaining counter that could be returned to the United States in the expected peace negotiations. The army had refused to supply the three divisions needed, while the rest of the navy expressed no enthusiasm for the idea. Yamamoto's own staff rejected an invasion of Hawaii because it was unlikely to attain surprise and run up against too many land-based planes. Yamamoto's chief of staff suggested a lesser operation of taking Midway and Johnston Islands, for they could serve as outposts from which a later operation against Hawaii might be mounted. The staff hoped that the American fleet would defend Midway, allowing a decisive battle in which it could be defeated. Even the senior staff officer, Capt. Kameto Kuroshima, was skeptical of this idea. He doubted that the American fleet would come out and thought Midway and Johnston would be hard to maintain.

Combined Fleet then considered a western operation in the Indian Ocean to destroy the British fleet, capture Ceylon (now Sri Lanka), and link up with the European Axis. The Japanese (or those Germans who thought along parallel lines) do not seem to have determined exactly what operations, after taking Ceylon, would be executed to achieve that link. The army objected again, however, being reluctant to allot the five divisions needed (two to take Ceylon) although the forces and transports were available. War games testing the idea did not suggest that the scheme was promising, although they were based on an overestimate of the British forces. Given the distances from Japanese bases, a full-scale drive all the way across the Indian

Ocean would probably not have been easier to support than an invasion of Australia. A large-scale carrier raid in the Indian Ocean was scheduled. Combined Fleet suggested a limited move against Northwest Australia and seizing the Darwin area, this too was rejected.

Yamamoto then revived a limited move against Midway, again arguing that it would draw the U.S. fleet into a decisive battle and push Japan's defensive perimeter far to the east. His representatives argued that Fiji and Samoa were too far from Japanese bases, and attacking them would not bring out the American fleet. The Navy General Staff's planners and some lower-level commanders, notably Admiral Inoue, and Adm. Nobutake Kondo, whose Second Fleet would carry out a Midway invasion, reasonably countered that those objections applied far more forcibly to Yamamoto's plans. The planners stressed that the New Caledonia-Fiji-Samoa drive would draw the Americans out and could be supported by land-based planes, unlike the Midway operation. Midway was not a good base, they countered, for defensive operations or to support an attack on Hawaii. It would be hard to supply and defend, and the small air units that could be based there were bound to suffer heavy losses to American attacks. These were strong arguments, while Combined Fleet's case was weak. And the army was unenthusiastic, correctly suspecting that Midway was an entering wedge for a full-scale assault on Hawaii.

Despite this resistance, Yamamoto threatened to resign and forced through his plan on April 5. The Japanese would take Midway after capturing Port Moresby and before launching the New Caledonia-Fiji-Samoa drive. After capturing Samoa, they would invade Hawaii. Many still opposed the Midway plan. But the Doolittle raid on Japan two weeks later ended this dissension. Preventing further humiliating attacks on the homeland merited high priority. Indeed, the army became enthusiastic about tackling Hawaii and began the necessary preparations. Against Yamamoto's inclinations, the Naval General Staff added yet another operation to the program. While the main forces attacked Midway, a secondary force would attack the Aleutian Islands.[8]

Japanese planning was belated and blundering. Between them, the Naval General Staff and Combined Fleet (although the latter's follies were worse) failed to concentrate Japan's limited resources on one clear line of endeavor and produced a sort of strategic stew. The carrier force, which had done little in the four months since Pearl Harbor, would now be overstrained. It had supported the Rabaul landing and the last part of the Indonesian campaign, but its help had not really been needed. As many officers complained, it had been used as a sledgehammer to crack walnuts instead of being given a worthwhile task such as breaking the American-Australian lifeline at an early date.

Invading Australia itself, however, might have been a mistake, even if it had been possible. Had the invasion gone forward without sinking the American carriers first and had the battle gone against the Japanese—the Allies certainly would have resisted fiercely—Japan might have been caught in a grinding campaign of attrition with long supply lines, especially costly in shipping. Indeed, it might have led to an earlier Japanese defeat.

## American Carrier Raids

Despite their weakness, the Americans were not passive. Their carriers covered convoys taking Marine and army forces to garrison islands on the route between the United States and Australia, raided outlying Japanese positions, and finally hit Japan itself. The attacks provided valuable experience and hampered Japanese plans.

The Americans suffered a loss on January 11, when, a Japanese submarine badly damaged the *Saratoga* as it returned from a patrol near Midway. The *Saratoga* went to Bremerton, Washington, for repairs. A raid on Wake Island was aborted when another submarine hit the task force's oiler.

After protecting the delivery of Marines to Samoa, task forces commanded by Admirals Halsey and Fletcher and built around the *Enterprise* and the *Yorktown* raided the Marshall and Gilbert Islands on February 1. An early raid on the Marshalls had been part of prewar plans, and the navy hoped that the attack would disrupt what was thought to be the enemy's most likely next move, an invasion of Samoa. The attacks, small and primitive by later standards, did little damage and twelve planes were lost. By later standards, Halsey should have used both carriers operating together, with the *Lexington* along as well, and struck only the Marshalls. But the Americans learned important lessons from the raid. Their pilots found that their guns frequently jammed and discovered how vulnerable the Douglas TBD Devastator was. It could only operate safely with fighter protection, contrary to prewar doctrine that rejected close fighter escort for torpedo bombers. They needed more fighters with better armor, self-sealing tanks, incendiary bullets that could set enemy planes on fire instead of just holing them, and identification friend or foe (IFF) gear so U.S. radars could distinguish between friendly and enemy planes.

More raids followed, although they did not divert forces from Southeast Asia. A strike on Rabaul was aborted when the enemy spotted the

Americans, but an air battle inflicted heavy losses on Japanese bombers and forced postponement of the Lae and Salamaua landings by five days. The *Enterprise* struck Wake and Marcus Islands, causing some damage. The ship's after-action reports repeated earlier lessons but noted the need for more reserve pilots and the problem of the Wildcat fighter's short range. It needed droppable tanks.

On March 8, the Japanese landed at Lae and Salamaua. The *Yorktown* had recently joined the *Lexington* for a renewed raid on Rabaul, but on March 10, they struck ships off Lae and Salamaua instead. Steaming off southern New Guinea, they sent off 104 planes, which crossed the island through a 7,500-foot pass in the towering Owen Stanley Range. It was a risky operation. The Wildcats' short range forced the carriers to operate closely inshore in poorly charted waters full of reefs, and there was a grave danger that bad weather would close the pass. The *Lexington*'s straining torpedo bombers only made it through by finding an updraft to help them over the highest point. Even the crews of the *Yorktown*'s lightly loaded TBDs, carrying bombs, were surprised to get through. This daring attack did more damage than any action since the start of the war and was more successful than the Allies realized. The Japanese were shaken. Postponing the attacks on Port Moresby and Tulagi by a month, they decided that fleet carriers from Nagumo's force should support operations. The Americans lost only one plane. Again, clearly the Wildcat was too short ranged, and their attacks had succeeded despite their bombs being poorly fused, going off on impact instead of penetrating enemy ships before exploding. Humidity caused radio malfunctions, and the dive-bombers' sights fogged as they plunged from cool high altitudes into steamy tropical air near the surface. Their bomb releases often failed. They also discovered that the early type of self-sealing tanks in the Wildcat were defective and had to be replaced.

Devised by Adm. Ernest King's staff and possibly originally inspired by President Roosevelt, the last carrier raid of early 1942 was the most spectacular and the most carefully planned—an attack on Japan itself. Nimitz had misgivings about it. With the navy's help, Lt. Col. James Doolittle, one of the great pioneers of aviation, had trained USAAF crews to take off modified B-25 twin-engine bombers from a carrier deck. (They could not land on it, though.) The *Hornet* and the *Enterprise* would approach Japan as closely as possible and launch the B-25s to attack targets in several Japanese cities. Afterward, the pilots would fly to bases in China. The task force ran into Japanese picket boats, and Doolittle had to take off prematurely. One B-25 hit the Japanese carrier *Ryuho*, delaying its completion by several months, and the raid caused a surprising amount of material damage. The premature launch and a failure to coordinate preparations properly with the Chinese caused the loss of all but one plane, which landed in Siberia, although most of the crews survived. The raid raised Allied morale and ended debate about the Midway plan among the Japanese. The Imperial Japanese Army committed four fighter groups to defend Japan that would have been better used elsewhere. It also generated a flurry of Japanese radio signals that proved helpful to American intelligence.

However, the raid was costly, aside from the loss of the planes. The Japanese overran the Chinese airfields the Americans had planned to use and slaughtered a huge number of Chinese civilians. As Nimitz had feared, the raid tied up two of his carriers at a crucial moment. They could not reach the Southwest Pacific in time to counter the next Japanese move.[9]

## Defending the Pacific Lifeline

The U.S. military quickly reinforced Hawaii after the attack on Pearl Harbor. With two understrength infantry divisions and considerable coast artillery, it may already have been too strong on the ground for any invasion the Japanese could mount, even had they attained air supremacy, which was becoming steadily more difficult. Between reinforcements and energetic repair efforts, the Hawaiian Air Force had 202 fighters and 78 bombers by New Year's Day 1942. A third division reached Hawaii in March.

The eastern approaches to Australia, and perhaps Australia itself, were wide open for a while. Fortunately, the Japanese did not use their carrier force to cover a major push in the region in early 1942. The Royal Australian Air Force in early 1942 had merely 177 planes, including 53 Hudson light bombers, but no modern fighters at all.

In December, planners decided to send a sizable air force to the Southwest Pacific. A group of heavy bombers, two medium bomber groups, a light bomber group, and four fighter groups (later reduced to three) were to join the heavy bomber group that had escaped the Philippines. The first units sent were badly mangled in the defense of Java.

Under pressure from Admiral King, Nimitz reluctantly sent a carrier task force under Admiral Fletcher to the South Pacific. A stream of ground and air reinforcements went to the islands between Hawaii and Australia that had been almost undefended when the war began. Only a New Zealand brigade group and two battalions of Fijians held Fiji, while fourteen hundred poorly armed Free French held New Caledonia. A few companies of New Zealanders held Western Samoa. The New Zealanders sent three more battalions to Fiji and a company to New Caledonia, while the Australians established a brigade and some antiaircraft guns at Port Moresby in New Guinea. Over the next few months, American Marines and soldiers garrisoned Samoa, Canton, Bora Bora, Palmyra Atoll, and Christmas Island. Two U.S. Army regiments went to New Caledonia in March; later, reinforced, they were organized into the Americal Division. In February and March, the Americans also decided to commit two infantry divisions to Australia and a third to New Zealand so that Australian and New Zealand units could stay in the Middle East instead of returning home. The Thirty-seventh Division, sent to New Zealand, later swapped places with the New Zealanders at Fiji. When the island line was completed, American and Allied ground troops and the few scattered air squadrons—many with obsolete planes—could at least stop the sort of small-scale attacks that had taken Wake and Rabaul. The area north of Australia was still practically undefended, apart from Port Moresby, which the Australians felt unable to either abandon or reinforce.

MacArthur reached Australia in March and assumed command of the new Southwest Pacific Area, comprising Australia, New Guinea, and the Japanese-held areas to the northwest. He was entirely independent of the navy's Pacific theater under Nimitz. The neighboring South Pacific Area, which included New Zealand, New Caledonia, the Solomons, and other islands to the north and east, was a subdivision of Nimitz's command.

MacArthur was instructed to hold "key areas of Australia." He had little to hold them with, though. For a time, in March, Australia was almost defenseless. Only poorly trained militia units (the equivalent of the American National Guard) were available, and the first American infantry division, the Forty-first, landed on April 6. The American airmen who had escaped from the Philippines and Indonesia were exhausted and demoralized, while newly arrived air units had no proper equipment or even training. Only 136 fighters were in commission in Australia, most belonging to the Forty-ninth Fighter Group, which had arrived in early February and was still in training. Of its 102 pilots, 89 had no experience in fighters, and 9 others had only fifteen hours' flying time in them apiece. There was one operational B-17 squadron and two dive-bomber squadrons.

Had the Japanese been able to attack Australia in March, they might have overrun its key areas despite their logistical difficulties. But even had they decided to attempt an attack, as opposed to cutting off the continent by seizing the islands east of it, they likely could not have moved fast enough to take Australia before its defenses were built up. By May, the Australians and Americans were much stronger; MacArthur's command was probably strong enough to repel a direct attack on Australia. Indeed, the Australian official historian concluded that by then the theater was "somewhat over-insured in ground troops."

In the combat zone in New Guinea, the Allied air forces approximately equaled that of their Japanese foes. There, despite poor command and miserable conditions, inadequate antiaircraft defenses, a lack of supplies and spare parts, and obsolete fighters, the Allies kept the Port Moresby base in operation and bombed Lae, Salamaua, and occasionally Rabaul. Admiral King already envisaged a step-by-step advance from the New Hebrides toward Rabaul.[10]

## The Indian Ocean Raid

The Japanese had rejected a major advance west but launched a major raid in the Indian Ocean. They hoped to destroy at least part of the British Eastern Fleet, neutralize any counteroffensive against their Southeast Asian conquests, and destroy merchant shipping in support of the Burma campaign.

Although Wavell and the British chiefs of staff feared a drive on Northeast India, the Royal Navy correctly thought that Ceylon would be the Japanese target. Its capture would allow the Japanese to dominate the eastern Indian Ocean, to threaten India, and (a point rarely noted) to take the Allies' last major source of natural rubber, which the Allies badly needed before America's synthetic rubber industry got going. The British had reinforced Ceylon by the end of March, sending the equivalent of two infantry divisions and, by the standards of the time, considerable air reinforcements there. This force would have given a Japanese invasion a difficult fight.

The British had a major but not formidable fleet in the Indian Ocean under Adm. James Somerville. The Royal Navy paid again for the fact that battleship admirals had dominated it between the world wars more thoroughly than they had the American or Japanese navies. Somerville's three carriers—*Indomitable*, *Formidable*, and *Hermes*, the last being old and small—carried only a few and mostly obsolete planes. In all, they had fifty-seven strike aircraft and less than forty fighters. Of the latter, only twenty-five Martlets (the British name for the Wildcat) and nine Sea Hurricanes were comparable to the Zero, and they would face hundreds of up-to-date Japanese planes on five big carriers and one light carrier. The *Formidable*'s air group was inexperienced. Not many land-based reconnaissance planes were available to support the carriers. Finally, most of Somerville's battleships were obsolete and many of his smaller ships in poor shape. The only advantages the British had were their shipborne radars, some radar-equipped torpedo bombers that could strike at night, and advance warning of attack from a partly deciphered Japanese signal. Everyone agreed that the Eastern Fleet must not be sacrificed, even to try to save Ceylon. Somerville knew that he could not face the Japanese in a major battle in daylight. Operating from a poorly equipped secret base in the Maldives, he maneuvered to stay out of Japanese range in daylight while tracking the enemy fleet and tried to strike it at night. But no chance to do so appeared.

The deciphered Japanese message gave the British sufficient warning to get the fleet and much of their merchant shipping clear of Ceylon. The Japanese struck Colombo, then Trincomalee. They destroyed two cruisers and the *Hermes*, which had been mistakenly detached from the main force, as well as much shipping. Although taking unjustifiable risks in his efforts to get at the enemy, Somerville maneuvered his force skillfully, but his few reconnaissance planes could not maintain continuous contact with the Japanese fleet. For his part, Nagumo knew from detecting British signals and encountering British carrier planes that their fleet must be near, but he never found it. Nagumo's force remained unhurt as Somerville broke off action and fled west, ultimately withdrawing to Kilindini in East Africa. He somberly wrote that the Japanese could take Ceylon at any time.

Despite inflicting considerable damage on the Eastern Fleet, the raid was a blunder. Nagumo's aircraft losses were not great, but most of his carriers needed to refit. The waste of time, effort, and trained men against a secondary target, before major battles with the Americans, was something the Japanese could not afford. Only two big carriers could support the Port Moresby and Tulagi landings. The Japanese did not draw any conclusions from their failure to find the British fleet.[11]

## Intelligence

An early success of signal intelligence had helped the British. The Allies had begun reading the most important Japanese naval cipher, the $D$ cipher, which the Allies called JN25b. They had also gained experience at traffic analysis, or the study of the pattern of enemy signals traffic, which could be revealing even when the messages could not be read.

The Japanese aided the Allies by committing two blunders: they did not encrypt call signs so it was easy to tell the sender and recipient of a message, and they repeatedly delayed adopting a new version of the code. A change originally scheduled for April 1 was delayed until June 1. By early

March, the Allies had read enough enemy signals to glean important information. Along with the British, American code breakers at Melbourne, Washington, and Hawaii all shared in the effort, but the Pearl Harbor station, headed by the brilliant Lt. Cdr. Joseph Rochefort, was the most important. In March, Rochefort forecast that the Japanese would attack in the New Guinea area and the central Pacific.

By the end of March, signs indicated that enemy aircraft were gathering at Rabaul for an operation in the south. During April, evidence increasingly pointed to a major operation against Port Moresby, with a secondary one in the Solomons. On April 14, the Allies learned that a new light carrier, *Shoho*, and cruisers were joining the enemy's Fourth Fleet at Truk in the Carolines. A day later, a rare completely deciphered message revealed that Rear Adm. Takeo Takagi's Fifth Carrier Division, with the carriers *Shokaku* and *Zuikaku*, was en route south. Other information pointed to a seaplane carrier going to New Guinea and the organization of two landing forces. By April 20, Nimitz was sure that the enemy aimed to take Port Moresby. Decrypts at the end of April helped confirm this and that the operation involved establishing a seaplane base off southeast New Guinea. On May 3, intelligence deciphered the general orders to Takagi's force and, on May 5 and 6, the plans and current position of the Port Moresby occupation force.[12]

## The Battle of the Coral Sea

The Americans had correctly deduced the elaborate and widespread Japanese plan. A small force would take Tulagi, formerly held by a small Australian force (it withdrew just before the Japanese arrived), and establish a seaplane base there while a larger force headed for Port Moresby. It would be supported by another group built around a seaplane carrier that would set up a seaplane base in the Louisiade Islands. Yet another force including the *Shoho* would safeguard both groups, while Takagi's big carriers provided more distant cover. The Japanese did not expect to meet American carriers.

Nimitz was determined to save Port Moresby, if possible, but the Doolittle raid left him with little to stop the Japanese. The *Lexington* was ordered from Pearl Harbor to join Fletcher's Task Force 17 with the *Yorktown*, which had been operating out of New Caledonia. Halsey's task force would come as soon as possible, but it needed at least five days to refit and replenish at Pearl Harbor. It returned there on April 25. So, unless the Japanese suffered unexpected delays, Halsey's force was unlikely to arrive in time.

Fletcher thus had only two carriers to face the enemy's three and had little shore-based air support. Neither the navy PBYs flying out of New Caledonia nor the USAAF units in MacArthur's theater could reconnoiter more than part of their respective areas, and radio communications in the region seem to have been quite unreliable. That situation was true, however, for both sides. Japanese shore-based planes would not prove successful, either. The odds were not as bad as the number of carriers suggested, for the *Shoho* could not have operated with Takagi's fleet carriers in any case. Thus, the two sides were evenly matched as far as the number of planes on the fleet carriers.

The *Lexington* joined Fletcher on May 1, but refueling proved lengthy and difficult. On May 2 Fletcher took the *Yorktown* force alone out into the Coral Sea to search for the enemy. On May 3, he received news of the landing on Tulagi. The next day, he struck the part of the landing force that was still there. The Japanese supporting forces had already left, while their big carriers were still far to the north. The Americans' strike was poorly coordinated, and they still used bombs with instantaneous fuses. Worse, however, was the pilots' struggle with the fogging of bombsights and windshields as had happened at Lae and Salamaua. Only after the Coral Sea did American dive-bombers get new sights and coatings for windshields that ended this problem. (They also realized, belatedly, that lower-approach altitudes would reduce fogging.) Between dive-bomber pilots attacking practically blind and the usual miserable performance of American torpedoes, only a few ships and landing craft were sunk. The Americans did destroy several flying boats, however, impairing Japanese reconnaissance.

On May 5, Rear Adm. Aubrey Fitch and the *Lexington* finally joined Fletcher's group. Over the next two days, the Japanese and Americans looked for each other, but both concentrated their searches in the wrong places. (Misinterpretations of partly deciphered signals by the intelligence specialists misled Fletcher into thinking that the enemy was to his northwest rather than the northeast.) The Americans were helped by the fact that until May 7 a front of bad weather hid them, while the Japanese carriers did not fly off searches of their own and relied instead on land-based planes. On May 6, Fletcher had several reports of enemy ships but not dependable ones. For instance, B-17s spotted and bombed the *Shoho* but missed. Fletcher rightly suspected that their target was only a light carrier. One of his dive-bombers narrowly missed finding the Japanese, while a Japanese flying boat did see the American carriers, but its report did not reach Takagi. Early on May 7, soon expecting the Japanese invasion force to cut through the Jomard Passage southeast of New Guinea, Fletcher detached American and Australian cruisers and destroyers under Rear Adm. John Crace to block it. This move weakened the already thin screen protecting the U.S. carriers. If the latter were lost, Japanese carrier planes could easily have sunk Crace's ships. They were lucky to survive attacks by both Japanese land-based planes and American B-17s, though they diverted some of the Japanese air effort.

Later that morning, both sides sighted each other's ships and sent off strikes but mistook minor forces for the other's big carriers. The disgusted Japanese pilots found that the carriers were merely a destroyer and the oiler and sank them. An American dive-bomber, meanwhile, found a small Japanese force. It tried to report sighting Japanese cruisers and destroyers—actually the ships it had seen were much smaller—but owing to a mistake in coding, this message was received as a report of carriers and cruisers. Fletcher sent off a big strike of ninety-three planes to hit the enemy ships. Fortunately, en route to its assigned targets, the American force spotted the *Shoho*. An overwhelming attack sank it. (The air near the surface was dry, so the dive-bombers could see their targets.)

Admiral Inouye postponed the Moresby invasion by two days, and the invasion force temporarily retreated. Late in the day, having been unable to find Fletcher's carriers, Takagi sent off a search-and-strike group of men trained in night landings. It too missed the U.S. carriers. En route home, after jettisoning their bombs and torpedoes, the Japanese finally stumbled on the American force, losing several planes to fighters. After dark, some Japanese planes apparently tried to land on the *Yorktown*, mistaking it for one of their own ships. The Japanese suffered serious losses on May 7 for nothing.

The next morning, Japanese and American carrier planes found each other's carriers almost at the same time. Takagi had already launched a strike "blind," but it was guided to the American carriers. Fletcher, meanwhile, had waited until his scouts actually found the enemy force.

The American attack was ragged, and in line with a pet idea of Admiral Fitch and Capt. Frederick Sherman of the *Lexington*, many dive-bombers were held back to fly anti-torpedo plane patrols and supplement the desperately few fighters defending the task force. The two air groups flew separately and were broken up by bad weather en route to the targets, with the dive-bombers getting separated from the torpedo planes. Some of the *Lexington*'s dive-bombers became lost and never did find the Japanese. The *Yorktown*'s dive-bombers, arriving first, made the mistake of orbiting to wait for the virtually useless torpedo bombers to catch up instead of attacking immediately. The Japanese had time to get ready; the *Zuikaku* successfully hid in a rainstorm. Fortunately, the Japanese defense was not efficient, but fogged windshields and sights again hampered the American dive-bombers. They nevertheless seriously damaged the *Shokaku*, knocking it out of the war for two months. Every American torpedo missed.

The American defense was not well managed, but it was the first time a U.S. carrier force had faced a large, combined dive-bomber and torpedo bomber attack. By later standards, the American fighters were poorly directed. Pilots were sent to intercept too near their carriers and too low to catch enemy dive-bombers before they pushed over into their dives. The dive-bombers assigned to anti-torpedo defense were really too slow for the task. They downed some Japanese planes but lost more themselves. One direct bomb hit and near misses by two others moderately damaged the *Yorktown* while at least two torpedoes and two bombs hit the *Lexington*. At first the *Lexington* seemed in no great danger. But broken aviation fuel lines filled some compartments with explosive vapor, and damage control missed this problem. On the afternoon of May 8, possibly set off by sparks from a motor-generator mistakenly left running, a series of explosions tore the carrier apart.

Both sides broke off action, and the Port Moresby invasion force went home. The loss of the *Lexington*, far more valuable than the *Shoho*, made the Coral Sea a tactical victory for the Japanese, but it was a strategic victory for the Americans. The Moresby invasion had been foiled, albeit temporarily. (The Japanese planned to renew it, after Midway was taken.) More important, the *Shokaku* and the *Zuikaku*, which had lost many planes, were unavailable for the next, more crucial battle.[13] The Japanese were sure that the *Yorktown* had been sunk or crippled, as well as the *Lexington*, which they mistook for the *Saratoga*. They had thought that the *Lexington* had been the carrier that was torpedoed in January; moreover, they thought it had been sunk, not simply damaged.

### Midway: Anticipation and Preparation

Thanks to Rochefort's unit, the Americans again knew the next Japanese target. By May 4, Rochefort's group, reading a quarter to a third of the JN25b code groups, was sure that the next attack would be in the central Pacific. Various clues pointed to Midway. Rochefort was satisfied with the evidence by May 11. On May 14, after a careful review, Nimitz concurred. He had some trouble, however, convincing Washington.

Admiral King continued to believe that the Japanese planned a renewed drive in the south, probably against Port Moresby. Others feared an attack on Hawaii or the West Coast, which had been hurriedly strengthened with air reinforcements and antiaircraft units. Aircraft plants in the region were camouflaged, and finished planes dispersed. The departure of the U.S. Eighth Air Force, the strategic bombing force that would be based in England, was delayed until after the result of the next Japanese move was known. (This postponement was an indication of what Washington might have done had if the Pacific Fleet had been defeated.)

U.S. intelligence used a ruse to confirm that Midway was the target. A fake message was sent in plain language reporting that Midway's water distillation system had broken down. The Japanese report of the message, which the Americans deciphered, helped confirm the code letters that the Americans had supposed designated Midway as the target. Late in May, Rochefort's unit deciphered most of Yamamoto's operations order, but on June 1 the Japanese finally changed ciphers. While the Americans were reasonably sure that the Japanese were heading for Midway, they could not know the precise timing or strength of the attack or the exact direction from which it would come. But, as Nimitz declared, intelligence was decisive at Midway. Without it, the Americans could not have prevailed.

When the *Yorktown* reached Pearl Harbor, yard workers made frantic efforts to patch it up. Full repair was estimated to take up to three months, but they did a remarkable job in two days. Still, damaged watertight doors were not fixed, and its knocked-out boilers could not be repaired, so, the crew thought the *Yorktown* could not steam at full speed.

Nimitz knew that even after Coral Sea, the Japanese had at least six carriers to throw at his three. He reinforced Midway as much as possible. The planes there were equivalent in numbers to an additional carrier air group, but most were obsolete, unsuited for the task at hand, or manned by pilots barely out of training. Most of the Marine fighters on Midway were Buffaloes. Only the PBY patrol planes were valuable. Six new TBF torpedo bombers, along with a handful of Wildcats and SBDs were the only up-to-date combat planes. But Midway was ready for an amphibious assault. The Marine ground forces were so strong and Midway so well fortified that, whatever the outcome of a battle at sea, it is unlikely that the single regiment Yamamoto planned to land could have taken it.[14]

At sea, the Allies in the Pacific were far weaker than they need have been. The *Saratoga* should have been available for Midway. Nimitz had urged that its repairs be finished as soon as possible, but the ship reached

Pearl Harbor on June 6, the day the battle of Midway ended. He later wrote that it could have sailed earlier if not for delays in forming an escort screen. Admiral Pye's old battleships, too slow to operate with the carriers, were based at San Francisco, and when they sortied during the battle, they used no less than eight destroyers that could have escorted the *Saratoga*.

But a deeper series of mistakes afflicted the Allies at Midway. When the Pacific war began, Churchill and other British strategists had considered but decided against sending British capital ships to Hawaii to form a concentrated Anglo-American striking force. (Before it was sunk, Churchill had wanted to send Force Z to Pearl Harbor.) The British tried to build a strong force in the Indian Ocean instead, still fearing a major offensive there after the April raid. They especially worried that the Japanese would seize Vichy French–held Madagascar and cut the supply route to the Middle East as well as India. Not trusting the French to stop the Japanese, the British decided to forestall the enemy by capturing Diego Suarez, the main naval base on Madagascar. Scheduled for May, that operation required a whole infantry division and an additional naval force, including the carrier *Illustrious*, from the Atlantic. That force could be supplied only by Force H, normally based at Gibraltar.

To offset the departure of Force H, Churchill had asked Roosevelt to send the carrier *Wasp* to join the British Home Fleet and deliver planes to Malta. Because of the Madagascar operation, the *Wasp* was not in the Pacific, while three British carriers were tied down in the Indian Ocean.

Belatedly, in mid-May, the anti-British Admiral King reluctantly asked the British to lend one of the carriers, not to Pearl Harbor, but to the southwest Pacific. He failed to reveal the real state of his carrier force. (The U.S. Navy did not acknowledge the *Lexington*'s loss until after the battle of Midway.) The British still expected an attack in the Indian Ocean and turned down's King request. (Indeed, in late April, Churchill had even suggested having the carrier *Ranger* and the new battleship USS *North Carolina* join the British Eastern Fleet.) By then it also would have been too late even for the British carriers based at Kilindini to have reached Hawaii, even had King asked for that.

Churchill had been right the first time. The true defense of the Allied position in the Indian Ocean was in the Pacific. Apart from other considerations, the Japanese could not risk a major move west without smashing their main enemy, the American Pacific Fleet. Had they managed to do so, no force that the British could gather in the Indian Ocean could have stopped them, no matter who held Madagascar. The three British carriers sent there, at the cost of diverting the *Wasp*, served no strategic purpose. One or two British carriers, plus the *Wasp* joining the Pacific Fleet, would have significantly strengthened Nimitz's force and given him a night search and torpedo attack capability U.S. carriers lacked.[15] The Americans' victory at Midway was not as close as is generally believed, but given the Allies' overall strength, it should not have been as close as it was.

Nagumo's carrier force, it should be noted, might have been stronger by one carrier had the Japanese made a greater effort to rebuild the *Zuikaku*'s air group as quickly as possible. Thanks to this deficit and their earlier blunders in the Indian Ocean and the Coral Sea, the force that the Japanese expected to fight the decisive sea battle of the war was weaker than the one sent against the unsuspecting ships in Pearl Harbor six months earlier.

Luckily for the Allies, the Japanese navy dissipated much of its strength with a typically overcomplicated plan. Nagumo's First Mobile Force, with the four big carriers, would attack Midway, support the landing of the Midway Occupation Force under Admiral Kondo, and fight the sea battle that the Japanese expected to develop days after Midway was taken. Kondo's force included the light carrier *Zuiho*, carrying planes to be based on the captured island. The main body, under Yamamoto's personal command and with the biggest battleships and the small carrier *Hosho*, stayed hundreds of miles behind Nagumo. Much of the main body—including the only Japanese ships with radar, the battleships *Ise* and *Hyuga*—was detached to support Adm. Boshiro Hosogaya's Northern Area Force in Aleutian waters. His command included the Second Mobile Force, with the light carriers *Junyo* and *Ryujo*, and the invasion force slated to attack the end of the Aleutian chain.

Many in the West long supposed that the Japanese attack on the Aleutians was a diversion to support the Midway operation, to confuse the Americans while Midway was taken, and possibly to crush them in a pincer between the Midway and Aleutian forces. Yet Japanese planning was more irrational than that. The Aleutians operation was an entirely separate affair. Mounting it at the same time as Midway was another expression of the overconfidence, or "victory disease," most Japanese later ruefully admitted afflicted them before Midway.

Nimitz and others later thought that the carriers committed to the Aleutians might well have supplied the decisive margin at Midway. Nimitz remarked that it was inconceivable that his three carriers could "by any combination of luck and skill have defeated" a properly concentrated Japa-

nese fleet of eight carriers and many other ships. Yet, *Junyo* and *Ryujo* were
not very effective carriers. *Junyo* was slow and was unable to keep up with
the larger carriers or to launch torpedo bombers, while *Hosho* and *Zuiho*
carried only a few second-line aircraft. Possibly only *Zuiho* could have operated successfully with Nagumo's force. Still, Yamamoto and the Naval
General Staff had so scattered their forces that at Midway, the Japanese actually had fewer planes than the Americans had. Nagumo's understrength
carrier air groups probably had only 225 combat planes against 233 U.S.
carrier planes and 115 planes based on Midway. Nagumo's force also had
4 reconnaissance planes and 17 seaplanes (the latter did most of the scouting), while the other carriers operating against Midway carried 21 obsolete
fighters, 18 obsolete bombers and the surface ships had 69 seaplanes. The
Aleutian force, meanwhile, had 18 Zeros, 18 torpedo bombers, 15 dive-
bombers, and 28 seaplanes.

The Japanese banked on taking the Americans by surprise and underestimated the forces they would meet. They expected to have plenty of time
to crush the Midway-based air force and take the atoll before the American
fleet, belatedly leaving Pearl Harbor, came out to fight. They also mistakenly thought they would meet probably only two and no more than three
carriers, believing that the Americans had lost two in the Coral Sea. And
thanks to an American deception operation in which a seaplane tender sent
signals on a frequency that carriers usually used, they concluded another
carrier was in the South Pacific. The Japanese expected their submarines to
spot the American carriers en route to Midway, but the submarine deployment plan was poorly thought out. The submarines were slated to take
up their stations too late, were delayed in their departure, and may have
been directed to the wrong places. An attempt to check Pearl Harbor itself
went awry. Repeating an operation carried out in March (a second bombing of Pearl Harbor in which only a high school's windows were shattered),
two flying boats were to fly from the Marshalls, refuel from submarines at
French Frigate Shoals, and overfly Hawaii to see if the carriers were still
there. But the Japanese found American forces at French Frigate Shoals and
cancelled the reconnaissance flight.

Submarine observations of activity around Midway, the sighting of
PBYs flying farther out than before, and their monitoring of American radio
traffic (which they could not understand), which suggested that the Ameri-
can fleet was already at sea—all of these factors should have caused the
Japanese to suspect that the Americans might have known or guessed the
Midway plan. Yamamoto did not take these signs seriously. Meanwhile, it

is not certain whether Nagumo knew of the delay in the submarine scouting effort or the failure of the Pearl Harbor reconnaissance mission.

The Americans planned an ambush. They deployed their carriers in two forces northeast of Midway, beyond enemy search range, and relied on Midway-based planes to find the enemy, who was expected to come from the northwest. When Admiral Halsey fell ill, Rear Adm. Raymond Spruance, a brilliant cruiser commander, took over Halsey's Task Force 16 with the *Enterprise* and *Hornet*. Admiral Fletcher, with Task Force 17 and the *Yorktown* under his direct command, exercised overall command but very loosely. The two task forces observed standard practice for 1942 and stayed well apart so the Japanese could not attack all the American carriers at once.

As the Japanese did, the Americans deployed their submarines poorly. They concentrated them tightly around Midway itself to counter an invasion rather than stationing them farther out, where they would have likelier encountered enemy carriers.

Nimitz told the task force commanders to "inflict maximum damage on the enemy by employing strong attrition tactics" and "be governed by the principle of calculated risk, which you shall interpret to mean the avoidance of exposure of your force to attack by superior enemy forces without good prospect of inflicting, as a result of such exposure, greater damage on the enemy." Evidently Nimitz did not regard Midway as an objective to be defended at all costs. Nor would he have engaged in a sea battle without the intelligence advantage. The Japanese Naval General Staff had been right in thinking the Americans would have let Midway go, had they not had an advantage they did not expect.[16]

### Midway: The Battle

On June 3, a Midway-based PBY spotted Kondo's invasion force, which B-17s bombed ineffectively from high level. That night a PBY torpedoed an oiler.

On the morning of June 4, Fletcher went against Nimitz's orders. Fearing that the Japanese might be ambushing him, he flew off a dawn search to the north as Nagumo launched a 108-plane strike against Midway. Depending on his seaplanes, Nagumo sent out a thin search effort, which was not expected to find anything.

A PBY sighted the Japanese carriers at 5:34 a.m., but its report gave a position forty miles out. At 5:45 a.m., another PBY spotted the Japanese planes heading for Midway. Midway's radar picked up the Japanese at 5:53

a.m. Thus, the Americans had discovered the Japanese nearly two hours before the enemy saw them. Thanks to radar, they would have known the Japanese carriers were near and their probable direction, even had the PBYs missed the enemy. Midway sent its planes against the enemy carriers. Against Nimitz's orders, it held back its fighters to defend the base rather than escort the bombers. That decision was likely a mistake.

At 6:07 a.m., Fletcher ordered Spruance "to attack enemy carriers when definitely located." He would follow as soon as he recovered his search planes. Spruance, knowing the short range of his torpedo bombers, decided to close the range a bit before launching. At 7:00 a.m., he ordered an attack. It seemed wise to strike as soon as possible, and he hoped to catch the enemy landing or refueling the planes that had attacked Midway.

Midway was hit hard, although human losses were light. The Japanese strike leader recommended a second attack. Shortly afterward, Midway-based B-26s and TBFs carrying torpedoes attacked the Japanese carriers. The Americans scored no hits and suffered horrible losses. At 7:15 a.m., Nagumo decided to hit Midway again and soon. Fatally disobeying Yamamoto's standing orders to keep a second strike ready with torpedoes and bombs suitable for attacking ships in case an American force suddenly appeared, Nagumo ordered planes rearmed with bombs suited for attacking land targets.

At 7:28 a.m., a scouting seaplane from the cruiser *Tone* that had been delayed in launching reported sighting American ships, although it did not report actually seeing American carriers until 8:20 a.m. The mere sighting of American ships where they were not expected, but, if present, would probably be accompanied by carriers, was alarming enough. (Contrary to what was long widely believed, the belated launch of *Tone*'s seaplane did not "save" the Americans. Had it been on time, it still would not have seen the Americans until later. The Japanese search was so inadequate that they were lucky to find the Americans as early as they did.) Nagumo *was* landed in a quandary both by failing to make a more intensive search effort before striking Midway at all and by assuming that a Midway-based air force would be the main danger. (However, the Japanese could not have known in advance that the Midway-based planes would be as ineffectual as they were.)

It is not quite certain when Nagumo received the report of the sighting of the American fleet. At 7:45 a.m., logs showed that he ordered suspension of the rearming effort with bombs and that the planes be rearmed with torpedoes—or probably did; Nagumo and others claimed that he did not learn of the Americans' presence until 8:00 a.m. or even later and that the reconstructed message log was in error. Regardless, rearming torpedo planes was time consuming. And continuing attacks by B-17s and later dive-bombers from Midway, although scoring no hits, forced the Japanese fleet into radical maneuvers that prolonged the process.

Nagumo was faced with a choice: launch a small strike—but not immediately, for no planes were ready on deck—or wait for the planes returning from Midway to land, complete rearming, and then launch a big, well-prepared attack. An early strike would perhaps have consisted of thirty-four to thirty-six dive-bombers, possibly escorted by twelve to twenty-four Zeroes, with a few torpedo bombers carrying "land" bombs. (Some sources hold that no fighter escort would have been available at all, although recent research indicates that this assertion is probably wrong.) Such an attack would not have saved his carriers because the American planes were already in the air before Nagumo could have acted. But to send off an early strike meant that many planes returning from Midway would run out of fuel and have to ditch. He concluded that launching a later, properly armed strike was more prudent. That choice was a mistake. Finally, having made his decision at about 8:30 a.m., Nagumo expected to have two carriers ready to strike by 10:30 and the rest no later than 11:00. He also ordered First Mobile Force to change course, but the new course mistakenly was calculated to close the distance between it and the Americans.

The course change, on top of the mistaken position report they had originally received, confused the Americans. Their patrol planes had been unable to keep contact with the Japanese, and the Midway-based planes attacking later did not make position reports as they went in to attack.

Spruance's decision to strike as early as possible was wise, but in many ways the attack was poorly conducted. The *Hornet*'s launch and the leadership of its air group, being the least experienced of the American carriers, were particularly poor. The low speed of the torpedo bombers alone would have made it hard to hold the attacking air groups together. The three carriers' air groups did not join up and flew in separate formations that broke up further en route to the target, leaving many attack planes flying with little or no escort. Finding the Japanese carriers proved difficult. The *Hornet*'s dive-bombers and their fighter escort, the strongest force dispatched, missed the Japanese entirely. After a series of blunders, all ten fighters and several dive-bombers ran out of gas and ditched. Lt. Cdr. John Waldron, the commander of the *Hornet*'s torpedo squadron, found the enemy only because he broke away from the rest of the air group and searched on his own. The *Enterprise*'s launch took so long that at 7:45 a.m., Spruance had the dive-bomber leader, Lt. Cdr. Clarence Wade McClusky, leave immediately instead of waiting for the rest of the air group. In the confusion, the *Enterprise*'s fighters mistook Waldron's unit for their own torpedo squadron and latched on to it, but finally got separated from it in the clouds. Low on gas, the *Enterprise* fighters had to turn back after reaching the Japanese force.

Fletcher's force launched later, at 8:38 a.m., sending off a smaller, better-coordinated strike. Unlike Spruance, he held back a reserve. Holding together better than the air groups of Task Force 16, the *Yorktown* planes flew more directly to their targets. But even they had bad luck, as four dive-bombers lost their bombs because of defective release mechanisms.

The torpedo bombers of all three carriers reached Nagumo's Force ahead of the dive-bombers. They were massacred. Of forty-one torpedo bombers, thirty-five were shot down, and not one scored a hit. Waldron's whole squadron was wiped out, with only one man surviving the battle. (Waldron's planes had been so low on fuel that they probably could not have returned in any case.) But the torpedo bomber attacks and the tiny escort of six Wildcats accompanying the *Yorktown*'s torpedo squadron pulled down and kept down the Japanese combat air patrol, delaying the Japanese preparation of their own attack. John Thach, leading the *Yorktown* fighters, skillfully fought the most important fighter action of the war against a superior force of Zeroes.

The *Yorktown* torpedo bombers' attack overlapped the arrival of the dive-bombers. The Japanese fighters were still low at 10:25 a.m. when the dive-bombers from the *Enterprise* and *Yorktown*, flying without escort, arrived high over the Japanese carriers at the same time. They plunged down. Caught in the middle of rearming planes, the crews of *Kaga*, *Akagi*, and *Soryu* were vulnerable. They had been nowhere near ready to strike and needed at least another half an hour to prepare. Now, torn by explosions and fires, the Japanese carriers were beyond saving. When the American dive-bombers pulled up from their attack a few minutes later, the United States had won the Pacific war.

Nagumo should probably have fled west immediately and surrounded his last carrier, *Hiryu*, with every possible escort ship. But he chose to fight. The *Hiryu*'s small retaliatory strike of dive-bombers damaged the *Yorktown* seriously. Fletcher had to shift to a cruiser and handed overall command to Spruance. A second strike from the *Hiryu*, this time by torpedo bombers, hit the *Yorktown* twice at 2:42 p.m. Badly damaged, it seemed as if it would sink, and the captain ordered it abandoned, prematurely. Meanwhile, dive-bombers flying from the *Enterprise*, including refugees from the *Yorktown*, sank the *Hiryu*.

The shocked Japanese sought a way to salvage something from the catastrophe. As they pondered bringing down the Second Mobile Force carriers from the Aleutians and uniting them with *Zuiho* and *Hosho*, they sent ships to shell Midway and tried to force a night surface battle on Spruance. But Spruance knew that his carriers would be helpless in such a fight and turned east during the night to avoid it. Early on June 5, Yamamoto ordered a general withdrawal but let the Aleutians operation go forward, perhaps hoping it would disguise the extent of the Midway disaster. The Japanese seized Attu and Kiska in the Aleutian chain, but this effort had little effect on the course of the war.

Spruance pursued the Japanese. His planes sank a heavy cruiser. The Japanese tried to tempt him into a night battle and draw him within range of bombers based on Wake Island, but he was too canny for these ploys to work. The *Yorktown* did not sink and was remanned; however, on June 6, a Japanese submarine sank it and an accompanying destroyer.

For the Japanese, that success was little recompense for losing four carriers and irreplaceable experienced aircrews technicians. Although the loss of 121 airmen was less severe than often reported, the Japanese could not afford it. They soon cancelled the New Caledonia-Fiji-Samoa drive and substituted an overland attack for a landing on Port Moresby. They now seized the port to protect the base at Rabaul, and their construction of a base at Guadalcanal went forward for the same purpose. The Japanese now were on the defensive; their remaining forward moves were to shield what they already had, not to cut off Australia or take Hawaii.[17]

It seems apparent that the American victory at Midway was not the miracle that many often supposed. The two sides were rather evenly matched in the actual battle area, and even concentrating every Japanese carrier under Nagumo's command would not have added as much to his strength than usually thought. Because the Japanese underestimated the Americans; supposed that they had the element of surprise and that the battle would develop in precisely the way they expected, and the consequential overwhelmingly focused on the threat of the Midway-based air force rather than on the U.S. carriers, which they believed to be badly outnumbered as well as far away; and neglected reconnaissance, they set themselves up to be sighted first and attacked first on June 4. The American carriers would have hit the Japanese first and hit them hard, even had

Nagumo not made the errors of deciding on an early second strike on Midway, of deferring a strike on the American fleet until the planes that had attacked Midway were safely recovered, and of ordering a change in course. Nor was he about to launch the strong attack that he wanted.

If anything, the surprising development at Midway is how badly the American attacks went. And while many often rightly emphasize that the sacrifice of the torpedo bombers contributed to the victory, it is by no means obvious that the Americans would have lost without it. Flying faster and higher, dive-bombers were far easier to protect than torpedo bombers. Given all the available fighter escort, dive-bombers striking alone might well have reached the Japanese carriers faster and struck successfully, if perhaps not quite as effectively as the unplanned sacrifice of the torpedo bombers.

As the Japanese Naval General Staff had seen, the whole strategy of Midway was wrong. A drive to cut off Australia would have been better calculated to harm the Allies and as likely to bring out the American fleet. Moreover, that drive would have occurred under more favorable circumstances. The Americans would have been farther from their base, and the Japanese fleet might have had the support of land-based planes.

The Japanese would not have won the war even had they destroyed the American fleet in 1942 at Midway or anywhere else. Within a few years, American industry would have rebuilt a navy far superior to Japan's even had had the entire Pacific Fleet been sunk. But the war would have been longer and far more costly. Had the Japanese won at Midway, they probably would have isolated Australia and then have tried to take Hawaii. While a direct attack on Oahu, which was strongly held, may well have failed, the Japanese might could have maintained control of the sea around Hawaii and starved out the defenders.

The war in Europe, too, would have lasted longer. The policy of defeating Germany first might not have survived a Japanese triumph over the Pacific Fleet, and the Pacific theater would have drawn American resources from Europe. Although the European Axis would almost certainly have been defeated, the destructive impact of enemy occupation would have lasted far longer, Europe would have been thoroughly wrecked, and Soviet power would probably have extended farther west than it did. A great deal ultimately depended on the outcome of Midway.[18]

# 11

## Conclusions

One of the most remarkable ideas about World War II is that the Axis powers nearly won it. This idea seems to be far more common in the former Allied countries than in Germany or Japan. It is strange that the heirs of what was, on the face of things, an enormously superior and victorious coalition seem to feel compelled to "scare themselves" by reflecting on how close they came to disaster.[1]

But the chances of a complete Axis triumph in the war that broke out in 1939 were probably nonexistent. It may be impossible to prove a negative—that Nazi Germany and Japan could never have won the war—but that conclusion is strongly indicated.

Portraying World War II as a series of narrow escapes from total disaster makes more interesting reading than showing it as a tedious effort to deal with foes who, however terrible, took on a task that was too big for them. Still, the notion is a curious one. Most of the revelations about Nazi and Japanese leadership and planning since 1945 have been unflattering. In many ways, Germany and Japan clearly ill judged their preparations for war, and not only Hitler's judgment (which actually may have been overly criticized) but also that of the professional heads of the German and Japanese armed forces was extremely erratic. They almost continually underestimated the strength and resolution of the Axis powers' three principal foes. An understandable reason for the popular assumption about the "narrow victory" may be the failure to separate the examination of the war itself, and especially the early German victories, from the disastrous political prelude to the war. To contemporaries, and observers looking back, the

French defeat of 1940 and the other disasters of the early war years were the horrible culmination of seven years of uninterrupted defeats the West had suffered at the hands of the Nazis. They could easily be seen as another phase in the democracies' seemingly endless suicidal bungling since 1918.

The validity of such ideas, however, should not prevent us from recognizing that World War II was a military conflict decided by the military strengths and weaknesses of the two sides. And, despite all the follies of the era between the world wars, Germany and Japan were never strong enough to win it. That Japan could never have defeated the United States, in the long run, is perhaps not very controversial, but many take the idea that Nazi Germany could have won the European phase of the war more seriously. The following discussion will concentrate, therefore, on European issues.

In retrospect, even some of the early German victories look less impressive. As we have seen, the Germans did not have overwhelmingly superior numbers of men or weapons. Even in weapons and technology, the German forces were superior only than their weakest foes: Poland, Norway, and the Balkan countries. Generally speaking, Germany's victories were owed to good leadership, thorough training, and the revolutionary use of tanks and tactical airpower. Against the western European powers, the Germans enjoyed no overall qualitative edge in military equipment and had a small advantage only in the air. Doctrine, organization, and leadership allowed the Germans to defeat the French with a speed and ease they never expected. Only the idiocies of a French military leadership that had "learned nothing and forgotten everything" since 1918 made it possible for the Germans to cut off much of the French Army and the British Expeditionary Force at one blow. Even in Poland and Yugoslavia, their leaders' blunders made an inevitable German victory much easier. Both armies tried to defend practically the whole frontiers of their respective countries instead of pulling back to defensible positions. But once the Germans encountered stronger foes, who had observed the Germans' methods and learned from others' fatal mistakes, things were likely to be different.

Several questions, military and political, must enter into any examination of Germany's chances to win the war after the fall of western Europe. The British had to struggle almost alone for a time, but they never could have defeated a Nazi Germany that controlled almost all of Europe west of the Soviet frontier. Much stronger forces had to be assembled. What were the chances of Britain, fighting? Was its doing so a narrow feat, a remarkable personal achievement of Churchill's? Was American intervention a chancy thing and only due to Roosevelt's clever manipulation or even to Hitler's blunder in openly declaring war in December 1941? If American intervention was inevitable, at least in the long run, could the Germans ever have defeated Britain before the United States came in or before it could bring its strength to bear? Could the Germans have defeated the Soviet Union quickly enough so they could focus solely on the war with the Western powers?

The analysis here is premised on the assumption that the entry of the United States into the war, at least if it could use Britain as a safe and reliable base, would have meant the eventual defeat of Germany. Without the bulk of the German Army being tied down in the east, it is hard to see how the Western powers could have invaded the European mainland. But the fact that an Axis victory in conventional land campaigns depended on Germany's invasion of the USSR, and the Soviets defeated that invasion, does not mean the whole Western war effort depended on the Soviet Union. Indeed, the Allies' conventional strategic bombing deprived Germany of vital fuel and brought about its total economic collapse by March 1945, even before the Allied armies marched deep in the Reich. Events in the east would not have affected the success of this effort much, as the Soviets tied down only a fraction of the Luftwaffe.

Two facts suggest the Western Allies enjoyed enormous superiority in air warfare. By 1943 the Western air forces in the Mediterranean theater alone outnumbered the whole Luftwaffe. And in 1944, even after Germany had fully mobilized for war, the United States alone outproduced it by more than two to one in planes, despite the fact that many of the American aircraft were large, expensive bombers while German production concentrated almost entirely on interceptors. The Germans were at most slightly ahead in jet fighters, but with short-lived and unreliable jet engines, their only advantage was in swept wings. Contrary to popular opinion, the German Me 262 and the British Meteor appeared in combat at about the same time. Many overlooked the latter because the British used it to counter the V-1 missile, and the Germans could not have acquired jets any sooner than they did. In any case, the development of atomic weapons gave the Western powers an advantage that ultimately would have won the war, whatever happened on the battlefields of Russia and the Mediterranean. Germany never had any prospect of building the bomb first. Even had the German atomic bomb project not remained stuck at the point it reached in 1942, Germany did not have the spare industrial capacity to devote to a Manhattan-type project.[2] Victory over the Soviet Union would not have ensured Germany's victory in the war, even though victory in the east would have made the Germans immune on land.

One aspect of the Western Allied war effort was fragile, namely, Ultra, the breaking of German ciphers. Some have depicted it as decisive in winning the war. If this effort was vital, then the Allies' victory in the war was hardly inevitable. Ultra was a valuable achievement but a vulnerable one. The Germans could have nullified the Allied effort had they been less recklessly confident about their communications security and correctly evaluated evidence suggesting that the Allies read their messages. They could have prevented the Allies' success completely had they used the Enigma machine correctly. Only weaknesses in their procedures and their failure to take precautions gave the Allies their chance, and some changes in the Enigma's design would have defeated the Allies despite the Germans' procedural mistakes.[3]

However, whether Ultra was the determining element in any of the decisive defensive battles of the war is doubtful. Deciphering German messages was not important in the Battle of Britain.[4] The role of reading enemy messages in the Battle of the Atlantic was greater but not decisive. The official British intelligence history cautioned that it was but one of many elements, warning that it should not be concluded that "reading the U-boat Enigma from the end of 1942 actually played a definitine part in defeating the second great U-boat campaign against the convoys, which was unleashed in December 1942 and called off in May 1943." Ultra saved many lives and shortened the war but seems to have been more important in the North African and the Mediterranean campaign—a secondary theater—than in either the vital defensive battles or the final campaign in Western Europe.[5]

After France fell, Germany had a military position and sufficient freedom of action to make Britain's defeat inevitable, if not quick or easy. Given the enormously greater resources under German control, if Britain had remained isolated, its position would have been hopeless. It might have been tempted to capitulate. But as we saw in chapter 2, it was not. The disclosure that the issue was ever discussed in the War Cabinet at all later shocked many people, but in fact there was not much discussion. Only Lord Halifax raised the issue seriously, and even he conceded that the likelihood of reaching acceptable terms with Hitler was highly unlikely. The cabinet did talk about the issue at length because the prime minister wished to conciliate the sulking foreign secretary and not because the latter had any support or even a settled belief in an alternative policy. The British military never favored giving in, and Churchill was the last man to do so. Moreover, it is a striking fact that the issue was settled before the success of the Dunkirk evacuation was clear. And while the BEF could have suffered far heavier losses, had the Germans conducted the destruction of the Allied northern pocket differently, it seems that its evacuation could never have been entirely prevented. The possibility of the British caving in never existed. They were determined to fight on. It was the French, in agreeing to an armistice rather than fighting on and establishing a government in exile, who were the odd men out in the Western alliance.

And Britain was never completely isolated. Even before the French armistice, the United States began a major military buildup and a policy of "all-out aid short of war," with President Roosevelt securing firm popular support for both. The fall of France reduced isolationists to an embittered minority. By Pearl Harbor, almost all the isolationist leaders thought they had been beaten. As foolish as the isolationists may have been, however, they were neither pro-Nazi nor friendly to Germany. Moreover, although most people never reconciled themselves to America's simply declaring war on Germany, Roosevelt's short of war policy did lead to America's effective entry into World War II, which took place with the shoot on sight order of September 11, 1941, and not with Pearl Harbor. Contrary to what is still generally said in textbooks, war with Germany began at least partly as a result of an intelligent American response to danger, not as the product of helpless drift and Hitler's suicidal impulses. Clearly Pearl Harbor did not trigger Hitler's final decision to declare war, which had been made already, and which Hitler regarded merely as a recognition of reality, which needed to be handled in such a way as not to impair German prestige and relations with Japan. Britain's valiant stand and America's participation in the war were inevitable. The formation of the Western component of what Churchill called the Grand Alliance was in some sense predetermined.

Given the forces that were ultimately to be arrayed against them, the Nazis' chances of victory thus were reduced to the possibilities of quickly defeating Britain by invasion or strangling the transatlantic supply line before the United States brought its strength to bear. Britain was an indispensable base for American intervention in Europe. Only from Britain could a serious land invasion or a strategic bombing campaign with conventional weapons be launched. Britain's survival in 1940 was probably essential to an Allied victory over Germany. Its survival was also indispensable for the Soviet Union. As we noted in chapter 6, when Hitler invaded the Soviet Union in 1941, he left fifty-four divisions and fifteen hundred planes, or 40 percent of the Luftwaffe's inventory, behind to handle the somewhat over-estimated British threat to occupied Europe. Had these forces been released for the operation against the Soviets, Germany would have defeated them.[6]

Superficially, three possible ways to defeat Britain seemed to exist after the fall of France: invasion, an air-sea blockade of its ocean supply routes (that is, success in the Battle of the Atlantic), and an indirect approach involving the conquest of what the Germans called "the periphery"—the Mediterranean and the Middle East.

Only a successful invasion could have quickly defeated Britain. However, as we saw in chapter 2, this was never possible. Hitler's understanding of his opponents was so limited that he was slow to perceive the need to finish them off, and his military seems to have been just as overconfident after France fell. Given the Luftwaffe's exhaustion and losses and the German Navy's lack of any landing craft, Germany could not follow up its victory in France with a quick improvised invasion. The Luftwaffe, while larger than the Royal Air Force, never had the margin of superiority generally supposed. It was never close to winning air superiority over southern England and would not have done so even had the Germans not mistakenly shifted their attacks from Fighter Command's bases to London at the beginning of September 1940. The many causes of this failure seem to have been "built in" to the Luftwaffe long before the war. Although Hitler was not reluctant or indecisive about the invasion, it would have failed even had the Germans secured domination of the air. During the worst period of the Battle of Britain, from August 24 to September 6, the Germans still made little progress toward knocking out Fighter Command. Indeed, the German commanders even suspected that driving it out of its southern bases would backfire, which is precisely why some favored the switch to London. There, the great fighter battle they sought had the opposite results from what they expected.

The modified barges that served as the inadequate landing craft would have been death traps in an attempted Channel crossing. Lacking an adequate surface fleet and air torpedoes or armor-piercing bombs capable of dealing with the Royal Navy's heavy ships, the Germans could not have prevented the British from sinking the invasion fleet despite air superiority. Even had a disorganized force somehow reached British beaches in September 1940, the British Army might well have driven it into the sea.

Next, an early victory in the Battle of the Atlantic was out of the question. With a small surface fleet left crippled by the Norwegian campaign, a U-boat force that was one-fifth of the size its commander estimated was needed to win, and only a few converted airliners able to reach convoys out on the ocean, a successful air-sea blockade was not possible in 1940. Over the longer term, the issue is more complicated. While the U-boat fleet could have been built up faster, Germany had no prospect of obtaining the three hundred boats Admiral Dönitz thought were needed in 1940 or 1941. The U-boats' freedom of action ebbed almost from the start of the Battle of the Atlantic as British planes ranged farther and farther out to sea, denying them the ability to stay on the surface, and then from the other side of the Atlantic, the American patrol area pushed east and finally encompassed Greenland and Iceland. Growing British strength, establishing the end-to-end escort, and breaking the U-boat cipher helped end the first period of U-boat success; but more important was the British reversing their mistaken reduction of the speed limit for independent merchant ships.

As seen in chapter 3, the defeat of the U-boats' heavy attack on convoy HG 76 in December 1941 convinced Dönitz's staff that "the writing was on the wall." Only the unexpected and unnecessary vulnerability of the Americans and the delay in providing heavier surface escort and air cover in the mid-Atlantic prolonged the struggle until the spring of 1943. A small increase in the number of very long-range planes (from ten to forty), the earlier delivery of escort carriers, and earlier recognition and use of the Blackett-Appleyard law of convoy size would have ensured a quicker victory in the Atlantic. Allied shipbuilding increasingly kept pace with losses even in 1942, and the disastrous losses of early 1943 did not portend Allied defeat, which many on both sides recognized at time. The 1943 crisis did not endanger Britain's survival but rather the Allies' ability to sustain offensives. It was very much the product of the Allies' taking a chance with their supply lines to launch an early offensive and of their misuse of already available aircraft that should have been deployed in the mid-Atlantic air gap.

Meanwhile, the fragile achievement of Ultra contributed to, but was not vital to, the turn in fortunes in the Atlantic. The two sides' rival cryptographic efforts arguably largely neutralized each other. For the Allies, knowing the German deployments was not the critical factor; instead, it hinged on the arrival of more planes and microwave radar that provided tactical location of the U-boats and close-in defense against them. In general, the Allies went from one tactical and technological innovation to another, some of which the Germans never even recognized, while the U-boats remained largely unchanged. As in the case of the Luftwaffe, the defeat of the German Navy seems to have been largely predetermined by the limitations of German's economy and prewar mistakes in planning that the military service itself made.

As we shall see later, the indirect approach of attacking the Allied position in the Mediterranean and Middle East, or inducing the Soviets to help, would not have led to the defeat of the Western powers. But an all-out commitment of German forces to such a policy ran athwart relations with Italy and Hitler's basic commitment to destroying the USSR.

It is widely believed that invading Russia was Hitler's fatal mistake. On the other hand, it is often asserted (although justification is rarely offered for this claim) that had the Germans beaten the Soviets, Germany would have won World War II as a whole—although neither the British nor the American leaders in 1941–1942, concerned as they were to ensure the Soviets' survival, thought that it would. But the Russian campaign was not an avoidable mistake. Nor was it ever likely that the Germans could have won it.

Our examination of Hitler's decision to attack the Soviet Union suggested that it was not contingent on particular events but the result of his basic outlook and of Germany's apparent freedom of action after its conquest of the western European mainland. Given Hitler's obsession with "Jewish Bolshevism," lebensraum, and the belief that the expected easy conquest of the Soviet Union would provide Germany with the raw materials it needed and improve Germany's strategic situation, it was not likely that he would forgo an attack once it seemed possible. To him, even after Britain's determination to fight on became clear, he was not embarking on the long-feared two-front war because there was no real land front against Britain at the time, and the Soviets would be conquered long before the Western powers could create one. (If anything, for Hitler, the threat that the United States would be in the war by 1942 was another argument for, not against, an early attack on the USSR.) Destroying the Soviets before a Western threat developed was actually Hitler's way out of the two-front dilemma. Eliminating that front—and not embracing the dubious idea of incorporating the untrustworthy and hated Bolsheviks in a Eurasian bloc— was the true and proper solution to Germany's problems for Hitler.

Nor did he encounter serious opposition to his decision. Indeed, it stemmed from ideas shared with most other Nazi leaders, and even the professional military, although generally more cautious than Hitler was, did not really regard the Soviets as serious opponents. They, too, shared the basic evaluation that if Germany could triumph so completely over its respected traditional rivals, the despised Soviets could be beaten with relative ease.

However, it seems that a Nazi defeat of the Soviet Union, while not inherently impossible, was never likely.[7] And the quick victory that the Germans banked on was never possible. Few criticisms of German planning would command such universal agreement as the judgment that victory in a single year's campaign was out of the question.[8] The Germans' assumption that it was possible to win without seriously fighting in the winter led straight to disaster in the winter of 1941–1942.

As we have seen, German planning was flawed from the start because they basically underestimated the Soviets' industrial and military strength, both in numbers and quality of weapons, and the Soviets' ability to improvise and recover from even staggering defeats. The Germans had no real conception of the extent of Soviet industrial development in the east, which let the Soviets carry on the war long after what the Germans imagined were their vital sources of supply had been captured. The erroneous assumption about the Soviets' need to retain those sources in the western USSR led to further wrong guesses about the strategic decisions the Soviets would make and to counting on the success of a particular scheme of maneuver early in the campaign. German battlefield failures were deeply embedded in poor preinvasion planning and intelligence. The planning phase neither resolved certain disputes between Hitler and the General Staff nor provided a guide on what to do should the enemy escape the "decisive" encirclement west of the Dnieper and Dvina Rivers. But many German weaknesses were built in and could not have been readily corrected even with better information and planning in 1940. German tank and vehicle production was quantitatively and qualitatively inadequate. Neither German-built trucks and wagons nor those obtained in occupied countries were suited to the poor roads in the Soviet Union. Nor could German industry have built the needed tracked carriers in time. The Germans also did not have the transport planes to make up the difference. They were not prepared to use or convert Soviet railroads, and their locomotives were not equal to the Russian winter.

Hitler's direction of the eastern campaign has drawn criticism, but much of it is unjustified. The primary accusations are that, at his instigation, the initial German encirclement drive in the center was too shallow and that by steering the German effort to the flanks of the front, he emphasized the conquest of Leningrad and Ukraine instead of driving on to Moscow, a strategically far more important objective that would have brought the main Soviet armies into a decisive battle. Further, having diverted forces to the north, Hitler then cut short the campaign there when, with a little more persistence, Leningrad would have been taken. Many also blamed him for the decision, too late in the year, to concentrate finally on taking Moscow after Leningrad was besieged and Ukraine overrun.

The last criticism simply blames Hitler for a mistake shared with the General Staff; indeed, most commanders, while not as recklessly as General Halder, overestimated what could be achieved in the final attack on Moscow. The criticisms of Hitler's earlier decisions, however, are also questionable. In most of these cases, if not all, a good argument can be made for his orders, and even a successful alternative would probably have not achieved more than marginally better results. Had the Germans tried a deeper encirclement at the start of the campaign, they would have found it even harder to close off the bigger pocket or pockets created. The infantry, marching on foot, needed to stop the Soviet troops from breaking out and would have been left even farther behind. Hitler's enforced caution about the first encirclement actually led to drawing more Soviet forces into the second big pocket at Smolensk and a bigger German success than would otherwise have eventuated. Further, the Fourth Panzer Group did not have enough infantry to capture Leningrad quickly in 1941.

While general strategic considerations would have justified Halder's and others' desire to concentrate on a drive straight to Moscow, it is not clear that this course was actually practical in the circumstances. Moreover, even had the Soviet capital fallen, Soviet resistance would not have collapsed. Much of the Soviet government was being evacuated to Kuibyshev (Samara); and while Moscow was an important rail hub, it was not the sole connection between the north and southwest of the Urals, as many have supposed. Nor could the Germans have occupied all of European Russia before winter. Had they taken Moscow in this way, they would have been left holding a vast salient with Soviet forces holding to the north and south. As it was, logistical considerations made it possible to attack Ukraine and win a great victory there well before attacking Moscow would have been possible. The delay in attacking Moscow (of only two to three weeks) and the Kiev victory not only eliminated an enormous force that would have threatened Army Group Center's southern flank if left alone, but allowed the drive on Moscow to be carried out with an additional panzer group that would have been unavailable earlier. An early drive on Moscow, which the Soviets expected (as they did not expect the turn south) would probably have bagged fewer Soviet forces than those destroyed at Kiev and Vyazma.[9]

Furthermore, given the Soviets' strength, none of the German victories in 1941 should have been possible. Stalin's refusal to recognize the danger until the last minute, despite ample warnings, and his dictation of a deployment that played into the Germans' hands made the great German triumphs possible. Had Soviet forces been alert and deployed rationally, the German attack would have misfired from the start, and the danger of a German victory over the Soviet Union would never have existed.

It seems likely that despite what was widely feared in 1942, the danger was past by the time of the 1942 campaign. Hitler, again, has been widely criticized for the strategy. Later many often suggested that the Germans should have renewed an offensive on the central front, forced a decisive battle on the Red Army, and captured Moscow instead of trying to seize the Caucasus. The basic defects of the Caucasus strategy have already been recounted. An examination of the actual situation in 1942, however, suggests that no other strategy was possible; in fact, though many disliked it, no one suggested a real alternative. The Germans simply did not have the strength to take Moscow (and even if they had, doing so would no more have ended the war in 1942 than it would have in 1941). Their objective had to be the Caucasus or nothing.

Again, only Soviet blunders gave the Germans some initial success in 1942. Given Hitler's erratic decision making in the summer of 1942, it is perhaps not possible to say with certainty whether the Caucasus could have been taken. But it seems highly probable that even had the Germans concentrated all their efforts on pushing south in the summer of 1942, gambling on leaving the formation of a defensive front to the east for later (and this is the opposite of what they are usually criticized for doing), they would still not have reached Baku. Given the physical obstacles and near impossibility of supplying even the inadequate forces allotted to Army Group A, it is not clear that the Germans could ever have supported an all-out drive over the mountains. Moreover, the Germans had had ample warning, even before the attack on the USSR, that they could not have used the captured oil fields themselves. Even if they had taken the fields intact—the only fields captured at Maikop were thoroughly wrecked—the transportation problem would have prevented a significant amount of oil from reaching Germany. To solve that problem, the Germans would have had to open a sea route through the Turkish Straits and the Mediterranean; however, British submarines and planes there were rapidly wiping out the Axis merchant fleet, which was already fully employed trying to supply forces in North Africa.

Even had the Germans defeated the Red Army and caused the collapse of the Soviet regime in 1941–1942, they could not have exploited Russia successfully in the near future. Their treatment of the conquered peoples, which was inseparable from the Nazis' basic ideology, inspired dogged resistance. Controlling and utilizing the conquered territories would have taken years. The most vital resource of all, oil, was not in prospect. The notion of a Eurasian bloc using the resources of a conquered Soviet Union to fend off an Anglo-American assault was a mirage, even disregarding the effects of Western nuclear weapons. Had the Western powers left the Nazis free to conquer the Soviet Union, the Nazis could have eventually wielded a conquered Eurasia into a deadly threat to the Western democracies. But while the Nazis were at war on both the eastern and western fronts, they never would have had the time and freedom needed to do this.

Finally, the Germans have often been criticized, with reason, for failing to see the importance of the Mediterranean and Middle East and acting there in time. Many have argued that had Hitler launched a serious offensive there instead of attacking the Soviets, he could have struck a deadly blow at the British.[10] Some have argued that the Axis could have defeated the British in the Mediterranean theater in 1941–1942, even while they were engaged in Russia, had readily available resources been used to support Rommel.[11]

Had the Germans reinforced their success in the spring of 1941, they undoubtedly could have overrun the Mediterranean and the Middle East; but given Hitler's basic ideas, it was not possible that he would choose to pursue this strategy instead of attacking the Soviets. In fact, Hitler and other German leaders were not as oblivious to the prospects in the south as has often been said. Mussolini, not Hitler, sabotaged the chance for an early joint Axis effort there. Only then did Hitler run up against the deadline imposed by the plan to attack the USSR in 1941. Mussolini's folly, Hitler's too tolerant treatment of the "senior" fascist leader, and the difficult political problems presented by the competing claims of Vichy France, Italy, and Spain prevented Hitler from acting promptly and decisively in 1940, as he should have, no later than the cancellation of the invasion of England. The prompt seizure of Malta and sending modest armored forces to North Africa would have enabled the Axis to take Egypt, made the costly invasion and occupation of the Balkans unnecessary, and, if successful enough, might even have secured valuable oil supplies for Germany without interfering seriously with the German invasion of the USSR.

As it was, in 1942, even with the limited forces and support given to Rommel, the Axis almost achieved victory in the Mediterranean. They nearly starved Malta into submission, and the success of the Allied convoys in June and August was a near thing. Rommel perhaps came close to victory in the desert at the start of July 1942, though possibly not as close as is often thought, for his force was weakened by earlier fighting, had outrun its air support, and had a long and tenuous land supply line. Even the last-throw effort in August might have ended differently had Malta, in turn, not starved him of supplies.

With more support in 1942, Rommel almost certainly could have overrun Egypt and perhaps the Iraqi oil fields as well. Hitler could have provided additional forces for him without any diversion from Russia, for twenty-nine divisions were idle in western Europe, which was not in danger of attack. As Rommel later noted bitterly, after the battles at El Alamein and the invasion of North Africa, his masters found it possible to throw forces into the futile and disastrous defense of Tunisia. These troops would have been invaluable for his offensive if they had been available earlier. It should also be noted that the British forces attacking his supply lines across the Mediterranean depended on Ultra to an unusually high degree for their effectiveness, perhaps more so than any other major striking force in the war. British survival and success in the Mediterranean arguably depended on the fragile achievement of the decryption effort.

However, there is little reason to think that losing the Mediterranean and the Middle East would have meant the defeat of the Western powers. The Cape of Good Hope route, not the Mediterranean, was the true lifeline of the British Empire. The closing of the Mediterranean from 1940 to 1943 (it had also been closed during part of World War I) was only an inconvenience to the Allies. The Middle East was an underdeveloped region that did not contain a major ally or indispensable resources at that time. Nor did it lead obviously to any place else. As Field Marshal Erich von Manstein pointed out, for logistic reasons it would not have been a good base for an attack either on the Soviet Union or India.[12] There was no prospect of a serious juncture between the European Axis and the Japanese in the area. Even the faction of Japanese planners favorable to a western drive envisaged at most taking Ceylon, not a major invasion of India or a move into the Middle East. In any case, given the threat that the Americans posed, Japan never had much of a chance of launching a major Indian Ocean campaign. Nor could the Italian fleet, which could not stand up to the British even in the middle sea, have operated successfully in the Indian Ocean. It lacked the aircraft carriers and supply ships needed for oceanic operations.[13]

Oil was the only commodity in the Middle East of great value to the Allies. But Britain's supplies during World War II came from the Americas. The oil of the Middle East was vital, not to the Allied war effort in general, but as the only nearby and convenient source of supply for British forces in the Mediterranean and Indian Ocean.[14] Losing the oil would have paralyzed any Allied threat to Germany from the southeast or to Japan from the southwest, but the decisive blows against Germany and Japan were not launched from those directions. The Americans were so unruffled by the prospect of losing the Middle East that on several occasions in 1941 they urged the British to abandon the area lest they sink too much of their military power there. Roosevelt, although not going that far, suggested once to Churchill that losing the Middle East could be withstood as long as the Allies kept command of the Atlantic.[15] Losing the Mediterranean and the Middle East would have been a most serious blow but a far from fatal one.

In short, the only victories the Axis might reasonably have hoped to win would not have affected the outcome of the war. In most respects, Germany and Japan were not strong enough to affect, or within range of, the vital spots of the major Allied powers. The Axis failed to prepare for war intelligently enough, and the Nazis capped this oversight by not mobilizing properly once the war began. Japan, furthermore, did not have the industrial strength to prevail against the United States. When the Nazis embarked on a war with enemies who were either geographically immune to the quick victories that the Nazi armored forces and tactical airpower produced in 1939–1940 or had the space and resources to survive the initial blows, the results were inevitably disastrous for the Germans and for the allies that depended on them to win.

# Notes

## 1. The Catastrophe

1. Stanley Payne, *A History of Fascism, 1914–1945* (Madison: University of Wisconsin Press, 1995), 173; Eberhard Jäckel, *Hitler in History* (Hanover, NH: Brandeis University Press, 1984), 67; Ernst Nolte, *Three Faces of Fascism: Action Française, Italian Fascism, National Socialism*, trans. Leila Vennewitz (New York: Holt, Rinehart and Winston, 1966), esp. 288–93, 302–3, 333, 402–7, 416–18; Norman Rich, *Hitler's War Aims*, Vol. 1 (New York: Norton, 1973), 3–10; Gerhard Weinberg, *The Foreign Policy of Hitler's Germany: Diplomatic Revolution in Europe, 1933–36* (Chicago: University of Chicago Press, 1970), 3, 7, 13–15, 20–23; H. R. Trevor-Roper and Gerhard L. Weinberg, *Hitler's Table Talk, 1941–1944: His Private Conversations*, trans. Norman Cameron and R. H. Stevens (New York: Enigma, 2000), esp. 53, 513; Eberhard Jäckel, *Hitler's Weltanschauung: A Blueprint for Power*, trans. Herbert Arnold (Middletown, CT: Wesleyan University Press, 1974); and Alan Levine, "Some Myths of the Struggle Against Fascism," *The World and I*, August 1987, 651–66. Hitler's peculiar personality and ideas have been best described, perhaps, not by orthodox biographers but by Nolte and Jäckel. Also worth consulting are Percy Schramm, *Hitler: The Man and the Military Leader*, trans. and ed. Donald S. Detwiler (Chicago: Quadrangle Books, 1971); and John Strawson, *Hitler as Military Commander* (London: Pen and Sword, 2003).

2. William Rock, *British Appeasement in the 1930s* (New York: Norton, 1977); Martin Gilbert, *The Roots of Appeasement* (New York: New American Library, 1966); Keith Middlemas, *The Strategy of Appeasement: The British Government and Germany, 1937–39* (Chicago: Quadrangle, 1972); Wolfgang J. Mommsen and Lothar Koettenoher, eds., *The Fascist Challenge and the Policy of Appeasement* (London: George Allen & Unwin, 1983); Levine, "Some Myths of the Struggle," 661–66; and Correlli Barnett, *The Collapse of British Power* (New York: William Morrow, 1972), 123–47, 166–232.

3. Rich, *Hitler's War Aims*, Vol. I, 81–131; Weinberg, *Foreign Policy of Hitler's Germany*, esp. 7–15, 75–76, 211, 216; Gerhard Weinberg, *The Foreign Policy of Hitler's Germany: Starting World War II, 1937–1939* (Chicago: University of Chicago

Press, 1980), esp. 14, 29, 36–38, 456, 462, 503–4, 513–14, 533–34, 549, 580, 612, 628–29, 675; and F. C. Jones, *Japan's New Order in East Asia, 1937–45* (Oxford, UK: Oxford University Press, 1954), 102–8.

4. R. J. Overy, *Why the Allies Won* (New York: Norton, 1995), 198–207; R. J. Overy, *War and Economy in the Third Reich* (Oxford, UK: Clarendon Press, 1994), 9–10, 18–23, 25–28, 196–99, 230–39, 241, 250, 252–56, 259–64, 276, 291; Berenice Carroll, *Design for Total War: Arms and Economics in the Third Reich* (The Hague: Mouton, 1968); and Sebastian Cox, introduction, *The Strategic Air War Against Germany, 1939–1945: Report of the British Bombing Survey Unit* (London: Frank Cass, 1998), xxvi–xxxiii. Overy's work is the most important corrective to some of the serious errors about the German war economy that marred almost all writing about World War II before the 1990s (including the present writer's *The Strategic Bombing of Germany, 1940–1945* [New York: Praeger, 1992]). Cf. also, Adam Tooze, *The Wages of Destruction: The Making and Breaking of the Nazi Economy* (New York: Viking, 2007), which argues that because Hitler knew that long-range rearmament plans were not going well and that Germany's chances were not good in a prolonged arms race, he accepted the risk of early war with the Western powers (294–95, 304, 311–21).

5. Geoffrey Megargee, *Inside Hitler's High Command* (Lawrence: University of Kansas Press, 2000), esp. ix–x, 27, 108, 123; Albert Seaton, *The German Army, 1933–45* (London: Sphere Books, 1983), esp. xxii, 55–61, 72, 75–76, 128, 140–41, 144; F. W. von Mellenthin, *Panzer Battles* (New York: Ballantine, 1971), xv; Milton Shulman, *Defeat in the West*, rev. ed. (New York: Ballantine, 1968), 22–24, 35–29, 41, 53; S. L. A. Marshall, introduction, *The Fatal Decisions*, ed. Seymour Freiden and William Richardson (New York: Berkley Books, 1958), xi–xii; Hanson Baldwin, *Battles Lost and Won: Great Campaigns of World War II* (New York: Harper & Row, 1966), 29, 394n80; and Karl-Heinz Frieser, *The Blitzkrieg Legend: The 1940 Campaign in the West*, with John T. Greenwood (Annapolis, MD: Naval Institute Press, 2005), 4–17.

6. Cajus Bekker (Hans Dieter Berenbrok), *The Luftwaffe War Diaries*, trans. Frank Ziegler (Garden City, NY: Doubleday, 1968), 137–40; Richard Hough and Denis Richards, *The Battle of Britain: The Greatest Air Battle of World War II* (New York: Norton, 1990), 43, 86–90; Stephen Bungay, *The Most Dangerous Enemy* (London: Aurum Press, 2000), 38, 40–41, 47–49, 52; Derek Wood and Derek Dempster, *The Narrow Margin: The Battle of Britain and the Rise of Air Power, 1930–1940*, rev. ed. (New York: Paperback Library, 1969), 42–43, 46–48; Klaus Maier et al., *Germany in the Second World War*, vol. 2, *Germany's Initial Conquests in Europe* (Oxford, UK: Clarendon Press, 1991), 33–62; Williamson Murray, *Strategy for Defeat: The Luftwaffe, 1933–1945* (Maxwell Air Force Base, AL: Air University Press, 1983), 1–30; Edward L. Homze, *Arming the Luftwaffe: The Reich Air Ministry and the German Aircraft Industry, 1919–1939* (Lincoln: University of Nebraska Press, 1976), 125–26, 209–11, 264–66; James Corum, *The Luftwaffe: Creating the Operational Air War, 1918–1940* (Lawrence: University of Kansas Press, 1997), 5–6, 125, 134–37, 141–44, 171–73, 179, 230–31, 267–69, 282–83; and E. R. Hooton, *Phoenix Triumphant: The Rise and Rise of the Luftwaffe* (London: Cassell, 1994), 98–99, 103–4, 107–9, 143, 150–57, 171.

7. David Woodward, *The Tirpitz and the Battle of the Atlantic* (New York: Berkley, 1965), 30–40; Corum, *The Luftwaffe*, 109–11, 176–78, 282; Weinberg, *Foreign Policy of Hitler's Germany* (1970), 176–77, 211, 216; Weinberg, *Foreign Policy of*

*Hitler's Germany* (1980), 28–29, 371, 514; Edward von der Porten, *The Germany Navy in World War II* (New York: Ballantine, 1974), 2–33; and Maier et al., *Germany and the Second World War*, 2:60–64, 176.

8. M. M. Postan, *British War Production* (London: Her Majesty's Stationery Office, 1952), 4–7, 87, 187; Barnett, *Collapse of British Power*, 8–12, 132–34, 168–84, 202, 211, 217, 224, 232, 474–76, 479, 482–83; S. W. Roskill, *The War at Sea, 1939–1945*, vol. 1, *The Defensive* (London: Her Majesty's Stationery Office, 1954), 29, 35–36, 53–58; Gregory Blaxland, *Destination Dunkirk: The Story of Gort's Army* (London: William Kimber, 1973), 6–12, 35, 53–59; Robert Jackson, *Before the Storm* (London: Cassell, 2000), 46–59; Levine, *Strategic Bombing of Germany*, 6–11; and Arthur Marder, *Old Friends, New Enemies: The Royal Navy and the Imperial Japanese Navy*, 2 vols. (Oxford, UK: Clarendon Press, 1981), 1:316.

9. Maier et al., *Germany and the Second World War*, 2:5, 9, 125; Mellenthin, *Panzer Battles*, 4–10; Alistair Horne, *To Lose a Battle: France 1940* (New York: Penguin, 1979), 132; Freiden and Richardson, eds., *Fatal Decisions*, 15–16; and Gerhard Weinberg, *A World at Arms: A Global History of World War II* (New York: Cambridge University Press, 1994), 48–52.

10. Adam Claasen, *Hitler's Northern War: The Luftwaffe's Ill-fated Campaign, 1940–1945* (Lawrence: University of Kansas Press, 2001), 12, 36–138; Maier et al., *Germany and the Second World War*, 2:191–219; Williamson Murray and Alan Millett, *A War to Be Won: Fighting the Second World War* (Cambridge, MA: Belknap Press, 2000), 65–68; J. L. Moulton, *The Norwegian Campaign of 1940: A Study of Warfare in Three Dimensions* (London: Eyre & Spottiswoode, 1966); and François Kersaudy, *Norway 1940* (New York: St. Martin's Press, 1991).

11. Most notably, Ernest R. May, *Strange Victory: Hitler's Conquest of France* (New York: Hill and Wang, 2000); and Frieser, *Blitzkrieg Legend*. Cf., John Ellis's comment in *Brute Force: Allied Strategy and Tactics in the Second World War* (New York: Viking, 1990), 4, that the Western European campaign was an "anomaly."

12. Frieser's *The Blitzkrieg Legend*, although invaluable, unduly plays down the Germans' qualitative advantages and probably greatly overestimates French air strength. Weinberg, *World at Arms*, 124–27; Horne, *To Lose a Battle*, esp. 113, 115–16, 161–64, 173–78, 181, 217, 233–582; William Shirer, *The Collapse of the Third Republic: An Inquiry into the Fall of France in 1940* (New York: Pocket Books, 1971), 592, 610–732; Hooton, *Phoenix Triumphant*, 203–82; Murray, *Strategy for Defeat*, 36–39; Maier et al., *Germany and the Second World War*, 2:229–78; L. F. Ellis, *The War in France and Flanders, 1939–1940* (Nashville: Battery Press, 1996), 22–23, 29–30, 39–40; Blaxland, *Destination Dunkirk*, 41–43, 71–89, 91, 107–9, 132; Brian Bond, *France and Belgium, 1939–1940* (Newark: University of Delaware Press, 1979), 79, 93–132; F. H. Hinsley et al., *British Intelligence in the Second World War*, vol. 1, *Its Influence on Strategy and Operations* (New York: Cambridge University Press, 1979), 163–164; and Mellenthin, *Panzer Battles*, 14–22.

## 2. THE BRITISH CARRY ON

1. Blaxland, *Destination Dunkirk*, 91–209; Robert Jackson, *Dunkirk: The British Evacuation, 1940* (New York: St. Martin's Press, 1976), 7–24; Bond, *France and Belgium*, 109–33; Ellis, *War in France and Flanders*, 5–52, 63–148; Roskill, *The War at Sea*, 1:201, 208–211, 216; Horne, *To Lose a Battle*, 555–84; and Shirer, *Collapse of the Third Republic*, 720ff.

2. Frieser, *Blitzkrieg Legend*, 291–314; Blaxland, *Destination Dunkirk*, 209–15; Horne, *To Lose a Battle*, 598–602; Maier et al., *Germany and the Second World War*, 2:290–94; Franz Halder, *The Halder Diaries: The Private War Journals of Colonel*

*General Franz Halder*, 2 vols. (Boulder, CO: Westview Press, 1975), 424; Bond, *France and Belgium*, 160–66; Murray, *Strategy for Defeat*, 38; Walter Lord, *The Miracle of Dunkirk* (New York: Viking Press, 1982), 293; and Hans-Adolf Jacobsen, "Dunkirk 1940," in *Decisive Battles of World War II: The German View*, ed. Hans-Adolf Jacobsen and Jürgen Rohwer (New York: Putnam, 1965), 53–66. For the arguments that the halt order was a "golden bridge," for the British see William Shirer, *The Rise and Fall of the Third Reich* (New York: Fawcett Crest, 1961), 963–68; Shulman, *Defeat in the West*, 71–72, 81; and Walter Ansel, *Hitler Confronts England* (Durham, NC: Duke University Press, 1960), 72–88.

3. Bond, *France and Belgium*, 135–56, 160, 177ff.; Horne, *To Lose a Battle*, 604–19; Shirer, *The Rise and Fall of the Third Reich*, 737–57; Blaxland, *Destination Dunkirk*, 227–347; Jackson, *Dunkirk*, 48–173; Ellis, *War in France and Flanders*, 159–237; Murray, *Strategy for Defeat*, 38; Bekker, *Luftwaffe War Diaries*, 126–29; Basil Collier, *The Defense of the United Kingdom* (London: Her Majesty's Stationery Office, 1957), 112–16, 124–27; Wood and Dempster, *The Narrow Margin*, 178–82; and Hough and Richards, *Battle of Britain*, 93–95.

4. J. R. M. Butler, *Grand Strategy*, vol. 2, *September 1939–June 1941* (London: Her Majesty's Stationery Office, 1957), 209–17; J. M. A. Gwyer and J. R. M. Butler, *Grand Strategy*, vol. 3, *June 1941–August 1942* (London: Her Majesty's Stationery Office, 1964), 21, 37–38; David Reynolds, *The Creation of the Anglo-American Alliance, 1939–1941: A Study in Competitive Co-operation* (Chapel Hill: University of North Carolina Press, 1982), 106–7, 109–12, 116–17, 148–49; Wood and Dempster, *The Narrow Margin*, 174–76; Philip Goodhart, *Fifty Ships That Saved the World: The Foundation of the Anglo-American Alliance* (Garden City, NY: Doubleday, 1965), 53–66; William L. Langer and S. Everett Gleason, *The Challenge to Isolation, 1937–1940* (New York: Harper, 1952), 487–88, 506, 566; and Winston Churchill, *Their Finest Hour* (New York: Bantam, 1962), 77–78, 122–23. Reynolds (*Creation of the Anglo-American Alliance*, 109–10) suggests that Roosevelt was not always confident that Britain would fight on or survive if it did so. This observation seems to be contradicted by the evidence that he himself cites and the fact that the president's instructions to American military planners were premised on Britain's continuing to fight successfully. Cf. Maurice Matloff and Edwin Snell, *Strategic Planning for Coalition Warfare, 1941–1942* (Washington, DC: Chief of Military History, 1953), 13–15. The chief study of Roosevelt's foreign policy, Robert Dallek's *Franklin D. Roosevelt and American Foreign Policy, 1932–1945* (New York: Oxford University Press, 1979), seems to find no evidence that FDR seriously doubted Britain's intention to persevere.

5. Churchill, *Their Finest Hour*, 78, 153; John Lukacs, *Five Days in London, May 1940* (New Haven, CT: Yale University Press, 1999), 106–24, 126–86; P. M. H. Bell, *A Certain Eventuality: Britain and the Fall of France* (Farnborough, UK: Saxon House, 1974), 38–43, 123–25; Bungay, *Most Dangerous Enemy*, 9–17; Reynolds, *Creation of the Anglo-American Alliance*, 107; Maier et al., *Germany and the Second World War*, 2:363; Gerhard Schreiber et al., *Germany and the Second World War*, vol. 3, *The Mediterranean, South-East Europe, and North Africa, 1939–1941* (Oxford, UK: Clarendon Press, 1995), 131–33, 137, 139, 197–98, 757; and Erich von Manstein, *Lost Victories*, ed. and trans. Anthony G. Powell (Novato, CA: Presidio Press, 1982), 155–56. Lukacs's *Five Days in London*, Reynolds's *Creation of the Anglo-American Alliance*, and Ian Kershaw's recent book, *Fateful Choices: Ten Decisions that Changed the World, 1940–1941* (New York: Penguin, 2007), 118, are excellent examples of the strained effort to show that it was a "near thing" that Britain continued to fight.

6. Butler, *Grand Strategy*, 2:307–8, 311–12; Churchill, *Their Finest Hour*, 358, 377–80; Roger Parkinson, *Blood, Toil, Tears, and Sweat: The War History from Dunkirk to Alamein, Based on the War Cabinet Papers of 1940 to 1942* (London: Hart-Davis MacGibbon, 1973), 90, 118; I. S. O. Playfair, *The Mediterranean and the Middle East*, vol. 1, *The Early Success Against Italy (to May 1941)* (London: Her Majesty's Stationery Office, 1954), 130–43; and Roskill, *War at Sea*, 1:296, 271.

7. Horne, *To Lose a Battle*, 635, 642–43; Shirer, *Collapse of the Third Republic*, 788, 790, 796, 803, 815, 826–30, 839–43, 864–65, 870–80, 885–89, 908; Paul Kecskemeti, *Strategic Surrender: The Politics of Victory and Defeat* (New York: Atheneum, 1964), 35–70; Guy Chapman, *Why France Fell: The Defeat of the French Army in 1940* (New York: Holt, Rinehart and Winston, 1968), 292; Churchill, *Their Finest Hour*, 157, 166–67, 172–73; and Maier et al., *Germany and the Second World War*, 2:18, 313.

8. Shirer, *Collapse of the Third Republic*, 919–27; Churchill, *Their Finest Hour*, 192–206; Roskill, *War at Sea*, 1:240–45; Playfair, *The Mediterranean and the Middle East*, 1:130–43; Parkinson, *Blood, Toil, Tears, and Sweat*, 54–55; and Maier et al., *Germany and the Second World War*, 2:19.

9. Halder, *Halder Diaries*, 1:622.

10. Rich, *Hitler's War Aims*, Vol. 1: 154, 157–60; Telford Taylor, *The Breaking Wave: The German Defeat in the Summer of 1940* (New York: Simon & Schuster, 1967), 19, 44–46, 52–59; Maier et al., *Germany and the Second World War*, 2:366–75; Schreiber et al., *Germany and the Second World War*, 3:185, 198–201; Horst Boog et al., *Germany and the Second World War*, vol. 4, *The Attack on the Soviet Union* (Oxford, UK: Clarendon Press, 1999), 14; Basil Collier, *The Battle of Britain* (New York: Berkley, 1969), 21; Bungay, *Most Dangerous Enemy*, 33, 109; Wood and Dempster, *The Narrow Margin*, 202; Halder, *Halder Diaries*, 2:487, 503–6, 515; Hough and Richards, *Battle of Britain*, 108; Ansel, *Hitler Confronts England*, 103–24; and Megargee, *Inside Hitler's High Command*, 87–92. Manstein's *Lost Victories*, 157–71, is interesting if captious and based too much on hindsight.

11. Barry Leach, *German Strategy Against Russia, 1939–1941* (Oxford, UK: Clarendon Press, 1973), 9, 47–51, 65, 69; Collier, *Battle of Britain*, 21–22; and Rich, *Hitler's War Aims*, 1:159–61. Cf. John Lukacs, *The Last European War: September 1939/December 1941* (Garden City, NY: Doubleday, 1976), 161, who ridiculously states that in July 1940 Hitler decided to finish off Russia before invading Britain.

12. Maier et al., *Germany and the Second World War*, 2:370, 375–77; Schreiber et al., *Germany and the Second World War*, 3:203–5; Halder, *Halder Diaries*, 1:530–34; Ansel, *Hitler Confronts England*, 178–83, 205, 208–11, 215–16, 238, 256, 262, 308ff.; Collier, *Defense of the United Kingdom*, 178–82; Taylor, *The Breaking Wave*, 199–273; Shirer, *Rise and Fall of the Third Reich*, 1000–9, 1026–1030; Murray, *Strategy for Defeat*, 44–45; and Shulman, *Defeat in the West*, 73, 78–80.

13. Churchill, *Their Finest Hour*, 220, 226, 241, 255, 257, 258, 301, 491; and Butler, *Grand Strategy*, 2:341–43.

14. Roskill, *War at Sea*, 1:247–51; Collier, *Defense of the United Kingdom*, 124–44, 219; and Roger Parkinson, *Summer 1940: The Battle of Britain* (New York: David McKay, 1977), 3–5, 19–20, 38–39, 41–42, 71.

15. Bungay, *Most Dangerous Enemy*, 99–107; Hough and Richards, *Battle of Britain*, 86–90, 98–102; Wood and Dempster, *The Narrow Margin*, 174–77; Parkinson, *Blood, Toil, Tears, and Sweat*, 12, 18; Collier, *Defense of the United Kingdom*, 108–11; and Ellis, *War in France and Flanders*, 307–9, 325.

16. Bungay, *Most Dangerous Enemy*, 107, 137, 370; Parkinson, *Summer 1940*, 89; Wood and Dempster, *The Narrow Margin*, 217, 252; and Hough and Richards, *The Battle of Britain*, 111.

17. Wood and Dempster, *The Narrow Margin*, 46–48; Bekker, *Luftwaffe War Diaries*, 133–37, 152; Corum, *The Luftwaffe*, 230–31, 271–72, 280, 282–86; Claasen, *Hitler's Northern War*, 170–73; Maier et al., *Germany and the Second World War*, 2:38; Murray, *Strategy for Defeat*, 12–13, 47; Werner Kreipe, "The Battle of Britain," in Freiden and Richardson, *Fatal Decisions*, 32; and Bungay, *Most Dangerous Enemy*, 32, 38, 40–41, 47–49, 52, 57, 374.

18. Bungay, *Most Dangerous Enemy*, 46–53, 71–84, 343, 374; Edward Sims, *The Greatest Aces* (New York: Ballantine, 1968), 36–37; Edward Sims, *The Aces Talk* (New York: Ballantine, 1974), 102–7; Mike Spick, *Luftwaffe Fighter Aces: The Jagdflieger and Their Combat Tactics and Techniques* (New York: Ivy/Ballantine, 1997), 46, 49–52; Hough and Richards, *Battle of Britain*, 198; and Wood and Dempster, *The Narrow Margin*, 48, 194, 360–61, 402–3. Bungay argues, most unconvincingly, that the Me 109's limited range was not of much importance in the Battle of Britain. This point runs counter to the views of all surviving German participants.

19. Bungay, *Most Dangerous Enemy*, 247, 260–61, 362; Spick, *Luftwaffe Fighter Aces*, 46–47; Mike Spick, *Allied Fighter Aces of World War II* (London: Greenhill, 1992), 69–70, 82; Francis K. Mason, *Battle over Britain* (Garden City, NY: Doubleday, 1969), 149; J. E. Johnson, *The Story of Air Fighting* (New York: Bantam, 1986), 159; Wood and Dempster, *The Narrow Margin*, 403; Hough and Richards, *Battle of Britain*, 311–14; and John Lundstrom, *The First Team: Pacific Naval Air Combat from Pearl Harbor to Midway* (Annapolis, MD: Naval Institute Press, 1984), 458–67, 477–81. Some sources maintain that the RAF adopted the "finger four" much later, crediting it to Douglas Bader in 1941.

20. Collier, *Defense of the United Kingdom*, 73, 168; Collier, *Battle of Britain*, 34–62; Spick, *Luftwaffe Fighter Aces*, 45; Bungay, *Most Dangerous Enemy*, 59–68, 288–89; and Wood and Dempster, *The Narrow Margin*, 105, 115–67, 279, 321.

21. Wood and Dempster, *The Narrow Margin*, 199–200; Bungay, *Most Dangerous Enemy*, 287; Hough and Richards, *Battle of Britain*, 113; Collier, *Defense of the United Kingdom*, 169–70, 219; and Johnson, *Story of Air Fighting*, 167.

22. Mason, *Battle over Britain*, 237; Corum, *The Luftwaffe*, 283; Hinsley et al., *British Intelligence*, 1:163–64, 176–81; Wood and Dempster, *The Narrow Margin*, 95–99, 112–13; Bungay, *Most Dangerous Enemy*, 127, 187–88; and Hough and Richards, *Battle of Britain*, 92, 325–27.

23. Bungay, *Most Dangerous Enemy*, 95–96; Parkinson, *Summer 1940*, 89–90; Hough and Richards, *Battle of Britain*, 102–3; and Wood and Dempster, *The Narrow Margin*, 88–89, 188–91.

24. Hough and Richards, *Battle of Britain*, 199–201, 221; Collier, *Defense of the United Kingdom*, 171; Wood and Dempster, *The Narrow Margin*, 19, 196–97, 252; Bungay, *Most Dangerous Enemy*, 137; and Parkinson, *Summer 1940*, 94.

25. Maier et al., *Germany and the Second World War*, 2:375, 378–81, 385; Bungay, *Most Dangerous Enemy*, 122–27, 203–6; Hough and Richards, *Battle of Britain*, 136–37, 140; Collier, *Battle of Britain*, 15, 49, 58–61; Wood and Dempster, *The Narrow Margin*, 211–16; and Taylor, *The Breaking Wave*, 108, 121–35.

26. Spick, *Luftwaffe Fighter Aces*, 57–58; Collier, *Battle of Britain*, 49–56; Bungay, *Most Dangerous Enemy*, 146–84, 199; Hough and Richards, *Battle of Britain*, 129–36; Parkinson, *Summer 1940*, 70, 96; and Roskill, *War at Sea*, 1:322–25.

27. Parkinson, *Summer 1940*, 105–48; Collier, *Battle of Britain*, 70–76; Wood and Dempster, *The Narrow Margin*, 259–74; Hough and Richards, *Battle of Britain*, 142–216; Bungay, *Most Dangerous Enemy*, 204–24; Collier, *Defense of the United Kingdom*, 184–99; Claasen, *Hitler's Northern War*, 163–69; and Bekker, *Luftwaffe War Diaries*, 157–63.

28. Bungay, *Most Dangerous Enemy*, 232–33, 237, 304; Hough and Richards, *Battle of Britain*, 216, 229; Wood and Dempster, *The Narrow Margin*, 279, 286–87; Collier, *Defense of the United Kingdom*, 203–4; Collier, *Battle of Britain*, 16, 78; and Parkinson, *Summer 1940*, 145, 153.

29. Johnson, *Story of Air Fighting*, 150–63; Parkinson, *Summer 1940*, 151–57, 217–20; Collier, *Defense of the United Kingdom*, 214–16; Collier, *Battle of Britain*, 87, 96–103; Bungay, *Most Dangerous Enemy*, 268–305; Wood and Dempster, *The Narrow Margin*, 286–318, 399–402; Hough and Richards, *Battle of Britain*, 219–41, 313–19; and Alan Deere, *Nine Lives* (New York: Beagle, 1970), 151–58.

30. Wood and Dempster, *The Narrow Margin*, 291, 309, 313, 322–31; Collier, *Defense of the United Kingdom*, 233–36; Hough and Richards, *Battle of Britain*, 241–45; Bungay, *Most Dangerous Enemy*, 304–6; and Collier, *Battle of Britain*, 104–5.

31. Shirer, *Rise and Fall of the Third Reich*, 1009–19; Collier, *Defense of the United Kingdom*, 224–25; Hough and Richards, *Battle of Britain*, 293–95; Parkinson, *Summer 1940*, 182, 184–85, 199–205, 208, 216; Maier et al., *Germany and the Second World War*, 2:370, 390–91; Halder, *Halder Diaries*, 583–84; Wood and Dempster, *The Narrow Margin*, 336, 343; Collier, *Battle of Britain*, 91, 117, 131; and Bungay, *Most Dangerous Enemy*, 317–36.

32. Wood and Dempster, *The Narrow Margin*, 313–41; Bungay, *Most Dangerous Enemy*, 308–35; Collier, *Battle of Britain*, 104–30; Spick, *Luftwaffe Fighter Aces*, 69; Collier, *Defense of the United Kingdom*, 236–42; Hough and Richards, *Battle of Britain*, 244, 258; and Donald Caldwell, *JG 26* (New York: Ballantine, 1993), 58–60.

33. Collier, *Battle of Britain*, 104–30; Wood and Dempster, *The Narrow Margin*, 342–60; Bungay, *Most Dangerous Enemy*, 323–44; Hough and Richards, *Battle of Britain*, 284–303; Collier, *Defense of the United Kingdom*, 245–49; Parkinson, *Summer 1940*, 178–79; and Maier et al., *Germany and the Second World War*, 2:370, 391.

34. Gwyer and Butler, *Grand Strategy*, 3:29; John Ray, *The Night Blitz* (London: Arms and Armour, 1996), 251–65; Postan, *British War Production*, 164–65; Constantine FitzGibbon, *Winter of the Bombs: The Story of the Blitz* (New York: Norton, 1957); and Norman Longmate, *Air Raid* (New York: David McKay, 1978), esp. 15, 26–27, 183–84.

35. Bungay, *Most Dangerous Enemy*, 372–373; Caldwell, *JG 26*, 68–69; and Murray, *Strategy for Defeat*, 80, 88.

36. Taylor, *The Breaking Wave*, 150–51; Parkinson, *Summer 1940*, 139, 151–52, 161, 167, 178, 216–20; Bungay, *Most Dangerous Enemy*, 291–92, 301, 368–69; and British Air Ministry, *The Rise and Fall of the German Air Force, 1933–1945* (New York: St. Martin's Press, 1983; originally published 1948 by British Air Ministry), 82.

37. Bungay, *Most Dangerous Enemy*, 297–98, 370; Collier, *The Battle of Britain*; B. H. Liddell Hart, *History of the Second World War*, 104; and Wood and Dempster, *The Narrow Margin*, 455–75.

38. Bungay, *Most Dangerous Enemy*, 291, 301, 368–69; and Parkinson, *Summer 1940*, 220. Cf. R. J. Overy, *The Air War: 1939–1945* (New York: Stein and Day, 1981), 42. "Even at the most dangerous moments the German air force was little closer to achieving the aim of air supremacy for long enough to permit a successful invasion than they had been at the beginning of the battle."

39. Johnson, *Story of Air Fighting*, 166–69; and Bungay, *Most Dangerous Enemy*, 289, 344, 374–75. Bungay, however, clearly overstates the case that the limitations of the Luftwaffe's equipment were not significant, arguing, for example, that the short range of the Me 109 was not important and that having a heavy four-engine bomber would not have helped the Germans. These arguments run

counter to the views of virtually all on the German side. It should be noted that the RAF, while far better led than the Luftwaffe, also made mistakes. Notably it failed to adopt appropriate fighter formations and tactics quickly, and it lacked coordination, to put it mildly, between 11 and 12 Groups and the wasteful Duxford Wing effort. Some felt that the otherwise useless Blenheim fighters and even the Defiants could have been used as intruders to disrupt German bomber operations over the European mainland.

40. Corum, *The Luftwaffe*, 280; Taylor, *The Breaking Wave*, 179–80, 188–89; Bekker, *Luftwaffe War Diaries*, 136, 182; Kreipe, "The Battle of Britain," 32–36; and Overy, *The Air War*, 41–42.

41. Wood and Dempster, *The Narrow Margin*, 183; Arthur Hezlet, *Aircraft and Sea Power* (New York: Stein and Day, 1970), 152, 154–56; and Chester Wilmot, *The Struggle for Europe* (London: Fontana, 1974), 30.

42. Alfred Price, *Blitz on Britain: The Bomber Attacks on the United Kingdom, 1939–1945* (London: Ian Allan, 1977), 86; *Rise and Fall of the German Air Force*, 49, 109; Kreipe, "The Battle of Britain," 26; Taylor, *The Breaking Wave*, 88; Roskill, *War at Sea*, Vol. 1: 326; Bungay, *Most Dangerous Enemy*, 115; Murray, *Strategy for Defeat*, 45; Maier et al., *Germany and the Second World War*, 2:370; and Ansel, *Hitler Confronts England*, 308–16.

43. Baldwin, *Battles Lost and Won*, 53; Taylor, *The Breaking Wave*, 287–90; Ansel, *Hitler Confronts England*, 316; Manstein, *Lost Victories*, 164–71; and Albert Kesselring, *Kesselring: A Soldier's Record*, trans. Lynton Hudson (New York: William Morrow, 1954), 71–80. Kenneth Macksey's *Invasion: The German Invasion of England, July 1940* (New York: MacMillan, 1980) is a fictional version of this idea.

44. Cajus Bekker, *Hitler's Naval War*, ed. and trans. Frank Ziegler (Garden City, NY: Doubleday, 1974), 168; Donald Macintyre, *The Naval War Against Hitler* (New York: Scribner, 1971), 54; Hough and Richards, *Battle of Britain*, 108; and Murray, *Strategy for Defeat*, 46.

## 3. The Battle of the Atlantic I

1. S. W. Roskill, *The War at Sea, 1939–1945*, vol. 2 *The Period of Balance* (London: Her Majesty's Stationery Office, 1956), 571; Churchill, *Their Finest Hour*, 508; and Winston Churchill, *The Hinge of Fate* (New York: Bantam, 1962), 109. Cf., however, the views of the semioffical U.S. Navy historian Samuel Eliot Morison in his *History of United States Naval Operations in World War II*, 15 vols. (Boston: Little, Brown, 1947–1962), 10:64: "Even in their palmiest days of 1942, the Axis submarines never came within measurable distance of victory."

2. Arthur Hezlet, *The Submarine and Sea Power* (New York: Stein and Day, 1967), 189.

3. Patrick Beesly, *Very Special Intelligence, The Story of the Admiralty's Operational Intelligence Centre, 1939–1945.* rev. ed. (New York: Ballantine, 1981); and F. H. Hinsley et al., *British Intelligence in the Second World War*, vol. 2, *Its Influence on Strategy and Operations* (Cambridge, UK: Cambridge University Press, 1981), 168–79, 225.

4. Marc Milner, *The Battle of the Atlantic* (St. Catherines, Ontario: Tempus/Vanwell, 2003), 107; Clay Blair, *Hitler's U-boat War* (New York: Random House, 1997), 37, 172; David Syrett, *The Defeat of the German U-boats* (Columbia: University of South Carolina Press, 1999), 3, 261, 264–66; and Maier et al., *Germany and the Second World War*, 2:384.

5. British Ministry of Defence (MOD), *The U-boat War in the Atlantic* (3 vols. in one) (London: Her Majesty's Stationery Office, 1989), 12; Morison, *History of*

*United States Naval Operations*, 10:11; Horst Boog et al., *Germany and the Second World War*, vol. 6, *The Global War* (Oxford, UK: Clarendon Press, 2001), 321–25; Timothy Runyan and Jan M. Copes, eds., *To Die Gallantly: The Battle of the Atlantic* (Boulder, CO: Westview Press, 1994), xxi; and Montgomery C. Meigs, *Slide Rules and Submarines: American Scientists and Subsurface Warfare in World War II* (Washington, DC: National Defense University Press, 1990), 75.

6. Peter Cremer, *U-boat Commander* (New York: Jove, 1986), 17–18; Tooze, *Wages of Destruction*, 397–400; Blair, *Hitler's U-boat War*, 40, 44, 46–47, 100, 276, 423; Syrett, *Defeat of the German U-boats*, 3; Maier et al., *Germany and the Second World War*, 2:62–64, 176; Bekker, *Hitler's Naval War*, 193, 333; Milner, *Battle of the Atlantic*, 33–38; and MOD, *U-boat War in the Atlantic*, 1:12.

7. Claasen, *Hitler's Northern War*; Maier et al., *Germany and the Second World War*, 2:347; and MOD, *U-boat War in the Atlantic*, 1:62–64.

8. Roskill, *War at Sea*, 1:18–19, 34–35, 355; Syrett, *Defeat of the German U–boats*, 7–9; Blair, *Hitler's U-boat War*, 70–79; Beesly, *Very Special Intelligence*, 25–26, 36; Milner, *Battle of the Atlantic*, 13–14, 31, 35; Martin Middlebrook, *Convoy* (New York: Morrow, 1977), 32; and Ian Buxton, "British Warship Building and Repair," in *The Battle of the Atlantic*, ed. Stephen Howarth and Derek Law (Annapolis, MD: Naval Institute Press, 1994), 80–99.

9. Roskill, *War at Sea*, 1:98–102, 106, 136–38; Beesly, *Very Special Intelligence*, 25–36; Bekker, *Hitler's Naval War*, 17–138; Milner, *Battle of the Atlantic*, 13–30, 37–38; MOD, *U-boat War in the Atlantic*, 1:3–26, 40; Blair, *Hitler's U-boat War*, 102, 131, 158–60; and Hezlet, *Submarine and Sea Power*, 124–28, 164–66.

10. Sonke Neitzel, "Deployment of the U–boats," in Howarth and Law, *Battle of the Atlantic*, 277–78; Milner, *Battle of the Atlantic*, 42–48; Roskill, *War at Sea*, 1:343–44; Maier et al., *Germany and the Second World War*, 2:343; Bekker, *Hitler's Naval War*, 186–91; and MOD, *U-boat War in the Atlantic*, 1:50–54.

11. MOD, *U-boat War in the Atlantic*, 1:62; Maier et al., *Germany and the Second World War*, 2:345; Blair, *Hitler's U-boat War*, 205, 222–23; and Macintyre, *Naval War Against Hitler*, 83–95.

12. Blair, *Hitler's U-boat War*, 205–6; MOD, *U-boat War in the Atlantic*, 1:62–64, 67–68; Roskill, *War at Sea*, 1:330–31; Maier et al., *Germany and the Second World War*, 2:302–27, 347; and Milner, *Battle of the Atlantic*, 49–50.

13. Milner, *Battle of the Atlantic*, 51–65; MOD, *U-boat War in the Atlantic*, 1:68–73; Neitzel, "Deployment of the U–boats," 278; Blair, *Hitler's U-boat War*, 247, 254, 262; Runyan and Copes, *To Die Gallantly*, 49; Roskill, *War at Sea*, 1:356, 451–53, 457–58; and Winston S. Churchill, *The Grand Alliance* (New York: Bantam, 1962), 92–106, 123.

14. Beesly, *Very Special Intelligence*, 46–53, 75–76; Macintyre, *Naval War Against Hitler*, 83–98; Maier et al., *Germany and the Second World War*, 2:347–53; Roskill, *War at Sea*, 1:331, 487–90; and James Tent, *E-boat Alert: Defending the Normandy Invasion Fleet* (Annapolis, MD: Naval Institute Press, 1996), 24, 33–50, 52.

15. Gordon Welchman, *The Hut Six Story: Breaking the Enigma Codes* (New York: McGraw Hill, 1982), 3, 11–12, 31–32, 77–82, 88–89, 96–102, 119, 125, 130–32, 163–99; Rebecca Ratcliff, *Delusions of Intelligence: Enigma, Ultra and the End of Secure Ciphers* (Cambridge, MA: Cambridge University Press, 2006), 14–20, 27–29, 36, 72, 127–36, 144–46, 181–85, 190–92, 195, 197, 214–16, 221–23; Hinsley et al., *British Intelligence*, 1:336–40; Hinsley et al., *British Intelligence*, 2:168–79, 220; Beesly, *Very Special Intelligence*, esp. 62–72, 99–100; Ronald Lewin, *Ultra Goes to War* (New York: Pocket, 1980), esp. 1–89, 113–40; Peter Calvocoressi, *Top Secret Ultra* (New York: Ballantine, 1980), 32; Milner, *Battle of the Atlantic*, 63–64;

and David Kahn, *Seizing the Enigma: The Race to Break the German U-boat Codes, 1939–1943* (New York: Barnes & Noble, 1998), esp. 32, 40, 60–62, 65, 72, 77, 91, 112–13, 129–30, 150–83.

16. Kahn, *Seizing the Enigma*, 183; Hinsley et al., *British Intelligence*, 1:168–70; Roskill, *War at Sea*, 1:457–58; Milner, *Battle of the Atlantic*, 57, 66–71; Boog et al., *Germany and the Second World War*, 6:368; MOD, *U-boat War in the Atlantic*, 1:75–78; Neitzel, "Deployment of the U–boats," 288–89; Beesly, *Very Special Intelligence*, esp. 99–100; and Blair, *Hitler's U-boat War*, 205, 309–10, 318.

17. MOD, *U-boat War in the Atlantic*, 1:77; Boog et al., *Germany and the Second World War*, 6:347–49; Kahn, *Seizing the Enigma*, 198, 205–6; Milner, *Battle of the Atlantic*, 79; and Blair, *Hitler's U-boat War*, 386–87.

18. Blair, *Hitler's U-boat War*, 318–19; Paul Sutcliffe, "Operational Research in the Battle of the Atlantic," in Howarth and Law, *Battle of the Atlantic*, 418–29; and Alfred Price, *Aircraft versus Submarine: The Evolution of the Anti-submarine Aircraft, 1912 to 1980* (New York: Jane's Publishing, 1980), 67–68, 78.

19. Blair, *Hitler's U-boat War*, 380; Neitzel, "Deployment of the U–boats," 278–85; Roskill, *War at Sea*, 1:467–70; Milner, *Battle of the Atlantic*, 57, 66–79; and MOD, *U-boat War in the Atlantic*, 1:79–82, 86–87.

20. Jan G. Heitman, "The Front Line: Convoy HG 76—the Offence," in Howarth and Law, *Battle of the Atlantic*, 490–507; A. B. Sainsbury, "The Front Line: Convoy HG 76—the Defence," in ibid., 508–15; Milner, *Battle of the Atlantic*, 78, 85–86; Blair, *Hitler's U-boat War*, 410–17; Boog et al., *Germany and the Second World War*, 6:362–366; MOD, *The U-boat War in the Atlantic*, 1:85, 90–91; and Macintyre, *Naval War Against Hitler*, 123–37.

21. Milner, *Battle of the Atlantic*, 35, 57; Bekker, *Hitler's Naval War*, 337; Blair, *Hitler's U-boat War*, 426; and Neitzel, "Deployment of the U–boats," 288–91. But cf., however, Sainsbury, "The Front Line," 513.

22. Boog et al., *Germany and the Second World War*, 6:349–50, 360, 361, 365; Kahn, *Seizing the Enigma*, 202–10; Syrett, *Defeat of the German U–boats*, 7; Blair, *Hitler's U-boat War*, 359, 386–87; Beesly, *Very Special Intelligence*, 115; and Hinsley et al., *British Intelligence*, 1:177–79.

## 4. THE RUSSIAN CAMPAIGN I

1. Gunther Blumentritt, "Moscow," in Freiden and Richardson, *Fatal Decisions*, 48; and Lukacs, *Last European War*, 3, 248–49.

2. Rich, *Hitler's War Aims*, 1:157, 204–11; Norman Rich, *Hitler's War Aims*, vol. 2 (New York: Norton, 1974), 409; Shulman, *Defeat in the West*, 97; Megargee, *Inside Hitler's High Command*, x, 89–92, 102; Seaton, *The German Army*, 148–51; Albert Seaton, *The Russo-German War: 1941–1945* (New York: Praeger, 1970), 36; Leach, *German Strategy Against Russia*, 9–13, 41–72, 86, 107; James McSherry, *Stalin, Hitler and Europe* (Cleveland: World, 1970), 2:140–41, 182; Halder, *Halder Diaries*, 506, 517, 520–23, 533–35; Horst Boog et al., *Germany and the Second World War*, 4:1–4, 14–17, 22, 26, 48, 244, 254–55; Schreiber et al., *Germany and the Second World War*, 3:133, 190, 204; Walter Warlimont, *Inside Hitler's Headquarters, 1939–1945* (New York: Praeger, 1964), 113–14; Trumbull Higgins, *Hitler and Russia: The Third Reich in a Two-Front War* (New York: Macmillan, 1966), 57–64, 73; Robert G. Waite, *The Psychopathic God: Adolf Hitler* (New York: Da Capo Press, 1993), 400; and Richard Stewart, *Sunrise at Abadan: The British and Soviet Invasion of Iran, 1941* (New York: Praeger, 1988), 30, 32–33, 46–47, 49.

3. Boog et al., *Germany and the Second World War*, 4:6, 48, 52–53, 137–52, 172–77, 220, 238–39, 244, 252–66, 270, 278–85, 324–25, 335, 337, 352–53; Leach, *Ger-*

*man Strategy Against Russia,* 77, 86, 89–114, 125, 136, 139, 146–47, 159, 178–81, 193, 205–6, 218–19, 230; Seaton, *Russo-German War,* 38–62; Seaton, *The German Army,* 163–69; Murray, *Strategy for Defeat,* 77–80; Megargee, *Inside Hitler's High Command,* 103, 108–11, 114, 130–31; Joel Hayward, *Stopped at Stalingrad: The Luftwaffe and Hitler's Defeat in the East, 1942–1943* (Lawrence: University Press of Kansas, 1998), 20, 62–71; and George Blau, *The German Campaign in Russia: Planning and Operations, 1940–1942* (Washington, DC: Center of Military History, 1988), 6–19, 22–26, 30, 42.

4. Megargee, *Inside Hitler's High Command,* x, 102–8; and Leach, *German Strategy Against Russia,* 136.

5. Boog et al., *Germany and the Second World War,* 4:220, 1108–24, 1132, 1135–36; Megargee, *Inside Hitler's High Command,* 123–24, 133; Leach, *German Strategy Against Russia,* 120–21, 136–45, 205–6; Seaton, *Russo-German War,* 170–75, 191, 218; Seaton, *The German Army,* 166–67; and Martin Van Creveld, *Supplying War: Logistics from Wallenstein to Patton* (New York: Cambridge University Press, 1977), 145–61, 173.

6. Manstein, *Lost Victories,* 206; Leach, *German Strategy Against Russia,* 176–91; Boog et al., *Germany and the Second World War,* 4:391–423; and Jäckel, *Hitler in History,* 71–72.

7. Leach, *German Strategy Against Russia,* 168; Boog et al., *Germany and the Second World War,* 4:220, 305, 318, 401–8, 495–99; Seaton, *Russo-German War,* 59–63; Earl F. Ziemke, *Moscow to Stalingrad: Decision in the East* (Washington, DC: U.S. Army Center of Military History, 1987), 7; David Glantz and Jonathan House, *When Titans Clashed: How the Red Army Stopped Hitler* (Lawrence: University Press of Kansas, 1995), 36–37; and Murray, *Strategy for Defeat,* 80. There are some variations in descriptions of the numbers of divisions that the Germans assigned to Russia, the number of tanks available, and the strength of the Luftwaffe. Some sources, such as Cajus Bekker's *Luftwaffe War Diaries* (219) and Gen. Paul Deichmann (in Seaton, *Russo-German War,* 63), give considerably lower figures for the Luftwaffe's effective strength at the start of the Russian campaign. The German official history Boog et al., *Germany and the Second World War,* 4: 331, denies that the Luftwaffe was permanently weakened by the battle against Britain, but cf. Murray (*Strategy for Defeat,* 80), who notes that the Luftwaffe had two hundred fewer bombers than it had the year before.

8. Schreiber et al., *Germany and the Second World War,* 3:525; Seaton, *Russo-German War,* 38; Walter Ansel, *Hitler and the Middle Sea* (Durham, NC: Duke University Press, 1972), 124; Blumentritt, "Moscow," 51; Weinberg, *World at Arms,* 204; Murray, *Strategy for Defeat,* 76; and Baldwin, *Battles Lost and Won,* 110–13. It should be noted that in the postwar era the issue of whether and how seriously the Balkan campaign delayed or otherwise interfered with the Russian campaign was a highly charged one for the British especially, who were entangled with emotional questions about the wisdom of their expedition to Greece in 1941 and whether it would have been better to complete the conquest of Libya instead.

9. Waldo Heinrichs, *Threshold of War: Franklin D. Roosevelt and American Entry into World War II* (New York: Oxford University Press, 1988), 21, 61–62, 224n7; Hinsley et al., *British Intelligence,* 1:430–31, 436–37; David E. Murphy, *What Stalin Knew: The Enigma of Barbarossa* (New Haven, CT: Yale University Press, 2005), esp. xvii, 39, 44–45, 87–88, 140–41, 174–75; David Glantz, *Stumbling Colossus: The Red Army on the Eve of World War* (Lawrence: University Press of Kansas,

1998), 96, 233, 245–51; and John Erickson, *The Road to Stalingrad* (New York: Harper & Row, 1975), 107.

10. Erickson, *Road to Stalingrad*, 14–108; Glantz, *Stumbling Colossus*, 7–10, 25–33, 41, 80–93, 96, 100, 102–6, 109, 111–12, 169–74, 184–85, 251; Seaton, *Russo-German War*, 17–21, 84–87; Harrison Salisbury, *The 900 Days: The Siege of Leningrad* (New York: Harper & Row, 1969), 17, 31, 59–62, 69; Glantz and House, *When Titans Clashed*, 7–9, 25–27, 37–39, 41, 42–43, 53; Andrei Kokoshin, *Soviet Strategic Thought, 1917–1991* (Cambridge, MA: MIT Press, 1998), 7–82, 105–8, 163–65; Ziemke, *Moscow to Stalingrad*, 8–12, 21–23; Robert Conquest, *The Great Terror: Stalin's Purge of the Thirties* (New York: Collier, 1973), 299–302, 645–54; and Murphy, *What Stalin Knew*, 29–30, 33–39, 44–45, 99, 134–37, 160, 176, 211–13, 223–24.

11. Boog et al., *Germany and the Second World War*, 4:526–47, 632–38, 763–71, 1112–26; Blau, *German Campaign in Russia*, 44–64; Glantz and House, *When Titans Clashed*, 43–58, 61; Seaton, *Russo-German War*, 93–142, 171–72; Leach, *German Strategy Against Russia*, 193, 197, 200–220; Megargee, *Inside Hitler's High Command*, 133–35; Blumentritt, "Moscow," 62–65; Van Creveld, *Supplying War*, 155–57, 168; Fedor von Bock, *The War Diary, 1939–1945*, ed. Klaus Gerbet and trans. David Johnston (Atglen, PA: Schiffer 1996), 281; and Halder, *Halder Diaries*, 2:991–1000, 1041–45, 1164–70.

12. Seaton, *Russo-German War*, 141–43, 151–52, 215–17; Boog et al., *Germany and the Second World War*, 4:533–37, 541–44, 548, 569–98, 602–3, 632–38, 762; Van Creveld, *Supplying War*, 176, 180; Seaton, *The German Army*, 178; Blau, *German Campaign in Russia*, 45–46, 48, 50–57, 59–70; Glantz and House, *When Titans Clashed*, 76–77; David Glantz, *Colossus Reborn: The Red Army at War, 1941–1943* (Lawrence: University Press of Kansas, 2005), 16; Leach, *German Strategy Against Russia*, 114, 223–24; Weinberg, *World at Arms*, 269; and Halder, *Halder Diaries*, 2:1040.

13. Glantz, *Stumbling Colossus*, 17; Glantz and House, *When Titans Clashed*, 65–67, 71–74; Ziemke, *Moscow to Stalingrad*, 7, 31, 45, 135, 300; and Erickson, *Road to Stalingrad*, 232–39.

14. Glantz and House, *When Titans Clashed*, 79–82; Ziemke, *Moscow to Stalingrad*, 37–44; Seaton, *Russo-German War*, 176–90; Blumentritt, "Moscow," 68–69; Blau, *German Campaign in Russia*, 75–85; Erickson, *Road to Stalingrad*, 212–22; and Boog et al., *Germany and the Second World War*, 4:670–73.

15. Shulman, *Defeat in the West*, 102; Blumentritt, "Moscow," 72–83; Blau, *German Campaign in Russia*, 83–100; Glantz and House, *When Titans Clashed*, 82–100; Ziemke, *Moscow to Stalingrad*, 49–242; Seaton, *Russo-German War*, 190–254; Murray, *Strategy for Defeat*, 107, 113–20; Erickson, *Road to Stalingrad*, 273–307; Glantz, *Colossus Reborn*, 23–24; Boog et al., *Germany and the Second World War*, 4:693–781, 1138–40; and Bock, *The War Diary*, 354–55, 357, 366, 375–77, 384.

## 5. The Mediterranean and the Middle East I

1. Playfair, *The Mediterranean and the Middle East*, 1:20, 41–49, 59, 74–76, 92–98, 190–95, 213, 244–45, 250; Butler, *Grand Strategy*, 2:310–11, 342; Roskill, *War at Sea*, 1:49, 271, 296–97; Donald Macintyre, *The Battle for the Mediterranean* (New York: Norton, 1965), 29–30; W. G. F. Jackson, *The Battle for North Africa, 1940–43* (New York: Mason and Charter, 1975), 21–23, 31–32; Correlli Barnett, *The Desert Generals* (New York: Ballantine, 1971), 7–9; Churchill, *Their Finest Hour*, 358, 361, 363, 366, 377–81; Harold E. Raugh, Jr., *Wavell in the Middle East, 1939–1941: A Study in Generalship* (London: Brassey's, 1993); and Ronald Lewin, *The Chief:*

*Field Marshal Lord Wavell, Commander-in-Chief and Viceroy, 1939–1947* (New York: Farrar, Straus and Giroux, 1980).

2. I. S. O. Playfair, *The Mediterranean and the Middle East*, vol. 2 (London: Her Majesty's Stationery Office, 1956), 2: 248; I. S. O. Playfair, *The Mediterranean and the Middle East*, vol. 3 (London: Her Majesty's Stationery Office, 1960), 363–68; Stewart, *Sunrise at Abadan*, 16–19, 26, 31–33; Dwight David Eisenhower, *The Papers of Dwight D. Eisenhower: The War Years*, ed. Alfred D. Chandler (Baltimore: Johns Hopkins University Press, 1970), 238–39; and Butler, *Grand Strategy*, 2:654–55.

3. Schrieber et al., *Germany and the Second World War*, 3:112–22, 152, 170, 174–75, 185–87, 198, 203, 206–10, 247, 252, 261, 273; Norman J. W. Goda, *Tomorrow the World: Hitler, Northwest Africa, and the Path toward America* (College Station, TX: Texas A & M University Press, 1998), 12, 52–53, 62; Ansel, *Hitler and the Middle Sea*, 9–13, 17; Jackson, *Battle for North Africa*, 21, 42; Playfair, *The Mediterranean and the Middle East*, 1:163–167, 257, 266; and Michael Glover, *An Improvised War: The Ethiopian Campaign, 1940–1941* (New York: Hippocrene, 1987), 23, 176–80.

4. Marc Antonio Bragadin, *The Italian Navy in World War II* (Annapolis, MD: Naval Institute Press, 1957), 4–20; Schrieber et al., *Germany and the Second World War*, 3:45–46, 92–98, 220, 247–52, 256–58; Jackson, *Battle for North Africa*, 26–28; David Wragg, *Swordfish: The Story of the Taranto Raid* (London: Cassell, 2004), 52, 60; Playfair, *The Mediterranean and the Middle East*, 1:92–98, 165–67; Macintyre, *Battle for the Mediterranean*, 1–19; Raymond de Belot, *The Struggle for the Mediterranean, 1939–1945*, trans. James Field, Jr. (Princeton, NJ: Princeton University Press, 1951), 35–29; Ellis, *Brute Force*, 229–34; Charles Jellison, *Besieged: The World War II Ordeal of Malta, 1940–1942* (Hanover, NH: University Press of New England, 1984), 31–42; Overy, *The Air War*, 52–53; Mellenthin, *Panzer Battles*, 178–79; Ian Cameron, *Red Duster, White Ensign* (New York: Bantam, 1983), 11–12; and C. E. Lucas Phillips, *Alamein* (Boston: Little Brown, 1962), 38.

5. Schrieber et al., *Germany and the Second World War*, 3:251–58; Playfair, *The Mediterranean and the Middle East*, 1:150–59; Macintyre, *Battle for the Mediterranean*, 23–27; and Wragg, *Swordfish*, 65.

6. Schrieber et al., *Germany and the Second World War*, 3:267–77; Jackson, *Battle for North Africa*, 29–34; and Barnett, *The Desert Generals*, 9–13.

7. Schrieber et al., *Germany and the Second World War*, 3:226–27, 231, 401–48.

8. Playfair, *The Mediterranean and the Middle East*, 1:201, 235–38; Roskill, *War at Sea*, 1:300; Wragg, *Swordfish*, 71–72, 83, 88–134; Macintyre, *Battle for the Mediterranean*, 36–38; Butler, *Grand Strategy*, 2:370; Schrieber et al., *Germany and the Second World War*, 3:443; Thomas P. Lowry and John W. G. Wellham, *The Attack on Taranto: Blueprint for Pearl Harbor* (Mechanicsburg, PA: Stackpole, 1995); and *The Royal Navy and the Mediterranean*, vol. 2, *November 1940–December 1941* (London: Whitehall Publishing, 2002), 10–13.

9. Goda, *Tomorrow the World*, 53–55, 64, 72–77, 134–35, 146, 161; Schrieber et al., *Germany and the Second World War*, 3:146, 187, 190, 193–94, 209–10, 221–33, 238; Ansel, *Hitler and the Middle Sea*, 19, 21–29, 72; Rich, *Hitler's War Aims*, q:166–76; and Ian Kershaw, *Hitler: 1936–1945 Nemesis* (New York: Norton, 2000), 325.

10. Ellis, *Brute Force*, 229–31; Jackson, *Battle for North Africa*, 50–86, 95; Playfair, *The Mediterranean and the Middle East*, 1:351–67, 371; Barnett, *The Desert Generals*, 10–53; Raugh, *Wavell in the Middle East*, 100–128; Schrieber et al., *Germany and the Second World War*, 3:645–53; and S. W. Roskill, *War at Sea, 1939–1945*, vol. 3, part 2, *The Offensive* (London: Her Majesty's Stationery Office, 1961), 390–91. Cf. Douglas Porch, *The Path to Victory: The Mediterranean Theater in World War*

*II* (New York: Farrar, Straus and Giroux, 2004), 142–43, for one of the few attempts to defend the decision not to go to Tripoli.

11. Jackson, *Battle for North Africa*, 65–68, 89–112; Playfair, *The Mediterranean and the Middle East*, 1:165–67, 391–448; Playfair, *The Mediterranean and the Middle East*, 2:223, 232–33; Glover, *An Improvised War*, passim; Butler, *Grand Strategy*, 2:379; and Raugh, *Wavell in the Middle East*, 134, 160, 180–81.

12. Schreiber et al., *Germany and the Second World War*, 3:654–62, 673–93; Jackson, *Battle for North Africa*, 95–96, 113–37; Playfair, *The Mediterranean and the Middle East*, 1:366–67; Playfair, *The Mediterranean and the Middle East*, 2:2–33; David Fraser, *Knight's Cross: A Life of Field Marshal Erwin Rommel* (New York: Harper, 1993); Mellenthin, *Panzer Battles*, 57; Hinsley et al., *British Intelligence*, 1:384–98; Raugh, *Wavell in the Middle East*, 142, 165, 184–94; Bragadin, *Italian Navy in World War II*, 68; and Ronald Lewin, *Rommel as Military Commander* (New York: Ballantine, 1968), 37. For critiques of Rommel, cf. Porch, *Path to Victory*, 197–208; and the German official history, Schreiber et al., *Germany and the Second World War*, 3:693–94.

13. Schreiber et al., *Germany and the Second World War*, 3:451–93; Ralph Bennett, *Ultra and Mediterranean Strategy* (New York: William Morrow, 1989), 29–32; Butler, *Grand Strategy*, 2:376; Raugh, *Wavell in the Middle East*, 112, 119, 134–45, 149–56; Parkinson, *Blood, Toil, Tears and Sweat*, 198–202; Playfair, *The Mediterranean and the Middle East*, 2:338–43, 371, 375–78, 380–89; Lewin, *The Chief*, 79, 86, 93–107, 112, 114; and Churchill, *Grand Alliance*, 55–65, 77–92.

14. Schreiber et al., *Germany and the Second World War*, 3:663–70; Macintyre, *Battle for the Mediterranean*, 56–57; Playfair, *The Mediterranean and the Middle East*, 2:62–70; Roskill, *War at Sea*, 1:428–31; and Hinsley et al., *British Intelligence*, 1:403–8.

15. Playfair, *The Mediterranean and the Middle East*, 2:83–105; Schreiber et al., *Germany and the Second World War*, 3:494–516; Roskill, *War at Sea*, 1:434–35; Anthony Heckstall-Smith and H. T. Baillie Grohman, *Greek Tragedy, 1941* (New York: Norton, 1961); Hinsley et al., *British Intelligence*, 1:406–9; and Bennett, *Ultra and Mediterranean Strategy*, 47–50, disagree on the value of Ultra information for the retreat in Greece.

16. Ian MacDougall Stewart's *The Struggle for Crete, 20 May–1 June 1941: A Story of Lost Opportunity* (Oxford, UK: Oxford University Press, 1966) is the best source. Unfortunately it was written before the intelligence background was available and so is a bit unfair to General Freyberg. Bennett, *Ultra and Mediterranean Strategy*, 51–62; Hinsley et al., *British Intelligence*, 1:415–21; Playfair, *The Mediterranean and the Middle East*, 2:121–49; Schreiber et al., *Germany and the Second World War*, 3:527–58; and Ansel, *Hitler and the Middle Sea*, passim.

17. Playfair, *The Mediterranean and the Middle East*, 2:56–57, 107–19; Jackson, *Battle for North Africa*, 153, 156–57, 204–12; Raugh, *Wavell in the Middle East*, 207–13; Churchill, *Grand Alliance*, 202–5, 207–13, 272–81; and Geoffrey Warner, *Iraq and Syria, 1941* (Newark: University of Delaware Press, 1979).

18. Churchill, *Grand Alliance*, 336–43, 418, 455–56; Shelford Bidwell and Dominick Graham, *Fire-Power: British Army Weapons and Theories of War, 1904–1945* (Boston: George Allen & Unwin, 1982), 177–78, 230; Raugh, *Wavell in the Middle East*, 231, 235–36; Jackson, *Battle for North Africa*, 158–64, 172; Barnett, *The Desert Generals*, 64–69; Playfair, *The Mediterranean and the Middle East*, 2:164–73, 248–54; Gwyer and Butler, *Grand Strategy*, 3:175–82; Hinsley et al., *British Intelligence*, 2:398–99; and Raymond Callahan, *Churchill and His Generals* (Lawrence: University Press of Kansas, 2007), 57, 67.

19. Adolf Hitler, *Blitzkrieg to Defeat: Hitler's War Directives, 1939–1945* (New York: Holt Rinehart and Winston, 1964), 78; Lewin, *Rommel as Military Commander*, 63; Playfair, *The Mediterranean and the Middle East*, 2:261; Fraser, *Knight's Cross*, 237; Bennett, *Ultra and Mediterranean Strategy*, 69; Erwin Rommel, *The Rommel Papers*, ed. B. H. Liddell Hart (New York: Harcourt Brace, 1953), 148, 191, 514; and Schreiber et al., *Germany and the Second World War*, 3:624–40, 706, 752.

20. Bragadin, *Italian Navy in World War II*, 120–24, 127, 130–43; Bennett, *Ultra and Mediterranean Strategy*, 70–80; Hinsley et al., *British Intelligence*, 2:281–83; Playfair, *The Mediterranean and the Middle East*, 2:276, 280, 296; Alan Levine, *The War Against Rommel's Supply Lines, 1943–1943* (Westport, CT: Greenwood/Praeger, 1999), 10, 16–19; Macintyre, *Battle for the Mediterranean*, 96–101; and Cameron, *Red Duster*, 96–110. The official history, Playfair's *The Mediterranean and the Middle East*, 2:296, maintains that the September convoy sustained Malta, except for the specified exceptions, until May 1942. This information does not seem consonant with other sources or the desperate efforts made to rush supplies long before that deadline.

21. Playfair, *The Mediterranean and the Middle East*, 2:341; Playfair, *The Mediterranean and the Middle East*, 3:2–102, 435; Mellenthin, *Panzer Battles*, 63–100; Hinsley et al., *British Intelligence*, 2:297, 302–3; Bennett, *Ultra and Mediterranean Strategy*, 90; Lewin, *Rommel as Military Commander*, 71–119; Bidwell and Graham, *Fire-Power*, 221–32, 254; Barnett, *The Desert Generals*, 61–124; Schreiber et al., *Germany and the Second World War*, 3:730–52; and Jackson, *Battle for North Africa*, 178–226.

## 6. The Hinge

1. Weinberg, *World at Arms*, 86–87, 176–78; Boog et al., *Germany and the Second World War*, 6:112–13; Trevor-Roper and Weinberg, *Hitler's Table Talk*, 545; Rich, *Hitler's War Aims*, 1: 242; Saul Friedlander, *Prelude to Downfall: Hitler and the United States, 1939–1941*, trans. Aline B. Werth and Alexander Werth (New York: Knopf, 1967), 36, 85, 89, 93, 201; James P. Duffy, *Target America: Hitler's Plan to Attack the United States* (Westport, CT: Greenwood/Praeger, 2004), 12–13, 16–18; Tooze, *Wages of Destruction*, 282; and Goda, *Tomorrow the World*, passim.

2. Steven Casey, *Cautious Crusade: Franklin D. Roosevelt, American Public Opinion, and the War against Nazi Germany* (New York: Oxford University Press, 2001), esp. 10–24; William Langer and S. Everett Gleason, *Challenge to Isolation, 1937–1940* (New York: Harper, 1952), 12–13, 487–88; Reynolds, *Creation of the Anglo-American Alliance*, 41; and Dallek, *Franklin D. Roosevelt*, esp. 75–76, 172–75.

3. Langer and Gleason, *Challenge to Isolation*, 11–137, 479, 480, 505–6; Dallek, *Franklin D. Roosevelt*, 70–71, 85, 101–2, 104; Manfred Jonas, *Isolationism in America, 1935–1941* (Ithaca, NY: Cornell University Press, 1966), 6–7, 15, 22–24, 27, 81, 87, 101, 106–15, 117–21, 130, 136–68, 199, 202–10, 237–38, 244–49, 262–74; Wayne S. Cole, *Roosevelt and the Isolationists, 1932–45* (Lincoln: University of Nebraska Press, 1983), 17–19, 29–34, 142–62, 243, 363–64; Dorothy Borg, *The United States and the Far Eastern Crisis of 1933–1938: From the Manchurian Incident through the Initial State of the Undeclared Sino-Japanese War* (Cambridge, MA: Harvard University Press, 1964), 89–90, 169–71, 319–90; and James Martin, *American Liberalism and World Politics, 1931–1941: Liberalism's Press and Spokesmen on the Road back to War between Mukden and Pearl Harbor*, 2 vols. (New York: Devin-Adair, 1964), 2:738–48, 766, 771–72, 776, 836, 843, 849, 870, 881–89, 1034–43.

4. Reynolds, *Creation of the Anglo-American Alliance*, 41–42; Basil Rauch, *Roosevelt, from Munich to Pearl Harbor: A Study in the Creation of Foreign Policy* (New York:

Barnes & Noble, 1967) (originally published 1950), 100–112; Wesley F. Craven and James Lea Cate, *Army Air Forces in World War II*, vol. 1, *Plans and Early Operations, January 1939 to August 1942* (Chicago: University of Chicago Press, 1948), 111, 125; Dallek, *Franklin D. Roosevelt*, 172–75; and Mark S. Watson, *Chief of Staff: Prewar Plans and Preparations* (Washington, DC: Office of the Chief of Military History, 1950), 17, 127, 138.

5. Goodhart, *Fifty Ships That Saved the World*, esp. 13–17; Watson, *Chief of Staff*, 95–96, 106; Matloff and Snell, *Strategic Planning*, 12–16, 24, 29, 34–45; Langer and Gleason, *Challenge to Isolation*, 479–80, 486, 505–7, 566, 748–69; Reynolds, *Creation of the Anglo-American Alliance*, 10–13, 23–25, 28, 43, 78–82; Mark Chadwin, *The Warhawks: American Interventionists before Pearl Harbor* (New York: Norton, 1970), 30; Dallek, *Franklin D. Roosevelt*, 229, 243–47; Joseph Lash, *Roosevelt and Churchill, 1939–1941: The Partnership that Saved the West* (New York: Norton, 1976), 135–42, 147, 202, 233; William Langer and S. Everett Gleason, *The Undeclared War, 1940–1941* (New York: Harper, 1953), 2, 197, 213–89; and Martin, *American Liberalism and World Politics*, 2:1045–57, 1139–41.

6. Jäckel, *Hitler in History*, 70–71; Friedlander, *Prelude to Downfall*, 99, 119, 152–54, 196–201, 300–302; Langer and Gleason, *The Undeclared War*, 29–34; Halder, *Halder Diaries*, 675; and Boog et al., *Germany and the Second World War*, 6:113–14, 167, 173–74, 309–10.

7. Langer and Gleason, *Challenge to Isolation*, 682–83; Langer and Gleason, *The Undeclared War*, 197, 200, 247, 269–70, 448, 542, 562–63, 753–58, 812, 819; Wayne S. Cole, *America First: The Battle against Intervention, 1940–1941* (New York: Octagon, 1971) (originally published 1953), esp. 15, 35, 37–41, 65, 75, 86–87, 90, 94–96, 103; Cole, *Roosevelt and the Isolationists*, 12–13, 363–64, 378, 411, 415–17, 419, 434, 456, 469; Wayne S. Cole, *Charles Lindbergh and the Battle Against American Intervention in World War II* (New York: Harcourt, Brace and Jovanovich, 1974), 135; Jonas, *Isolationism in America*, 113–14, 199, 206, 226–31, 236–39, 244–49, 269–73; and Rex Stout, ed., *The Illustrious Dunderheads* (New York: Knopf, 1942), 25, 28, 30, 32, 39, 42, 43, 53, 57, 72–75, 84, 103, 108, 156–58, 166, 178.

8. Reynolds, *Creation of the Anglo-American Alliance*, 201–5; Langer and Gleason, *The Undeclared War*, 422–28, 458, 489, 522, 569, 736; Lash, *Roosevelt and Churchill*, 298; Heinrichs, *Threshold of War*, 40–45, 48, 70, 83–85, 107, 109, 113; *Army Air Forces in World War II*, 1:314, 317–42; Friedlander, *Prelude to Downfall*, 205–11; Dallek, *Franklin D. Roosevelt*, 261–67, 273; and Eliot Janeway, *The Struggle for Survival: A Chronicle of Economic Mobilization in World War II* (New Haven, CT: Yale University Press, 1951).

9. Dallek, *Franklin D. Roosevelt*, 276–77, 281–86; Langer and Gleason, *The Undeclared War*, 575–79, 663–92, 742–43; Watson, *Chief of Staff*, 401–9; and Heinrichs, *Threshold of War*, 85–90, 108–12, 117, 146–60, 165.

10. Jäckel, *Hitler in History*, 72–74; Boog et al., *Germany and the Second World War*, 6:114, 310–13; Ansel, *Hitler and the Middle Sea*, 107, 121n3; Weinberg, *World at Arms*, 238, 250; and Friedlander, *Prelude to Downfall*, 204, 207, 210–13, 255–59.

11. H. H. Arnold, *Global Mission* (New York: Harper, 1949), 214; and *Hearings Before the Joint Committee on the Investigation of the Pearl Harbor Attack*, 79th Cong., 39 parts (Washington, DC: Government Printing Office, 1946), part 5, 2310–14.

12. Heinrichs, *Threshold of War*, 166–68; Boog et al., *Germany and the Second World War*, 6:319–29; Jäckel, *Hitler in History*, 74; Morison, *History of United States Naval Operations*, 1:79–80, 84–86, 109–13; Friedlander, *Prelude to Downfall*, 290–94, 302–3; Dallek, *Franklin D. Roosevelt*, 285–91, 310; Lash, *Roosevelt and Churchill*, 418–28; Langer and Gleason, *The Undeclared War*, 732–60; and Cole, *Charles*

*Lindbergh*, 197–99. Cf. the very different interpretation of Reynolds, *Creation of the Anglo-American Alliance*, 212–13, 218–19; and of Robert Divine, *Roosevelt and World War II* (New York: Pelican, 1970) for the argument that Roosevelt may never have been fully reconciled to America's all-out participation in the war.

13. Heinrichs, *Threshold of War*, 118, 132–44; Dallek, *Franklin D. Roosevelt*, 299–306; Jäckel, *Hitler in History*, 70–71; Borg, *United States and the Far Eastern Crisis*; Robert Butow, *Tojo and the Coming of the War* (Princeton, NJ: Princeton University Press, 1961); Herbert Feis, *The Road to Pearl Harbor: The Coming of the War between the United States and Japan* (Princeton, NJ: Princeton University Press, 1950); Gordon Prange, *Pearl Harbor: The Verdict of History* (New York: St. Martin's, 1987); Jones, *Japan's New Order*, 170, 192–94, 218, 308–12, 316, 457–62; and Churchill, *Grand Alliance*, 495, 502.

14. Jäckel, *Hitler in History*, 76–85; Ian Kershaw, *Hitler: 1936–1945 Nemesis* (New York: Norton, 2000); Trevor-Roper and Weinberg, *Hitler's Table Talk*, 488; Friedlander, *Prelude to Downfall*, 305–9, 312–14; Rich, *Hitler's War Aims*, 1:242–46; Boog et al., *Germany and the Second World War*, 6:113–14. Cf. Weinberg, *World at Arms*, 262; Megargee, *Inside Hitler's High Command*, 137; Waite, *The Psychopathic God*, 403, 409; and Murray, *Strategy for Defeat*, 88, for arguments that Hitler was recklessly contemptuous of the Americans or actually sought his own destruction.

15. Dallek, *Franklin D. Roosevelt*, 312; Langer and Gleason, *The Undeclared War*, 937–41; and Reynolds, *Creation of the Anglo-American Alliance*, 220.

16. Boog et al., *Germany and the Second World War*, 6:116–29, 860, 889, 902–3; Megargee, *Inside Hitler's High Command*, 170–72; Higgins, *Hitler and Russia*, 199; and Trevor-Roper and Weinberg, *Hitler's Table Talk*, 237, 299–301. Some have claimed that Hitler already knew the war was lost in December 1941; see, for example, Schramm, *Hitler*, 26–27, 161. This point has been the basis for some far-reaching speculations, as in Waite's *The Psychopathic God*, esp. 377, 409. Such claims seem to place excessive reliance on a vague account General Jodl gave several years later about Hitler's despair and may reflect only a fit of nerves on Hitler's part during the crisis in Russia that did not represent his normal views. The evidence points rather to Hitler's realizing that the war could not be won in the late summer of 1942; however, even then he may not have accepted that this idea meant total defeat.

17. Kershaw, *Hitler*, 444; Ian Kershaw, *The "Hitler Myth": Image and Reality in the Third Reich* (New York: Oxford University Press, 1987), 185–87; and Marlis Steinert, *Hitler's War and the Germans: Public Mood and Attitude during the Second World War*, ed. and trans. Thomas de Witt (Athens: Ohio University Press, 1977), 131, 150, 160.

18. Gwyer and Butler, *Grand Strategy*, vol. 3, part 1, 25; ibid., part 2, 513; Boog et al., *Germany and the Second World War*, 6:607, 863–71, 879–80; British Bomb Survey Unit, *Strategic Air War Against Germany*, xxvi–xxx; Murray, *Strategy for Defeat*, 102; Overy, *War and Economy in the Third Reich*, 26–30, 254, 343; Werner Abelshauser, "Germany, Guns, Butter and the Economic Miracle," in *The Economics of World War II: Six Great Powers in International Comparison*, ed. Mark Harrison (Cambridge, UK: Cambridge University Press, 1998), esp. 152, 156; and Tooze, *Wages of Destruction*, 497–98, 507–8, 552 ff. Tooze violently attacks Speer's reputation, arguing that his achievements were largely owing to Dr. Todt's efforts, reinforced by payoffs of earlier programs and the increased mobilization of money, material, and labor, especially the exploitation of slave labor.

19. Christina Goulter, *A Forgotten Offensive: Royal Air Force Coastal Command's Anti-shipping Campaign, 1940–1945* (London: Frank Cass, 1995), xviii, 278–86, 299–301; Hinsley et al., *British Intelligence*, 2:197–99; Roskill, *War at Sea*, 2:259, 263–64; Boog et al., *Germany and the Second World War*, 6:438, 492; and Levine, *Strategic Bombing of Germany*, 47, 196.

20. Craven and Cate, *Army Air Forces*, 1:104, 105, 139, 274–281; and Matloff and Snell, *Strategic Planning*, 48, 87, 95.

21. Gwyer and Butler, *Grand Strategy*, 3:37–38, 325–99; Churchill, *Grand Alliance*, 533, 544–55, 569–70; and Matloff and Snell, *Strategic Planning*, 97–123.

## 7. THE BATTLE OF THE ATLANTIC II

1. John K. Waters, foreword, in Homer Hickam, Jr., *Torpedo Junction: U-boat War off America's East Coast* (New York: Dell, 1991), xiii.

2. Cremer, *U-boat Commander*, 69; Milner, *Battle of the Atlantic*, 57, 83–85, 89–97; Hickam, *Torpedo Junction*, passim; Michael Gannon, *Operation Drumbeat: The Dramatic True Story of Germany's First U-boat Attacks along the American Coast in World War II* (New York: Harper & Row, 1990); MOD, *U-boat War in the Atlantic*, 2:2–6, 10–13, 20; Boog et al., *Germany and the Second World War*, 6:369–79; Morison, *History of United States Naval Operations*, 1:125–57, 229–31, 237–42, 252–56; Beesly, *Very Special Intelligence*, 109–13; Roskill, *War at Sea*, 1:136–37; and ibid., 2:95–105. Cf. Blair, *Hitler's U-boat War*, 434–39, 444–523, 591, 692–94, for a basically unconvincing defense of Admiral King, although Blair corrects individual criticisms made of him.

3. Gary E. Weir, "A Truly Allied Undertaking," in Howarth and Law, *Battle of the Atlantic*, 101–17; Morison, *History of United States Naval Operations*, 1:290–95; Blair, *Hitler's U-boat War*, 694; and Clay Blair, *Hitler's U-boat War: The Hunted, 1942–1945* (New York: Random House, 1998), 168–69.

4. Boog et al., *Germany and the Second World War*, 6:326–31; and Blair, *Hitler's U-boat War*, 561.

5. Blair, *Hitler's U-boat War: The Hunted*, 9, 313, 626–27, 659; Boog et al., *Germany and the Second World War*, 6:402–3; MOD, *U-boat War in the Atlantic*, 2:44; ibid., 3:5–7; Paul Kemp, *Underwater Warriors* (London: Cassell, 1996), 183–84; Meigs, *Slide Rules and Submarines*, 189; Eberhard Roessler, "U-boat Development and Building," in Howarth and Law, *Battle of the Atlantic*, 133–35; Morison, *History of United States Naval Operations*, 10:6–62, 338; Hezlet, *Submarine and Sea Power*, 229–30, 235–37; V. E. Tarrant, *The Last Year of the Kriegsmarine* (London: Arms and Armour Press, 1991), 20–25, 48–50, 206; United States Strategic Bombing Survey, *German Submarine Industry Report* (Washington, DC: Government Printing Office, 1947), 3–5, 23–24, 27–28, 29; Eberhard Roessler, *The U-boat: The Evolution and Technical History of German Submarines* (London: Arms and Armour Press, 2001), 168–88, 198, 208–10, 214–31, 240–42; and Albert Speer, *Inside the Third Reich* (New York: Avon, 1971), 358.

6. Beesly, *Very Special Intelligence*, 115–19; Kahn, *Seizing the Enigma*, 212–14; Hinsley et al., *British Intelligence*, 2:228–31; Milner, *Battle of the Atlantic*, 107; Price, *Aircraft versus Submarine*, 196; and Meigs, *Slide Rules and Submarines*, 33–36, 54.

7. Boog et al., *Germany and the Second World War*, 6:373–89; Blair, *Hitler's U-boat War: The Hunted*, 28, 47–48, 50, 72–77, 248; MOD, *U-boat War in the Atlantic*, 2:25–29, 39, 42, 50; Milner, *Battle of the Atlantic*, 101, 107–25; and Roskill, *War at Sea*, 2:107–11, 209–11.

8. Milner, *Battle of the Atlantic*, 131–36; Roskill, *War at Sea*, 2:201, 215–17; Boog et al., *Germany and the Second World War*, 6:389–91; Morison, *History of United*

*States Naval Operations*, 10:39; Syrett, *Defeat of the German U-boats*, 17; MOD, *U-boat War in the Atlantic*, 2:69–70, 73; and Neitzel, "Deployment of the U-boats," 294.

9. Blair, *Hitler's U-boat War: The Hunted*, 176–78, 231–36; Hinsley et al., *British Intelligence*, 2:548–59; Beesly, *Very Special Intelligence*, 158–66; Kahn, *Seizing the Enigma*, 225–30; and MOD, *U-boat War in the Atlantic*, 2:88.

10. Milner, *Battle of the Atlantic*, 137–38; Michael Gannon, *Black May* (New York: Dell 1999), 119; Sutcliffe, "Operational Research in the Battle of the Atlantic," 418–29; and Arthur Marder, *From the Dreadnaught to Scapa Flow: The Royal Navy in the Fisher Era, 1904–1919*, 5 vols. (London: Oxford University Press, 1970), 91, 100.

11. Roskill, *War at Sea*, 2:351–52, 363; Milner, *Battle of the Atlantic*, 99, 142–46; Middlebrook, *Convoy*, 309–10, 312–13; Blair, *Hitler's U-boat War*, 103–6, 148–52, 164–65; Price, *Aircraft versus Submarine*, 96, 99, 127, 145–46; Syrett, *Defeat of the German U–boats*, 15–16, 182; and Boog et al., *Germany and the Second World War*, 6:396–97.

12. Middlebrook, *Convoy*, passim; Milner, *Battle of the Atlantic*, 135–46; Roskill, *War at Sea*, 2:356, 365–67; MOD, *U-boat War in the Atlantic*, 2:83–84, 88–89; Price, *Aircraft versus Submarine*, 127, 131; Boog et al., *Germany and the Second World War*, 6:394–95; Bekker, *Hitler's Naval War*, 330; Beesly, *Very Special Intelligence*, 179–85; and Morison, *History of United States Naval Operations*, 10:334–42, 357–58.

13. Boog et al., *Germany and the Second World War*, 6:397–405; Roskill, *War at Sea*, 2:366–79; Milner, *Battle of the Atlantic*, 147–55, 157–69; MOD, *U-boat War in the Atlantic*, 2:96–112; Morison, *History of United States Naval Operations*, 10:65–132; Syrett, *Defeat of the German U–boats*, 25–180, 259–64; Beesly, *Very Special Intelligence*, 177–97, 196–97; Price, *Aircraft versus Submarine*, 154–68; Gannon, *Black May*, passim; and William Y'Blood, *Hunter-Killer: U.S. Escort Carriers in the Battle of the Atlantic* (New York: Bantam, 1992), 53–104

14. Morison, *History of United States Naval Operations*, 10:10; Syrett, *Defeat of the German U–boats*, 182–85, 203, 207; Blair, *Hitler's U-boat War*, 161–62, 167–69, 426, 444; Milner, *Battle of the Atlantic*, 171; Cremer, *U-boat Commander*, 161–62; and Hezlet, *Submarine and Sea Power*, 181.

15. Macintyre, *Naval War Against Hitler*, 402, 405–6; and Beesly, *Very Special Intelligence*, 180–82.

16. Middlebrook, *Convoy*, 31–35, 308–9; Macintyre, *Naval War Against Hitler*, 401; and Milner, *Battle of the Atlantic*, 35.

## 8. The Russian Campaign II

1. Ziemke, *Moscow to Stalingrad*, 283–84, 286–87, 298, 302, 306–8; Murray, *Strategy for Defeat*, 316; Hayward, *Stopped at Stalingrad*, 3–9, 12–13, 15–22; Boog et al., *Germany and the Second World War*, 4:695; Boog et al., *Germany and the Second World War*, 6:3–5, 102, 120–26, 131–32, 844, 850–54, 857–60, 862n70, 865–69, 882, 897; Blau, *German Campaign in Russia*, 109–15, 176–77; Nolte, *Three Faces of Fascism*, 361; Michael Howard, *Grand Strategy*, vol. 4, *August 1942–September 1943* (Her Majesty's Stationery Office, 1972), 33; Hinsley et al., *British Intelligence*, 2:83, 91–92, 98; and Leach, *German Strategy Against Russia*, 146–47. For critiques of Hitler's failure to resume an offensive on Moscow, cf. Blau, *German Campaign in Russia*, 177; Wladyslaw Anders, *Hitler's Defeat in Russia* (Chicago: Regnery, 1953), 80–87; and my own remarks in "Was World War II a Near-run Thing?," *Journal of Strategic Studies* 8, no.1 (March 1985): 55.

2. Ziemke, *Moscow to Stalingrad*, 296–98, 300–303; Blau, *German Campaign in Russia*, 124–25; Boog et al., *Germany and the Second World War*, 6:131–32, 882, 886, 894, 898–903; Hayward, *Stopped at Stalingrad*, 21; and Seaton, *Russo-German War*, 255–56.

3. Blau, *German Campaign in Russia*, 121–24; Ziemke, *Moscow to Stalingrad*, 286–90; Bock, *The War Diary*, 429, 439, 464; Megargee, *Inside Hitler's High Command*, 177–79; Hayward, *Stopped at Stalingrad*, 21–26; and Weinberg, *World at Arms*, 299. Seaton's otherwise excellent work perhaps unduly downplays the importance attributed to Stalingrad in Directive 41. Cf. Seaton, *Russo-German War*, 255–58, 267–70.

4. Hayward, *Stopped at Stalingrad*, 17–18, 50–51, 103–5, 128–29; Boog et al., *Germany and the Second World War*, 6:863–71, 878–80, 1040–41; Blau, *German Campaign in Russia*, 114–20, 128–32, 136–38; Seaton, *The German Army*, 191; Ziemke, *Moscow to Stalingrad*, 126, 241–42, 284–86, 293–96, 325; United States Strategic Bombing Survey, *The German Locomotive Industry During the War* (Washington, DC: Government Printing Office, 1947), 4–7, 12–13; Seaton, *Russo-German War*, 228n12, 240, 258; Murray, *Strategy for Defeat*, 94, 119–22; and Halder, *Halder Diaries*, 2:1392.

5. Boog et al., *Germany and the Second World War*, 6:904–6; Blau, *German Campaign in Russia*, 130; and Seaton, *Russo-German War*, 27.

6. Seaton, *The Russo-German War*, 257–65; Erickson, *Road to Stalingrad*, 335–52; Ziemke, *Moscow to Stalingrad*, 261–82, 304–21; Glantz and House, *When Titans Clashed*, 105, 111–16; Weinberg, *World at Arms*, 413; Boog et al., *Germany and the Second World War*, 6:933–41; Hayward, *Stopped at Stalingrad*, 13–15, 64–128; and Manstein, *Lost Victories*, 239–40.

7. Ziemke, *Moscow to Stalingrad*, 322–59; Seaton, *The Russo-German War*, 271–79; Glantz and House, *When Titans Clashed*, 117–22; Hayward, *Stopped at Stalingrad*, 131–47; Blau, *German Campaign in Russia*, 142–55 (Blau interprets Directive 45 as a reversion, after deviations, to the original Directive 41); Halder, *Halder Diaries*, 2:1488, 1490–91; Tooze, *Wages of Destruction*, 477–80; Boog et al., *Germany and the Second World War*, 6:959–95; and Paul Carell, *Hitler Moves East, 1941–1943* (New York: Ballantine, 1971), 533–43.

8. Andrei Grechko, *Battle for the Caucasus*, trans. David Fidlon (Moscow: Progress, 1971); Erickson, *Road to Stalingrad*, 376–81; Ziemke, *Moscow to Stalingrad*, 360–81, 453–54; Hayward, *Stopped at Stalingrad*, 148–50, 155–59, 164–73; Boog et al., *Germany and the Second World War*, 6:1022–59; Blau, *German Campaign in Russia*, 156–58, 162–63; Manstein, *Lost Victories*, 239–40; and Carell, *Hitler Moves East*, 542–61, 572–74.

9. Ziemke, *Moscow to Stalingrad*, 357–58, 382–97, 441–44, 458–68; Seaton, *The Russo-German War*, 278–79, 288–310; Erickson, *Road to Stalingrad*, 382–461; Hayward, *Stopped at Stalingrad*, 155, 184, 191–99, 302, 219; Mellenthin, *Panzer Battles*, 197–98; Murray, *Strategy for Defeat*, 181; Blau, *German Campaign in Russia*, 158–64, 167–68; and Glantz and House, *When Titans Clashed*, 121–22.

10. Erickson, *Road to Stalingrad*, 453–72; Ziemke, *Moscow to Stalingrad*, 441–50, 455–57, 468–502; Boog et al., *Germany and the Second World War*, 6:1073, 1084, 1091–94, 1111–1195; Glantz and House, *When Titans Clashed*, 133–47; Seaton, *The Russo-German War*, 306, 310–51; Murray, *Strategy for Defeat*, 150–52; Bekker, *Luftwaffe War Diaries*, 287–94; Carell, *Hitler Moves East*, 621, 662, 671; Weinberg, *World at Arms*, 451–52, 1040; Kurt Zeitzler, "Stalingrad," in Freiden and Richardson, *Fatal Decisions*, 137–58; Seaton, *The German Army*, 195–96; Antony Beevor, *Stalingrad* (New York: Viking, 1998), 227, 267–68, 273, 299–336; Hay-

ward, *Stopped at Stalingrad*, 222–330; Manstein, *Lost Victories*, 292–440; Ziemke, *Moscow to Stalingrad*, 471, 479; Alan Clark, *Barbarossa: The Russian-German Conflict 1941–1945* (New York: Perennial, 2002), 249–73; and Alexander Stahlberg, *Bounden Duty: The Memoirs of a German Officer, 1932–45*, trans. Patricia Crampton (London: Brassey's, 1990), 215, 222, 228–29, 233.

11. Kershaw, *The Hitler Myth*, 189–94; and Steinert, *Hitler's War and the Germans*, 128–29, 131, 156, 163, 168, 224–27, 240–41.

12. Blau, *German Campaign in Russia*, 178; and Murray, *Strategy for Defeat*, 122. Cf. Higgins, *Hitler and Russia*, 225, 278.

## 9. The Mediterranean and the Middle East II

1. Playfair, *The Mediterranean and the Middle East*, 3:108, 109, 113–43, 155; Macintyre, *Battle for the Mediterranean*, 119–23; Schreiber et al., *Germany and the Second World War*, 3:713, 723; Boog et al., *Germany and the Second World War*, 6:635–51; Jackson, *Battle for North Africa*, 230–43; Mellenthin, *Panzer Battles*, 100–109; Bennett, *Ultra and Mediterranean Strategy*, 97–106; Lewin, *Rommel as Military Commander*, 123–34; Hinsley et al., *British Intelligence*, 2:319–24, 327–29, 334–40; and *Royal Navy and the Mediterranean*, 2:195–97, 200, 215, 217.

2. Boog et al., *Germany and the Second World War*, 6:119–26, 652–56, 706; Playfair, *The Mediterranean and the Middle East*, 3:174–75, 193–95; Bennett, *Ultra and Mediterranean Strategy*, 120; Bekker, *Hitler's Naval War*, 252–56; and Gwyer and Butler, *Grand Strategy*, 3:444–45.

3. Playfair, *The Mediterranean and the Middle East*, 3:155–95; Levine, *War Against Rommel's Supply Lines*, 19–21; Cameron, *Red Duster*, 118–170; and Brian Cull, *Spitfires over Malta*, with Frederick Galea (London: Grub Street, 2005), 98–99, 105.

4. Gwyer and Butler, *Grand Strategy*, vol. 3, part 2, 447–51, 453–61; Hinsley et al., *British Intelligence*, 2:342, 352–56, 366; Bennett, *Ultra and Mediterranean Strategy*, 117–20; Playfair, *The Mediterranean and the Middle East*, 3:202–5; and Jackson, *Battle for North Africa*, 245.

5. Hinsley et al., *British Intelligence*, 2:366, 374–88; Playfair, *Mediterranean and the Middle East*, 3:197–98, 205, 213–78; Desmond Young, *Rommel* (New York: Harper, 1950), 103–4; Barnett, *The Desert Generals*, 136–75; Lewin, *Rommel as Military Commander*, 138–64; Fraser, *Knight's Cross*, 312–35; Mellenthin, *Panzer Battles*, 110–49; Boog et al., *Germany and the Second World War*, 6:667–718; and Jackson, *Battle for North Africa*, 249–93.

6. Bekker, *Hitler's Naval War*, 255–56; I. S. O. Playfair, *The Mediterranean and the Middle East*, vol. 4 (London: Her Majesty's Stationery Office, 1966), 277–78; and Boog et al., *Germany and the Second World War*, 6:716–19.

7. Jackson, *Battle for North Africa*, 299–305; Mellenthin, *Panzer Battles*, 153–57; and Barnett, *The Desert Generals*, 195–96.

8. Boog et al., *Germany and the Second World War*, 6:728–30; Niall Barr, *The Pendulum of War: The Three Battles of El Alamein* (Woodstock, NY: Overlook Press, 2005), 70–174; Jon Latimer, *Alamein* (Cambridge, MA: Harvard University Press, 2002), 54, 58–72; Lewin, *Rommel as Military Commander*, 167–74; Hinsley et al., *British Intelligence*, 2:374–80, 392–93; Bennett, *Ultra and Mediterranean Strategy*, 125, 131, 135–37; Jackson, *Battle for North Africa*, 312–33; Barnett, *The Desert Generals*, 201–39; and Mellenthin, *Panzer Battles*, 161.

9. Gwyer and Butler, *Grand Strategy*, vol. 3, part 2, 613–14; Howard, *Grand Strategy*, 4:51–59; Hinsley et al., *British Intelligence*, 2:106; Playfair, *Mediterranean and*

*the Middle East*, 3:362–67; Jackson, *Battle for North Africa*, 323; and Barnett, *The Desert Generals*, 329–31.

10. Bragadin, *Italian Navy in World War II*, 166–88, 203–14; Playfair, *Mediterranean and the Middle East*, 3:301–7, 314–25; Levine, *War Against Rommel's Supply Lines*, 21–22, 24–25; Cameron, *Red Duster*, 184–96, 206–31; Macintyre, *Battle for the Mediterranean*, 149–62, 166–84; and Sam Moses, *At All Costs: How a Crippled Ship and Two American Merchant Marines Reversed the Tide of World War II* (New York: Random House, 2007).

11. Bennett, *Ultra and Mediterranean Strategy*, 136; Playfair, *Mediterranean and the Middle East*, 3:326, 377–78; Boog et al., *Germany and the Second World War*, 6:716, 741; Rommel, *The Rommel Papers*, 266–67, 288–89; and Levine, *War Against Rommel's Supply Lines*, 25–27.

12. Lewin, *Rommel as Military Commander*, 183–204; Barnett, *The Desert Generals*, 238–47; Latimer, *Alamein*, 89–117; Michael Carver, *El Alamein* (London: Fontana, 1975), 24–74; Playfair, *Mediterranean and the Middle East*, 3:367–69, 381–91; Bennett, *Ultra and Mediterranean Strategy*, 140–52; Boog et al., *Germany and the Second World War*, 6:748–69; Mellenthin, *Panzer Battles*, 172–73; and Barr, *Pendulum of War*, 218–82. There is some argument about whether and how Rommel intended to deal with Alam Halfa. Some maintain that he intended to bypass it entirely, but Mellenthin, whose account seems more likely, contradicts this view. There is a notable difference in interpretation between the Germans and the British. German memoirs and historians agree that Montgomery forfeited a great chance to destroy the Panzer Army, while British writers mostly defend Montgomery's caution.

13. Jackson, *Battle for North Africa*, 352–79; Barnett, *The Desert Generals*, 283–308; Carver, *El Alamein*, 75ff; Boog et al., *Germany and the Second World War*, 6:767–68, 775–84; Lewin, *Rommel as Military Commander*, 205–39; Hinsley et al., *British Intelligence*, 2:438–51; Bennett, *Ultra and Mediterranean Strategy*, 154–72; Playfair, *Mediterranean and the Middle East*, 4:3–63; Latimer, *Alamein*, 118ff; and Levine, *War Against Rommel's Supply Lines*, 28. Much argument has been evoked by Barnett's claim (*The Desert Generals*, 284) that the second Alamein battle was unnecessary because, given the North African invasion, the Axis forces would have had to retreat in November in any case and could have been overtaken and destroyed in the open far more cheaply. Barnett even suggested that it was fought for political reasons to provide a supposedly "independent" British victory over the Axis before the British war effort was wholly subsumed in the combined Anglo-American effort. While technically correct, Barnett overlooked the point that both the British and Americans were anxious for an early victory at Alamein before the invasion to impress the North African French and Spanish with an Allied success. The British, moreover, wanted to recover the Libyan airfields quickly and before the next Malta convoy.

14. Dwight D. Eisenhower, *Crusade in Europe* (New York: Avon, 1968), 41–42, 72; Omar Bradley, *A Soldier's Story* (New York: Popular Library, 1970), 193; Matloff and Snell, *Strategic Planning*, 102, 111–14, 175–77, 179–97, 200–203, 234–56, 272, 278–80; Gwyer and Butler, *Grand Strategy*, vol. 3, part 2, 563–80, 597, 621–36, 677–81, 684–91; and Levine, *War Against Rommel's Supply Lines*, 32–36.

15. George F. Howe, *Northwest Africa: Seizing the Initiative in the West* (Washington, DC: Department of the Army, 1957), esp. 677; Eisenhower, *Crusade in Europe*, 72; Keith Sainsbury, *The North African Landings, 1942: A Strategic Decision* (Newark: University of Delaware Press, 1979), 9, 171–73; Bennett, *Ultra and Mediterranean*

*Strategy*, 372; and George Mowry, *Landing Craft and the War Production Board, April 1942 to May 1944*, War Production Board Special Report no. 11 (Washington, DC, 1946).

16. Levine, *War Against Rommel's Supply Lines*, 36–41; Morison, *History of United States Naval Operations*, 2:28, 31–33, 182–84; Howard, *Grand Strategy*, 4:111–39; Playfair, *The Mediterranean and the Middle East*, 4:115–30, 152; Bennett, *Ultra and Mediterranean Strategy*, 186–88; Mark Clark, *Calculated Risk* (New York: Harper, 1950), 57–70; and Eisenhower, *Papers of Dwight D. Eisenhower*, 410–11, 461, 469–72, 493.

17. Eisenhower, *Crusade in Europe*, 103–20; Levine, *War Against Rommel's Supply Lines*, 55ff; Playfair, *The Mediterranean and the Middle East*, 4:130–55, 158–63, 165–79; Howe, *Northwest Africa*, 74, 185–87, 255–65, 277–95, 310–18, 321, 336–47; and Jackson, *Battle for North Africa*, 380–408.

## 10. The Pacific

1. Jerome Cohen, *Japan's Economy in War and Reconstruction* (Minneapolis: University of Minnesota Press, 1949), xi, 25, 49–52, 104, 110, 216; Masatake Okumiya and Jiro Horikoshi, *Zero!*, with Martin Caidin (New York: Ballantine, 1957), 36–40, 49–50, 53–56; Carl Boyd and Akihiko Yoshida, *The Japanese Submarine Force and World War II* (Annapolis, MD: Naval Institute Press, 1995), xi–xiii; W. J. Holmes, *Underseas Victory* (New York: Zebra, 1979), 30, 58–61; H. P. Willmott, *Empires in the Balance: Japanese and Allied Pacific Strategies to April 1942* (Annapolis, MD: Naval Institute Press, 1982), 57–62, 83–86, 455; Chester Nimitz and E. B. Potter, *The Great Sea War: The Story of Naval Action in World War II* (New York: Bramhall House, 1960), 420–21; Marder, *Old Friends, New Enemies*, 1:296–306; and James Belote and William Belote, *Titans of the Seas: The Development and Operations of Japanese and American Carrier Task Forces during World War II* (New York: Harper & Row, 1975), 21–32.

2. Churchill, *Grand Alliance*, 495, 508; Marder, *Old Friends, New Enemies*, 1:36–40, 48–49, 52–55, 62, 66–69, 142–47, 194–98, 201, 218–33; Willmott, *Empires in the Balance*, 95–129; Alan Warren, *Singapore 1942: Britain's Greatest Defeat* (London: Hambledon and London, 2002), 7, 23–46; Roskill, *War at Sea*, 1:41–42; Brian Linn, *Guardians of Empire: The U.S. Army and the Pacific 1902–1940* (Chapel Hill: University of North Carolina Press, 1997), 174, 177–78, 190–92, 237–38; Matloff and Snell, *Strategic Planning*, 22–25, 36, 67–73; Butler, *Grand Strategy*, 2:326–35; Gwyer and Butler, *Grand Strategy*, 3:271–88; Lionel Wigmore, *The Japanese Thrust* (Canberra: Australian War Memorial, 1957), 8–10, 14, 18–19, 41–45, 58, 72–75, 82–83, 95–101, 136; and Raymond Callahan, "Churchill and Singapore," in *Sixty Years On: The Fall of Singapore Revisited*, ed. Brian Farrell and Sandy Hunter (Singapore: Eastern University Press, 2002), 156–72.

3. Gordon Prange, *At Dawn We Slept* (New York: Penguin, 1982), 10–11, 25–27, 45, 64–65, 104–5, 113, 159–63, 182–83, 261–63, 280, 402–11, 420, 476, 543–45, 547–48, 575; Prange, *Pearl Harbor*, 46–47, 140–43, 290, 326–27, 389–400, 403, 408–18, 426–27, 446–47, 471–73, 485, 489–93, 500–501, 514, 565–66; Willmott, *Empires in the Balance*, 140; Nimitz and Potter, *Great Sea War*, 197; Michael Slackman, *Target: Pearl Harbor* (Honolulu: University of Hawaii Press, 1990), 73; Homer Wallin, *Pearl Harbor: Why, How, Fleet Salvage and Final Appraisal* (Washington, DC: Naval History Division, 1969), 44, 45–49, 51–59, 92, 175, 192–93, 276; W. J. Holmes, *Double-Edged Secrets* (New York: Berkeley, 1981), 87; Belote and Belote, *Titans of the Seas*, 3–9; Frederick Sherman, *Combat Command* (New York: Bantam, 1982), 1–4, 10, 20, 320, 322; and Marder, *Old Friends, New Enemies*, 1:332n46.

4. Morison, *History of United States Naval Operations*, 3:209–14, 218–20, 256–57; Louis Morton, *Strategy and Command: The First Two Years* (Washington, DC: Department of the Army, 1962), 147; Craven and Cate, *Army Air Forces*, 1:280–81; Harold Buell, *Dauntless Helldivers: A Dive-Bomber Pilot's Epic Story of the Carrier Battles* (New York: Dell, 1992), 68, 108–9; Lundstrom, *The First Team*, 8–14, 26–27, 76; John Lundstrom, *The First South Pacific Campaign: Pacific Fleet Strategy, December 1941–June 1942* (Annapolis, MD: Naval Institute Press, 1976), 18–19; Robert Cressman, *USS* Ranger: *The Navy's First Flattop from Keel to Mast, 1934–46* (Washington, DC: Brassey's, 2003), 181, 183, 188–89, 347; Belote and Belote, *Titans of the Seas*, 21–32; H. P. Willmott, *Barrier and the Javelin: Japanese and Allied Pacific Strategies, February to June 1942* (Annapolis, MD: Naval Institute Press, 1983), 198–99; Sherman, *Combat Command*, 320; and Pat Frank and Joseph Harrington, *Rendezvous at Midway: U.S.S.* Yorktown *and the Japanese Carrier Fleet* (New York: John Day, 1967), 44, 125.

5. John Lundstrom, *Black Shoe Carrier Admiral: Frank Jack Fletcher at Coral Sea, Midway, and Guadalcanal* (Annapolis, MD: Naval Institute Press, 2006), 14–48; Willmott, *Empires in the Balance*, 144–46; Holmes, *Double-Edged Secrets*, 46; Sherman, *Combat Command*, 51–52; Lundstrom, *The First Team*, 33–44; Belote and Belote, *Titans of the Seas*, 43–44; Okumiya and Horikoshi, *Zero!*, 86–88; and Gregory Urwin, *Facing Fearful Odds: The Siege of Wake Island* (Lincoln: University of Nebraska Press, 1997), esp. 305–40, 407–23, 516–23.

6. Roskill, *War at Sea*, 2:6–7, 18–19; Morton, *Strategy and Command*, 159, 161–63; S. Woodburn Kirby, *The War Against Japan*, 5 vols. (London: Her Majesty's Stationery Office, 1957), 1:163, 252–57; Willmott, *Empires in the Balance*, xiii, 95, 104–5, 126–28, 219–20, 229–37, 311; Christopher Shores, Brian Cull, and Yasuho Izawa, *The Bloody Shambles* (London: Grub Street, 1992), 1:55–65; and Gwyer and Butler, *Grand Strategy*, 3:275, 311, 318, 342, 366–81, 465–66.

7. Okumiya and Horikoshi, *Zero!*, 57, 84–88; Willmott, *Empires in the Balance*, 147–54, 181–217, 264–76, 282–309, 336–65, 398–432; Holmes, *Underseas Victory*, 89–92; Clay Blair, *Silent Victory: The U.S. Submarine War Against Japan* (New York: Lippincott, 1975), 106–7, 132–35; Walter D. Edmonds, *They Fought with What They Had: The Story of the Army Air Forces in the Southwest Pacific, 1941–1942* (Washington, DC: Center for Air Force History, 1992), x–xiv, 14, 18, 20–26, 30, 51, 59, 65–67, 70–71, 74–77, 441–43; William Bartsch, *Doomed at the Start: American Pursuit Pilots in the Philippines, 1941–1942* (College Station, TX: Texas A & M University Press, 1992); Louis Morton, *Fall of the Philippines* (Washington, DC: Department of the Army, 1953), 32–37, 43, 55–58, 64, 79–82, 86, 141, 152, 161, 254, 256–57, 261; Craven and Cate, *Army Air Forces*, 1:201–13, 218, 372–74, 400; Morton, *Strategy and Command*, 151–53; Matloff and Snell, *Strategic Planning*, 82–87; Gwyer and Butler, *Grand Strategy*, vol. 3, part 2, 407–19, 465–69; Wigmore, *The Japanese Thrust*, 41, 51, 122–23, 136, 142, 146, 196, 255, 285–86; Morison, *History of United States Naval Operations*, 3:277–380; Kirby, *War Against Japan*, esp. 1:163, 252–57, 260, 324, 325, 350, 353, 442–48, 456–61, 463, 466; Shores, Cull, and Izawa, *The Bloody Shambles*, 1:122, 138, 142, 159, 241–51, 261, 273, 297, 313, 384; Louis Allen, *Singapore, 1941–1942* (Newark: University of Delaware Press, 1979); Raymond Callahan, *The Worst Disaster: The Fall of Singapore* (Newark: University of Delaware Press, 1977); Warren, *Singapore 1942*; Marder, *Old Friends, New Enemies*, 1:220, 229, 231, 365, 378, 385–88, 404, 411–506; and Roskill, *War at Sea*, 2:2–8.

8. Willmott, *Empires in the Balance*, 437–40, 456–59; Willmott, *Barrier and the Javelin*, 39–56, 65–79, 117–19; Samuel Milner, *Victory in Papua* (Washington, DC:

Department of the Army, 1957), 10–13; Gordon Prange, *Miracle at Midway*, with Donald Goldstein and Katherine Dillon (New York: McGraw-Hill, 1983), 14–15, 21–28, 30; Jonathan Parshall and Anthony Tully, *Shattered Sword: The Untold Story of the Battle of Midway* (Washington, DC: Potomac Books, 2005), 26–40, 42–45; John J. Stephan, *Hawaii under the Rising Sun: Japan's Plans for Conquest after Pearl Harbor* (Honolulu: University of Hawaii Press, 1984), xiii; Marder, *Old Friends, New Enemies*, 2:81–84; Mitsuo Fuchida and Masatake Okumiya, *Midway: The Battle that Doomed Japan* (New York: Ballantine, 1968), 54–73; and Lundstrom, *First South Pacific Campaign*, 9, 25, 43–46. Some authors, notably the brilliant British historians F. C. Jones (in *Japan's New Order in East Asia*, 402–4) and H. P. Willmott have argued that the Japanese should have concentrated their efforts on overwhelming the British and destroying the latter's position in the Middle East oil fields. This strategy, they argue, *might* have knocked Britain out of the war. Their arguments are impressive but do not explain what operations would have accomplished this goal or how they could have been sustained logistically. And to adopt such a strategy, Willmott notes, would have exposed Japan to the Americans or, more exactly, would have meant passing up any chance of Japan knocking out the American fleet, its main foe, when that was possible. Cf. Eric Bergerud, *Fire in the Sky: The Air War in the South Pacific* (Boulder, CO: Westview Press, 2000), 29–33.

9. Lundstrom, *First South Pacific Campaign*, 39, 78; Lundstrom, *The First Team*, 27, 62–76, 107–8, 112–53, 160–61; Frank and Harrington, *Rendezvous at Midway*, 50–59, 66–68, 74–75; Belote and Belote, *Titans of the Seas*, 44–54, 67, 75–79; Holmes, *Double-Edged Secrets*, 77–80; Willmott, *Barrier and the Javelin*, 56–58, 60–63; Morison, *History of United States Naval Operations*, 3:259–68, 387–98; Duane Schultz, *The Doolittle Raid* (New York: St. Martin's Press, 1989); Craven and Cate, *Army Air Forces*, 1:438–44; and Lisle Rose, *The Ship That Held the Line: The U.S.S. Hornet and the First Year of the Pacific War* (Annapolis, MD: Naval Institute Press, 1995), 56–67.

10. Morton, *Strategy and Command*, 103, 198–255; Craven and Cate, *Army Air Forces*, 1:409–17, 419–26, 430–38, 471–83; Edmonds, *They Fought With What They Had*, 439–41; Linn, *Guardians of Empire*, 246; Clive Howard and Joe Whitley, *One Damned Island after Another* (Chapel Hill: University of North Carolina Press, 1946), 43; Willmott, *Barrier and the Javelin*, 123–24, 139–55, 163–68, 182, 192–97; Matloff and Snell, *Strategic Planning*, 87–95, 115–17, 151–54, 162; Martin Caidin and Edward Hymoff, *The Mission* (New York: Lippincott, 1964), 27–30, 68–87, 101–3; Thomas E. Griffith, Jr., *MacArthur's Airman: General George C. Kenney and the War in the Southwest Pacific* (Lawrence: University Press of Kansas, 1998), 49–52; and Lundstrom, *First South Pacific Campaign*, 49–60.

11. Marder, *Old Friends, New Enemies*, 2:94–145; Churchill, *The Hinge of Fate*, 149–50, 159–60; Belote and Belote, *Titans of the Seas*, 68–75; Kirby, *War Against Japan*, 2:115–27; Shores, Cull and Izawa, *The Bloody Shambles*, 1:383–431; John Prados, *Combined Fleet Decoded: The Secret History of American Intelligence and the Japanese Navy in World War II* (New York: Random House, 1995), 274–78; Michael Smith, *The Emperor's Codes: The Breaking of Japan's Secret Ciphers* (New York: Arcade 2001), 12; Willmott, *Empires in the Balance*, 440–46; Gwyer and Butler, *Grand Strategy*, 3:482, 484–87; and Roskill, *War at Sea*, 2:22–32.

12. Holmes, *Double-Edged Secrets*, 71–80; Willmott, *Barrier and the Javelin*, 174–82; Prados, *Combined Fleet Decoded*, 300–307; Morison, *History of United States Naval Operations*, 4:13; Belote and Belote, *Titans of the Seas*, 82–83; and Prange, *Miracle at Midway*, 18–20.

13. Morison, *History of United States Naval Operations*, 4:11–64; Lundstrom, *Black Shoe Carrier Admiral*, 135–203; Sherman, *Combat Command*, 71–93; Okumiya and Horikoshi, *Zero!*, 95–106; Willmott, *Barrier and the Javelin*, 203–87; Belote and Belote, *Titans of the Seas*, 83–100; Lundstrom, *The First Team*, 167–305; Buell, *Dauntless Helldivers*, 68, 87; and Frank and Harrington, *Rendezvous at Midway*, 83–141.

14. Holmes, *Double-Edged Secrets*, 95–107; Prange, *Miracle at Midway*, 38–39, 74–75, 120, 126; Morison, *History of United States Naval Operations*, 4:79–87; Willmott, *Barrier and the Javelin*, 293–305, 310–12, 340–41; Nimitz and Potter, *Great Sea War*, 224; and Prados, *Combined Fleet Decoded*, 315–18.

15. Willmott, *Barrier and the Javelin*, 331–35; Nimitz and Potter, *Great Sea War*, 226; Gwyer and Butler, *Grand Strategy*, 3:490–91; Roskill, *War at Sea*, 2:37–38; Morison, *History of United States Naval Operations*, 4:81; Marder, *Old Friends, New Enemies*, 2:25, 28, 151, 191–92; Churchill, *Grand Alliance*, 518, 550; and Churchill, *The Hinge of Fate*, 160, 193–204, 262–63.

16. Belote and Belote, *Titans of the Seas*, 104–5; Nimitz and Potter, *Great Sea War*, 224–25; Parshall and Tully, *Shattered Sword*, 46, 54, 95–97, 99–102; Willmott, *Barrier and the Javelin*, 100–113, 343, 347–52; Prados, *Combined Fleet Decoded*, 329; Holmes, *Double-Edged Secrets*, 107–8; Prange, *Miracle at Midway*, 121–23, 137–39, 176; and Boyd and Yoshida, *Japanese Submarine Force*, 79.

17. Prange, *Miracle at Midway*, 160–358; Parshall and Tully, *Shattered Sword*, 117–384; Lundstrom, *Black Shoe Carrier Admiral*, 220–301; Morison, *History of United States Naval Operations*, 4:101–56; Belote and Belote, *Titans of the Seas*, 104–34; Willmott, *Barrier and the Javelin*, 363–510; Lundstrom, *The First Team*, 313, 324–426; Frank and Harrington, *Rendezvous at Midway*, 164–337; Prados, *Combined Fleet Decoded*, 337–38; and Milner, *Victory in Papua*, 56. Important new information from Japanese sources has caused a considerable revision of the Japanese side of Midway, but a significant degree of uncertainty still exists about some matters, notably, whether and when Admiral Nagumo received certain reports and whether Japanese fighters could have accompanied an early strike against the U.S. fleet. For a defense of Nagumo, arguing he was denied crucial intelligence before the battle and only belatedly received important reports during it, see Dallas Isom, *Midway Inquest: Why the Japanese Lost the Battle of Midway* (Bloomington: Indiana University Press, 2007). In my opinion, the defense is unconvincing.

18. Nimitz and Potter, *Great Sea War*, 247; and Parshall and Tully, *Shattered Sword*, 422–27.

## 11. Conclusions

1. Cf., most notably, the German official history, especially the conclusions in Boog et al.'s *Germany and the Second World War*, vol. 6; but this view has been common among Germans at least since the 1950s, even though some thought they could have defeated the Soviets.

2. David Irving, *The German Atomic Bomb: The History of Nuclear Research in Nazi Germany* (New York: Simon & Schuster, 1967); Speer, *Inside the Third Reich*, 300–305; Alfred Price, *Battle Over the Reich* (New York: Scribner, 1976), 149; and Levine, *Strategic Bombing of Germany*, 189–202.

3. Welchman, *Hut Six Story*, 3, 163–69; and Calvocoressi, *Top Secret Ultra*, 32. But cf. Ratcliff, *Delusions of Security*.

4. Hinsley et al., *British Intelligence*, 1:177–79.

5. Hinsley et al., *British Intelligence*, 2:547–48, 554–56, 563; and Russell Weigley, *Eisenhower's Lieutenants: The Campaign of France and Germany, 1944–1945* (Bloomington: Indiana University Press, 1980), 53.

6. Seaton, *The Russo-German War*, 222, 590. For a similar assessment, see Carell, *Hitler Moves East*, 323.

7. My interpretation on this point differs from that in my article "Was World War II a Near-run Thing?," 52–56.

8. See, for example, Manstein, *Lost Victories*, 175; Seaton, *The Russo-German War*, 222; and Anders, *Hitler's Defeat in Russia*.

9. Cf. chapter 4 of this volume; Leach, *German Strategy Against Russia*, 223–24; and Seaton, *The Russo-German War*, 217, 226–54.

10. For example, Shirer, *Rise and Fall of the Third Reich*, 1087; Shulman, *Defeat in the West*, 112, 116; and Kreipe, "The Battle of Britain," 35–36.

11. For example, Rommel, *The Rommel Papers*, 148, 191–93, 511–15; Warlimont, *Inside Hitler's Headquarters*, 132; and Barnett, *The Desert Generals*, 181–82.

12. Manstein, *Lost Victories*, 161.

13. De Belot, *Struggle for the Mediterranean*, 265.

14. Gwyer and Butler, *Grand Strategy*, vol. 3, part 2, 455; and Wesley Craven and James Lea Cate, *Army Air Forces in World War II*, vol. 2, *Europe: Torch to Point-Blank, August 1942 to December 1943* (Chicago: University of Chicago Press, 1949), 617.

15. Gwyer and Butler, *Grand Strategy*, vol. 3, part 2, 125–39; Watson, *Chief of Staff*, 401–5; and Robert E. Sherwood, *Roosevelt and Hopkins: An Intimate History* (New York: Grosset and Dunlap, 1965), 314–18.

# Index

# About the Author

**Alan Levine** is a historian, with a doctorate from New York University, specializing in World War II and the Cold War. He teaches at Borough of Manhattan Community College in New York City. He is the author of a dozen books, most recently *Bad Old Days: The Myth of the 1950s* (Transaction Publishers, 2008) and *Stalin's Last War: Korea and the Approach to World War II* (McFarland, 2005). Two of his earlier books, *D-Day to Berlin: The Northwest Europe Campaign, 1944–45* (Praeger, 2000) and *The War Against Rommel's Supply Lines: 1942–43* (Praeger, 1999), have recently been reprinted in paperback.